ROBERT LEVERING, MILTON MOSKOWITZ, and
MICHAEL KATZ are a team of business journalists and researchers. They are the authors of *The Computer Entrepreneurs* and the
bestselling *Everybody's Business: An Almanac*.

WINNING STRATEGIES

☐ **YOUR CAREER: How to Plan It—Manage It—Change It by Richard H. Buskirk.** Whether you're in school, on your first job, or in a position that is dead-end or wrong-way, this remarkable and practical guide is for you. The product of wide professional experience, filled with fascinating case histories, this book is meant not just to be read but to be used. Its goal is yours: the career and success you deserve.   (625595—$3.95)

☐ **CONCEPT OF THE CORPORATION by Peter F. Drucker.** An up-to-date edition of the classic study of the organization and management policies of General Motors—the company that has become the model for modern large-scale corporations across the world.   (621972—$3.95)

☐ **HOW TO START AND MANAGE YOUR OWN BUSINESS by Gardiner G. Greene.** If you run a small business, you need all the help you can get—and this is the book that gives it all to you. It includes information on financial strategies, selecting professional services, developing and marketing your product, the psychology of negotiating, contracting with the government, and everything else you need to know to be your own boss, create your own company, and make a good profit! (625021—$4.95)*

☐ **CORPORATE ETIQUETTE by Milla Alihan.** Why do some executives quickly rise on the corporate ladder, while others, seemingly just as qualified, remain bogged down on the lower echelons? An eminent business consultant clearly spotlights all the trouble areas where minor gaffs can turn into major roadblocks to advancement in this essential guide to getting ahead in the fast-changing business world of today.   (625498—$3.95)

*Price slightly higher in Canada

THE

100

BEST

COMPANIES
TO WORK FOR
IN AMERICA

Robert Levering
Milton Moskowitz
and Michael Katz

Ⓢ
A SIGNET BOOK

NEW AMERICAN LIBRARY

To Carol, indomitable spirit
To Lois and George

NAL PENGUIN BOOKS ARE AVAILABLE AT QUANTITY DISCOUNTS WHEN USED TO
PROMOTE PRODUCTS OR SERVICES. FOR INFORMATION PLEASE WRITE TO PREMIUM
MARKETING DIVISION, NAL , 1633 BROADWAY, NEW YORK, NEW YORK 10019.

Published by arrangement with Addison-Wesley Publishing Co.

This book previously appeared in a Plume edition.

 SIGNET TRADEMARK REG. U.S. PAT. OFF. AND FOREIGN COUNTRIES
REGISTERED TRADEMARK—MARCA REGISTRADA
HECHO EN CHICAGO, U.S.A.

SIGNET, SIGNET CLASSIC, MENTOR, ONYX, PLUME, MERIDIAN
and NAL BOOKS are published by NAL Penguin Inc.,
1633 Broadway, New York, New York 10019

First Signet Printing, April, 1987

     3   4   5   6   7   8   9

PRINTED IN THE UNITED STATES OF AMERICA

CONTENTS

ACKNOWLEDGMENTS

We had help from many quarters in the pursuit of these companies. We are grateful, first of all, to Harriet Rubin, who suggested the idea for this book. We would have been lost if not for the indefatigable research and fact-checking done by Harry Strharsky and Carol Townsend. We received recommendations of good companies from many people. The most productive recommenders were Robert Kahn, Alexis Park, Robert Kneely, and Gary Levering. Finally, we want to thank the dozens of people we interviewed at the companies themselves. They were our best sources.

PREFACE TO THE NAL EDITION

Companies never stand still. They are changing every day—and since the May 1984 publication of *The 100 Best Companies to Work for in America*, we have carefully monitored the advances and setbacks of the companies on our original roster. We have also been deluged by letters from all parts of the country. Most of them approved our choices, but some people questioned why their companies were not included. Others disputed some of our selections, and a few passionate ones praised us for *not* including their companies. (Two letters from employees of American Broadcasting Companies were notable in the latter respect.)

We also welcomed the nominations of new candidates. We decided then, based on the evidence we collected, that substantive changes were in order. After a careful review, including visits to new companies and old, we replaced six of our original choices with new ones.

The companies that appeared in the first edition but failed to make this one are:

- Borg-Warner
- Walt Disney Productions
- Hospital Corporation of America
- Merck
- Philip Morris
- Ralston Purina.

The companies that replaced them are:

- Federal Express
- Fisher-Price Toys
- Northrop
- Recreational Equipment
- Remington Products
- Steelcase.

The reasons for the addition of these six companies are spelled out in their profiles. They are a varied bunch, ranging in size from Recreational Equipment (1,000 employees) to Federal Express (30,000). Two—Federal Express and Northrop—are publicly owned. Two—Remington Products and Steelcase—are privately owned. One, Recreational Equipment, is a consumers' cooperative. And Fisher-Price is a division of another company, Quaker Oats, which is not one of the "100 Best." We talked extensively to employees at all these companies—and once again, we found that the best arbiters of workplace environments are the people who work in them.

Dropping companies was much more difficult for us; we literally agonized over each decision. To some extent, it was simply a matter of relativism: we found better ones. The companies we excised may still provide fine workplaces, better than the ones maintained by the vast majority of firms in the United States. But for one reason or another, in our minds they did not measure up to the companies replacing them.

Companies were not eliminated solely because of financial reverses that led to large-scale layoffs of employees. If that had been the criterion, we would not have been able to keep John Deere, Polaroid, Levi Strauss, Inland Steel, and Baxter Travenol, among others. Our thesis is that the companies on our roster are good for their people—in bad times as well as good times. So with companies undergoing stormy times, we examined carefully how they dealt with their people. Levi Strauss closed 20 plants and reduced their payroll by 5,000 persons. Baxter Travenol closed its plant in Hays, Kansas, and chopped 2,000 from its work force. We thought both companies went to extraordinary lengths to soften those blows for the affected employees. If every company closing a plant did as well, we wouldn't need the plant-closing legislation that has recently been proposed.

We did not find evidence of the same kind of concern at Philip Morris, one of the biggest profit-makers in corporate America. Plunging sales at its Miller beer subsidiary has made Philip Morris tougher on its employees. It won a strike at its big brewery in Milwaukee, it reduced its Miller work force by 8 percent, it never opened a brewery that it built in Ohio, and it instituted an across-the-board 7 percent cut in personnel in its New York headquarters office. It was not a happy time in Marlboro country.

Two of the companies dropped from the roster—Merck

and Walt Disney—were targets of strikes by their unionized employees in 1984. The strikes were settled, and the workers have returned to their jobs. But everything has not returned to normal. We visited Disneyland several months after the strike. Unlike our first visit, when the management encouraged us to interview anyone we wished, we were expressly forbidden full access to the workers. We did, however, manage to talk with a wide variety of employees. Several expressed considerable bitterness because they feel the management has betrayed the ideals of founder Walt Disney. Nearly all said they felt Disney has lost "the family touch" and is becoming overly concerned with making money, with the result that it has begun to seem little different from other big corporations. Clearly, Disney's new top executives have a big job ahead of them if they want to recapture the part of Walt's dream that has made Disney a special place for the people working there.

We also talked with a number of Merck employees who were still upset with the company after the settlement of their strike. No one disputed that Merck still pays top dollar—higher than any other pharmaceutical company and better than almost any other firm in any industry. But the highly profitable firm simply had not convinced its workers that a wage freeze was called for. About 4,000 Merck workers were on strike for five months before they finally agreed to a contract that closely resembled the management's initial offer. "They raped us," said one union leader representing workers at the Merck plant in West Point just outside of Philadelphia.

Borg-Warner is not the company it was. Two-thirds of its 68,000 U.S. employees are now in the service sector, including an army of security guards working for William Burns International, where both wages and morale are low. Apparently, the philosophy of teamwork, open communication, and respect for the individual articulated so well by company chairman James Beré has not been extended to those people. Hospital Corporation of America is another company that conceded to us it could not guarantee that the conditions in Nashville headquarters are replicated in the hospitals it operates across the country. Ralston Purina, under a new management, is trying to shed the folksy image it once had and is on its way toward becoming a faceless food conglomerate. It bought from ITT the nation's largest bread baker, Continental Baking, maker of Twinkies and Wonder Bread, and we could find little to differentiate the employee relations at Ralston's Jack in the Box chain from those that caused us to exclude McDonald's from our list (see Epilog).

Our standards have remained the same. Above all, we look for the special feeling that exists where management and employees work together rather than square off in "we vs. they" confrontations. We look for companies that are bringing out the best in their people. And we feel that the best guides to those companies are the employees themselves.

The new edition gave us the opportunity to correct any error, no matter how minor, that appeared in the original edition. We sent each profile to the company itself and asked for corrections and updated information. We also invited the companies to take issue with any of our judgments they thought were off base, although we reserved the right to reject these comments.

Infallible we're not. We therefore welcome comments from readers who, because of their firsthand experiences with some of these companies, object to their inclusion on our roster. We also continue to welcome recommendations of companies we may have overlooked. Send your comments to Everybody's Business, 1537 Franklin Street, San Francisco, CA 94109.

Robert Levering
Milton Moskowitz
Michael Katz

February 1985

INTRODUCTION: BEYOND TECHNIQUE

Finding a good place to work is not easy. It's not easy for a job hunter, and it wasn't easy for us.

Over the years everyone hears about great places to work—that such-and-such a company has a country club for employees, that a certain firm has such a terrific profit-sharing plan that a $5-an-hour warehouseman retired with a half-million dollars, or that some corporations treat their people so well that executive recruiters find it impossible to lure them away. But how do you go about finding America's superlative employers?

We had some ideas to begin with. One of us has covered the business scene for more than 25 years. All three of us had worked together to produce *Everybody's Business: An Almanac*, a book published by Harper & Row in 1980, which profiled 317 large companies.

Our previous research made us painfully aware that we were entering unexplored territory. It's odd—but telling—that American companies are rarely examined from the standpoint of their employees. The literature of business is rich with stories about companies and analyses of their operations. The *Wall Street Journal* chronicles these activities so well that it has become the largest-selling daily newspaper in the nation. During the course of a year, *Business Week*, *Forbes*, and *Fortune* publish 103 issues that are crammed with lists, tables, and charts tracking the progress of companies in a multitude of categories. And there are hundreds of trade magazines that rank, grade, and otherwise evaluate companies in their industrial settings: biggest hotels, biggest candy makers, biggest airlines, and on and on.

Yet none of these sources regularly spotlights the human condition inside business. They don't, as a rule, tell how employees are treated. They don't discuss which companies have the best benefit programs. They hardly ever do company-by-company comparisons of workplace environments.

We knew we had to cast a wider net to confirm our hunches and inspire new ones. If a company is a good place to work, its employees make no secret of it. Talking about where you work is one of the most common pastimes in America (and who isn't at least curious about whether the grass is greener somewhere else?). The better employers usually acquire a good reputation within their communities and within their industries. We realized that, at first, reputation would have to be our guide, so we resorted to the grapevine.

We asked all kinds of people to recommend great places to work: friends, relatives, executive recruiters, management consultants, market researchers, publishers, public relations counselors, business school teachers, newspaper reporters, magazine editors, radio and TV news staffers, advertising agency employees. We literally solicited prospects from everyone we met, including doctors and dentists we visited. A notice that we were looking for superior workplaces appeared in three widely circulated business publications. We rarely conducted interviews inside a company without asking the people we were talking with for additional recommendations.

After we had compiled a list of 350 candidates, we wrote to all of them for information about themselves and their employee policies. We received a wide range of responses. Some sent elaborate descriptions of their employee philosophy; at the other extreme was a terse letter informing us that the company was already besieged with job applications and that the last thing they needed was more attention of this kind; still others, suspecting a vanity press venture, told us they chose "not to participate."

Sifting through this material and listening to what people told us, we narrowed our candidate roster to 135 companies. But we quickly realized that the material was thin and rather lifeless, and that the only way to get in-depth information and lend substance to hearsay was to look for ourselves at every company on our list. We took a deep breath and telephoned our travel agents.

We crisscrossed the country for the better part of a year, visiting 114 companies in 27 different states—from a textile mill in South Carolina to a plywood coop in Oregon, from banks on Wall Street to oil companies in Texas. In between plastic trays of airline food, we settled down to lengthy conversations with employees, from the factory floor to the executive suite. We typically interviewed at least half a dozen people at each company, and sometimes we talked with several dozen. We made a point of asking the companies to set up interviews with people who had previously worked elsewhere. We found group interviews to be particularly useful, because comments by one person would spark reaction from another.

It was heartening to discover how well earned are the reputations of the companies on our list; people really like to work at these places. Employee satisfaction is a factor you can't measure by reading company pamphlets. It's one thing to listen to presidents or chairmen talk about the great companies they head; they do it all the time. It's something else to talk, as we did, to the head of the mailroom at Time Inc., or an usher at the Los Angeles Dodgers stadium, and to see the pride they felt about working for their companies.

People are proud to work for companies that treat them well. They become linked to these companies in more than just an employer/employee relationship. It's the presence of this feeling more than any other, perhaps, that sets these 100 companies apart from the great mass of companies in America.

Our methods were journalistic rather than scientific. We did not try to impose a preconceived set of standards. The firms vary too much for systematic comparison. Working in a bank in Southern California is very different from working in a steel mill in Indiana. And IBM, with over 200,000 U.S. employees, is a world apart from Celestial Seasonings, with about 200 workers.

Despite the diversity, almost every one of the "100 Best" has something distinctive to offer its employees. At some the benefits are very tangible, from the huge fortunes attainable at Trammell Crow to the 25-cent gourmet lunch prepared by a French chef at Merle Norman Cosmetics or the million-dollar employee center with swimming pools, Jacuzzis, and handball courts at ROLM. Other places, like Gore and Kollmorgen, offer unusual management styles. Each company is unique, but there were certain themes we heard over and over again, and the urge to draw a kind of composite picture of the ideal company is irresistible. Beyond good pay and strong benefits, such a company would:

1. Make people feel that they are part of a team or, in some cases, a family.

2. Encourage open communication, informing its people of new developments and encouraging them to offer suggestions and complaints.

3. Promote from within; let its own people bid for jobs before hiring outsiders.

4. Stress quality, enabling people to feel pride in the products or services they are providing.

5. Allow its employees to share in the profits, through profit-sharing or stock ownership or both.

6. Reduce the distinctions of rank between the top management and those in entry-level jobs; put everyone on a first-name basis; bar executive dining rooms and exclusive perks for high-level people.

7. Devote attention and resources to creating as pleasant a workplace environment as possible; hire good architects.

8. Encourage its employees to be active in community service by giving money to organizations in which employees participate.

9. Help employees save by matching the funds they save.

10. Try not to lay off people without first making an effort to place them in other jobs either within the company or elsewhere.

11. Care enough about the health of its employees to provide physical fitness centers and regular exercise and medical programs.

12. Expand the skills of its people through training programs and reimbursement of tuition for outside courses.

We found, in general, that small companies are better than big companies—as places to work. So you will find here some companies you may never have heard of, like Odetics or Moog. The big companies on our roster have maintained many small-company traits: they break down their operations into small units, they push responsibility down into the ranks, they don't mangle people. We were pleased also to find three divisions of large companies that qualified (though their parent companies didn't): Bell Labs (American Telephone & Telegraph), Physio-Control (Eli Lilly), and Westin Hotels (United Airlines).

Midway through our process the Thomas Peters/Robert

Waterman book, *In Search of Excellence*, was published. We examined their list of "excellent" companies with interest to see how it compared with our "100 Best." Finding some overlap but also significant divergences, we observed that management for profits, growth, and contented stockholders does not always yield a good place to work. We rejected many companies to which they gave accolades—Boeing, National Semiconductor, Frito-Lay, and McDonald's (see the Epilog), to name a few.

By the time we completed our research we had gained a better understanding of the difference between the traditional employer/employee relationship, which is often adversarial, and the kinds of practices we encountered on our journey. We feel that the "100 Best" may be part of the first wave in a major change that will affect for the better the way all of us think of our jobs and conduct our businesses. A phrase that expresses this change is "beyond technique." Whether a technique is drawn from a management handbook or an organization psychologist, the whole framework tends to be manipulative: "we" are looking for a way to get "them" to work harder or do something we want them to do. (One of the most alienated groups of employees we met was a Japanese-style quality circle at a Honeywell bomb factory in Minneapolis.) Among the "100 Best" we found many firms which have transcended that manipulative framework and achieved a sense that "we are all in it together." This unwritten pact among employees often begins with one or more key individuals who genuinely care about the quality of the experience of everyone in the company.

It can be argued that both conventional managerial techniques and the innovative practices described in this book enhance productivity and create a healthy economy. But the "100 Best" offer an added benefit of such high value that it's difficult to place on the same scale: a working life for thousands of people really worth living and worth looking forward to every waking day.

A NOTE ON THE RATINGS

In the grading session which produced the ratings that open each company profile, we asked the following questions:

1. *Pay.* How well does the company pay, relative to the

other 99 companies and relative also to the other companies in its industry?

2. *Benefits*. How varied and strong are the benefit programs? Does the company have profit-sharing? Does it match employee savings? Can employees buy company stock at a discount? Does it have some unusual benefits?

3. *Job Security*. Do employees have to live in fear of being laid off? The highest mark, five points, was reserved for such companies as Hewlett-Packard, Procter & Gamble, IBM, Delta Air Lines, and Digital Equipment Corp., all of which have a no-layoff policy.

4. *Chance to Move Up*. Is it possible for an employee to rise from a low level to a high one? Does the company have good training programs?

5. *Ambience*. What unique qualities does the company have, what styles of working (or playing) that set it apart from all others?

We found that in some instances we lacked the information to make very precise distinctions and that in others we were comparing apples with oranges. Nonetheless we thought it useful to provide a quick overview of each company's attributes.

■■■■■	means it ranks at the very top
■■■■	means it's superior
■■■	means it's average (in this group)
■■	means it's below average (in this group)
■	means it's at the bottom (of this group)

One other note. The number of employees, specified at the top of each profile, is usually the U.S. figure. We have generally noted at the end of the profile, in the section headlined "Main employment centers," the number working overseas.

ADVANCED MICRO DEVICES, INC.

AMD is the fifth-largest maker of silicon chips in the United States. U.S. employees: 8,000.

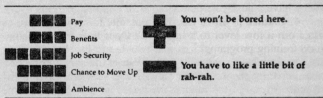

■■■ Pay		You won't be bored here.
■■■ Benefits		
■■■■ Job Security		
■■■ Chance to Move Up		You have to like a little bit of rah-rah.
■■■ Ambience		

Jerry Sanders is a folk hero in Silicon Valley. AMD's president and founder personifies the brash, go-go spirit of the world's preeminent high-tech center. He wears loud clothes and gold chains; he drives to work in one of his six cars, including a Rolls-Royce Corniche convertible, a Bentley convertible and Rolls four-door sedan; he owns three fancy homes—in San Francisco, Bel Air, and Malibu.

A combination of evangelist, politician, and supersalesman, Sanders is a nonstop talker. Virtually no journalist writes an article about Silicon Valley without some colorful quotes from him.

At the end of 1983, Sanders threw a gigantic Christmas party for 4,000 AMDers and their guests at San Francisco's Moscone Center, site of the 1984 Democratic National Convention. It was the office party to end all office parties. The *San Francisco Examiner* said it outdazzled "even Hollywood's tribute to the Queen of England" earlier in the year. The huge hall was decked with 24,000 giant balloons and hundreds of Christmas trees and poinsettias. The feast included 8,000 pounds of seafood, one-and-a-half tons of roast beef, 16,000 pastries, 2,000 pounds of cheeses, and 500 gallons of ice cream. So no one would go thirsty, 25 bars were scattered throughout the arena amidst two large stages where 37 violinists and several big-name entertainers and bands performed.

Sanders himself rode into the hall in a sleigh. Justifying the massive Christmas treat, he said, "The bottom line is people are not just machines. I believe people make the difference. And I believe they will do an extraordinary job if fairly treated." As the *Examiner* said, "Envious other Bay Area employees might call it royal treatment." The 1984 Christmas party was even bigger, featuring the rock group Chicago.

AMD employees appreciate the Sanders style. Some typical comments: "Jerry always makes us feel like we are a big part of his success. He is always so positive, no matter how bad it gets," said Charlene Greene, a communications traffic manager. Greene came to AMD in 1972, only three years after the company was founded. "Jerry ties us into the company because he recognizes that people are looking for more than just a job," explained Kathy Ryan of the accounts receivable department. "I like the fact Jerry is so visible," said Ernadene Angus of the analog marketing group. She says she never saw the president of Signetics, a smaller company where she worked for several years.

Though Sanders operates as AMD's charismatic leader, he does not rule autocratically. Instead, AMD has a highly fluid management structure. Many AMDers consider themselves "team members" rather than employees. A company newsletter in 1982, for example, showed photos of 19 different AMD "teams," including "The Super Rabbits Team," "The Mail and Literature Distribution Team," "The Quality Control Receiving Inspection Team," and three "MOS Static RAM Design" teams.

The teams are part of "directorates," each of which is led by a "managing director," whom Sanders calls "my centurions." Each directorate has its own engineering, manufacturing, and sales operations. As Geoff Tate, managing director of microcomputer systems, put it, "The entire company is structured entrepreneurially."

Sanders's own background was in sales. Before he founded AMD, he was a marketing director at Fairchild, one of the first companies to manufacture semiconductors (the formal name for the silicon chips that comprise the innards of computers and other electronic equipment). So, it's not surprising that AMD is run almost like the sales department of a big food company. There are always one or more sales campaigns going on. The walls of AMD's factories are lined with posters from these various sales and incentive campaigns.

Physically, AMD's offices are indistinguishable from dozens of other high-tech companies in Silicon Valley. They occupy sprawling warehouse-like facilities, with beige or sand-colored exteriors. Unlike neighbors such as Tandem Computers, no attempt has been made to create a fern-bar atmosphere in the waiting rooms or the offices. Functionality is the byword. But the colorful advertising posters on the walls set AMD apart.

One poster displays a color photo of a bunch of asparagus, commemorating "The Age of Asparagus" (symbolizing a crop that takes its time to nurture, then grows very rapidly, presumably just like AMD). Another, a recruiting poster for professionals and engineers, shows an executive in a business suit riding a surfboard as an ocean wave is breaking behind him. In big letters it reads, "Catch the Wave!"

The sales campaign environment permeates the entire organization. One of the most notable campaigns occurred in 1980, when AMD launched an "American Dream" campaign. If AMD reached $200 million in sales that year, Sanders told his people he would give two employees Cadillac Sevilles and one the "American Dream"—a house. Every employee's name went into the hat for a drawing in case the goal was reached. Sure enough, AMD surpassed the goal. Not one to miss a chance for the dramatic, Sanders had local media accompany him on his unannounced visit to the home of the winner. With the TV cameras whirring, Sanders handed Jocelyn Lleno, an AMD factory line worker, a check for $1,000. She was to receive the same amount every month for the next 20 years to buy her house.

AMDers seem to thrive on the sales campaign atmosphere. Here are some sample comments from a roundtable discussion with a half-dozen employees, including three engineers, an accounting department staffer, and two office staff managers:

"It seemed like a fast-paced, exciting place when I joined AMD. It has stayed that way."

"I am never bored. I never feel like I am stagnating. Lazy people don't fit in here."

"People here are positive thinkers. Things are half full rather than half empty."

"Nobody pays attention to job descriptions around here.

If you do not find somebody's toes to step on here, you are not working."

The constant emphasis on sales makes AMD a great place for someone interested in high-tech marketing. The company's entire sales force holds an annual conference in Hawaii to learn about the latest chips and AMD slogans. Those who expect a vacation are sorely disappointed to learn that they have little free time in paradise. Most of their time is structured, including organized sporting events. It's all part of helping veteran AMDers "imbue the more recent arrivals with the AMD culture," according to Sanders.

Though the company's reputation was built on its elite sales force, AMD spends increasing amounts of time and money on research and development. It is trying hard to make up for the initial years, when the company merely duplicated the chips created by others, most notably Fairchild and National Semiconductor. AMD emphasized quality—manufacturing chips without defects. "Quality is never having to say you're sorry" is one AMD slogan prominently plastered on the wall in the reception area of the executive offices.

More recently, AMD is designing its own chips. In 1981, AMD ranked third among the top 1,200 American companies in percent of sales spent on research and development. Sanders claimed that AMD would spend 20 percent of its 1983 sales on R&D, which could make it number one. That translates to many openings for electrical and computer engineers.

Those who land jobs with AMD should realize that pay is based strictly on merit. Bob Crossley, who was human resources director in 1983, said, "We do not have a service awards program. There are no pins or watches for being able to stay around here. We believe people work for money, and we give them a chance to make it." (Crossley left AMD in 1984 to join an anti-nuclear group.) In December 1984, AMD issued $14 million in profit-sharing checks—equivalent to 19.2 percent of people's salaries.

Despite its fast pace, AMD has been one of Silicon Valley's most stable employers. Though the company laid off some workers during the 1974–75 recession, Sanders promised there would be none as the semiconductor industry took a nose dive in 1981. He kept his word. AMD was one of the few chip makers not to lay off people in 1981–83. For several months in early 1982, salaried employees were expected to work 10 percent more hours for the same pay. No professionals quit during the belt-tightening, though a few clerical staffers moved elsewhere.

There are few executive perks at AMD. There's no executive dining room. The one exception is that vice-presidents receive a Mercedes. "It's our company Chevy," one new vice-president explained.

But the VPs have to fight for parking spaces with those who arrive in their Chevys, Toyotas, and Volkswagens. There isn't even a reserved parking space for Sanders. When he arrives late, he has to put his Rolls across the street in the overflow parking lot, just like anyone else. He wouldn't have it any other way.

Main employment centers   23 plants in California's Silicon Valley, where 6,000 people work; four in Austin, Texas, and two in San Antonio. Another 7,000 AMD employees work in Malaysia, Singapore, and the Philippines.

Headquarters   Advanced Micro Devices, Inc.
901 Thompson Place
Sunnyvale, CA 94086
408-732-2400

BEST PLACES FOR WOMEN TO WORK

Citcorp	Hallmark Cards	Northwestern
Control	IBM	Mutual Life
Data	Levi Strauss	J. C. Penney
Doyle Dane	Mary Kay	Recreational
Bernbach	Cosmetics	Equipment
Federal	Nordstrom	Security
Express		Pacific Bank
		Time Inc.

ANALOG DEVICES, INC.

Analog Devices makes components and systems that translate real-world signals (measurements of weight and temperature, for example) into the digital language of computers. U.S. employees: 2,750.

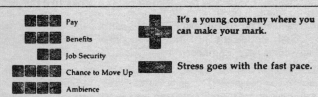

Pay

Benefits

Job Security

Chance to Move Up

Ambience

It's a young company where you can make your mark.

Stress goes with the fast pace.

This is a young high-tech company—the average age of employees is 29—founded and headed by an engineer, Ray Stata, who doesn't mind being described as a "humanist." In fact, he relishes it.

Analog Devices fosters a climate where the individual employee will feel free to shoot for the moon—as long as shooting for the moon jibes with corporate objectives. A company manual states: "While acknowledging the necessity for policies, procedures, and basic management control systems, we attempt to hold these to a minimum and invest more effort in developing sound human judgment. This reflects our belief that individual judgment is generally more reliable than rules and regulations."

Stata has talked often about the importance of challenging people to perform at the limit of their potential. And he doesn't believe you can do that with rules. "We try to break the procedural syndrome whereby managers impose themselves on others," he says. "We're not trying to eliminate all hierarchy but to cut the counterproductive values generated by the rules. The greatest limitation in traditional organizations is that people farther down the ladder always consider themselves less valuable and less creative human beings."

One way Analog tries to modify the traditional, hierarchical patterns of American business is by a "parallel ladder program." The traditional route an engineer might travel looks like this:

Engineering Supervisor
Functional Manager
Product Line Manager
Director
Vice-President

Analog has created a parallel path for engineers who don't want to travel the managerial route. It looks like this:

Senior Project Engineer
Staff Engineer
Senior Staff Engineer
Division Fellow
Corporate Fellow

The title of corporate fellow represents the ultimate position an engineer can achieve in climbing this ladder. In compensation, responsibility, and influence, it's comparable to corporate vice-president on the managerial side. The company named its first corporate fellow, Ivar Wold, in 1981. However, he soon left Analog to start his own software company. Toward the end of 1983 there were no corporate fellows, but six engineers had reached the rank of division fellow.

The people working at Analog's New England facilities are quick to tell you that they feel management wants them to expand their horizons. Anne Marie Flynn, formerly a teacher and now a marketing specialist at Analog, put it this way: "If you can cut it here, you get a chance to do anything." Harry Kasparian, a systems product line manager, said Analog is a far more open company to work for than his two previous New England workplaces: Foxboro and Metcalf & Eddy.

Whatever Analog is doing, it's making some fast tracks. The company turns out a long line of products that amplify, condition, convert, and display analog electrical signals. It makes its own semiconductors—and they account for 70 percent of the company's business. It pioneered in the development of circuits that could convert such measurements as temperature, pressure, and flow into a digital form usable by computers.

Ray Stata once assessed the company's prowess as follows: "We derive our competitive strength primarily from technical innovation in the area of linear circuits and process technology. We achieved this by nurturing the image of Analog Devices as a mecca for a vanishing breed of linear technologists in a world which has become increasingly digital."

A typical product from Analog Devices is a converter that enables you to see a digital readout when a grocer weighs a sack of potatoes on a scale. It's a product, in other words, that converts pound-and-ounce measurements into a digital display.

Not yet 20 years old, Analog leaped from sales of $60 million in 1972 to over $300 million in 1984, with an even greater jump in profits. The company has never had a layoff.

Analog looks for engineers who are "free spirits"—almost a contradiction in terms—and who can work in a corporate mold. To inculcate this spirit, the company installed Crawford W. Beveridge as vice-president of human resources in 1982. An ebullient, red-bearded Scotsman, Beveridge originally joined Hewlett-Packard in Europe and worked for H-P for nine years before joining Digital Equipment Corp., where he was European personnel manager. At Analog, he's striving for a balance between H-P and DEC. At H-P, he said, he never realized how controlled he was until he left the company. On the other hand, he said, DEC "had no structure at all."

Analog has a strong benefits program. The company provides life, medical, dental, and disability insurance at no cost to employees and their families. In 1984, Analog introduced what it calls "The Investment Partnership," a tax-deferred, long-term savings program under which the company makes a monthly contribution equal to 5 percent of each employee's earnings and also matches employee contributions up to an additional 2 percent of earnings. In addition, 1984 also saw the debut of a universal employee bonus program that pays out money quarterly if certain profit and sales goals are met. These goals are high—25 percent sales growth and 23 percent return on assets. And the bonuses double if a "model" performance is reached—say, a 35 percent leap in sales instead of 25 percent.

The pressure to perform here is therefore strong. It's not a place where you can loaf. Ray Stata's goal, after all, is to hit $1 billion by 1990.

Analog has another interesting feature. Its venture capital arm, Analog Devices Enterprises, scours the technological landscape looking for suitable, long-term investments in people who are pushing against frontiers. It has pumped money into about 12 new ventures—and the beauty of it is that Analog doesn't have to put up any of its own money. It's all advanced by Standard Oil of Indiana, which trusts Analog's judgment on these matters. In return, Standard of Indiana gets stock in Analog. It now owns 17 percent of the company.

Main employment centers   Analog remains primarily a New England company, although it now has plants in Greensboro, North Carolina; Limerick, Ireland; London; and Shiroyamacho, Japan. Employees number 1,200 at or near its Norwood headquarters, which is 10 miles southwest of Boston. Another 1,200 work north of Boston at Wilmington, where Analog produces its semiconductors. The components group is based at Burlington, Massachusetts. Another 1,600 work overseas.

Headquarters   Analog Devices, Inc.
2 Technology Center
Norwood, MA 02052
617-329-4700

ANHEUSER-BUSCH COMPANIES

ANHEUSER-BUSCH COMPANIES, INC.

Anheuser-Busch brews more beer than anyone else in the world. U.S. employees: 38,000.

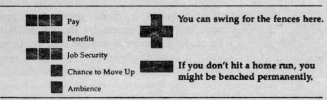

■■■ Pay	**You can swing for the fences here.**
■■ Benefits	
■■■ Job Security	
■ Chance to Move Up	■■ **If you don't hit a home run, you might be benched permanently.**
■ Ambience	

You've seen crowds at football games crying maniacally, "We're number one, we're number one." Anheuser-Busch is a little like that. They're the world's largest brewer of beer, and they wear that title with braggadocio. If you work for this company, you're continually reminded that you're fighting in a beer brawl and that you have to be rough and tough to win. The attitude was exquisitely expressed by August A. Busch III, scion of the founding family and absolute ruler of this company, when he was asked during the early 1970s about Miller Brewing's thrust to unseat Anheuser-Busch from its throne. "Tell Miller to come right along," he said, "but tell them to bring lots of money."

Everything this company does reinforces this "don't mess with me" image: the Clydesdale horses, the A-and-Eagle symbol in use since 1872, the upbeat "King of Beers" commercials. "We're the best and we know it. That makes us special." Those words of exhortation were issued to the troops in 1983 by Dennis P. Long, who is president of Anheuser-Busch, Inc., the brewing subsidiary of the umbrella company, Anheuser-Busch Companies. Long grew up in the Irish section of the south side of St. Louis. He joined the brewery, which is on the south side, when he was 17. "I got a job with the brewery," he once told an interviewer, "because my father, a construction worker, told me to do it. 'Find a good, solid St.

Louis company, like the brewery. Go to work.'" Long signed on as an office boy. He was named president in 1979, when he was 42 years old.

Some would say there's a soppiness intertwined with the swaggering. Long puts it this way: "This is a magical place. People who walk through here are amazed at the spirit. The interest, involvement, and feeling of belonging are apparent. As corny as it may sound, I still get an incredible thrill when someone asks where I work and I say, 'Anheuser-Busch.' I feel I'm part of something special."

Long's sentiments appeared in the *Anheuser-Busch Eagle*, the company's newspaper, a rah-rah sheet of the first order. The same issue carried an article by the editor, Bill Mueller, in which he said, "I wonder if anyone else out there ever feels like I do when I see an Anheuser-Busch commercial. Sure, all the commercials make me feel proud to be a part of A-B, but the Christmas spot with the Clydesdales especially gives me a chill. And when I read the business pages in the newspaper and see how A-B sales records continue, I'm proud I work for A-B."

Now you can understand why people walk around Anheuser-Busch wearing T-shirts emblazoned, "I'm a Miller killer." Or why, when we asked a secretary over the phone whether Anheuser-Busch was a good place to work, she snapped back, "You better believe it. I've been here thirty-eight years."

The toughness comes out in many ways. This is a company bent on succeeding, and it pushes its people to go the extra mile. In 1976, it toughed out the Teamsters in a bitter 95-day strike. The company absolutely refused to grant amnesty to strikers accused of violence. And after the strike was over, the brewery gave bonuses of $1,000 in stock to 2,815 white-collar workers who helped out during the strike.

In 1982, Jesse Jackson, the civil rights leader, threatened to boycott Anheuser-Busch if the company didn't sign a pact with his organization, PUSH, pledging to take various actions to promote minority economic development, especially the selection of black distributors. Other big companies—Coca-Cola and Miller Brewing, for example—signed such agreements with PUSH. But Anheuser-Busch flatly refused, saying that with a minority employee representation of 18 percent, it had nothing to be ashamed about. When Jackson went to different cities to urge the boycott of Budweiser and other A-B brands, the company sent along a black vice-president, Wayman Smith, to refute what Jackson was saying. In the end, Jackson and the brewery reached a boycott-ending agreement that was widely seen as a victory for August Busch. It certainly did not pin the company down to specific, remedial actions—and Jackson conceded that there might have been some communications problems.

Anheuser-Busch could be an especially interesting place right now because it seems to be trying to make the transition from an authoritarian family business to a professionally managed company, except that it's not clear that August Busch will ever give up much power. Robert S. Weinberg, who used to work at the brewery as a planning executive (a lot of planning is done there these days) and who now runs a St. Louis consulting firm, told *Industry Week* magazine in 1982, "There are very few old-timers left. All the key people around now were hired, picked, or approved by Mr. Busch. He has literally created the present organization." And he apparently still reserves the key decisions for himself. *Industry Week* also interviewed Busch, who said this about his management team: "The minute they're out of bed in the morning, I want them immediately thinking about making their areas of work better. We don't ask our managers to work twelve-hour days, but most of them do."

A-B has been working to catch up with other companies. A quality-of-life work program was started in 1974. The top managers of the company now have face-to-face meetings with employees to respond to questions. There's an employee assistance program that offers free, confidential counseling on any personal problems. There's an ombudsman to whom complaints about one's boss can be brought. An employee suggestion program introduced in 1982 yielded 2,500 cost-saving ideas—and a participation rate of 24 percent in 1984, resulting in company savings of $250,000.

The benefits at Anheuser-Busch are not as comprehensive as they are at many other companies. There's no profit-sharing program, for example. But Anheuser-Busch keeps careful tabs on what other breweries pay, and it claims to offer the best wages in the industry. People who work in the breweries themselves are covered by union contracts. The average wage rates in 1983 at breweries in four different cities were: St. Louis, $14.00 an hour; Houston, $13.85 an hour; Tampa, $13.74 an hour; Jacksonville, $13.50 an hour.

Everyone who works for the company is entitled to two free cases of beer a month. And if you work in the St. Louis headquarters, you will feel a part of history. Three of the buildings in the headquarters complex have been designated as historic landmarks. The Brew House has been brewing beer since 1892. The Clydesdale stables date from 1885. And some company executives have offices in the grade-school building that August Busch, Jr., attended when he was a child. The brewery, still the largest in the A-B network, is open for tours every day — and 350,000 tourists troop through there every year. It's one of the sights of St. Louis.

Main employment centers   A third of the 18,000 brewery employees work in the St. Louis area. Other breweries are in Newark, New Jersey; Los Angeles; Jacksonville and Tampa, Florida; Houston; Columbus, Ohio; Merrimack, New Hampshire; Williamsburg, Virginia; Fairfield, California; and Baldwinsville, New York. The company also operates can manufacturing plants in Jacksonville and Gainesville, Florida; Columbus, Ohio; and Arnold, Missouri. Anheuser-Busch also runs four theme parks, at Tampa, Williamsburg, Dallas/Fort Worth, and Langhorne, Pennsylvania; and it's the proud owner of baseball's St. Louis Cardinals, winner of the 1982 World Series. And A-B now owns the nation's second-largest baker, Campbell Taggart, which is headquartered in Dallas and operates more than 80 plants in the U.S., Europe, and Brazil.

Headquarters   Anheuser-Busch Companies, Inc.
One Busch Place
St. Louis, MO 63118
314-577-2000

apple computer
The Most Personal Computer Company

APPLE COMPUTER, INC.

Apple makes personal computers. U.S. employees: 5,600.

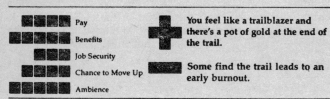

■■■■	Pay	
■■■■	Benefits	You feel like a trailblazer and there's a pot of gold at the end of the trail.
■■■	Job Security	
■■■	Chance to Move Up	Some find the trail leads to an early burnout.
■■■■■	Ambience	

Everyone who works at Apple gets an Apple computer because of a policy called the "Loan to Own" program. All Apple employees—from assembly-line workers to vice-presidents—are loaned the computer (an Apple IIe, IIc, or Macintosh with a disk drive and monitor) just two months after joining the company. Ten months later the computer is theirs, no strings attached.

Apple's across-the-board, $1,500 to $2,000 bonus is uncommonly generous, even for California's Silicon Valley, noted as the land of perks. One Apple executive explained the rationale: "'Loan to Own' spreads the gospel of personal computing. Besides, it's good for the morale."

Apple's undeniably high morale attracts many to the company. A "Rah, Rah Apple" atmosphere pervades Apple's facilities. Everywhere you turn, you see the distinctively colorful Apple logo—from decals on employees' cars, to lapel pins, to paperweights on the desks of secretaries. At the young company's second annual stockholders' meeting, held in early 1983, hundreds of Apple employees cheered spontaneously every time one of the company executives was introduced and even when the most innocuous sales or profit figure was announced.

The annual meeting reflected the heady days of the early years at Apple, the company that launched the personal computer industry in May 1977 with the Apple II computer. Two years earlier, Steve Jobs and Steve Wozniak, who were 21 and 26 years old at the time, built the first Apple I in Jobs's garage. They had sold Wozniak's Volkswagen bus for $1,300 to get the capital to produce the first machines. By the end of 1982, Apple had annual sales of nearly $600 million, qualifying it for the Fortune 500 list and making Apple the first company in history to make the coveted list in less than five years. Apple topped $1 billion in sales in 1984. Not even such companies as Xerox and Polaroid grew so big so quickly. It's a success story of dreams, of legends.

By late 1983 the competition from IBM and the dozens of others who had joined the personal computer fray began to take its toll. The company's product Lisa, the computer with the "mouse," won plaudits within the industry but few customers. The value of Apple stock plunged from over $60 a share to less than $20. Yet those who work at Apple aren't about to throw in the towel. There's an attitude that somehow they'll manage to pull success out of the fire. And the introduction in early 1984 of the popular Macintosh seemed to ignite the troops again. Employees believe they are doing more than making and selling computers: they are on a social mission. Again and again, Apple people explain that Apple exists to bring technology to individuals. Just as bicycles enable people to move more rapidly from place to place, so computers permit people to extend their intelligence. They insist Apple is selling "a revolutionary tool." In the world before Apple, the power of the computer was reserved for large companies or governments. But in the post-Apple world, it can be made available to everyone.

Apple practices this gospel at home. There are virtually no typewriters in the main offices. Executives are expected to type their letters and memos on their own Apples.

Because they feel they invented the personal computer, Apple people think they are the ideal leaders of the movement. Implicit in the Apple cosmology is a "We'll show the bastards" mentality. By "bastards," Apple people mean IBM and other large corporations. Though Apple is growing at a rate enviable to the most hard-bitten Wall Street analyst, a subtle 1960s-style youth culture is pervasive. The average age of employees is 30. Jeans are acceptable attire for corporate vice-presidents.

The counter-corporate culture attitude extends beyond dress. Every new Apple employee is given a sheet that describes "Apple Values." The sheet was the result of a task force of a dozen Apple employees at all levels who spent several months interviewing co-workers regarding their attitudes about working at Apple, according to Ann Bowers, the former dean of Apple University (dedicated to in-house training and the indoctrination of the company's beliefs). She told us: "Most people come to Apple with a dream. It's where they thought they could make a difference."

When we met over lunch with a dozen employees (mostly nonsupervisory) at the Cupertino headquarters, we saw evidence of the Apple dream. Some of the comments we heard:

"There's a lot of spirit behind our products," said one engineer.

"People will not tolerate mediocrity at Apple," explained a woman who writes user manuals. "Some of that sense comes from the spirit of Steve Jobs. He's got a strong sense of aesthetics."

"We believe in computer power to the people," said a marketing supervisor. "People develop an emotional attachment to personal computers. It's not a rational thing, but we see it all the time. That makes us feel like we're doing something special."

Finding managers who can fit in at Apple is not easy, according to Bowers. "We are looking for people who are coaches and team builders and expanders, not controllers of people. We see ours as a Third Wave company [referring to Alvin Toffler's book with that title]. Many of the managers we hire are Second Wave. They do not trust people." They have a phrase to describe what happens to such managers: they are "Appleized." (Between 15 and 20 percent of Apple's managers are women or minorities.)

In mid-1983 the company hired John Sculley, formerly president of Pepsi-Cola, as Apple's president. Steve DeVaughn, manager of investor relations, told us that before he was hired, it was a "prerequisite that Sculley hold values consistent with our corporate culture." There are hints that Sculley is being "Appleized." An article in the *Wall Street Journal* in October 1983 stated: "Mr. Sculley says Apple's opulent executive offices in its new headquarters building—dubbed

Apple Values

Empathy for Customers/Users: We offer superior products that fill real needs and provide lasting value. . . . We are genuinely interested in solving customer problems and will not compromise our ethics or integrity in the name of profit.

Achievement/Aggressiveness: We set aggressive goals, and drive ourselves to achieve them. We recognize that this is a unique time, when our products will change the way people work and live. It's an adventure and we're in it together.

Positive Social Contribution: As a corporate citizen, we wish to be an economic, intellectual, and social asset to communities where we operate. But beyond that, we expect to make this world a better place to live. We build products that extend human capability, freeing people from drudgery and helping them achieve more than they could alone.

Individual Performance: We expect individual commitment and performance above the standard for our industry. Only thus will we make the profits that permit us to seek our other corporate objectives.

Team Spirit: Teamwork is essential to Apple's success, for the job is too big to be done by any one person. Individuals are encouraged to interact with all levels of management, sharing ideas and suggestions to improve Apple's effectiveness and quality of life. It takes all of us to win. We support each other, and share the victories and rewards together.

Quality/Excellence: We care about what we do. We build into Apple products a level of quality, performance, and value that will earn the respect and loyalty of our customers.

Individual Reward: We recognize each person's contribution that flows from high performance. We recognize also that rewards must be psychological as well as financial, and strive for an atmosphere where each individual can share the adventure and excitement of working at Apple.

Good Management: The attitudes of managers toward their people are of primary importance. Employees should be able to trust the motives and integrity of their supervisors. It is the responsibility of management to create a productive environment where Apple values flourish.

'The Big Pink' for the color of some interior walls—will be replaced soon by more humble offices to preserve 'Apple values.'"

Besides egalitarianism, another strong part of the Apple belief system is sharing the wealth. An estimated 300 Apple employees (almost all of whom are less than 40 years old) have become millionaires. The company regularly distributes a percentage of quarterly profits to employees. For the first quarter of 1983, this bonus augmented salaries by 12 percent.

Pay is already good at Apple. According to Jay Elliot, vice-president of human resources, Apple pays higher than Hewlett-Packard or IBM for comparable jobs. The company is also one of the few firms in America to offer stock options to all employees. That means the company gives employees the right to purchase a specified number of shares of Apple stock in the future at the same price the stock is selling for when the option is initially granted. Assembly-line workers receive options to buy 200 shares (50 a year for four years), while middle managers get options to buy from 5,000 to 20,000 shares.

Apple has also marked corporate successes with gifts. When the company had its first $100 million sales quarter, all employees were granted an extra week's paid vacation. For Christmas in 1982, all received an AM-FM radio with headphones; the previous year, everyone was given a solar-powered calculator.

Main Employment Centers   Cupertino, San Jose, and Garden Grove, California; Carrollton, Texas.

Headquarters   Apple Computer, Inc.
20525 Mariani Avenue
Cupertino, CA 95014
408-996-1010

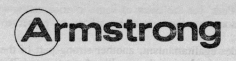

Armstrong

ARMSTRONG WORLD INDUSTRIES, INC.

The world's largest flooring manufacturer and one of the biggest furniture makers in the United States under the Thomasville label. U.S. employees: 18,600.

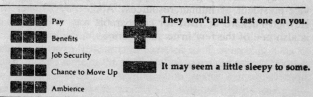

▮▮▮ Pay		**They won't pull a fast one on you.**
▮▮▮ Benefits		
▮▮▮ Job Security		
▮▮▮ Chance to Move Up		**It may seem a little sleepy to some.**
▮▮▮ Ambience		

Armstrong celebrates its 125th year in 1985. Two years earlier, the company's board of directors elected its ninth president. Like his predecessors, Joseph L. Jones has spent his entire career with Armstrong, joining the company in 1947.

Playing an important role in the continuity of management is the Armstrong Manor. A remodeled farmhouse, Armstrong Manor sits on the outskirts of Lancaster, Pennsylvania (population 70,000), in the heart of Pennsylvania Dutch country. When driving the 65 miles between Philadelphia and Lancaster, it's common to pass Amish farmers in their horse-drawn buggies. Newly hired sales trainees since the mid-1920s have lived at the Manor while undergoing Armstrong's three-month orientation and training program. About 85 to 90 trainees go through the Manor each year. Except for the gourmet-quality Manor food, the facility resembles a college fraternity house. Rooms have dormitory beds and study desks. There's a comfortable lounge where the new recruits can watch TV in the evenings or sit around and talk.

The Manor fosters its own brand of old-school pride. Alums of the Armstrong Manor Class of '48, including some who left the company long ago for jobs elsewhere, recently held their thirty-fifth reunion. From time to time, a company accountant suggests tearing down the Manor. But the top officers, all Manor alumni, won't hear of it.

Tradition and sentiment still matter to Armstrong. Every Christmas season, the company holds a Christmas carol songfest at the corporate headquarters. People come to the large auditorium in the red brick schoolhouselike building. Many employees especially look forward to singing the Armstrong carol, "A Holiday Wish," the company's own tribute to the holiday season, penned many Christmases ago. Good Friday, Easter Monday, and two days each at Thanksgiving, Christmas, and New Year's are among the company holidays.

When we visited the corporate headquarters one evening last spring, a pinochle tournament, sponsored by the Armstrong Activities Association, was under way in the same auditorium. It could have been a small-town church social. As dozens of people at card tables sat hunched over their hands, several women were standing at a refreshment table selling homemade pies, cakes, and cookies.

Armstrong employees in Lancaster speak proudly of their company's "small-town atmosphere." Yet Armstrong is hardly a small corporation. It has long been a Fortune 500 company (1983 sales: $1.4 billion) and one of the country's biggest advertisers. It's the world's largest resilient flooring manufacturer. It's also one of the biggest makers of carpets, ceiling materials, and furniture (Thomasville). It has 54 plants in eight different countries, 41 of them in the United States.

Lancaster is the home of the company's largest plant. Armstrong also employs a number of commercial artists, interior designers, and product stylists in Lancaster. Most work in a modern technical center complex on the edge of town, creating the designs and colorings for the new varieties of flooring, carpets, and ceiling patterns the company announces annually. Several hundred engineers and scientists share the 682-acre technical center site. They figure out how to translate the designers' concepts to mass production. Other artists, designers, and craftspeople work in Armstrong's interior design center in downtown Lancaster. One floor of the building is used like a Hollywood studio to create room scenes that are photographed for the company's ads in national magazines.

Armstrong people point with pride to the interior-design center. Rather than allow Lancaster's decaying downtown business district to die altogether, the company invested several million dollars in the late 1970s to build the center. Several department stores, banks, and other businesses have followed Armstrong's lead, and the downtown area has been revitalized.

Armstrong has acquired a reputation for aggressive marketing, tops in its field. Consider Armstrong's entry into the carpet business. Though Armstrong did not sell its first carpet until 1968, *Forbes* reported that it had become number two in only a decade.

This kind of success appears to stem in part from the highly trained and motivated sales force. *Fortune* once quoted a flooring contractor as saying, "If you ever listen to one Armstrong salesman, you can pick out another Armstrong man anywhere you happen to find him." A former Armstrong president acknowledged that his company "tends to submerge the individual personality and develop the corporate personality," though he insisted that "it takes individuals rather than conformists to be good performers."

Armstrong gets most of its new sales and management people directly from university campuses. "College recruiting is our lifeblood," according to Bill Van Pelt, an Armstrong personnel manager. "We're not necessarily looking for the brightest, but we want people who are able to communicate and have a positive attitude."

"We're very big on the career concept here," added Jack Jordin, vice-president of human resources. Promotion from within is gospel at Armstrong, except for certain technical jobs. Employee turnover is low, especially after the first few years. Few people at Armstrong have worked elsewhere.

The company started recruiting people from the campuses in the 1920s, long before it was fashionable or considered practical to do so. Early company trainees were called "Armstrong chicks." As one Armstrong executive recalled, they learned to "live and die for Armstrong" at the Armstrong Manor.

Because the company has long believed that it offers not jobs but careers (something said by many companies, but it is clearly more than rhetoric at Armstrong), it has had an almost paternalistic approach to job benefits. It was one of the first, if not the first, company in the United States to provide dental care for employees (1909). It also led the way in extra pay for overtime (1913), paid vacations (1924), and group life insurance (1931). About one-third of Armstrong's 13,000 hourly workers are unionized.

Armstrong's Operating Principles

1. To respect the dignity and inherent rights of the individual human being in all dealings with people.

2. To maintain high moral and ethical standards and to reflect honesty, integrity, reliability, and forthrightness in all relations.

3. To reflect the tenets of good taste and common courtesy in all attitudes, words, and deeds.

4. To serve fairly and in proper balance the interest of all groups associated with the business—customers, stockholders, employees, suppliers, community neighbors, government, and the general public.

People who join Armstrong can expect to work hard. As personnel manager Van Pelt explained, "This is a hardworking community around here. When you drive to work you might see the Amish in their fields working with their hands with all the manual equipment. They know the value of a buck. I think that rubs off on us."

Armstrong's emphasis on ethics might also be traced to the influence of the Pennsylvania Dutch. A few years ago, *American Banker* magazine quoted the company's president as saying that company executives are indoctrinated, from start to finish, with the company's principles and methods. In 1960, when the company celebrated its centennial, it had a team of researchers study what typified Armstrong. They cited the "Operating Principles," which are reproduced on many pieces of company literature (see above).

Everybody is on a first-name basis at Armstrong. Everyone, from president to factory line worker, eats in the company cafeteria. It is a plain, Horn & Hardart-style facility where people tend to eat quickly and dash back to work. There is no executive dining room.

Because Armstrong's headquarters are in a small town, people who work there can expect to get to know many of their co-workers socially as well. Nancy Sauer, a staff assistant in the residential builder sales department, explained, "You see Armstrong people on the volleyball court or in the church choir. Your friends in the company are often the same friends outside."

To Sauer this means, "It's not all business all the time. My boss and my boss's boss know something about me as a person. There are always the few extra minutes of talk about the family. They don't just treat me as a floor and carpet salesperson, they're also interested in what I do outside."

Main employment centers Lancaster, Pennsylvania: almost 5,000 (of the total in the Lancaster area, 700 work in the technical center); Thomasville, North Carolina: 3,000; Dalton, Georgia (main carpet plant): 1,000. About 3,000 of Armstrong's employees, mostly foreign nationals, work outside the United States.

Headquarters Armstrong World Industries, Inc.
Liberty and Charlotte Streets
P.O. Box 3001
Lancaster, PA 17604
717-397-0611

ATLANTIC RICHFIELD COMPANY

ARCO ranks as the sixth-largest oil company in the United States. U.S. employees: 45,800.

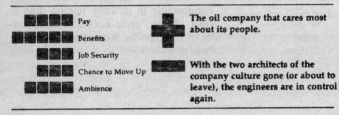

Pay

Benefits

Job Security

Chance to Move Up

Ambience

The oil company that cares most about its people.

With the two architects of the company culture gone (or about to leave), the engineers are in control again.

Here's a big oil company trying to act as if it were not—at least not like any other big oil company. For example, in the middle of 1983, Bill Kieschnick, the president of ARCO, invited employees to tell him what they thought about the company's style and values. He issued this invitation via the company's weekly newspaper, the *ArcoSpark*. More than 100 employees took up Kieschnick's offer and sent him their opinions. Among the responses were letters running to four and five pages. And 90 percent were signed.

The newspaper, in itself, is one reason someone might decide to work here, since it may well be the best internal paper published in the corporate world. A tabloid staffed by professional journalists and photographers who are given a wide degree of freedom to pursue stories, it doesn't fawn over management. Nor does it engage in rah-rah journalism. And it's not afraid to print criticism of the company or the petroleum industry. At one point, the *ArcoSpark* carried a letter from the wife of an employee who objected to the paper's running a photograph of Chairman Robert O. Anderson's office because it showed a nude painting that hung on the wall; she didn't think that a paper carrying such an image should come into the home. The *ArcoSpark* also ran an article written by Senator William Proxmire that sharply attacked the Political Action Committees that have been mounted by ARCO and other companies to fund political campaigns. "One PAC representative," wrote Senator Proxmire, "has been quoted as saying that when he makes a contribution, he buys legislation! That is corruption, pure and simple."

It may be that ARCO is different because it's so new. Other oil companies, around for many years before ARCO was born, have encrusted policies and practices. Rigidity is one of their trademarks. But the more likely reason for ARCO's differences is Robert O. Anderson, a remarkable character who's more comfortable in cowboy regalia than in gray pinstripes. A product of the "great books" culture implanted at the University of Chicago by Robert M. Hutchins, Anderson went to Philadelphia in 1965 to take the reins of Atlantic Refining, a tired remnant of the old Rockefeller oil trust. He proceeded, with the help of a former Harvard Business School teacher, Thornton Bradshaw, to create the company we now know as Atlantic Richfield. Anderson and Bradshaw moved the corporate headquarters, first to New York and then clear across the country to Los Angeles. They merged Atlantic with Richfield and parts of Sinclair.

But they were careful to pay attention to the quality of the company. And the corporation they crafted does stand out in the petroleum industry. It's a major supporter of the arts and is committed to the improvement of the public education system. Its philanthropic budget is much bigger, relative to its size, than that of other oil companies. It saved *The Observer*, a leading British Sunday newspaper, from falling into the hands of Rupert Murdoch. It helped rescue *Harper's* magazine in the United States. It broke with other members of its industry on several political and social issues. And, thanks to a big oil find on Alaska's North Slope, it emerged as one of the most powerful companies in the industry, dependent, happily, on domestic sources.

ARCO thus has the trappings of a big oil company leavened by frequently repeated expressions of social concern. It's a company determined to do well by the people who work there and by the people who live in its plant communities. Bill Kieschnick reaffirmed these concerns when he succeeded Anderson as chief executive in 1982. "If we can't go home at night and tell our families what we do and feel okay about it, then we have a problem," he said.

If you do work for ARCO, you're paid very well—

and the fringe benefits are outstanding, as they are at the other big oil companies. The ARCO Savings Plan, for example, enables employees to sock away up to 12 percent of their pay—and the company will match the first 2 percent, two-for-one. You have a choice of five ways to invest those savings: interest-bearing cash accounts, U.S. government E bonds, ARCO stock, a broad-based stock fund, or combinations of the previous four options. It's a plan that can add up to big bucks. A 1982 survey of 5,000 employees showed that more than 60 percent were influenced by the benefit program in joining ARCO—and 83 percent said benefits help to keep them at ARCO.

Every week, in the *ArcoSpark*, all jobs open in the company—throughout the world—are listed so that employees may have first crack at them. Some 20 jobs are posted every week—and 8 people usually apply for each opening. Seven out of 10 of these jobs are filled by people already working for ARCO. Early in 1983, for example, the company was looking for a paralegal associate in its Los Angeles headquarters office, salary ranging from $21,437 to $36,310, depending on qualifications and experience; a drafting supervisor for the Bakersfield, California, oil and gas exploration unit, salary ranging from $27,000 up to $43,000; and an employee relations representative in Houston, salary range $33,000 to $52,000.

When ARCO recruits on school campuses, it looks primarily for technical people. About 77 percent of its college recruits come from engineering and the sciences. Very few liberal arts graduates are hired. A strong effort has been made to recruit and promote minority and female employees. About 17 percent of ARCO's employees are now minority-group members. However, there is no black officer—and only one female officer, Cameron Cooper, ARCO's treasurer.

Women make up 6.8 percent of the managerial ranks. In 1980, ARCO transferred 35-year-old Peg Fisher from West Texas to Prudhoe Bay, Alaska, where she supervised 50 crew members working on an oil rig. She was probably the only female rig supervisor in the industry. She made more than $50,000 working 26 weeks in Alaska. Sandra Thomas, a shift supervisor at ARCO's Houston refinery, says: "I was the first black woman hired in the refinery. I started in the maintenance pool, then worked in the coker. When I moved to the butane recovery unit, I became the first woman to qualify as a 'still-man'—the person responsible for the unit. Now I supervise five people and make sure the towers that manufacture petroleum products are running smoothly." Sandra Thomas's remarks were made in an official ARCO publication on women in ARCO, but just the fact that the company is willing to stick its neck out and put forth women as role models indicates the commitment. An unsolicited comment came our way from Patricia Criscione, who joined ARCO in 1980 as a file clerk in the natural gas department in Dallas. She was promoted twice within a year, and she said ARCO's concern extended beyond the workplace. Although she had been with the company for less than six months, she was able to tap an emergency fund for a no-interest loan to meet a family crisis.

ARCO's social consciousness is reflected in its generous donations to social service organizations, and in its encouraging employees to work for community groups. It gives annual community service awards to employees who have made outstanding contributions. ARCO is also one of the few companies that will match employee and retiree gifts, up to $20,000, on a two-for-one basis. Let's say, for example, that you're flush enough to give $20,000 to your alma mater. ARCO will match that donation with $40,000. Other big companies in the nation match only dollar-for-dollar—and have limits as low as $1,000. Three times in the past 10 years ARCO has published a report, "Participation," that details its social responsibility activities—and each one has included a critique of its programs by an outsider. Self-criticism is not a hallmark of corporate behavior.

There's frequently a gap, of course, between what a company preaches and what it practices. The 1,100 people who were thrown out of work in Anaconda, Montana, when ARCO shut down the copper smelter there in 1980 would not give the company high marks. ARCO bought Anaconda in 1977—and it probably rues the day. Some people who have worked at ARCO say that while the company talks a good show, inside the walls it resembles any other stratified, bureaucratic business. There are office politics at the ARCO Tower headquarters in Los Angeles, and there's not much mixing between upper- and lower-level people. The higher up you go in the building, the more lavish the offices—until you reach the very top, where the chairman and president work in acres of carpeted elegance.

In 1984, uneasiness spread through the company as a result of belt-tightening, terminations, the sale of virtually all the metals businesses, and a sinking feeling that the corporate culture was undergoing a profound change. Even as this malaise was spreading, however, ARCO held an extraordinary conference, bringing to Los Angeles the presidents of 30 retiree clubs across the country. ARCO underwrote the entire meeting, including the travel expenses of the wives who accompanied their husbands. The point of the meeting was to explore the needs of people who have retired from the company and to discuss avenues of support from the company. It was believed to be the first conference of its kind ever sponsored by a corporation—another sign that Atlantic Richfield still cares about its people.

Main employment centers   ARCO has operations in 47 states. Biggest states (from an employee population standpoint) are: Texas (11,000), California (9,000), and Pennsylvania (5,400). Some 2,000 people work in Alaska, and their average wage is $50,000 a year. Three thousand employees work outside the United States, more than two dozen in China, where ARCO is drilling for oil in the South China Sea.

Here are the ten colleges most frequently represented among ARCO employees (showing the number of degrees obtained from each school): Texas A&M (466), University of Texas (435), UCLA (267), University of Houston (239), North Texas State University (229), University of Southern California (222), Drexel (222), University of Oklahoma (218), Texas Tech (209), and Southern Methodist University (203).

Headquarters   Atlantic Richfield Company
515 South Flower Street
Los Angeles, CA 90071
213-486-3511

AT&T BELL LABORATORIES

Bell Labs is the research-and-development arm of AT&T. Employees: 19,000.

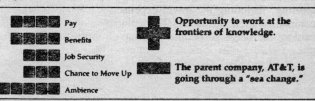

■■■■ Pay		Opportunity to work at the frontiers of knowledge.
■■■■ Benefits		
■■■ Job Security		
■■■ Chance to Move Up		The parent company, AT&T, is going through a "sea change."
■■■■■ Ambience		

Bell Labs has 19,000 employees—and 23,000 computer terminals. That quickly tells you something about the nature of this place, certainly one of the most prestigious scientific research organizations in the world. The fact that it's tucked into the confines of AT&T has not prevented Bell Labs from developing a culture of its own, one that's related to its mission: to break down the barriers to knowledge, especially in —but not limited to—the field of telecommunications.

The transistor was invented at Bell Labs. So were sound movies, modular phones, and the display on digital watches. Vitamin B1 was first synthesized here. In 1978, two Bell Labs scientists, Arno Penzias and Robert Wilson, were awarded Nobel Prizes for their discovery of faint background radiation, a discovery that confirmed the theory that the universe was created billions of years ago by a "big bang." They are the sixth and seventh Nobel laureates to come from Bell Labs. In August 1983, Bell Labs received its 20,000th patent. So this is a very heady place. The people at Bell Labs are often working on the leading edge of their disciplines. If you like witnessing or being part of breakthroughs, it's an exciting place to be.

Bell Labs provides the closest approximation to an academic environment that you can find within the walls of a commercial establishment. It's a collegial atmosphere. Scien-

29

tists work in labs the way they would at a medical research institution or advanced engineering school. Various disciplines are represented at Bell Labs: electrical engineering, chemistry, biology, computer science, physics, psychology. There's a sharing of information, an opportunity to trade wisecracks over the lunch table with some brainy colleagues.

The Bell Labs complex at Murray Hill, New Jersey, looks like a college campus, with lawns and trees surrounding the building. Inside, there's a maze of corridors lit by fluorescent lights, and off the corridors are small rooms, which serve as offices and laboratories, both big and small. You see an array of garb—jeans and open shirts, shorts and sandals during the summertime, a fair number of business suits. You know you are not in a regular business office.

In 1984, the staff included 2,747 Ph.D.'s, 4,648 people with master's degrees, and 2,791 others with bachelor's degrees. And many are still going to school. An in-house education center has enrolled more than half the employees in courses covering everything from accounting to computer science. These courses are given on the premises or at outside schools where Bell Labs will pick up the tuition. More than 3,000 Bell Labs employees were enrolled in tuition-reimbursement programs in 1984. One two-year in-house program of study enables employees to get the equivalent of a master's degree in computer science, and Chuck Kierschenmann, head of Bell's continuing education department, claims it is "technically just as rigorous as any university graduate course."

Bell Labs also follows academic practice by having a monthly lecture series addressed by experts who are working in exotic areas that, on the face of it, have nothing to do with the work there. Recent lectures dealt with bridge-building, bird navigation, and whale songs.

There are many advantages to working for Bell Labs. The pay is good, the benefits are super. The company, for example, picks up 100 percent of your medical and dental insurance premium—for you and all your dependents. You can sock away up to 6 percent of your salary into a savings-and-investment plan—and for every dollar you put up, Bell will put up sixty-seven cents. So it can be a fairly cushy place.

At the same time, the pressure to perform is strong—it's

peer pressure from colleagues. You're also not going to be working in a dingy laboratory with outmoded equipment. The Bell labs are sparkling clean, and the people are generally working with state-of-the-art equipment. The Bell scientists also get a chance to go to lush watering holes when their professional societies gather for meetings. The company picks up the tab. This is also a very big place. What other research-and-development outfit is working on an annual budget of $1.9 billion?

R.D. Gordon, a computer scientist from Purdue University, whose work in marrying computers with television can be seen at Disney's Epcot Center in Orlando, Florida, was worried when he came to Bell Labs because he was used to a "small-company environment." But he said that in his first year there, "I became totally convinced that this place has all the advantages of a small place and all the opportunities of a large corporation. It really surprised me."

It's not easy to be hired by Bell Labs. As Gordon says, if you just get to the interview stage, you must already be someone "who can walk on water." But then it becomes a question of how well you would fit into a particular laboratory. Each Bell lab can have a different personality—some are outgoing, some ingrown. So before a candidate is hired, he or she will be interviewed by five or six people from the lab most likely to hire the prospect.

Being smart doesn't necessarily mean that you will automatically succeed at Bell Labs. Dr. C. Kumar N. Patel, an Indian-born physicist who has been with Bell Labs for more than 20 years, explained recently some of the other conditions for success: "Every person hired by Bell Labs comes with technical excellence. But doing science or technology is more than working in your own lab or subgroup. It requires convincing your colleagues of the importance of your work.

"The easiest way to enter this culture is making contacts in nontechnical situations, for example at lunch. In my area we have tea available in late afternoon.

"In the Bell Labs culture, it is not derogatory to ask questions. It is merely a way to get information. Being assimilated does not mean giving up your own values. If you want to change the values of the dominant culture, you can do it only from within.

"Once you are assimilated into the Bell labs culture, you

gain visibility. Some visibility is informal—people in your area get to know you as knowing a lot about a certain subject. Some is formal—you can ask for, and be given, the chance to give talks at professional society meetings.

"This visibility makes possible another necessary condition of success—perceived, as opposed to actual, excellence. You can be very good in a closed lab, but no one will necessarily know. You must be good in public."

There's a tension at Bell Labs between doing good basic research and the need to produce a product for the corporate owner. The apparatus used by the phone companies around the country—the phones themselves, the elaborate switching systems—were developed at Bell Laboratories. The ultimate justification of Bell Labs has been the technological breakthroughs that could be converted into products used by the phone companies.

But the breakup of AT&T brought a new ballgame. One immediate effect on Bell Labs was the transfer of some 3,000 scientists and engineers to Bell Communications Research, which serves as the research-and-development arm of the independent phone companies—a mini Bell Labs, if you will.

At Bell Labs in 1984, a sense of urgency—and some uneasiness—was growing among staff members because of the expected pressure to come up with usable products in shorter periods of time. After all, AT&T will be competing directly against IBM in the burgeoning field of electronic transmission of data. If anyone can take on IBM in computers, it's probably Bell Labs. So the Bell Labs people may have to become more bottom-line oriented.

The management, of course, sees it as a golden opportunity. The breakup, they point out, frees Bell Labs "to pursue potential applications wherever théy take us." Before they could not. If the labs invent something like the transistor in the future, AT&T will get first crack at exploiting its end uses.

The pioneering scientific work done at Bell Labs has been so impressive that it has often been called "a national treasure." The question is: will this heady atmosphere change? *Business Week*, for one, believes it already has. In a special report in its December 3, 1984, issue, the magazine concluded that Bell Labs has become "just another corporate research & development facility tethered to the bottom line." We didn't feel that in a half-day visit we made to Bell Labs'

Indian Hill facility outside Chicago in September 1984. Security is much tighter than it used to be (you need to get clearance every time you move to another building), but there was a collegial easiness about the place that you don't find in most corporate research labs. It still looks like a good place to work. Jeremy Bernstein, science writer for the *The New Yorker*, did a close inspection of Bell Labs in *Three Degrees Above Zero*, a book published in late 1984 by Charles Scribner's Sons. Bernstein asserted in his introduction that if the fundamental character of Bell Labs does change, "then the United States will have lost one of its great technological assets. That, I believe, *would* be total folly."

Bernstein's book concludes with words from Arno Penzias, who said, in part:

"If people are doing an outstanding job, we let them alone, and we're going to continue to do that.... As long as there is a healthy Bell Laboratories we need fundamental research desperately. Fundamental research is our window to the universities, to the scientific community.... If I hire the fifth-best theoretical physics student in the country I can get away with it, but if I hire the fifteenth-best I am wasting my time. We are looking for number two or number three, and we want to compete with the best universities for number one. That is where we are. I am a high-pressure guy, and I didn't take this job to conduct a going-out-of-business sale."

Main employment centers   In New Jersey, Holmdel, 3,800; Murray Hill, 3,500; Whippany, 2,600; Piscataway, 1,800; and Short Hills, 1,200 employees. The other big facility is the Indian Hill Laboratory in Naperville, Illinois, outside Chicago, where 4,700 people work.

Headquarters   Bell Laboratories
600 Mountain Avenue
Murray Hill, NJ 07974
201-582-3000

TRAVENOL

BAXTER TRAVENOL LABORATORIES, INC.

Baxter Travenol makes medical care products including intravenous solutions (of which it's the world's leading supplier)
and dialysis equipment for people with failed kidneys. U.S.
employees: 21,000.

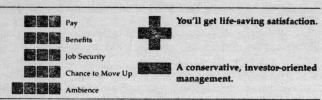

■■■ Pay	**+**	**You'll get life-saving satisfaction.**
■■■ Benefits		
■■■ Job Security		
■■■ Chance to Move Up	■■	**A conservative, investor-oriented management.**
■■■■ Ambience		

Michele J. Hooper is happy with this suburban Chicago
company that supplies many of the products you see in hospitals. A black and a graduate of the prestigious business school
at the University of Chicago, she joined Baxter in 1976 and
was promoted seven times in eight years. When we saw her in
the summer of 1983, she was director of operations for
Baxter's biggest unit, the parenteral products division,
whence come the intravenous solutions and the equipment to
inject them into the bloodstream of patients. A few months
later she had moved on again, in charge of a new unit having
to do with reimbursement of claims (a crucial area in today's
health-care industry). Two promotions later, she was, in early
1985, a Travenol vice-president responsible for strategic planning. Hooper, who worked at a drug company in Pennsylvania before coming to Baxter, said that when she arrived
here, "I came thinking like a typical M.B.A. I'd be here two
years, get a promotion and slip away to climb the corporate
ladder somewhere else. I'm here eight years and I really enjoy
it. I like coming to work. This is a very fast growing company, still undefined. You can go in and have your decision
make an impact."

Marilyn Terry Mercer is also pleased to be here. She

worked for 10 years at IBM before coming to Baxter in 1982 and is impressed with the mobility of the place and her access to top managers. "Here," she said, "I feel that I can make something happen." Mercer was promoted in 1983 to a division presidency, and in 1984 she joined the management staff for the company's information businesses.

Another ex-IBMer who has risen quickly at Baxter is Rick Adam, who joined the company in 1980. He heads up the information businesses group (code words for hospital and other medical computer software operations), and in 1983, at age 36, he was elected a corporate vice-president. Contrasting IBM with Baxter, he told us: "IBM is fine for a $30 billion company. It may be the best $30 billion company around. But here you get more of a chance to have a direct impact. It's a folksy place, yet it's big enough, at $2 billion, to have a worldwide impact."

Baxter Travenol does have a worldwide impact because it has emerged as one of the giants of the exploding health-care industry. The career opportunities that have opened up here resulted from Baxter's "smarts" in constantly improving its products and exploring new areas. Unlike some other companies in this industry, it has a superlative quality-control record. You may not have heard of Baxter Travenol because it hasn't gotten into trouble with product disasters.

Baxter Travenol has carried out its mission in health care with close attention to financial return to investors. As of 1983, it had 28 years, back-to-back, in which sales and earnings had increased by at least 20 percent *every year*. That incredible record (no other company could match it) was smashed in 1984 when cost containment efforts in the health-care industry resulted in a sharp decline in profits.

Baxter Travenol works hard to maintain a family feeling, which is not easy when you have facilities all over the place —there are 19 manufacturing plants in the United States alone. But it uses a variety of techniques. Every year it gives plant awards: outstanding large plant, outstanding small plant, most improved large plant, most improved small plant; and there are also awards to plants for exceptional performance. Top management travels to the award-winning plants for the presentations.

In 1983, when we saw Vernon Loucks, the young, preppy-looking chief executive of Baxter, he had just returned from such a presentation to the Hays, Kansas, plant—and he was tickled by a letter he had already received from a production worker whom he had stopped to talk to; the note began, "Dear Vern." A year-and-a-half later it was a different story, as the company, jolted by its first setback in three decades, announced that it would close the Hays plant to consolidate production of intravenous devices at its plant in Mountain Home, Arkansas. It was a blow to the Kansas community where Baxter employed 700 people. Some employees described it as a "bolt from the blue." Loucks himself called it the most "agonizing" decision he had ever had to make. The company cushioned the blow to Hays workers with this closeout package:

- The plant was to be phased out over a 12-month period;
- Employees would receive four weeks of pay, plus one week for each year of service (the plant was opened in 1968);
- Employees over 40 years of age received an additional four weeks of pay;
- Employees over 50 got an additional four weeks for a total of eight additional weeks;
- Health insurance coverage continued for six months after the last day worked;
- Profit-sharing contributions were paid out in full whether the employee was fully vested or not;
- Any employee already enrolled in an educational course would continue to receive reimbursement; and
- Children of employees on Baxter Travenol scholarships will continue to qualify for such aid.

In addition, a counseling service was opened to help employees find new jobs.

When the company celebrated its fiftieth birthday in 1981, 50 employee ambassadors from 50 Travenol (they call the company both "Baxter" and "Travenol") facilities in 18 countries traveled to Deerfield headquarters to mark the occasion. And these people were not top brass at all; they represented rank-and-filers.

Baxter Travenol keeps a close watch on labor costs, holding them down by avoiding unions, and by placing its factories in small towns such as Kingstree, South Carolina; North Cove, North Carolina; and Mountain Home. Those are low-wage towns where Baxter Travenol can instantly become the best payer around. And then it builds a loyal work force by providing stable employment with good fringe benefits. There's a Baxter plant in the Mississippi Delta town of Cleveland, which makes intravenous solutions and disposable hospital products. L.C.Dorsey, a Mississippi civil rights activist who grew up in the Delta, describes the Cleveland plant as "one of the best places to work," although she adds that white males held all the supervisory posts while black women were rarely promoted.

Baxter Travenol also holds down labor costs by automating plants. But it has had no company-wide layoffs.

Baxter's folksy chairman, William B. Graham, is a University of Chicago-educated lawyer who joined the company in 1945. No one disputes that he was the chief architect of Baxter's growth. When he came aboard, annual sales were $1.5 million. They're now close to $2 billion. He served as chief executive officer from 1953 to 1980. In 1983 he was 72 years old. Baxter has an outgoing, athletic president in Loucks, who graduated from Yale and the Harvard Business School. Loucks played football at Yale—and one member of Baxter's board of directors is former adman Clinton E. Frank, and all-time Yale football great. Loucks runs marathons and is the force behind the emphasis on physical fitness at Baxter; he was 48 in 1983. Wilbur H. Gantz, executive vice-president, was named chief operating officer in 1983, which means he is second-in-command to Loucks; he also runs marathons (a tip to would-be advancers at Baxter Travenol).

Also in the top management ranks is an echelon of military types. Steven Lazarus, senior vice-president, is a former Navy captain. Dr. Robert A. Patterson, a physician and senior vice-president, was Surgeon General of the U.S. Air Force, with the rank of lieutenant general, before joining Baxter in 1976. And Warren D. Johnson, vice-president, was also a lieutenant general in the Air Force, serving as director of the Defense Nuclear Agency before retiring in 1977.

Baxter takes good care of its own people. It maintains a strong benefits program to which it keeps adding all the time. In addition to the standard items (medical and dental insurance, group life insurance), it includes the following:

• Profit-sharing—the company kicks in 7 percent of pre-tax profits to the pool to be divided;

• A deferred thrift plan, enabling employees to save pre-tax money (thereby reducing their tax liability)—the company matches each dollar saved with fifty cents of its own, up to a maximum of $500;

- Subsidized day care—the company picks up one-third of the cost of tuition at two day-care centers near its Deerfield headquarters; enrolled in 1984 were 60 children of Baxter employees;

- At some locations a flex-time policy permits employees to report to work at 7:30 A.M., 8:00 A.M., or 8:30 A.M., whichever is most convenient for them;

- Summertime hours—everyone works an extra hour Monday through Thursday so that the office can be closed Friday afternoons;

- Incentive to bring in your friends—the company will pay you $350 or $500 (depending on the job filled) if you recommend someone who is hired by the company.

The 1,500 people at the corporate headquarters in Deerfield, 30 miles northwest of Chicago's Loop, occupy one of the most spectacular corporate offices in America. Designed by Skidmore, Owings & Merrill, it sits on 188 acres, only half of which are in use. It consists of a series of ten low-slung buildings interconnected by glass-enclosed bridges, flanked by sloping lawns and man-made ponds, one of which has a fountain patterned after the one in London's Hyde Park. Three enclosed garages can handle 1,500 automobiles. However, the most spectacular feature of the headquarters facility is the cafeteria. It has a wonderful feeling of openness because there are no posts or pillars holding up the roof, which is suspended by 98 steel cables radiating from two 35-foot masts. More than three-quarters of the headquarters staff eat there regularly, including the top officers. There is no executive dining room. A mile-and-a-half running track loops around the site.

When the complex went up in 1976, it did not have a physical-fitness facility. Now it has. Loucks, quickly seeing the error of his ways, approved the conversion of one area into a gymnasium where employees can work out and take classes. More than 900 Baxter Travenol people—more than half the staff at Deerfield—pay an annual fee of $70 to participate in activities there. In 1983, Baxter also opened an outdoor half-mile jogging track for employees at its Round Lake, Illinois, facility, not far from Deerfield. Cutting the ribbon to open the track was England's world-class miler, Sebastian Coe. He's a friend of Vernon Loucks's. Coe was featured on the front cover of the 1981 annual report of Baxter Travenol.

If you come to this company, bring your jogging shoes.

Main employment centers   Chicago area: 6,500; North Cove, North Carolina: 2,600; and, Mountain Home, Arkansas: 1,500. Of Baxter's 31,000 employees, 10,000 work overseas.

Headquarters   Baxter Travenol Laboratories, Inc.
One Baxter Parkway
Deerfield, IL 60015
312-948-2000

BEST PLACES FOR BLACKS TO WORK

Cummins Engine	Hewlett-Packard IBM	Los Angeles Dodgers
Federal Express	Levi Strauss	Polaroid
General Electric		Time Inc.

Leo Burnett Company, Inc.

LEO BURNETT COMPANY, INC.

Leo Burnett is the largest ad agency in Chicago. U.S. employees: 1,600.

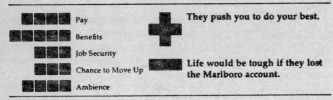

■■■■ Pay	➕ **They push you to do your best.**
■■■■■ Benefits	
■■■ Job Security	
■■■ Chance to Move Up	■■ **Life would be tough if they lost the Marlboro account.**
■■■■ Ambience	

What other company gives away 1,000 apples every day? The Leo Burnett advertising agency in Chicago does. There's a bowl of red apples in the reception rooms on every one of the 11 floors the company occupies in the Prudential Building on Randolph Drive near Lake Michigan. Apples became a company trademark after a combination receptionist-telephone operator-accountant put them out when the agency first opened its doors on August 5, 1935, in the midst of the depression. Visitors used to walk away munching apples, some of them saying, "It won't be long before Leo Burnett is selling apples on the street corner instead of giving them away." This wisecrack ended up in a Chicago newspaper column—and, as the agency likes to explain today, "we became more determined than ever to make better and better ads and give away more and more apples. We hope we're still living up to that first one; we *know* we're doing it with the second."

Burnett is now one of the largest advertising agencies in the world—it ranks eighth in the U.S standings—but it's unique in that it's the only one of the giant American ad shops that's not headquartered in New York City. Nor does it maintain any presence in New York save for a tiny contact office. The agency that invented the Jolly Green Giant, the Marlboro

40

Man, the lonely Maytag repairman, Tony the Tiger, Charlie the Tuna, Morris the Cat, and the Pillsbury Doughboy was born in Chicago and insists, almost patriotically, on remaining there. The late Leo Burnett, the ex-newspaperman who founded the agency, once said: "Any canvass of New York agencies will show, of course, that a lot of their star performers were originally cow-milking yokels from the Midwest. I suppose we can be proud of that, but I think Chicago advertising has now reached the point where we can stop being a way-station for talent, and that making good in Chicago is in every way as rewarding as making the grade in New York.

"To paraphrase an old saying, if you can't make a good ad in Chicago, you can't make one anywhere!"

Leo Burnett, who came from St. Johns, Michigan, and who worked as a reporter on the *Peoria Journal* before beginning his advertising career with Cadillac Motor in Detroit, died in 1971 at age 79, but he left his mark on this agency, in more ways than just his name. The company's symbol, from the start, was a hand reaching for stars, the explanation being: "If you reach for the stars, you may not always get one, but you won't come up with a handful of mud either." Burnett was a stern taskmaster who had high standards for the ads that came out of his shop. Among his convictions were these:

"Good advertising lifts up, not tears down."

"Nothing is ever good enough around here."

"Clichés are unacceptable."

"We want people to say, 'What a great product,' not 'What a great ad.' "

This drive for creative excellence is still the propelling force at the Burnett agency. It has a small roster of accounts, but they are all big advertisers: Philip Morris, United Airlines, Kellogg, Procter & Gamble, Oldsmobile, McDonald's, Nestlé, Pillsbury, Star-Kist, Union Oil. And while Burnett insists on operating from Chicago, its clients come from all over the country. In terms of number of flights out of Chicago, Burnett ranks as the third biggest customer at O'Hare Airport—after Sears, Roebuck and Arthur Anderson & Co. Burnett people who fly are, of course, required to fly client United Airlines unless they're going to a city where United doesn't fly. And you will always find the Burnett people in the first-class section. The agency does not believe in sending people by coach.

In a business noted for its volatility, Burnett has long-term relationships with clients and employees. The agency has 10 clients that go back more than 25 years. Nearly all its client relationships go back more than 10 years. As for employees, at the start of 1983, of the 1,540 people working in Burnett's Chicago office, 33 had been there more than 30 years, 103 between 20 and 29 years, 315 from 10 to 15 years. So, 451, or 30 percent of the work force, had more than 10 years' service.

Burnett people show intense loyalty. At least they speak passionately about working there. Adell Zine, who works in accounting and who completed her fortieth year with the agency in 1984, says it's "a company with a heart. I thought that after I was married, I would quit. But I didn't because I enjoy coming to work here." Marcia Garrett, a receptionist, came to the agency from a schoolteaching career. She thought at first that she would be bored, "but that was nineteen years ago." Garrett says she sees many people who leave the agency and then return to confess, "I'm glad to be back." She works on the executive floor at Burnett, and so she sees the chairman and the president, about whom she relates, "There are times when I've had an idea about an account, and they listen to me. You're not just a receptionist. They respect you."

Mark Hazeltine, an account executive on Allstate Insurance, worked at other agencies before coming to Burnett—and he says that even though Burnett is bigger, there's "less red tape here. And you're challenged more." Hazeltine says, "If you're looking for the cushiest companies to work for, this one will never make your list because you work long hours here. But you can walk out of here sometimes and be amazed at what you can do."

Kent Middleton, a 28-year-old copywriter, speaks mostly about the opportunity he has to work with very bright, creative people. "We don't have any rules at Burnett," he says, "because there are so many people in charge that you are not ruled by the whims of one man. And you can bend the rules if you have good reasons to bend them." Middleton says he expects to be fired one day—that's the nature of the agency business. "All my friends have been fired. You just sit and wait. But Burnett is amazing.... We don't do boring soap commercials. We even managed to get Procter & Gamble to do decent advertising."

As to the continuing influence of Leo Burnett, Hazeltine describes meetings where people scream at each other over which is the best advertising approach, when someone will suddenly say, "What would Leo think?" And it does make everyone stop and think.

Burnett people are justifiably proud of their athletic prowess. In 1984, the agency fielded a 26-person track team in the annual Corporate Cup Relays sponsored by *Runner's World* and finished fifth competing against companies (General Electric, IBM, Ford, AT&T, Rockwell) with many thousands more employees to draw upon. Burnett's Frankfurt office sent Klaus Kuester, who won a gold medal in the 1,500-meter event with a meet record time of 4:12:4.

Burnett has a super benefits package for its employees—profit-sharing, pension plan, annual bonus, comprehensive medical insurance, an adoptive aid program that will pay up to $3,000 to help an employee adopt a child—but the features that really stand out are the informal ways in which it shows its concern. Marcia Garrett will tell you that when she called in sick and said she was going to the hospital the next day, Burnett sent a company car to take her, "even though I was perfectly capable of getting there myself." In 1980, when the agency handled one billion dollars of advertising for the first time, everyone in the New York and Hollywood offices—50 people altogether—were flown to Chicago, first class of course, to share the festivities at the agency's annual breakfast celebration.

Two events every year galvanize Burnett people. One is Anniversay Day on August 5. The agency goes to great lengths to have a special theme for the day and special gifts of very high value for every employee. In 1982, it was an expensive glass jar filled with high-quality jams and jellies, one package of jams and jellies for each client. In previous years it was a model train, statues, customized bottles of wine. In addition, on Anniversay Day every employee in every Burnett office (the agency now has 30 offices outside the United States) receives one dollar for every year of the agency's life. In 1984, that meant $49 for every person on the payroll around the world. The other big event is Bonus Day in the second week of December. The entire agency force troops out of the Prudential Building to the Hyatt Regency Hotel on Wacker Drive for a full breakfast and report from the agency's

Taking the Gobbledygook
Out of Employee Handbooks

If you're looking for a sedative, head for your nearest employee handbook, the document issued by a company to explain its policies and benefits to the people who come to work there. An exception is Leo Burnett's. Called "The Star Reachers Handbook," it's written in language everyone can understand. Here are some examples from the Burnett handbook:

"What we call our business day starts at 9:00 A.M. and keeps going until 5 o'clock, with one hour out for lunch. The lunch hour is the same for those who go out to eat and those who prefer to stoke up at their desks."

"Part of our people philosophy is to make the necessary travel as pleasant as possible. For these reasons our travel policy is to fly first class, stay in first-class hotels and live and work under first-class conditions."

"The Burnett Profit Sharing Plan was established in 1943.

"Here's a brief explanation of how the plan works.

"Each year the company contributes a portion of its profits into a separate trust fund, held by a large Chicago bank, and credits you with your share. Generally speaking, your share will be 15 percent of your total annual compensation—that is, base pay, overtime and bonus. The percentage could be less but 15 percent has been contributed in every year—except for one of the very early years—since the plan began. By the way, 15 percent is the maximum contribution allowed by federal law."

"Sick time. There may not be another policy like ours anywhere. For employees who have been with us for at least 2 years, the policy simply reads, 'you will receive full salary whenever you are sick.' This is particularly important for employees stricken with a serious illness, and allows them to concentrate their energies on getting well. Employees with less than 2 years of service may receive up to 10 paid sick days in a calendar year. . . . If you're sick for over 56 consecutive days, sick pay stops and the company's disability plan takes over."

And here are some guidelines for Burnetters who are traveling on business:

"Meals: With clients, good business judgment. Alone: First class—but reasonable.

"Entertainment: With the client: good business judgment. Alone: A movie and a drink is okay, but that's about it."

top managers. They also show a film of Leo Burnett's last appearance—and that makes it a teary-eyed occasion. And then the bonuses are awarded. They can be quite substantial, 15 to 20 percent of one's pay. Kent Middleton said that when he opened his envelope in 1982, he had to sit down. "On that day," he says, "you wouldn't want to be working anywhere else in the world."

Main employment center   Chicago, where 1,500 people work. Another 2,100 work in overseas offices.

Headquarters   Leo Burnett Company, Inc.
Prudential Plaza
Chicago, IL 60601
312-565-5959

BEST EMPLOYEE NEWSPAPERS

Atlantic Richfield   **Publix Super Markets**
General Mills   **Time Inc.**

CELESTIAL SEASONINGS, INC.

CELESTIAL SEASONINGS, INC.

Celestial Seasonings makes herbal teas packed in artful boxes that carry uplifting messages. Employees: 200.

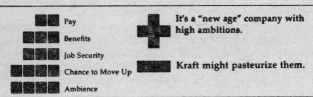

■■ Pay	✚ It's a "new age" company with high ambitions.
■■■ Benefits	
■■■ Job Security	
■■■■ Chance to Move Up	▬▬ Kraft might pasteurize them.
■■■■■ Ambience	

This is the smallest company in this book, but it's not likely to remain so small. Between 1978 and 1983, sales tripled to reach $27 million. Coming into 1983, the company had 200 employees. And it's clear this is a company committed to growth. Mo Siegel, founder, leader, and driving force, has said, "I want Celestial Seasonings to enter the twenty-first century as one of America's leading corporations." It's unlikely to do that now, at least under its own steam. In May 1984 Celestial Seasonings was acquired by one of the largest food companies in the United States, the Kraft Foods division of Dart & Kraft. Whether this new parentage turns out to be positive or negative has yet to be determined. People might still look at Celestial Seasonings as a chance to get in on the ground floor.

"Ground floor to what?" you might ask. Although Celestial Seasonings has fooled around with other products from time to time, it's basically a one-product company: herbal tea. To be sure, there are 27 varieties in the line, each packed in a colorful, animated, Disneylike carton, each package carrying an inspirational message, such as "Nothing cures like time and love" (songwriter Laura Nyro) or "To live is to change and to be perfect is to have changed often" (Cardinal Newman) or "The closer we are to nature, the closer we are to God" (Goethe)—but it's still just a tea company. However, no one who knows Mo Siegel believes he will be satisfied with the status quo. Herbal hair shampoos and conditioners were introduced in 1983 under the name Mountain Herbery. And new food products emphasizing natural ingredients are expected to flow next from this Boulder, Colorado-based company.

Boulder is an important feature about working for Celestial Seasonings. Unless you're one of a handful of people assigned to a regional sales office, that's where you will be working. It's not exactly a fate worse than death. Boulder is a breathtaking town set in the foothills of the Rocky Mountains, just 20 miles northwest of Denver—and 1,000 miles from Kraft's headquarters outside of Chicago. It's the home of the University of Colorado, and it's developing a high-tech presence (Storage Technology, NBI, Cobe Labs). Much of the new development has the look of the Silicon Valley south of San Francisco. Boulder may also have a fair claim to the title "health capital of the country." If everyone in town is not out running or bicycling, they look as if they're about to be. Celestial Seasonings was the original sponsor of the Red Zinger Bicycle Classic, a bike marathon that has since been taken over by the nearby Coors brewery and renamed the Coors' Classic.

There's nothing high-tech about Celestial Seasonings, although its teabag-making line is highly automated. The company plans to put up a modern facility north of Boulder in 1987, but it now occupies five old buildings on the outskirts of town, and they look like buildings you could find in the East Bronx. Nothing fancy, including Mo Siegel's office, which is just to the left of the cramped switchboard-receptionist cubicle as you enter the main building. He has a book-lined office, the cases being filled with sets of the *Encyclopaedia Britannica* and the Great Books. When we encountered him in the summer of 1983, Siegel was crouched over a Lisa computer trying to punch out a statement on the overarching values of the company. His preliminary draft emphasized the importance of "God" and "family"—and he said to us that he knew he would have trouble getting his staff to accept those two concepts. Siegel, in 1983, was 33 years old. He never went to college, but he became a millionaire by the time he was 26—by selling herbal tea. He likes to think of himself as a philosopher. And he has a disarming, Socratic way of putting questions to people who are interviewing him. S.J. Guffey, a writer in the Denver office of the Associated Press, once described him as "a guy with the moral conviction of Abraham Lincoln, the drive of Lee Iacocca, and the whimsy of E.T."

Siegel does run an interesting show at Celestial Seasonings. "What is important," he says, "is creating a condition in which the work force feels better about their lives, because what is good for labor should be good for management and vice versa." There's an easy informality about Celestial Seasonings, but people are clearly there to work. An employee stock-ownership trust used to own 10 percent of the stock and as a result of the Kraft purchase, the average employee received a check equivalent to 70 percent of his or her annual salary. There's a gain-sharing program that pays cash dividends to employees twice a year if corporate goals are exceeded. The company also has a thrift plan enabling employees to save up to 16 percent of their pay—and up to the 6 percent level, the company will match half the contribution. After joining Celestial Seasonings, you get a free company T-shirt. On your birthday you receive a $25 check. At Thanksgiving you get a $50 check. And at Christmas there's a $100 check for everyone. There are no time clocks at the plant. There are no unions. And the place seems to have a sense of humor. Tacked up on one wall was the headline: "Price, Quality, Speed—Pick Any 2."

Celestial Seasonings has been a company where people can spread their wings. Helen Harring arrived there as a secretary in 1979, and she was later put in charge of automating the office with word processing stations. A janitor who thought money could be saved by having a fleet of trucks to transport teas to the marketplace instead of hiring outside truckers was given the job of organizing such a fleet. Frank Boruff, the plant manager, came to Celestial Seasonings after 10 years at General Foods. There's much more team effort here, he says, and the company is "smaller, younger, and more creative." Many of his neighbors work for IBM, and Boruff says they envy his being able to go to work in jeans every day.

Getting a job at Celestial Seasonings is not easy. Turnover is low, and for every opening, there are more than 100 applications. Boruff says he rarely has to advertise for plant openings because he has so many unsolicited applications on hand. And he says that 75 percent of these applications begin by saying something like, "I'm applying to Celestial Seasonings because I am a longtime user of your products, and I really appreciate what you are doing." But Mo Siegel is not one who's averse to tapping talent in big corporations. He has brought into Celestial Seasonings alumni from Quaker Oats, Procter & Gamble, Heublein, Campbell Soup, and PepsiCo. Indeed, Siegel has an inordinate admiration for the competence of some big American companies. He's a great fan of Mary Kay. And he's in awe of what the Watsons built at IBM. Among his teachers, he freely admits, are Norman Vincent Peale, Peter Drucker, and Mortimer Adler.

So there's an enigma about Mo Siegel and the company he built, a tension that makes Celestial Seasonings an exciting place to be. More often than not, Siegel is described as a refugee from the hippie culture of the 1960s. The name of his company comes from the name of a girl friend of Wyck Hay, the brother of John Hay, who cofounded the company with Siegel in 1971. As recently as 1983, the *New York Times* described Celestial Seasonings as "one of the most remarkable business successes to arise out of the late 1960s counterculture." It pains Siegel to read these descriptions. He doesn't identify with this heritage. But now that he runs a successful business, he's described as turning his back on his heritage and looking to create a new General Foods or Norton Simon. An article in the *Denver Post* in 1983 took this tack, declaring: "It isn't quite Procter & Gamble now, but it's a long way from the volleyball games which they used to play during lunch hours. A smooth corporate image prevails." These articles, aligning him with the big corporate culture of America, irritate Siegel just as much as the ones that talk about his coming out of the hippie culture.

What Siegel says he's trying to do is build a *big* company that's a *good* company, that has some values. He puts it this way: "I want Celestial Seasonings to be something of a social experiment, as well as a really button-down, topnotch company."

In July 1983, when we saw Siegel, we asked him if Celestial Seasonings would ever sell stock to the public. He snapped back, "No comment." Two months later came the prospectus from the Wall Street investment banking house Goldman Sachs, offering 23 percent of the shares to the public at $13.50 a share. Included in the offering were shares owned by more than 40 individuals, many of them employees. The biggest seller was Mo Siegel, who put up for sale 104,000 of his one million shares. Part of the proceeds from the sale of company stock was to be used to buy land in Boulder, where the company planned to put up a new headquarters-and-plant complex.

But the stock sale never came off. After going public on November 3, 1983, at $13.50 a share, and after the stock was actually traded on the over-the-counter market for four days, the entire offering was canceled in the wake of some bad news for the company. A woman with a broken hip tried to relieve her suffering by downing 18 cups of Celestial Seasonings' Comfrey tea, brewed from the leaves of the comfrey plant. She had a bad reaction: blurred vision. Subsequent tests of the tea disclosed traces of atropine, which can be a highly toxic drug. Celestial Seasonings moved quickly to retrieve all the Comfrey tea packages from the marketplace. At the same time, it withdrew the public offering. Buyers of the stock got their money back. The company couldn't risk going ahead with the sale since buyers might very well sue Celestial Seasonings, claiming that important information had been withheld from them.

Celestial Seasonings did not cover itself with glory in this crisis. When it first announced the withdrawal of the stock offering, it blamed the cancelation on a supply problem with one of the herbs it uses. Only later did the Comfrey tea disaster surface. Mo Siegel, reflecting a few days later on how the company reacted, told the *New York Times*: "After spending a decade trying to get people healthy, we shot ourselves in the foot."

It was thought then that Celestial Seasonings would reenter the market later with a public offering. Instead, it sold out to Kraft. Whether this move will change the culture at Celestial Seasonings remains to be seen. So far—up to early 1985—it doesn't seem to have had that effect. The benefit programs were maintained. The company continued to use its own distribution system. And six months after the purchase no emissary had been dispatched from Chicago to Boulder to ride herd on the new subsidiary, although a Kraft marketing whiz was expected to be transferred there in early 1985. It

Celestial Seasonings' Beliefs

Excellence

We believe that in order to make this world a better place in which to live, we must be totally dedicated to the endless quest for excellence in the important tasks which we endeavor to accomplish.

Our Products

We believe in marketing and selling healthful and naturally oriented products that nurture people's bodies and uplift their souls. Our products must be superior in quality, a good value, beautifully artistic, and philosophically inspiring.

Dignity of the Individual

We believe in the dignity of the individual, and we are totally committed to the fair, honest, kind, and professional treatment of all individuals and organizations with whom we work.

Our Employees

We believe that our employees develop a commitment to excellence when they are directly involved in the management of their areas of responsibility. This team effort maximizes quality results, minimizes costs, and allows our employees the opportunity to have authorship and integrity in their accomplishments, as well as sharing in the financial rewards of their individual and team efforts.

We believe in hiring above-average people who are willing to work for excellent results. In exchange, we are committed to the development of our good people by identifying, cultivating, training, rewarding, retaining, and promoting those individuals who are committed to moving our organization forward.

Our Environment

We believe in fostering an environment which promotes creativity and encourages possibility thinking throughout the organization. We plan our work to be satisfying, productive, and challenging. As such, we support an atmosphere which encourages intelligent risk-taking without the fear of failure.

Our Dream

Our role at Celestial Seasonings is to play an active part in making this world a better place by unselfishly serving the public. We believe we can have a significant impact on making people's lives happier and healthier through their use of our products. By dedicating our total resources to this dream, everyone profits: our customers, consumers, employees, and shareholders.

appeared that Kraft was urging its new subsidiary to spend more on advertising. But we talked to several Celestial Seasonings employees, and they insisted that nothing had changed as a result of the Kraft ownership. Barnet Feinblum, vice-president of finance and administration and one of the oldest employees in Mo Siegel's company (he began there in 1976), told us: "I'm still wearing my jeans and cowboy boots."

Main employment center   Boulder.

Headquarters   Celestial Seasonings, Inc.
1780 55th Street
Boulder, CO 80301
303-449-3779

CITICORP⊕®

CITICORP

Citicorp makes more money than any other bank in the country. U.S. employees: 36,000.

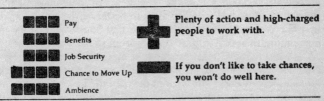

■■■ Pay	✚ Plenty of action and high-charged people to work with.
■■■ Benefits	
■■■ Job Security	
■■■■ Chance to Move Up	■■ If you don't like to take chances, you won't do well here.
■■■■ Ambience	

"This is the only place in town where the elevators are crowded at 11:30 at night," explained one young Citibanker. "Maybe we're just seventy thousand workaholics."

Citicorp attracts a distinct breed: people who relish action. People who thrive on competition. People who love pressure. Stuffy banker types need not apply. For Citicorp is hell-bent on changing the nature of banking, and it wants people who prefer living in the eye of a hurricane.

Outsiders have long considered Citicorp, based in New York City but with tentacles all over the United States and the world, as banking's trend setter. It has paved the way for virtually every advance in modern banking, from creating negotiable certificates of deposit (in 1961), to being the first bank to launch automated teller machines on a large scale in the late 1970s, to establishing an elaborate satellite network for electronic banking and moving ahead with interstate banking in the early 1980s. One of its innovations, the bank holding company, propelled it outside of banking. Citicorp is the bank holding company of which Citibank is the largest unit.

Sometimes Citicorp pushes too much. It created an uproar in 1983 when it tried to force customers with balances of less than $5,000 to use automated tellers instead of the human variety. The bank quickly reversed itself, but not before competitor Chemical Bank put up signs declaring, "Our Tellers Love People."

For the most part, however, Citibank's brash moves have paid off, especially on the bottom line. It is not only the largest bank in terms of assets, but Citicorp also ra ıks first in profits. That's exactly what former Chairman Walter Wriston saw as the goal of all the bank's seemingly frenetic activity. To achieve maximum profits, Wriston instituted a "meritocracy" within the bank. That means people are rewarded according to their performance rather than by seniority. And money is good at Citibank. The head of personnel, Rick Roesch, told us that Citicorp aims to be the best-paying bank. In 1982 Wriston himself became the first banker in history to make more than one million dollars from salary and bonuses.

"Meritocracy" goes far beyond mere compensation. Behind locked doors on an executive floor of Citicorp's Park Avenue headquarters sits a room devoted to "key management resources." Pinned on a board in the office are the photos and biographies of about 200 managers, considered to be the bank's up-and-coming superstars. The only people permitted entry into the room are the bank's senior executives. They make sure the superstars get special attention and job transfers to acquire a broad-based experience at the bank.

The superstars are not the only ones who move around at Citibank. Job changes are frequent, partly because people are expected to create their own niches. Chairman Wriston told prospective employees, "Each new job I've accepted (except for the one I now hold) didn't exist before I took it."

Citicorp also puts a high premium on promotion from within. Of the 29 top managers at the bank, most are career Citibankers. All have been with Citicorp for at least 10 years, with one exception: a consumer services executive picked up in 1975 from General Mills (hardly the sort of company many banks would look to for personnel).

Everyone at Citibank talks of the competitive atmosphere. It seems to be built into the system. Personnel Vice-President Roesch admitted that "we intentionally overstaff with high-caliber entry-level management associates. That is, we always hire more than the baseline requirements for a job. But you don't have to fear stapling papers around here for the next 35 years." The bank expects that with so many overachievers working together, they will create new jobs and opportunities for both themselves and the bank.

On the other hand, some people cannot keep up with the pace. Stories run the circuit at the bank of successful executives who "pull the plug" and move to Vermont or New Hampshire for a more peaceful existence.

Citibank is also the kind of place that can be difficult for someone working directly under some of the overachiever types. "Some of the aggressive people are rough on those under them," explained one young manager.

There have also been instances when the bank itself has been accused of taking shortcuts. *Fortune* detailed the case of dubious international currency trading practices during the mid-1970s in a 1983 article entitled "The Maverick Who Yelled Foul at Citibank." The bank eventually paid various governments for back taxes without admitting guilt in the case.

People are not, however, vying against each other within a predetermined hierarchy at Citicorp. "It's very decentralized here," explained a young manager in the data processing department. "There are lots of small organizations at Citibank, so you feel you can rise to the top of something." Another young Citibanker, a black woman in the commercial lending department, agreed: "There's lots of horizontal doors here as opposed to just vertical ones. This institution has flexibility. It's easy to move around."

Another good feature of the competitive atmosphere at Citibank is the lack of an old-boy network, common at many other banks and financial institutions. Results are all that matter at Citibank. It does not make any difference what school you went to or whom you happen to be related to.

"I came here because I knew that if I busted my fanny and worked hard I would be able to get ahead," explained a young auditor from New York City. "People are just watching how good you are and how much you work." The auditor explained that Citibank does not believe in elaborate training. "They throw a lot at you and sit back and watch how you do. If you do well, they throw more."

The auditor finds the system stimulating. "It's exciting. There is a spirit of camaraderie here at the bank that is tremendous."

Main employment centers   The 59-story Citicorp Center skyscraper, at 53rd Street, with its distinctive slanted solar-panel roof, is located across Lexington Avenue from the 39-story headquarters building on Park Avenue. More than half of the two buildings are occupied by Citicorp. Outside New York State, Citicorp has more than 500 offices in 40 states and the District of Columbia. Citi is represented by corporate finance offices in key commercial centers across the country; savings and loan associations in California, Illinois, and Florida; credit-card processing operations in Colorado, South Dakota, and Maryland; and mortgage lending offices and industrial banks in 36 states. Overseas, Citicorp has banking and other financial services offices in 91 countries. The total worldwide employment of 72,000 is about evenly divided between the United States and overseas operations. About 1,000 of the Citi employees outside the United States are American citizens.

Headquarters   Citicorp
399 Park Avenue
New York, NY 10043
212-559-1000

⊂⊐ CONTROL DATA

CONTROL DATA CORPORATION

Control Data makes mainframe and minicomputers, sells computer services, and runs a financial credit company. U.S. employees: 47,000.

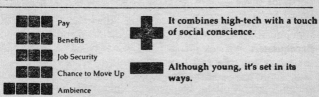

	Pay
	Benefits
	Job Security
	Chance to Move Up
	Ambience

It combines high-tech with a touch of social conscience.

Although young, it's set in its ways.

Control Data's headquarters tower looks as impersonal and imposing as one of the company's mainframe computers. Only a protruding Control Data logo disturbs the mirrorlike efficiency of the green-tinted windows on the 14-story building. To make the *Brave New World*-ish vision complete, Control Data's striking headquarters rises far above the other warehouse-type buildings in a high-tech industrial park just south of the Minneapolis-St. Paul airport.

You get a very different impression of Control Data, however, if you go to one of the top floors of the sleek high rise and look down at the other side of the property. Just beyond the employee parking lots, you can see the company garden. About 600 CDC employees and their families farm their own tomatoes, corn, squash, and other vegetables in a four-acre plot. A garden club presents a Golden Hoe Award each year to the employee who grows the biggest vegetables. From the high rise you can also see five softball fields and a hydroponic greenhouse on the roof of a research facility. The greenhouse produces lettuce sold at bargain rates to Control Data employees.

The contrast between "The Tower," as the high rise is known, and the community garden plot symbolizes much about working for the big computer maker. Control Data offers a wealth of benefits and employee programs as exten-

57

sive as any in American industry. First and foremost, Control Data provides extensive training for its troops. "We need to train and retrain people in this industry," Frank Dawe, vice-president of personnel and administration, explained. "An engineer is obsolete after five years, so we must keep them up to date."

Almost every Control Data facility in the world has its own training center, complete with a battery of PLATO computer terminals. Through its PLATO computerized educational system, Control Data claims it is second only to the Department of Defense in training Americans. PLATO has individualized courses for entire elementary and high school curricula, as well as for specialized advanced courses. More than 100 colleges and universities have PLATO courses on their campuses, and there are specialized PLATO courses for training airline pilots, bank tellers, and retail buyers, among many others.

It's no surprise then that Control Data has dozens of PLATO courses aimed at its own employees. Each manager and most engineers are *required* to take a minimum of 40 hours a year of training—most of which is done using PLATO. In 1982, Control Data managers spent an average of 47 hours in training, 70 percent on PLATO computers. That translated into one-quarter-million hours of training time for managers. By the end of 1984, all Control Data employees had spent one and one-half million hours in training.

PLATO training courses range from "Basic Math Skills" and "Beginning Typing" to "Disk Drive Fundamentals" and "Reactor Power Oscillation Due to Xenon Poisoning." Even employees who want to get a high school diploma can take all the GED courses on PLATO.

All managers must take courses each year on affirmative action. Control Data has long been a leader in corporate social responsibility. In the late 1960s, it made it a point to locate a production plant in the depressed area of north Minneapolis. It hired people from that area and claims it is "now one of our most productive facilities."

The north Minneapolis plant was not a one-shot affair. Chairman William Norris once defined Control Data's mission as "addressing society's major unmet needs as profitable business opportunities." (Norris founded the company in

1957.) The slogan permeates company literature and forms the basis of much of the company's business strategy. In a low-key way, Control Data sees itself as trying to save the world through computer technology. In particular, the company sees constituencies in minorities (computer plants in ghettos, and PLATO in schools and prisons), small businesses (Control Data Business Centers, where small businesses can rent time on big computers), and small farmers (Control Data Ag Centers). CDC doesn't attract the flamboyant Elmer Gantry-type evangelists; it appeals more to YMCA-type do-gooders, provided they also possess a strong Calvinist interest in making money. "No project is considered philanthropy; each is intended to return a profit," explains one company brochure.

Savvy, a women's magazine, rated Control Data as one of the best places for women to work in America, citing its special efforts to promote women into upper management. In 1981, Control Data became one of the few large companies to elect a woman employee to the board of directors. She's Lois Dickson Rice, senior vice-president of government relations. Though many companies have added women to their boards, they are usually outside directors, rather than full-time employees.

In some cases, the company has provided PLATO terminals at home for women to continue working after having a child. One technical editor was given both a PLATO terminal and a Wang word processor. She now comes to the office only once a week to attend a staff meeting.

Vera Walters, an assembly-line worker, thinks highly of the level of communication at Control Data. She especially appreciates how supervisors insist on explaining exactly how the part she is working on fits into the finished product. Not only are assemblers given classroom instruction on how their part of the production fits into the overall computer, they are also taken to other assembly plants to see what happens to their part in the later stages of production.

Walters also benefits from the flexible hours, a program enabling employees to pick their own arrival time. Their workday ends eight hours later, excluding lunch.

Because Control Data is constantly getting involved in new fields and enterprises, many CDC people feel they are working in an ever-changing atmosphere. "It's like Minnesota weather," engineering consultant Carroll Skiba said. "If you do not like it today, wait until tomorrow."

CDC considers itself firmly rooted in the Midwest. "We're a good, solid Middle American-type company," explained Roger Baldelli, the marketing vice-president of the peripheral-products division. "We're conservative, not a high flyer. Though we're willing to take risks, we don't go too far out. This is not the place for a Silicon Valley job hopper."

Control Data decidedly does not have the atmosphere of many of the relaxed and informal Silicon Valley high-tech companies. Most men at headquarters wear suits and ties. One division even asked that all its engineers wear ties lest any customers get the idea that CDC is too laid back. Nor has Control Data sought to foster egalitarianism. Top executives have a garage of their own (though they have to pay for space in it), while other managers have a parking lot closer to the building than other employees. How far you have to trudge through the snow does make a difference on many a Minnesota winter day.

And Control Data's employee handbook would put off anyone looking for an unstructured environment. It summarizes policies and refers to various policy manual numbers (like 6:14:22 for business travel accident insurance). The manual spells out in distinctly non-laid-back terms that "Drinking alcoholic beverages is not appropriate at events held during the normal work day for the purpose of recognizing employee accomplishments, such as service anniversaries, promotions, transfers and terminations." So much for the Friday afternoon beer bust.

John Shier, a microcircuits engineering consultant (the technical equivalent to a manager), previously worked for several high-tech firms in California's Silicon Valley. He prefers living in Minnesota because it is "less congested and easier to make friends." Unlike the fast-paced life in California, he says that "Control Data takes a longer-term view of things. There's an expectation that people will be here for twenty years, but not in the same job." People are expected, even encouraged, to move around in the company. Education is the vehicle for the changes, as people who want to get ahead or try out different fields within the company can pick from among dozens of courses in the training centers.

The company even provides a service for employees thinking about starting their own business. It's called EEAO (Employee Entrepreneurial Assistance Office). Of the more than 600 who have used the EEAO since its inception in 1979, 57 of them have gone out on their own.

Those who stay—and most CDC employees consider it a lifetime commitment—can avail themselves of one of the largest number of distinct employee programs in the country:

• EAR (Employee Advisory Resource), a 24-hour counseling service available to employees or their families, first introduced in 1974. EAR counselors can be called for advice about either personal problems (alcohol, drug, marital, health, financial) or for work-related difficulties.

• Peer Review, a sophisticated grievance procedure. If an employee cannot resolve a complaint with his or her supervisor or that person's boss, the employee can contact EAR, which assigns a representative to try to resolve the dispute. If that doesn't work, a review board is set up, consisting of an EAR representative, two employees at the same level in the company, and one company executive. The peer and executive members are selected by a random drawing. The board votes on the case and submits its findings to a company vice-president for a final decision.

• ESN (Employee Services Network), a tape library of hundreds of recordings. Any employee can make a collect call to the ESN library and listen to a tape on topics ranging from "Where to look for a used car" to "What you should know about a Keogh retirement plan."

• WiserWays, an inflation-fighting program that sponsors a huge discount buying program for employees for everything from eyeglasses and new cars to microwave ovens and home games of the Minnesota Twins or Vikings.

In 1981, CDC added to the list a job security program called "rings of defense strategy," occasioned by a downturn in business. It set up an employment placement center that placed 400 people in internal job openings. Volunteers were asked to take time off without pay to pursue schooling or stay home with their children. The nearly 2,000 who did received $50 a month to maintain their company health benefits. And finally, Control Data introduced SWAT (Special Workforce Action Teams), composed of CDC employees who typically worked for 90 days at jobs previously done by outside contractors. About 300 employees worked at SWAT jobs such as fixing the sprinkler system, painting basements, and purging old files. As a result of the rings of defense, Control Data had to lay off fewer than 1.5 percent of its U.S. employees during the 1981–82 recession.

Main employment centers   Most of the people involved in the computer side of the business work in the Minneapolis area. About 13,500 are considered "technical." Others include educators, sales personnel, and financial service representatives. Eight thousand work for Commercial Credit Company, Control Data's financial services subsidiary. Its main office is in Baltimore. In November 1984, Control Data announced that it was putting Commercial Credit up for sale.

Headquarters   Control Data Corporartion
8100–34th Avenue South
P.O. Box O
Minneapolis, MN 55440
612-853-8100

BEST EMPLOYEE COMMUNICATIONS

Federal Express	Pitney Bowes	Time Inc.
Marion Labs	Tandem Computers	Viking Freight
Physio-Control		

TRAMMELL CROW COMPANY

A large developer of office buildings, industrial parks, and warehouses. U.S. employees: 1,250.

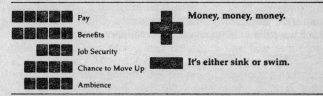

■■■■■ Pay	**Money, money, money.**
■■■■■ Benefits	
■■■ Job Security	
■■■■ Chance to Move Up	**It's either sink or swim.**
■■■■ Ambience	

Don't consider working for Trammell Crow unless you want to be a millionaire. The company may well have more millionaires per capita than any other in the United States—over 5 percent of its work force. But even if the chance to make a lot of money weren't there, Crow's working environment is hard to beat.

Crow is owned by its partners, about 100 of them spread across the country in 50 different regional offices. Each of the partners owns a sizable percentage of the properties he helps to develop (there are as yet no female partners). Senior partners also get a piece of the action on most other new Crow properties. The company owns and manages more than 3,000 projects encompassing 160 million square feet of commercial space, including warehouses, shopping centers, and high-rise office buildings. That's why becoming a Crow partner can be extremely lucrative. *Forbes* estimated founder Trammell Crow himself to be worth more than a half-*billion* dollars, ranking among the three dozen richest people in the United States.

But Trammell Crow doesn't even have a private office. At the Dallas headquarters on the thirty-fifth floor of the LTV Center, he shares a large "bullpen" area with other partners, secretaries, and accountants.

Crow told us he has never had a private office, except for

63

a short stint in the Navy. "Having everybody together is the best way to communicate. Everybody can see everybody else. You're available. You can get more done."

Crow also sees another dimension. "I think that a major component of a successful business is love. How are these people going to know I love them if they cannot see me?" he asked. A soft-spoken man, Crow conveys a sense of religious conviction without sounding at all as if he is pontificating or preaching.

Many young people have been attracted to the company because of Trammell Crow's personality. One of his young associates calls him "expansive, a visionary, generous. I have been stimulated and expanded being with him." He is also held in high regard within the industry. "His handshake is better than a contract; he has an outstanding reputation," competitor Jerry L. Speyer told the *New York Times*. Arthur J. Mirante, head of New York operations for competitor Cushman & Wakefield, added, "He has an exquisite reputation because of the quality of the projects he builds and people who work for him."

Crow is not a somber place. Having fun is central to Crow's philosophy of business. "We're all teammates here," Crow said. "We don't work here, we have fun."

Ned Spieker, partner in charge of the San Francisco office, echoed that sentiment: "We make a lot of money in our business. After a while, money is not the reason we work. We do it because it's fun."

The Crow management board of 12 senior partners meets four or five times a year. In the previous year, one meeting was held at Spieker's ranch in Northern California, where the group went duck hunting. They also went rock climbing together in Maine and snowmobiling in Montana.

There's no regular timetable for the board gatherings. Like everything else about the company, Crow people prefer schedules to be fluid. "The kind of people who are good at real estate don't respond well to structure," explained Spieker.

Once a year all the partners come to Dallas. Yet their two- or three-day meetings are not all business. They have typically spent part of their time talking with people who have nothing to do with real estate. In recent years guests have included Henry Kissinger, Gerald Ford, futurist John

Naisbitt, the late Herman Kahn, and aerobics instructor Dr. Kenneth Cooper.

The reason, according to managing partner Don Williams, is that "we're concerned about the whole person. We try seriously to be a business family. We want to have fun. We want to enjoy it. It's our company. We're not going to sell it."

Crow owns and leases about 95 percent of all its developments. Some of the more prominent ones are Peachtree Center in Atlanta, Embarcadero Center in San Francisco, the San Jacinto, Diamond Shamrock, and Bryan Towers in Dallas, Charlotte Plaza in North Carolina, and the 275-acre Hamilton Lakes development in Chicago. Trammell Crow is the lead developer in the $1 billion redevelopment of New York City's Times Square. In 1983, Crow ranked number one among all U.S. real estate developers, putting in place more than $1.2 billion worth of new construction.

Crow emphasizes high-quality projects. According to Williams, "We build quality. If the market is good, quality pays. If the market is not good, you'd better not have the second-best project."

Almost all the decisions on what projects to build and how to build them are done by the regional partners. They conceive the project, buy the land, hire the architect and contractor, build it, lease it, and then manage it. Communication between regional offices and Dallas is extremely informal; the emphasis is on what Crow calls "a consensus style of management."

Regional offices also organize their territories as they see fit. In Houston, the area is divided according to the type of property—warehouses, office buildings, or shopping centers —whereas in San Francisco it is done geographically— downtown, East Bay (Oakland), South Bay (San Jose).

Final decisions on hiring are done by regional partners. Individual partners often visit local business schools to interview candidates. Because partners often communicate with each other, a partner in Boston, for instance, may tell a partner in Atlanta about a prospect he has interviewed at Harvard.

It helps to have recently graduated with an M.B.A. from Harvard, Stanford, or some other prestigious business school if you want to join Crow as a potential partner. Virtually all of the 62 new recruits the company hired in 1984 were recent M.B.A.'s. Though M.B.A.'s are notoriously fickle, more than 80 percent of the 175 or so who've joined Crow in the past dozen years are still with the firm.

Chief financial officer Joel Peterson explained that many M.B.A.'s would not fit in at Crow. Peterson, who happens to be a Harvard M.B.A., said, "People who need a lot of certainty in terms of career path or job definition wouldn't like it here. Nor would those who are perquisite-oriented. We don't provide people with private offices, fancy titles, or country club memberships."

Crow looks for other traits as well. According to Spieker, "We look for somebody you would like to go out and have a beer with." He estimates that about 90 percent of Crow partners are joggers. "You won't find any overweight people here. I don't know of any who smoke."

Above all, Crow insists that those who join the company be "nice people." According to Trammell Crow, "When I was younger, I noticed that many successful businessmen seemed like very nice people. I thought that, of course, they were able to be nice after they had become successful. But as I've grown older, I've seen that they were nice all the way along. Nice people succeed more."

A newly hired Crow employee is typically assigned to lease new tenants for a Crow warehouse or office building. It's sink or swim at Crow. "There's no formal training process. They have to learn the business on their own," explained Peterson. "People have to be self-disciplined and self-motivated."

That doesn't mean people don't receive guidance from the partners. But it may come in unanticipated ways. Partner Ned Spieker said he learned a lot about real estate while jogging around downtown San Francisco at 5:00 A.M. with Trammell Crow.

The salary is a flat $18,000 a year—the same amount received by Trammell Crow, managing partner Don Williams, and all other partners. Extra income has to come from sales commissions or ownership of a property. When a new leasing agent finds a tenant for space, he or she is immediately given a lump-sum commission based on a percentage of the lease.

Crow starts its newcomers as leasing agents because it sees itself as "a marketing company." As Don Williams put it,

"Most developers see themselves as builders or investors. We don't. We are in the business of selling space to our customers, the tenants." As a new recruit learns the ropes in sales, he or she takes more responsibility. After a minimum of three years, those who show an ability to bring in money for the firm are asked to become partners. That typically means being given an ownership stake of 10 to 20 percent of a Trammell Crow property the new partner works on. The new partner makes no financial investment to get this stake, only an investment of time and, by all accounts, considerable effort. As time goes on, newer partners acquire ownership in more and more new Crow properties. In a period of seven to ten years, Crow partners usually become, in the words of one partner, "financially independent," that is, millionaires.

Everybody who becomes a Crow partner starts at the bottom. The company promotes only from within. Trammell Crow explained that he does not hire people with previous real estate experience because "we want them to go our way. We want everybody to go our way."

Of course, not everyone who works for Trammell Crow is hired as a potential partner. The company has secretaries, file clerks, and various professionals such as accountants and attorneys. They share the profits of this highly profitable enterprise, too. At least one Trammell Crow secretary retired as a near millionaire. Here's how: the partners set aside a 10 percent ownership stake in every third or fourth property the company develops. Income from that property is put into an employee profit-sharing trust. Each year a nonpartner Trammell Crow employee can expect an amount equal to as much as 75 percent of his or her annual income to be placed into his or her trust account.

These contributions add up quickly. "People can retire from here at the age of 55 and never miss a paycheck," said Peterson.

Main employment centers   Dallas (200); Houston (60); Atlanta (40); Chicago, (30).

Headquarters   Trammell Crow Company
                        3500 LTV Center
                        2001 Ross Avenue
                        Dallas, TX 75201
                        214-979-5100

CRS SIRRINE

CRS SIRRINE, INC.

A large architecture, engineering, and construction management firm, CRSS also has an interior design division and a construction division. U.S. employees: 3,000.

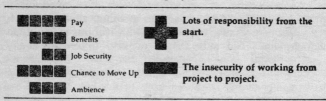

■■■■ Pay		**+** Lots of responsibility from the start.
■■■ Benefits		
■■ Job Security		
■■■■ Chance to Move Up		**■** The insecurity of working from project to project.
■■■ Ambience		

"Nobody owns any turf around here," the late Bill Caudill, guru and cofounder of the firm, used to tell newcomers to CRSS. He meant it, too. There are no enclosed offices in the headquarters of the Houston-based firm. This philosophy applies to Caudill and other top executives, whose spaces look pretty much like those of everyone else. People regularly move from one part of the building to another, and the shoulder-high partitions between workspaces are constantly being shifted around.

The fluidity illustrates much of what it's like to work for CRSS and Caudill, who disagreed with the popular notions of architects as renaissance men. Though he admired the work of such architects as Frank Lloyd Wright, Le Corbusier, Mies van der Rohe, and Walter Gropius, CRSS's founder declared, "The prima donnas have had their day. Now the architect is a team."

The team concept has been used at CRSS for years. Today it means architects work in groups of six to eight people, with each group working on three to six different projects at a time. Members of a CRSS team usually see the project through to the end. They can then learn various facets of the business—from dealing with clients to handling on-site difficulties. According to Michael Shirley, a senior design architect, "Each group forms almost a fraternal brotherhood. People cover for each other."

Shirley explained that a few years ago the teams were organized differently—by function, so that there was a design team, a production team, and a construction team for each project. He said that restructuring the company is part of the CRSS style, part of the flexibility of the place. "Very seldom do you feel like you have a ceiling over your head and have nowhere to go. Everything changes around here every couple of years."

Steve Parshall, vice-president of research, joined CRSS in 1977. He finds "CRSS is always growing, always presenting a new opportunity. Working at CRSS requires an ability to change and respond, to be a good 'gypsy'—to be ready at any moment to join a new project team." He added, "The environment here is really challenging. It's not like working in a traditional office, but rather a workshop or a studio, with the latest technology, such as CAD [computer-aided design] equipment and personal computers, side by side with more conventional technology, such as models and drawings."

New employees nevertheless get the chance to rub shoulders with the top people in the company. Carter Rohan, an architecture graduate of the University of Houston, explained, "Unlike what you hear in architecture school, that you do not see executives in big firms, you see the top people all the time here. You work directly with them. The concept is to understaff and give people lots of responsibility."

The stimulating environment—and its reputation as an innovator—has led some to liken working at CRSS to attending a graduate school. It also attracts many young architects and other construction professionals who stay at CRSS for only a few years before moving on.

The sites of CRSS projects can be almost anywhere in the world. Caudill and his cofounders (John Rowlett and Wallie Smith), all Texas A&M architecture graduates, launched the firm to design schools. Since 1946 CRSS has designed 443 elementary and high schools, as well as over 100 colleges and universities, including 60 from scratch.

CRSS today handles other large projects, such as hospitals, corporate headquarters, hotels, and large industrial projects, such as pulp-and-paper mills and food processing facilities. In 1984, the company was the largest construction management company and the largest architecture/engineering design firm in the United States. Some notable examples of CRSS's work are the Philip A. Hart Senate Office Building in Washington, D.C., the Gulf Tower in Houston, King Saud University in Saudi Arabia, the El Gezirah Hotel in Cairo, Egypt, the headquarters of Hercules in Wilmington, Delaware, and of Mountain Bell in Salt Lake City.

Like other architecture and construction firms, CRSS offers little job security. There may or may not be another project waiting in the wings when one job is completed. Or a new project may require extensive travel to another part of the globe.

Those who do well can progress very rapidly. Many of the company's top executives are in their early thirties. Bill Peel was made vice-president of development while in his late twenties. An architecture graduate of Texas A&M, Peel considers CRSS a "family-oriented firm. Banquets for clients always include wives or husbands."

Peel, who used to work for 3DI, another Houston-based architecture and construction firm, says CRSS is more than a job for many who work there—it's a way of thinking. There's something about the place that encourages people to sit around talking about the philosophy of what they are doing. He drew a sketch for us on one of the many blackboards scattered around the headquarters to illustrate a favorite company theme. Using three circles to represent designers, technologists, and managers, Peel explained, "Few people are all three; most are one or a combination of two of them. That's why teams are important."

CRSS was one of the first companies in its industry to initiate a flexible benefits program for employees, enabling each person to tailor his or her benefits package. An integral feature of the plan is a tax-sheltered savings option, which the company partially matches.

As could be expected, CRSS designed its own headquarters. It's an unusual building, as it cannot be seen from the street. The ground-level parking lot is the roof of the building. But the structure isn't actually underground since the building sits on a hill. The windows face a beautiful wooded area. It's hard to believe that only a few yards in the other direction is Houston's notorious West Loop freeway that carries a quarter-million cars a day.

One wall inside the headquarters displays more than 300 different architecture awards CRSS has won for buildings it has designed throughout the world. CRSSers call it their "Ego Wall."

Main employment centers   six-hundred-sixty-two work in Houston; 1,346 work in Greenville, South Carolina, at the engineering group headquarters. Another 505 work in Denver with a construction subsidiary; and 109 work at their interior architecture division in San Francisco.

Headquarters   CRS Sirrine, Inc.
1177 West Loop South
Houston, TX 77027
713-552-2000

CUMMINS ENGINE COMPANY, INC.

Cummins makes diesel engines for trucks, buses, farm tractors, workboats, and other applications. It is the largest supplier of engines to makers of heavy-duty highway trucks. U.S. employees: 14,770.

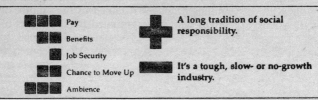

■■■ Pay	✚ A long tradition of social responsibility.
■■ Benefits	
■ Job Security	
■■ Chance to Move Up	■■ It's a tough, slow- or no-growth industry.
■■■ Ambience	

"I am not sure our internal practices are as good as our image." That was the frank opinion of Ted Marston, vice-president, industrial relations, when asked about Cummins as a good place to work.

At many companies such a statement would not mean much, since few companies have Cummins's reputation as a corporate good guy. Largely because of the efforts of former chairman and major stockholder Irwin Miller, Cummins has long insisted that a company has social responsibilities as well as purely economic ones. The company has consistently contributed 5 percent of pretax profits to charitable causes. It has promoted racial equality both by funding groups such as the Delta Foundation in Mississippi and by making sure that blacks hold management positions within Cummins itself. And the company has helped to transform its hometown of Columbus, Indiana, from just another small farm-belt town into a showpiece for some of the world's most illustrious architects.

Marston's comment reflects the problem of ensuring that the same principles apply within the company as well. It appears that as far as professionals and managers are concerned, the company has lived up to its high standards. But Marston frankly concedes it has not done so well with the hourly, largely unionized work force. Cummins and at least one of the unions are addressing the problem, however, and the company has made some major innovations despite the grim recession that gripped the auto and truck industry in the early 1980s. One advance was the extension of profit-sharing to the entire work force. Previously, this benefit was reserved for top executives, but in February 1984 it was extended to all employees —with quarterly cash payouts pegged to the company's return on sales. In 1984, it resulted in an average payout of $2,000 to each employee.

In 1977, the *New York Times* ran a feature article entitled "Whiz Kids at Cummins Engine." It talked of the "influx of bright young executives who were groomed for the rigors of higher responsibility." Cummins has acted as a magnet to many such people partly because of its outstanding reputation as a corporate citizen. Some have participated in the company's executive-on-loan program that pays managers to spend time working for a charitable organization such as the Delta Foundation.

At Cummins they found a company willing to hand over major responsibilities to young people. "It's a hard-driving company," reports Joe White, vice-president for personnel and public affairs, who joined Cummins in 1982 after serving for years as an outside consultant. "Your plate is full all the time. Not everyone responds well to that. If you just want a job, Cummins is not a good place. A lot is expected of you here." Those who respond well have been able to move up rapidly. The current chairman, Henry Schacht, became president at age 39.

Besides its sterling reputation for social responsibility, Cummins is often cited as one of the best-managed companies. "Headhunters consider Cummins a prime target," Marston explained. "They have an up-to-date, permanent file on us. After five years here, a young manager can command his own price."

Some young managers are also attracted by Cummins's hometown. Located 40 miles from Indianapolis and 80 miles from Louisville, Columbus (population 30,000) might seem as if it's in the middle of nowhere for those used to urban life. And there have been reports of some young managers imported from New York who left after concluding that Columbus was a social wasteland. But it is undeniably an architectural oasis. There are homes, churches, and office buildings by the biggest names in contemporary architecture (like Eero Saarinen and I. M. Pei), sculpture by Henry Moore, a school by Caudill Rowlett Scott, and even a golf course by Robert Trent Jones. Cummins's new corporate headquarters, designed by the Kevin Roche–John Dinkeloo architectural firm, is a white, airy, one-story structure that extends for three blocks in the middle of the town. It surrounds a five-story red brick building that was part of a complex that housed the first Cummins plant and offices. Just a block away is a large city park, complete with an old-fashioned covered bridge.

Physical attractiveness aside, some talk of Columbus as a great place to raise a family. It has good schools, cultural amenities, no crime to speak of, and is very church-centered (mostly Protestant, as there are few Catholics or Jews): the all-American town. At the same time, single women don't find it so great because it's so difficult to find single men, according to Marston.

Even this seeming paradise has had a rough time. The recession affecting the auto industry hurt Cummins, causing the company to lay off over 2,000 employees in 1981 and 1982. Some were recalled in 1983, but no one expects employment levels ever to be the same at Cummins any more than at any other major auto industry producer.

Despite the downturn in its businesses, Cummins has launched several innovative programs. Its first major experiment was a new plant built in 1973 in Charleston, South Carolina. Rather than follow the more traditional labor-management relationships, Cummins reduced the number of supervisory levels and expanded the job descriptions of plant workers so that they would be able to do more tasks. Some Charleston managers then went to Jamestown, New York, where Cummins opened another plant in 1975. Similar work styles have been created there.

Perhaps more significant for those in Columbus has been the experience of Cummins's Atlas Crankshaft subsidiary in Fostoria, Ohio. According to Louis Baumbarger, president of UAW Local 336, "The union has made Atlas a good place to work."

In particular, Baumbarger cites the Quality of Work Life

program initiated by the UAW's national office. Among other things, the QWL program involves getting labor and management people together in relaxed settings to talk about improving the work situation. Baumbarger says that as recently as contract talks in 1975, "I was told quality is not my concern. But now they agree that the amount of scrap we produce is the concern of the working people."

Baumbarger said, "The QWL program has led to changes in the role of supervisors, so that they do not police the work force anymore. There are fewer supervisors now. There's more employee involvement. We're not just someone who pushes the buttons and makes machines run."

As proof of how much things have improved, Baumbarger reported that the number of written grievances went down from 600 to 75 in one year. "We settle things more informally now."

Cummins officials have applied lessons learned in Charleston, Jamestown, and Fostoria to their biggest plant in Columbus. The workers there may have a traditional work environment on the job, but the company has always been more egalitarian than most smokestack manufacturers. There are no executive dining rooms or reserved parking places.

A few miles outside Columbus is Ceraland, a company-operated physical-fitness-and-recreation center. There's a large swimming pool that entire families often visit on hot summer days, a small lake surrounded by campsites, and an outdoor theater. Since Columbus is located in the middle of a basketball-crazy state, Ceraland also has two full-size indoor basketball courts.

Main employment centers   Columbus, Indiana, area: 9,500; Atlas plant in Fostoria, Ohio: 1,280; Charleston, South Carolina: 815; Jamestown, New York: 915. Another 5,830 work overseas, mostly foreign nationals.

Headquarters   Cummins Engine Company, Inc.
Box 3005
Columbus, IN 47202-3005
812-377-5000

DANA CORPORATION

Dana makes axles, transmissions, clutches, frames, engine parts, and universal joints for cars and trucks, as well as a variety of valves, pumps, and motors for industrial equipment. U.S. employees: 25,000.

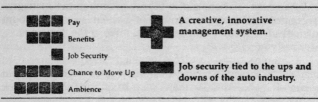

			A creative, innovative management system.
Pay			
Benefits			
Job Security			
Chance to Move Up			Job security tied to the ups and downs of the auto industry.
Ambience			

Dana is rewriting the book on American management. Many trappings of traditional management—organization charts, policy manuals, a large corporate staff, written reports and memos—have fallen by the wayside here.

People at Dana headquarters in Toledo point to a 1969 meeting of the board of directors as a turning point. The new company president, Ren McPherson, is said to have plunked a foot-high stack of policy manuals on the boardroom table and asked which ones were really important. When he didn't get a satisfactory answer, he tossed all the manuals into a wastebasket and said he would put everything essential from the manuals onto one piece of paper. At the next meeting he produced the one-page document.

Dana today has no policy manuals. McPherson's one-page policy sheet (updated in 1981 and again in 1983) is still circulated to all Dana people. Among its iconoclastic precepts are: "We discourage conformity, uniformity, and centralization. . . . We believe people should be involved in setting their own goals and judging their own performance. The people who know best how the job should be done are the ones doing it. . . . We do not believe in company-wide procedures. If an organization requires procedures, it is the responsibility of the manager to create them. . . ." Even that sheet has been reduced to a shorter version called "40 Thoughts."

Unusual words on paper represent only part of the quiet revolution going on at Dana. In place of well-defined organization charts and budgets, the company has created a number of new forms. Like "Hell Week." About 200 managers from Dana's divisions come to Toledo in the first week of December to meet with the company's policy committee (the top nine executives). Managers from each division give the committee their future sales and profit projections along with requests for capital expenditures for the next year. The committee hears each of them in turn before sitting down on Friday to make decisions. On Friday afternoon the managers troop into the auditorium known as "The Pit"—a tiered room that looks like a college lecture hall—to hear the decisions.

The emphasis during Hell Week is on the process rather than budgets themselves. The late Stan Gustafson, who was president of Dana when we visited there in 1983, told us: "We found that people worship at the altar of budgets. So we threw out our budgets a long time ago."

Dana promotes from within. Gustafson, who died on December 26, 1983, had been with the company since 1958. All members of the policy committee have put in at least 20 years. Gerry Mitchell, the chairman, joined Dana in 1944. He may be the only head of a major American corporation who did not graduate from high school. He started as an hourly laborer in a machine shop. The newest policy committee member, in 1984, was Woody Morcott, North American president.

The top people at Dana make regular visits to Dana plants. In the first half of 1983, Mitchell and Gustafson visited 30 plants. In 1984, Mitchell and Morcott visited a total of 50 plants between them. In each case, they first go through the plant and shake hands with employees at their individual workstations, stopping to answer any questions. Everyone calls them "Gerry" and "Woody." They then give a presentation to the entire plant force, followed by a question-and-answer period. The company invites retirees and laid-off employees to the presentations.

In all plants, the company puts up posters with a drawing of Mitchell headlined: "Ask Me." Attached are notepads for employees to talk back to the chairman. Ten letters a week reach Mitchell, and he replies to each one. The whole purpose is communication. As Dana's one-page policy sheet states, "We believe direct communication with all of our people eliminates the need for third-party involvement."

Times have been tough in the automotive industry, resulting in a large number of laid-off workers at Dana. From 30,000 domestic employees in 1978, the company went to 18,200 in early 1983—a 40 percent decline. The force was back to 25,000 at the end of 1984. Dana took great pains to find employment for those it laid off, from helping them to fill out resumes to providing opportunities at other Dana plants. Two new Dana distribution centers—in Fogelsville, Pennsylvania, and Hilliard, Ohio—are staffed largely by workers who had been laid off elsewhere.

The majority of Dana plants have been unionized for years, many by the United Auto Workers. Gustafson and Mitchell conducted their plant visits in the same manner whether it was a union or a nonunion facility. They wanted everyone in Dana to identify with the company. "If you don't feel a part of the company, it won't be a good place to work," said Gustafson.

To bolster identification with the company, most Dana plants have a small company store with dozens of items bearing the Dana logo, from baseball caps, T-shirts, and running sweatsuits to shoe horns, golf balls, and bumper stickers. About one-quarter-million dollars' worth of goods a year are sold through the Dana identity centers. Dana also encourages its people to buy shares of stock in the company. For each dollar an employee puts up to buy Dana stock, the company contributes another 30 cents. In 1983, employees bought 846,000 shares with $17 million of their own money and $5 million of the company's. About 70 percent of all Dana employees are stockholders. At the UAW-organized plant in Lima, Ohio, 57 percent of the workers are stockholders.

Since 1969, Dana has used various productivity plans. They are variations of the Scanlon Plan, a scheme that enables workers to share in productivity gains. Before a gain-sharing plan is adopted, at least three-quarters of a plant's workers have to vote their approval. Under a Scanlon Plan, committees composed of workers and supervisors meet regularly to discuss suggestions on how to improve productivity—better methods, different equipment, or changes in paperwork. The committee forwards its ideas to a plantwide screening committee, usually composed of the plant manager, several other managers, and nonsupervisory representatives from the production committees. If the process reduces costs or increases output, the workers receive a bonus equal to 75 percent of the savings (the company gets the other 25 percent).

This bonus is tacked onto a worker's paycheck once a month. The company claims the Scanlon Plans have had dramatic results. A clutch plant in Auburn, Indiana, for instance, instituted new procedures that resulted in making 75 clutches an hour instead of 55; the new methods come out of Quality Circle sessions at the plant. Such changes can have a dramatic effect on a worker's paycheck. In an example from a Dana Perfect Circle Division camshaft plant, it was estimated that an employee might receive about $145 a month as his or her Scanlon bonus.

Several employees we talked with like working in Dana's environment. Gary Gilsdorf, an 18-year veteran, has had a typical Dana management career. He started as a personnel clerk, became a buyer in the purchasing department, then a production line foreman, and is now in the industrial relations department at the corporate headquarters. He said, "You don't have to go through 12 layers of bureaucracy to do everything because of the policy sheet." He added that Dana makes it easy for a person who wants to have a variety of experiences in the company. "Dana isn't just interested in specialists. There are lots of opportunities for growth. You can be more rounded."

The company's training center, called Dana U, provides intensive management seminars both at the corporate office and in the field. Supervisors who complete five Dana U courses are awarded a diploma of a "Certified Dana Supervisor." Over 575 had completed the courses by 1984.

Dana U's main office is in the campuslike corporate headquarters in an affluent suburban area of Toledo. Set in the middle of an 84-acre plot, the red brick main building could just as easily be sitting in the middle of the restored Colonial Williamsburg in Virginia. The pieces of furniture in the reception room, dining room, and boardroom are authentic antiques dating from 1760 to 1800. Across the street from Dana's headquarters is Inverness Country Club, scene of numerous professional golf tournaments.

Dana's 40 Thoughts

Remember our purpose—to earn money for our shareholders and increase the value of their investment.

Recognize people as our most important asset.

Promote from within.

Remember—people respond to recognition.

Share the rewards.

Provide stability of income and employment.

Decentralize.

Provide autonomy.

Encourage entrepreneurship.

Use corporate committees, task forces.

Push responsibility down.

Involve everyone.

Make every employee a manager.

Control only what's important.

Promote identity with Dana.

Make all Dana people shareholders.

Simplify.

Use little paper.

Keep no files.

Communicate fully.

Let the people set goals and judge their performance.

Let the people decide, where possible.

Discourage conformity.

Be professional.

Break organizational barriers.

Develop pride.

Insist on high ethical standards.

Focus on markets.

Utilize assets fully.

Contain investment—buy, don't make.

Balance plants, products, markets.

Keep facilities under 500 people.

Stabilize production.

Develop proprietary products.

Anticipate market needs.

Control cash.

Deliver reliably.

Help people grow.

Let Dana people know first.

Do what's best for all of Dana.

These beautiful facilities seem only partly occupied, however. Though the company has nearly 35,000 employees worldwide, there are only 83 on the corporate staff in Toledo, including clerical staff and maintenance people. So the headquarters seem more like a meeting facility for people working in some of the more than 100 plants across the country, and a place of refuge for corporate officials who spend most of their time on the road. The day we visited Toledo, Dana's corporate helicopter was sitting on its pad in front of the main building, propellers turning, ready to whisk an official away to anywhere the company considered the action to be.

Main employment centers   Most Dana plants are relatively small, and they are located primarily in Ohio, Michigan, Indiana, Pennsylvania, and North Carolina.

Headquarters   Dana Corporation
4500 Dorr Street
Toledo, OH 43615
419-535-4500

MOST UNUSUAL BENEFITS

Free Taxi Ride Home:
Time Inc.
*Free Saturday Night
Movies:* **Merle
Norman
Cosmetics**
First-class Air Travel:
Leo Burnett
Free Airline Passes:
Delta Air Lines
Fridays Off in May:
Reader's Digest
*Paid Week Off at
Christmas*
Northrop
Free Home Computer:
Apple Computer

Free Lunch: **Hewitt
Associates, Merle
Norman
Cosmetics (25
cents), J.P.
Morgan,
Northwestern
Mutual Life**
Leased Automobile:
Nissan
*Bonus for
Recommending New
Hires:* **Baxter
Travenol, Security
Pacific Bank,
Tandem Computers**
$3,000 Adoption Aid:
Leo Burnett

DAYTON HUDSON CORPORATION

DAYTON HUDSON

Dayton Hudson is one of the nation's largest operators of stores (department stores, discount stores, bookstores, apparel stores). Employees: 107,000.

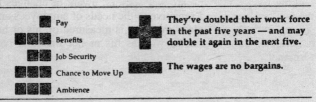

■ Pay
■■■ Benefits
■■ Job Security
■■ Chance to Move Up
■■■ Ambience

They've doubled their work force in the past five years — and may double it again in the next five.

The wages are no bargains.

There are not many places in the country where you *can't* work for Dayton Hudson. It has more than 1,100 stores in 48 states. The only states missing its presence are Hawaii and Vermont—and they will probably fall to the ongoing expansion of this Minneapolis-based retailer by 1987.

Communities should welcome Dayton Hudson with open arms. The company has an almost legendary reputation in its hometown for down-the-line support of the cultural and social service activities that bind a city together. And this is true also of Mervyn's, a California-based chain of apparel stores that Dayton Hudson acquired in 1978.

For nearly 40 years Dayton Hudson has, as a matter of policy, allocated 5 percent of its pretax profits to charitable contributions, an amount about five times the level of giving at the nation's major corporations. It was the inspiration for the Five Percent Clubs launched in Minneapolis and other cities during the early 1980s. Asked once whether government welfare programs resulted from the failure of the private sector to meet these needs, Kenneth N. Dayton, member of the founding family and chairman of the company's executive committee, responded: "I suppose there's a lot of truth to that. You know the government does respond to needs. If the public has needs, and if they cannot be met in other ways more efficiently, then the government steps into the void."

That's hardly the kind of statement corporate leaders are accustomed to making.

The question is: Does corporate citizenship translate into good working conditions? In Dayton Hudson's case, the answer is a resounding yes. Within reason you can do your own thing here in a hassle-free environment, whether you're attached to a Dayton or Hudson department store or a Target discount store or a B. Dalton bookstore.

This is a company that's clearly on the move, and it's looking for people who are self-starters, aware of changes in the marketplace—and sensitive to the needs of employees and society. A Dayton Hudson manager is measured on his or her community involvement as well as his or her financial performance and the means by which it is achieved.

The different chain operations are given considerable autonomy. For example, they don't have to buy corporate services (legal, research) offered by headquarters staffers in Minneapolis. They can go to outside suppliers and compare prices and other factors. However, all the statistics on how you're doing come to roost in Minneapolis, where they are scrutinized carefully. If you do well, you may be tapped for a higher position, perhaps in another location. And you may even be asked to move your skills to another part of the retail ball field—say, switch from discount stores to bookstores.

Minneapolis headquarters—in the IDS skyscraper that's the tallest building between Chicago and San Francisco—maintains a database on the 8,000 salaried people in the United States so that openings can be filled with the appropriate person. In 1984, Dayton Hudson made over 70 placements using this system. The company's goal is to fill 85 percent of its top 600 positions with people already in the company. Ed Wingate, senior vice-president, says: "We are not into hiring stars. We're more interested in the right match."

The corporate staff in Minneapolis is lean—only 275 people (for a $7 billion company), most of them in support functions such as finance, legal, and planning. And the turnover is high with managers coming in from the field and then returning. The upward route in this company is through the field, working in the stores—or as a buyer. Each division operates as an autonomous unit. Of the five operating retail units, three are headquartered in Minneapolis.

Dayton Hudson has expanded in two ways. It has bought other companies, such as Hudson's in Detroit and Mervyn's in California. And it has started retail chains from scratch—Target and B. Dalton, for example. Whatever it's doing seems to be working. The company's success has turned it into prime territory for raiders. Slumping Montgomery Ward stocked its upper management ranks with a team of managers out of Target. But mobility has become a way of life in the retail world. While Dayton Hudson prides itself as an up-from-the-ranks company, in 1985 three of the top five officers were relative newcomers. President Boake A. Sells came aboard in 1983, vice-chairman Gerald R. Gallagher joined the company in 1977, and executive vice-president P. Gerald Mills arrived in 1978.

They all report in to Minneapolis but the operating units do not have to adhere to a set of rules promulgated by headquarters. Mervyn's, a chain started in 1949 by Mervyn Morris, maintains its own well-developed style. It has all the earmarks of a close-knit, family operation, especially in such areas as upward and downward communications. There's a homey feeling about Mervyn's, something you may not be able to say about some other Dayton Hudson outfits. Rather than try to stifle this individuality, Minneapolis headquarters people are proud of it, and one gets the feeling that they wish the rest of the company were more like Mervyn's. Indeed, so delighted is Minneapolis with Mervyn's that it has pumped money into it in an eastward thrust across the country. When Mervyn's was acquired, it had 47 stores; it had more than 120 at the start of 1985.

More than half the 107,000 people who work for Dayton Hudson are sales personnel—and a big chunk of those, upward of 60 percent, are part-timers, working fewer than 40 hours a week. That's common in the retail industry, and it varies by season. At Christmastime 1984, the Dayton Hudson work force approached the 120,000 mark. The store personnel are not represented by unions—and whether they get benefits depends on how many hours they work and in which unit they work (it can vary from division to division). At Mervyn's part-timers who work at least 80 hours a month are eligible for full benefits. Benefits for the salaried staff are good. They get comprehensive medical insurance, long-term disability, a pension program. They also participate in a savings and stock purchase plan: every dollar they sock away up to 5 percent of their pay, the company matches with a 50-cent contribution.

Dayton Hudson has doubled its work force in the past five years, and another doubling seems possible in the next five. Between 1985 and 1989 the company is planning to open more than 500 new stores, including 140 Mervyn's units, 70 new Targets, and 300 new bookstores.

Main employment centers Stores in almost every state in the United States. Dayton's, Hudson's, Target, and B. Dalton are headquartered in Minneapolis; Mervyn's has its home base in Hayward, California; and Lechmere is run out of Woburn, Massachusetts. The three main employment states are Texas, California, and Minnesota.

Headquarters   Dayton Hudson Corporation
777 Nicollet Mall
Minneapolis, MN 55402
612-370-6948

JOHN DEERE

DEERE & COMPANY

Deere is the world's largest manufacturer of farm equipment.
U.S. employees: 34,000.

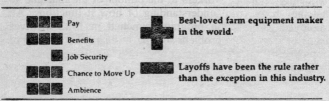

■■■ Pay		
■■■ Benefits	✚	**Best-loved farm equipment maker in the world.**
■ Job Security		
■■■ Chance to Move Up	■■	**Layoffs have been the rule rather than the exception in this industry.**
■■■ Ambience		

When you line up the three big Midwest makers of agricultural equipment against each other, Deere is the company of choice. The product lines of the three companies are similar, their workers are all represented by the United Auto Workers, but still, Deere does something that sets it apart from International Harvester and Caterpillar Tractor.

One explanation seems to be that Deere has made the right business decisions—both in automating its plants and motivating its employees to feel they have a stake in the company. In any case, it seems to be the least hated of the farm equipment makers even though it slashed its payroll by 31 percent in the 1980s.

Deere has some of the most highly automated plants in American industry but it has been careful to "engineer" employee satisfaction into these facilities. For example, when it expanded its tractor capacity at Waterloo, Iowa, in the late 1970s, it decided that a plant with 13,000 people was too big to manage, so it split up the business. It built a new engine plant and a new tractor assembly factory. Left in the center of Waterloo was an old components facility—and Deere broke that up into four "factories within a factory." The result was more autonomy for the workers. The drawback was that employees no longer had the feeling they were building a tractor, because they were now separated from the final product.

Deere tried to reinstill worker pride by stepping up quality inspection of each part instead of waiting for the tractor to be completed to do this testing.

It's clear that Deere is doing something differently from other players in its industry—and that difference comes down to making its employees, including unionized plant workers, feel as though they are partners in the business. One signal result is the acceptance by employees of automation. When Deere installs a new piece of machinery in a plant, it will frequently send line workers to the builder of the machine so that they have a full understanding of how it functions. An employee participation program launched in 1982 involves teams of workers in problem-solving groups. The number of employees submitting suggestions for changes or improvements doubled between 1980 and 1984. And the company is proud of having set records in employee safety. In 1984, the hay and forage equipment plant in Ottumwa, Iowa, broke a farm equipment industry mark by completing more than 3.9 million hours without a single lost-time accident.

When it comes to working conditions, Deere is a clear winner. Its plants are modern and clean. *Industry Week* called its tractor works in Waterloo "the ultimate state-of-the-art manufacturing facility." Its headquarters center, set on a 1,000-acre, wooded site seven miles southeast of downtown Moline, Illinois, ranks as a spectacular architectural achievement, called by some the "Versailles of the cornfields."

The main building, a glass-and-steel structure designed by the late Eero Saarinen, opened in 1964. It was supplemented in 1978 by a new building designed by Kevin Roche and John Dinkeloo, two architects who had worked with Saarinen. Among the features of the Deere headquarters complex are a 400-seat auditorium; glass-enclosed bridges that connect the flanking structures with the main building; two lakes, one of which has an island holding a large bronze sculpture by Henry Moore; a Japanese rock garden; and a product-display building, which has a three-dimensional mural by Alexander Girard. The mural is made up of more than 2,000 historical items from the period 1837 to 1918. It was in 1837 that John Deere developed the first successful self-cleaning steel plow.

Deere's concern for workplace conditions extends to the factory floor. M.R. Montgomery, a reporter for the *Boston*

Globe, visited Deere facilities in 1982 and was impressed by the cleanliness. "Foundries," he wrote, "can be the first circle of hell in the industrial cosmos. They are filled with smoke and the fireworks of 2400-degree molten iron, with dust and soot and sand from the casting molds. Deere may run the only foundries in North America with not even a cigarette butt on the floor." R.J. Bernhard, manufacturing engineering manager at the engine works, told Montgomery, "Nobody ever put ashtrays on a production line, and we had one every 20 feet. The workers thought it was funny. And we'd go through and if we found a butt on the floor, we'd pick it up and put it in the ashtray." As Montgomery reported, Wayne Schoville, superintendent of the Deere foundry in Waterloo, Iowa, "is convinced that pride in place becomes pride in work, and it is true for everyone in the plant. To him, the workers are not divided into white-collar and blue-collar—they just have different responsibilities. They are not thinkers and laborers, brains and brawn—each one is a responsible employee."

This attitude may explain why at Deere, unlike many other manufacturing companies, the assembly-line workers are making close to what the machine tool and foundry workers are making. At other places, the assembly-line worker is at the bottom of the totem pole, earning far less than other production workers.

This attitude may also explain why Deere commands more employee loyalty than its competitors. Workers at Deere's tractor plant told the *Boston Globe* reporter about the time someone had left a screwdriver inside an engine. The crew that assembled it wrote to the owner, without prompting, "We apologize. We do not want to make junk."

The recession of the early 1980s was a testing time for Deere and other companies in its industry. International Harvester and Massey-Ferguson almost went under. Caterpillar Tractor endured a nine-month strike that left a sour taste in everyone's mouth in Peoria, Illinois. Deere fared better but did not escape unscathed. It reduced its work force from 65,100 to 45,000, and after the Caterpillar strike was settled, Deere signed a new UAW contract that froze wages. (The average hourly wage at Deere and Caterpillar is $18—$24.45 with benefits.) The union agreed to the freeze to help Deere out in a tough economy.

However, the ink was hardly dry on the signed agreement when Deere announced that it was going to have large hydraulic excavators supplied from Japan, where they would be produced by Hitachi Construction for shipment back to United States dealers. According to the UAW, it would mean the loss of 275 jobs at the Davenport, Iowa, plant. Bill Deadmon, who works at the Deere Plow & Planter Works in Moline, said, "This time we were willing to bend with the company to make them remain profitable. Then, they turn around and hit you with something like this. It smacks us right in the face." Deere denied that any United States jobs would be lost, claiming the excavators were a new line which can be made more efficiently in Japan, but Stan Callahan, president of UAW Local 291, in Davenport, said, "It's a bitter pill to swallow. They should have invested in us—we were willing to invest in them."

Investment in its people is what Deere is generally known for. It has a strong engineering and professional staff, and it has backed them by traditionally spending 5 percent of sales on research and development, almost as much as IBM. It trains its own people and rarely hires from the outside. In 1984 the average age of its senior officers was 51, and they had been with Deere an average of 24 years. If you were a salaried employee at Deere, you were permitted to earmark 1 percent to 6 percent of your earnings for the purchase of John Deere stock, with the company matching every dollar of yours with 75 cents of its own. However, in 1982, when farmers cut back on their purchases, the company froze the pay of salaried employees and suspended contributions under the stock purchase plan. In 1983, the match was reinstated at the 25-cent level. And in 1985 a profit-sharing plan for the hourly and clerical work force went into effect.

Main employment centers   Quad cities on the Illinois-Iowa border, eleven thousand; Waterloo, Iowa, 9,000; Dubuque, Iowa, 4,300. Eleven thousand work overseas.

Headquarters   Deere & Company
John Deere Road
Moline, IL 61265
309-752-8000

DELTA AIR LINES, INC.

Delta flies to over 75 U.S. cities and to London, Frankfurt, and (as of April 1985), Paris. Employees: 37,000.

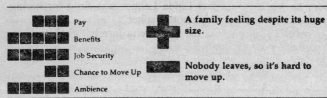

■■■	Pay	✚	A family feeling despite its huge size.
■■■■	Benefits		
■■■■	Job Security		
■■	Chance to Move Up	▓	Nobody leaves, so it's hard to move up.
■■■■	Ambience		

One of the most publicized corporate love affairs is between Delta employees and their airline.

In 1982, for instance, a retiring Delta pilot took out a full-page ad in the *Atlanta Constitution* (at a cost of $8,000) to tell readers that "it has been my privilege to work with the finest group of human beings that God ever created" in "an organization that has been exceedingly well managed."

A few weeks later, three stewardesses announced that they and other Delta employees were pledging nearly $1,000 apiece to buy a $30 million Boeing 767 jet for the airline. "We just wanted to say thanks for the way Delta has treated us," one of the women explained. By December they had raised enough pledges to buy the 767. Seven thousand employees turned out at the Atlanta airport for the christening of "The Spirit of Delta."

Such expressions of affection may sound like the concoctions of a public relations flack. Not so. A large number of Delta employees genuinely love their company. They continually talk about the "the Delta family feeling."

Byron Carroll, a Delta mechanic for 18 years, told a reporter why he had contributed to the employee 767: "Delta's been good to me and my family. When my dad died, the company helped my wife and kids fly to the funeral, sent flowers, and several managers wrote letters. It meant a lot to me that they cared."

The company newsletter is filled with stories of the good family members. There's a regular "Feather in Your Cap" award given for service above and beyond duty, such as the flight attendant who drove a passenger from Houston to Beaumont, Texas, for a funeral she would otherwise have been unable to attend because she missed her connecting flight.

Like many families, Delta has the reputation of being conservative and upright—perhaps a touch on the prudish side, as when stewardess Linda Lehner was fired for baring her backside to a *Playboy* photographer.

Much of the credit for the "Delta family" goes to C.E. Woolman, who founded the line as a crop-dusting service in the rural South during the mid-1920s and ran it till his death in 1966. A longtime Delta mechanic recalls that Woolman referred to him and others as "son" and took an interest in the personal lives of those who worked for him.

Woolman's attitude has been institutionalized in Delta's employee benefits program, called by *Business Week* "one of the most generous in U.S. industry." It's a cradle-to-grave approach, with disability payments based on the number of dependents, a retirement pension pegged at 60 percent of income, and extensive medical and dental coverages. The entire program is paid for by the company.

On top of that package, Delta employees, like those at other airlines, qualify for one of the best perks in American corporate life: free air travel. After 10 years of service, Delta employees and their spouses are granted annual passes good for unlimited travel anywhere on the Delta system, and reduced rates on other airlines. It's a rare airline employee who doesn't take advantage of free flight privileges for quick jaunts to Europe or across the country.

The benefits are nice, but what many Delta employees cite as the best part of working for the company is job security. The year 1982 saw the airline industry beset with pay cuts, wage freezes, and layoffs—even a bankruptcy (Braniff International). Yet Delta reiterated its long-standing policy of no layoffs and declared an across-the-board *pay hike* of 8.5 percent.

Not laying off anyone in the "family" has meant some

juggling of personnel during hard times. During the 1973 oil embargo, when Delta's schedules were sharply curtailed, the company reassigned 600 pilots and stewardesses. Delta's president, David C. Garrett, Jr., explained to *Business Week*: "We put them to work everywhere we could—loading cargo, cleaning airplanes, selling tickets, making reservations.... Sure, that was a blow to the size of their paychecks, especially in the case of the pilots, but they still got paychecks and they kept their seniority and all their medical benefits."

Delta employees take such reassignments in stride, for they see themselves as working on the same team—no wonder, since the company makes an effort to pick only people it considers to be "team players." Job interviews are said to be informal, even casual. Delta wants to know whether someone wants to make a lifelong commitment to the airline. Delta can afford to be selective, with nearly 250,000 job applications on file.

On the other side of the picture, Delta's not the place for someone looking for a quick road to the top. There's hardly any turnover, and the company promotes almost exclusively from within. Except for those with special skills, such as pilots or lawyers, Delta employees start at entry-level jobs. It's common for baggage handlers to be college graduates; a few are even Ph.D.'s. The nine members of the senior management team average 28 years with the airline; the president started as a reservations agent in 1946.

The company's president once told the *New York Times*: "If we ever become unionized, it will be because we've made mistakes." Though aggressively nonunion, the airline doesn't engage in classic union-busting tactics. Far from it. Delta's top brass tries to make unions unwelcome by being especially nice to employees. Labor union officials have noticed that after contracts are signed with other airlines, Delta will quietly give its workers a nickel or dime an hour more than that offered under the union contract.

Keeping the unions out also means top Delta management goes to great lengths to keep in touch with employees. Small groups of workers meet at least every 18 months with the senior management of their department. Frank exchanges of opinions are encouraged. At one regional sales office, for instance, employees complained about worn-out waiting room furniture. Within weeks, the personnel staff in Atlanta made sure the furniture was changed. The management refused, however, a request for day-care facilities at the sales office, but the explanation for their refusal satisfied virtually everyone. Flight attendants select their own uniforms through a similar kind of interaction.

Being nonunion has a practical side, as well. Without the rules and restrictions inherent in a union contract, Delta can move employees wherever needed. It's the primary reason cited for the company's profitability; Delta earned twice as much money during the last decade as its nearest competitor. Though it was the sixth-largest airline in terms of passengers flown in 1982, *Forbes* predicts it will be number one by 1990.

But it's not going to be easy. In 1983, the company posted its first annual loss in 36 years. Characteristically, the company's top 48 executives took a cut in their own pay for the next year. Three months later, the airline froze the salaries of the 32,000 nonunion employees for six months, but ordered no layoffs. A company spokesman told the *Wall Street Journal*: "The attitude I see here is one of grim damned determination."

Main employment centers   Atlanta, Boston, Cincinnati, Dallas/Fort Worth, Memphis.

Headquarters   Delta Air Lines, Inc.
Hartsfield Atlanta International Airport
Atlanta, GA 30320
404-765-2600

digital

DIGITAL EQUIPMENT CORPORATION

Digital is the nation's largest manufacturer of minicomputers.
U.S. employees: 60,000.

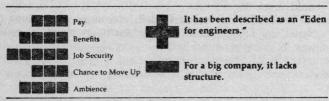

■■■ Pay	**+** It has been described as an "Eden for engineers."
■■■■ Benefits	
■■■■■ Job Security	
■■■ Chance to Move Up	For a big company, it lacks structure.
■■■■ Ambience	

You won't find many companies in America that have created as many new jobs as Digital Equipment has over the past decade. In 1973, Digital had 12,000 employees; by 1985, it had 86,700 (60,000 in the United States). This explosive growth reflects Digital's spectacular success in designing and selling minicomputers. It was the first company to make a computer that could be used on or near desks or in factory aisles where people could punch in instructions directly on a keyboard and see results displayed on a video screen. Presto, the interactive computer!

Kenneth Olsen's ideas about computers germinated when he was an engineer at the Massachusetts Institute of Technology's Lincoln Laboratories. He also knew what kind of company he wanted to have; as he once explained, "When we left MIT in 1957 to start Digital, we had ideas that were so unique we gave up trying to explain them. You know, I could have been happy at MIT. But we wrote papers on our ideas about interactive computers, and people laughed or shrugged. So we had to get out and show them. We had some unique business ideas too—we would not take government money, we insisted on making a profit right away, we insisted we were manufacturers and not researchers, and we said growth was not our goal. To a lot of people here, these are still important ideas, and they help to keep things in perspective."

Digital doesn't look like a California high-tech company—for one thing, the parking lot is filled with *American* cars—but it has some similar attributes. It's not a 9-to-5, white-shirt culture. People communicate on a first-name basis. And it doesn't have a lot of rules. Peter Christy, a Digital engineer who was working in 1983 at Trilogy, a California-based company partly owned by Digital, told us that when people are hired, they are not automatically slotted into specific job functions. "You tell them what the problem is and say, 'I want you to go out and tell me what needs to be done.'"

The look and feel of Digital, and its people, belong to New England. Maynard, Massachusetts, is about 20 miles west of Boston, and when you enter the town by car, you instantly feel you have entered a time warp going back to the late nineteenth and early twentieth centuries, when mean textile barons hired children to work in their mills for pennies an hour. And indeed, that is Maynard's heritage. Dominating the town, from a bluff, is a complex of red buildings that housed one of the largest textile mills in New England, American Woolen. In the early 1900s, 14-year-olds worked in the mill for six cents an hour. Maynard remained a one-industry town until 1950, when American Woolen closed down its big mill on the banks of the Assabet River. When Digital was started in 1957, it leased 8,680 square feet in the mill. As it grew, it took over more and more space, finally buying the entire mill in 1974.

Rather than build a new glass-and-steel structure for itself, Digital elected to remain in the mill. Digital has worked hard to make it a comfortable place to work. The red brick walls have been exposed. The wood-plank floors have been retained. It has high ceilings and large windows. One of the relics from the past is a clock tower. The clock has four faces, each nine feet in diameter, and it has never been electrified. Each week an employee climbs 120 steps to the top of the tower to wind the clock.

The curse of all companies that grow rapidly is the comparable growth of a stifling bureaucracy. It's a danger Digital managers work to avoid. They try to maintain the "small company" feeling by pushing responsibility down to lower levels and breaking down staffs into small teams. Gordon Bell, who headed a staff of 5,000 engineers before leaving in

1983, believed that "large groups are always less efficient than small ones." He held teams down to 30 persons, and instead of promoting smart engineers to managers, he kept them at the bottom of the organization, where they are happy doing what they know how to do, but gave them much more money—sometimes more than their bosses.

The looseness of the place offends some efficiency-minded engineers who want everything to run by the book. But self-management is part of Digital's charm. Win Hindle, one of Digital's top officers, says, "People are responsible for the success of the projects they propose. He who proposes, does." Founder Ken Olsen puts it this way: "I believe that the worker always knows more about his job than the boss."

Digital is conservative—it doesn't borrow money, for example—but sometimes acts like a maverick. It parted company with most other firms in its industry and other industries as well by putting its salespersons on straight salary rather than paying them commissions. Dangerous, you might think. Would salespeople work without an incentive? They seem to at Digital. The Digital sales force has produced the orders—and the turnover, 14 percent a year, is among the industry's lowest.

There's clearly a high level of morale here. Ruth Hoover, a secretary, joined Digital in 1973 after her four children were all grown up. She liked it a lot, she said, "because they let you do what you want to do." She liked it so much that she recommended the company to her husband, an electrical engineer who had worked at two big companies, Raytheon and Sylvania. He did join Digital, in 1977, and said the difference between this company and his former employers "is like night and day."

In 1984, we went to a meeting of field sales managers, and we were impressed with their youth, diversity, enthusiasm, and sense of humor. The meeting was a "visionary" one in that it tried to determine the conditions Digital would face in 1990. The day-and-a-half session opened with stirring film clips of talks made by the late Martin Luther King, Jr.

Another reason for the high morale is that Digital never lays off people. That policy was sorely tested in 1982, which was a difficult year, and when Wall Street security analysts questioned Olsen about it at that time, he replied, "We never promised never to have layoffs, but it seems common sense to avoid it. When a company has to have a layoff, it's most often the management's fault. So at least for a while, we should take the licking, not the employees. In a recession, people want to test me to see if I'm brave enough to have a layoff. I'm willing to take that ridicule because it's paid off to hold on to our people. I don't have layoffs to prove how brave I am. At some time, if it's the wise thing to do, we may do it.

"But we have a big investment in those people. So keeping them, when we know things are going to turn around, is good business. It's also good business for our people to have confidence that we will not lay them off just to help our profit short-term. Their faith in the company is important. We might have layoffs someday, very reluctantly. Hopefully never."

That resolve was tested again in late 1983, when Digital reported a 75 percent drop in profits for the quarter. Wall Street responded by a selloff that reduced the price of Digital's stock by 25 percent. And *Fortune* raised the question of whether the company had grown middle-aged. But Digital said it would not lay off its employees.

Main employment centers   Digital has major facilities in 14 Massachusetts communities: Maynard (the corporate headquarters, with 5,350 employees), Acton, Andover, Boston, Hudson, Franklin, Littleton, Marlboro, Shrewsbury, Southboro, Springfield, Westborough, Westfield, Westminister. There are other manufacturing facilities in Connecticut (Enfield), New Hampshire (Salem, Nashua), Maine (Augusta), Vermont (Burlington), Arizona (Phoenix, Tempe), California (Mountain View), Colorado (Colorado Springs), New Mexico (Albuquerque), and South Carolina (Greenville). Outside the U.S., where more than 26,000 are employed, Digital has manufacturing plants in Puerto Rico, Ireland, Germany, France, Scotland, Taiwan, and Hong Kong.

Headquarters   Digital Equipment Corporation
146 Main Street
Maynard, MA 01754
617-897-5111

Donnelly

DONNELLY CORPORATION

Donnelly makes mirrors, windows, and other glass products, including nearly all the rearview mirrors found in U.S. automobiles. Employees: 800.

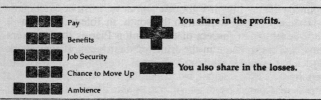

■■■ Pay	✚ **You share in the profits.**
■■■ Benefits	
■■■■ Job Security	
■■■ Chance to Move Up	■■ **You also share in the losses.**
■■■■ Ambience	

Personnel executives from other companies (and from other countries) trek regularly to Holland, Michigan, to learn how Donnelly does it. Most people are surprised to learn that Donnelly makes 98 percent of the rearview mirrors found in American-made automobiles. These mirrors and other glass products, including outside mirrors for trucks, automotive vanity mirrors, fixed and side windows for cars, and glass for liquid crystal displays, are made in Donnelly's four plants in Holland. Annual sales are in the neighborhood of $75 million. The company was founded in 1905 and remains a completely privately owned firm; most of the shares are presumably held by members of the founding Donnelly family.

Even people who don't know about Donnelly's lockhold on the rearview mirror market may have heard of Donnelly as a company that has succeeded through application of the Scanlon Plan to harmonize labor-management relationships. It's a case history in participative management that has been written up by the *Harvard Business Review*, the Conference Board, and the authors of the recent book *Working Together*.

Donnelly operates on the notion that people can be responsible human beings, even in the workplace. They don't have to be *told* what to do; they can decide for themselves. The goal at this company is self-management. These ideas stem from the Scanlon Plan, named for the late Joseph Scanlon, an accountant who worked with the steelworkers union in the 1930s to come up with a labor-management plan that would save the LaPointe Steel Company. The company was threatened with extinction because of seemingly intractable conflicts between labor and management. It was rescued—and Scanlon went on, at the Massachusetts Institute of Technology, to build his theory, the Scanlon Plan, which was later adopted by a handful of companies that swear by it. Donnelly is one of them—it adopted the plan in 1952. Another, close to Donnelly in the Dutch Calvinist region of western Michigan, is Herman Miller. Another, to the south, in Toledo, is Dana.

An important aspect of the Scanlon Plan is that workers must be able to share in the fruits of their labor. If they work harder and smarter, they should be rewarded along with the shareholders who benefit from increased productivity. So the plan encompasses both participative management and profit sharing. There's no standard way of implementing the plan. Each company develops its own policies and practices. The imperative common to all plans is *equity*.

There's nothing hit-or-miss about the way Donnelly operates. That is, just because it's democratic doesn't mean it's disorganized. The company has adopted rules and regulations covering everything, and they are all spelled out meticulously in a 106-page handbook, "You and Your Company," which covers every base from "Absentee Percentages" to "Workers Compensation"—all with a decided lack of humor.

Donnelly does have an up-from-the-ranks tradition, and you can move here from factory floor to the managerial ranks. Many have done it. There's a supervisory level consisting of 19 people—eight came up from the factory floor. Jud Scholten started as a glass cleaner in 1957—now he's the corporate secretary. Ken Armstrong started in 1957 as a quality control technician; he's now treasurer of Donnelly. The systems manager, Kay Hubbard, who's in charge of computer operations, joined the company as a secretary in 1972.

Donnelly's reputation as a good employer draws applicants like a magnet. They keep coming in looking for production jobs because they have heard it's a friendly place where it's possible to move up.

At Donnelly, time clocks have been removed and everyone is salaried. A Donnelly employee works in a team of 10 people. You are trusted to keep your own records but you are responsible to other members of the team. If you're late because of an illness in the family, for example, your work will be covered by another team member. You will have a primary job but are expected to be able to do the jobs done by other members of your team. So if you're consistently absent or not performing well during working hours, you have to answer not to the company but to the other members of your team. Each team sets its own production goals, within the framework of the larger company-wide objectives—and goals are also set for each individual member of the team. These production rates can vary from individual to individual, depending on experience, the job being performed, and worker capability. Your team is linked to other teams through your team leader. Monthly focus meetings bring together representatives from all the work teams.

Pay scales at Donnelly are established by the company in conjunction with the judgments of team members. Areawide surveys are conducted every year to ensure that the base pay at Donnelly is competitive with rates paid at other companies. The determination of when you move up at Donnelly is made basically by your team members or team manager. When employees decide on a general increase in the base pay, it's coupled with a cost-reduction drive—that is, every employee is charged with thinking of ways to reduce expenses for the company. In 1970, for example, employees voted to boost the base pay by 10 percent and set a cost-reduction target of $610,000; savings of $643,000 were achieved by the employees.

All job openings are posted at Donnelly, and employees are invited to bid on them. There is a rule that no one can be displaced by technological improvement. If someone's job is eliminated, he or she is given a chance to work in another area. People with seniority can bump others with fewer years of service. A Donnelly Committee functions to consider all grievances and set policies in compensation and benefits. It meets once a month, and meetings can sometimes consume more than three hours. Represented on this committee are employees from all parts of the company. It's a miniature "Town Hall," what with every 50 employees electing a representative for a two-year term. A representative can be recalled if constituents are unhappy with their representation. The only management representative on the committee is the president. Two-thirds are production workers, one-third office staff. All decisions made by this committee must be adopted unanimously. The committee is responsible for preparing an annual wage package for submission to the board. In 1984, it called for a 7 percent wage hike.

Donnelly employees share in the profits through a bonus plan rigged to the company's return on investment. Bonuses are paid monthly. The company is first allowed to make a 5.2 percent return on its investment. Once that is achieved, profits go into a pool, 56 percent of which is retained by the company; the remaining 44 percent is divided among employees. It's not divided equally. The more money you make, the higher your bonus. Typically, the bonus augments your salary from 7 to 12 percent. If a 5.2 percent return is not achieved, a "negative bonus" is recorded—and it will have to be "paid back" before bonuses are given to employees.

The benefits at Donnelly are good. The company pays the entire medical insurance premium for employees and their dependents. There's a pension plan. At Christmastime, every employee receives "a ham or other main course of the Christmas dinner."

John F. Donnelly, who brought the Scanlon Plan to Donnelly Mirrors and who retired in 1982 after 50 years as head of the company, was once asked by *Harvard Business Review* why other companies don't adopt these ideas. He replied: "They're afraid of losing authority." And he added, "Because that's the way it's been done, and that's the way organizations are structured. They're mostly modeled after the military, and it's difficult for people to conceive of any other system working. I would be the last one to say that we don't use authority in this company. We do. But, to the extent that you have to rely on the authority of your position, you're a questionable manager. If you are not in the position to get people to accept ideas because they're sound, and if you are not willing to accept an idea because it's sound, then you're really not a good manager."

Between 1964 and 1971, Donnelly's productivity— amount of output per unit of direct labor—went up nearly 50 percent. Since 1965 Donnelly's sales have mushroomed from $3 million to $75 million and its number of employees from

200 to 1,000. Between 1975 and 1984 productivity—measured by sales per employee—went up by 110 percent.

Main employment center   Holland. Of the 1,000 employees, 200 work at Donnelly's one overseas plant in Ireland.

Headquarters	Donnelly Corporation
	49 West 3rd Street
	Holland, MI 49423
	616-394-2200

WHERE THE BIG BOSSES MEET REGULARLY WITH THE TROOPS

Dana	Johnson Wax	Pitney Bowes
Electro	Marion Labs	Tandem
Scientific	Mary Kay Cosmetics	Computers
Federal Express	Physio-Control	Viking Freight

DOYLE DANE BERNBACH
INTERNATIONAL INC.

DOYLE DANE BERNBACH
INTERNATIONAL INC.

Doyle Dane Bernbach is the seventh-largest advertising agency in the United States. U.S. employees: 2,100.

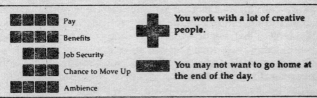

■■■■ Pay	✚ **You work with a lot of creative people.**
■■■■ Benefits	
■■■ Job Security	
■■■ Chance to Move Up	■■ **You may not want to go home at the end of the day.**
■■■■ Ambience	

Remember the classic Volkswagen ads, the ones that made a virtue of understatement? Or the sidesplitting TV commercials for Alka-Seltzer? Do you recall the "Avis Is Only Number 2, We Have to Try Harder" ads? All were created by Doyle Dane Bernbach, an advertising agency that handles more than $1.4 billion worth of advertising a year and ranks seventh in terms of the amount of advertising handled in the United States.

Working for an ad agency can promise insecure moments. Who knows that you have created those beautiful ads? What if the biggest account walks out? Marketing types on the client's end may have no appreciation of the subtleties of fine art and fine writing. And as you get up in years, you may wonder how long you are going to last in a business often characterized as a young people's business, intent on the new. Doyle Dane, or DDB, as it's sometimes called, has managed to grapple with those questions so successfully that it's regarded as the shop of choice on Madison Avenue.

Ned Doyle, Maxwell Dane, and William Bernbach, the three admen who founded this agency in 1949, have all departed from the scene. Doyle and Dane have retired. Bernbach died on October 2, 1982, at the age of 71. But the spirit they breathed into this agency seems to live on. It's a spirit based on respect for the individual and dedication to doing good work. DDB spearheaded the "creative revolution" in the advertising business. Led by Bill Bernbach, DDB people created ads that had humor, wit, warmth, and excitement. They didn't slavishly kowtow to clients. They didn't talk down to consumers. And they demonstrated that such sensibility sells. Bernbach once explained: "It is ironic that the very thing that is most suspect by business, that intangible thing called artistry, turns out to be the most practical tool available to it. For it is only artistry that can vie with all the shocking news events and violence in the world for the attention of the consumer."

In carrying out that philosophy, the Doyle Dane people had a profound impact on the entire advertising business, and they built a big agency that bred among employees—and even ex-employees (many of whom return)—an intense loyalty comparable to what you find in close-knit families. Bob Levenson, for years one of the agency's top copywriters, said: "When I tell someone anywhere in the world that I work for an advertising agency, they say, 'Oh.' But when I tell them that the agency I work for is Doyle Dane Bernbach, they say, 'Ah!'" Frank Camardella, a senior art director, returned to the agency in 1980 after being away for 12 years; he says of other agencies where he worked, "I could smell the fear in the halls. I felt the tenseness." Bob Kuperman, who started in the New York office in 1963, left in 1972, and returned to the Los Angeles office in 1982, said: "I got lonesome and wanted to come home."

Not everyone who works in an advertising agency is a writer or artist, but the enthusiasm felt by the creative people seeps through this entire agency. Harriet Messinger, who works in traffic (they see that the ads get out), still looks forward each day, after 15 years, to coming to work. "It's a warm, delicious feeling," she says. Messinger also reports that when you meet ex-DDBers at advertising functions, they tell you "their hearts have never left here."

Salaries in the ad agency business are high—and Doyle Dane is no exception. Of the agency's total revenues of $200 million in 1983 (an agency's income is roughly 15 percent of the advertising dollars it places), $118 million, or nearly 60 percent, went to wages and benefits, which works out to an average of $35,000 per person. There aren't many businesses like that. The company has a standard benefits program: medical insurance, group life, and a very good deferred profit-sharing plan, too: only twice has it ever missed paying the maximum allowed by the IRS—15 percent of an employee's compensation. Doyle Dane is also one of the few publicly held agencies; its stock is traded on the over-the-counter market.

But it's not the benefits and salary so much as the intangibles that make Doyle Dane a good place to work. Employees seem to want to stick around. One-quarter of them have been there at least 10 years—and the agency just reached its thirty-fifth birthday. There's an annual luncheon for all 10-year employees, at which awards of stock are given out: employees celebrating 10 years with the company receive ten shares; 15 years, 15 shares; 20 years, 20 shares; and 25 years, 25 shares. Doyle Dane stock was selling at $18 a share toward the end of 1984. (Employees hold about one-third of all the stock in Doyle Dane.) Some other extraordinary aspects of DDB include:

• Respect for your private opinions. If you don't want to work on a liquor or candy account (because of these products' effects), you're encouraged to say so. For many years the agency refused to handle a cigarette account, but it took one at the end of 1982.

• Job-posting. It's common in many industries, but not in the advertising business. Every position in the agency that's open is listed inside first so that employees can have first crack.

• Time off to work in community service or on political campaigns that are important to you. When Martin Luther King, Jr., was assassinated, the agency closed its doors for the day. Maxwell Dane, active in the American Civil Liberties Union and Businessmen for the End of the Vietnam War, was Number 3 on the Nixon "enemies" list.

• Intramural sports. Many companies have teams, but did you ever hear of one footing the expenses for a tournament involving four different offices? Yes, it happened at DDB in 1982, when softball teams from the New York, Los Angeles, and St. Joseph, Missouri, offices went to Kansas City "to get people together on a very social level."

The Los Angeles office, incidentally, won the tournament. Barry Loughrane, who was then president of DDB-West, pitched four winning games and batted 6 for 15. Here's a snippet of a report in the DDB house publication: "And then there were the L.A. women. New York watched in awe an

L.A. infield of women at first, second, and third base, something it had never seen."

When Bill Bernbach died in 1982, there was an outpouring of emotion in the entire advertising community, a testimony to the kind of place Doyle Dane Bernbach had become under his leadership. A letter appeared in *Advertising Age* from Louis A. Magnani, president of another ad agency, Marsteller. He quoted from a letter he received from Sam Katz, who once worked for DDB and is now an adman in Sweden. It read in part: "Nobody mentioned, for example, that [Bernbach] hired an awful lot of bums—neurotics, drunks, complainers, kooks of every description . . . because he saw a vein of talent in them. . . . I personally and literally owe him my life. He brought out what talent I had. . . . You know what his chief deep-down achievement was? Let me tell you. A lot of those people didn't have homes. They had a place to live, but they didn't like going there. So he made home for them at DDB. . . . I used to see them playing ball in the corridors. 'Why don't you go home?' I used to ask. One would say he was waiting for his wife to put the kids to bed. Another would say the trains were too crowded. A third would say he was waiting for type. And on and on. But the truth was that they hated to leave the office, they were so happy and comfortable there."

Yes, DDB is a place with that kind of heritage. Sign up if you can—and if you can hit and field, New York may be especially partial to you. After all, Barry Loughrane has now moved to New York to become president and chief executive officer of the agency.

Main employment centers   Doyle Dane Bernbach employs 3,350 people, 850 in the New York office, 1,250 overseas. There are Doyle Dane offices in Los Angeles, San Francisco, and Denver. DDB-owned agencies in the United States are Milici/Valenti Advertising in Honolulu; Cargill, Wilson & Acree, Atlanta; Fletcher/Mayo, St. Joseph, Missouri; Bernard Hodes Advertising, New York; Tallir, Philips, Ross, New York; Rapp & Collins, New York. And there are DDB offices in 17 other countries.

Headquarters   Doyle Dane Bernbach International Inc.
437 Madison Avenue
New York, NY 10022
212-415-2000

ESTABLISHED 1802

E. I. DU PONT DE NEMOURS & COMPANY, INC.

Du Pont is the largest chemical company in the United States.
U.S. employees: 100,000.

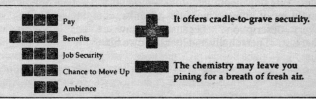

■■■ Pay	✚ It offers cradle-to-grave security.
■■■■ Benefits	
■■■ Job Security	
■■■ Chance to Move Up	■■ The chemistry may leave you pining for a breath of fresh air.
■■ Ambience	

Tradition means a lot at Du Pont. It's one of the oldest companies in the country, founded as a gunpowder manufacturer in 1802. A painting of Thomas Jefferson with founder Eleuthere Irénée du Pont adorns a wall in the chairman's office.

A chief element of the Du Pont tradition involves a benevolent attitude toward employees. In the early part of the century, the company decentralized its management structure and became one of the first big companies to be run by committee rather than by a single man. Du Pont is still highly decentralized, and the executive committee, composed of the top officers of the company, meets weekly to make major decisions and discuss up-and-coming younger employees.

Du Pont also pioneered in the field of employee benefits with a pension and retirement plan in 1904, company-paid life insurance in 1919, vacations in 1934, health insurance in 1936, and a disability pay plan in 1937. Today's Du Pont has a published policy that it will maintain a balanced set of benefits that are as good as or better than its competitors'. For instance, employees are paid in full for up to six months for injuries or illnesses that are *not* job-related.

Scientific breakthroughs are yet another part of the professional tradition of Du Pont. During the first half of this century, Du Pont labs created such products as moisture-proof cellophane, tetraethyl (anti-knock compounds for gasoline), Freon (for refrigeration), neoprene (synthetic rubber), nylon (the first synthetic fiber), Lucite (the first molded plastic), and Teflon (a tough plastic finish). The tradition has continued to the present, as Du Pont scientists have managed to come up with 88 distinct products in the past two decades, including Kevlar (used in bullet-resistant vests and tires), SilverStone coating, aca (for medical diagnosis), and Nomex fire-resistant fibers.

Someone who joins Du Pont becomes part of this proud tradition—a history that has much to recommend it. But it is not the place for someone who is looking for a quick rise to the top or a fluid, entrepreneurial environment.

"We react like a fast-moving iceberg," explained Robert Armstrong, a principal Du Pont recruiter. "We tend to be conservative. We promote almost exclusively from within, and nearly everybody starts in an entry-level position."

Once hired, people tend to stay with Du Pont. Forty-six percent of all Du Pont employees have been with the company more than 15 years, and the average length of service for Du Pont retirees exceeds 30 years.

Such long associations with a company breed close ties among workers. Du Pont's chairman, Edward Jefferson, who joined the company as a research chemist, once said, "We're a company of friends." For many Du Ponters, it's more than just friends. Of the U.S. work force of 100,000, nearly 7,000 are married to another Du Ponter. There are 80 married couples, for example, at Du Pont's plant in Cape Fear, North Carolina.

One of the largest instances of this inbred work environment is Wilmington, Delaware. Nearly 27,000 Du Ponters work in the Wilmington area, either at the headquarters, at research centers just outside the city, or at the manufacturing facilities. The corporate headquarters in downtown Wilmington includes two 14-story, block-long, tan brick buildings erected at the turn of the century. One of the buildings includes the Hotel Du Pont, originally built to make sure out-of-town guests had a place to stay, as Wilmington then had no other hotels.

Though the company itself has no executive dining rooms, some top managers regularly eat in one of the two first-class restaurants on the bottom floor of the hotel/office building. This practice is the exception, not the rule. Top executives are not only accessible in Wilmington, but approachable. People refer to each other by their first names. Since most top managers came up through the ranks, they have lots of old friends scattered throughout the organization.

Du Ponters tend to socialize with each other outside of work. Some critics of the company say too much emphasis is placed on socializing with others in the company, but sometimes promotions are based on out-of-work contacts. Nearly 10,000 Wilmington-area employees belong to the Du Pont Country Clubs. There are four 18-hole golf courses, three in Wilmington, one in nearby Newark, Delaware, plus tennis courts and facilities for dining and social gatherings.

People also get to know their fellow Du Ponters outside the Wilmington area. It's a rare Du Pont manager who does not get transferred. It used to be part of the Du Pont tradition.

Du Pont still attracts many of the top scientific researchers. Nearly 3,500 Du Ponters have Ph.D.'s, including the chairman of the board. The company spent more than $1 billion on research and development in 1984. About half of the 4,000 Du Pont scientists work in one of the 30 buildings that constitute the Experimental Station, built on a bluff overlooking the Brandywine River in Wilmington. In 1984, Du Pont opened an $85 million life sciences research complex near Wilmington for biomedical studies.

Du Pont scientists are "encouraged to pursue their own interests," says Dr. Fred Oettle, who taught chemistry at Columbia University before joining Du Pont. The engineers and chemists work in small teams. According to Oettle, "It's relatively easy to find your own niche."

The company stresses its outstanding safety record—20 times better than the chemistry industry and 85 times better than all manufacturing industries, according to the National Safety Council. Du Pont's "audit" teams regularly survey each of the 140 Du Pont plants to make sure company safety regulations are enforced. The *Wall Street Journal* once said, "Concern about safety and health takes on a slightly manic air at Du Pont. Safety slogans sprout from almost every available wall space." Company employees and retirees have received free medical checkups since 1916, and Du Pont has maintained a cancer registry since 1956. Its Haskell Lab conducts constant studies of the effects of various chemicals to which

Du Pont workers are exposed. Du Pont has, however, lobbied against stricter government controls over chemical production processes.

Only 38 percent of Du Pont workers eligible for union membership belong to unions. Most of those who are in unions join independent locals, some of which are an outgrowth of the Workers Councils set up by Du Pont during the 1930s. In 1981, workers at 14 Du Pont plants in the South voted overwhelmingly against representation by the United Steelworkers of America, after the union's long organizing drive.

One of Du Pont's traditions that has died, however, is the running of the company by the du Pont family. The last du Pont to run the company stepped down as chairman in 1972. None is in the wings to take over, although a half-dozen du Pont family members still sit on the board of directors.

Traditions die hard at Du Pont.

Main employment center   Wilmington. Other plants throughout the United States.

Headquarters   E. I. du Pont de Nemours & Company, Inc.
1007 Market Street
Wilmington, DE 19898
302-774-1000

EASTMAN KODAK COMPANY

Eastman Kodak is the world's largest photographic company. U.S. employees: 86,000.

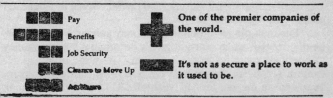

Pay	
Benefits	One of the premier companies of the world.
Job Security	
Chance to Move Up	It's not as secure a place to work as it used to be.
Ambiance	

Merchants in Rochester, New York, wait eagerly every year for the Friday following March 15. They put streamers in their windows to herald the day. They advertise in newspapers and on radio and television. They mount special sales. The banks are in there pitching alongside the merchants.

They all want a piece of the enormous wage dividend paid annually by Eastman Kodak, the area's largest employer. It's not an inconsequential piece of change. Kodak has 54,000 employees in Rochester, and in 1984 they shared in a payout of more than $165 million, which averages out to $3,000 a person.

Of course, not everyone gets $3,000. The more you make, the more you get. The wage dividend is based on a formula related to the payout of dividends to stockholders. The formula, in recent years, has awarded employees between $24 and $36 for every $1,000 earned in the previous five years.

The annual wage dividend is not a substitute for poor wages. Kodak pays well—and for every dollar it pays in direct wages, it spends another 50 cents on fringe benefits. Treating its people well, as part of an extended family, is a tradition that goes back to the company's founder, George Eastman, who was forced to leave school when he was 14 after his father died, leaving the family penniless. That was in

111

1868. He began experimenting with photography when he was 24 years old. He worked as a bank clerk during the day and experimented in his mother's kitchen at night. His first Kodak camera came out in 1888. A year later he introduced the first commercial transparent film in rolls.

Eastman gave away his fortune while he was still alive. He was a great benefactor of the Massachusetts Institute of Technology, the University of Rochester, the Rochester Institute of Technology, the Eastman School of Music, Tuskegee University, Hampton Institute, and dental clinics in Rochester and five European cities.

Eastman pioneered on the company side as well. In 1898 he distributed, as an outright gift, a substantial sum of money to every person who worked for him. The wage dividend became a formal program in 1912, and it has been paid every year except the depression year of 1934. In 1919 Eastman gave one-third of his stock holdings in the company to his employees. Before he died in 1932, by his own hand, he had in place at Kodak a retirement plan, life insurance, and disability benefits. In this respect he was far ahead of other business leaders.

It was paternalism, to be sure, but it bred a fierce loyalty among employees, so much so that sons and daughters of Kodak employees often aspired to—and did—work at Kodak Park in Rochester.

Kodak has an up-from-the-ranks policy. It's almost unheard of for the company to fill any important position from the outside. It's also almost unheard of for other companies to pry people away from Kodak. One headhunter told *Dun's Review:* "We tried to get someone out of there, and we might as well have tried to get a three-year-old away from his mother."

Though the company has grown to gargantuan size, Kodak people are still encouraged to tinker on their own, much as George Eastman did. Kodak has one of the largest research budgets in U.S. industry: $3 million a day. In 1984, the company set up a Venture Board to sponsor ideas that come from employees and that "are outside the realm of photography and chemicals."

Eastman Kodak is a world unto itself. In Rochester, for example, it maintains a medical department staffed by 200 people, including 30 full-time physicians and approximately

60 nurses. Its Employee Center has a 20-lane bowling alley, a pistol range, and a 2,500-seat theater. Then there's the Eastman Savings & Loan Association, which the company established some years back but which is now owned and run by the employees.

Kodak's Suggestion Plan is the granddaddy of them all, having been started in 1898. Kodak takes this Suggestion Plan seriously. If a suggestion results in out-of-pocket savings for the company, the award is equal to 15 percent of the savings achieved in the first two years of use. If a suggestion results in a new product, the award is equal to 3 percent of the sales achieved in the first year. A person who submits an idea that is rejected receives a written explanation of why action was not taken.

In recent years Kodak has given awards averaging $3 million annually to more than 30,000 people who turned in ideas. Kodak has more people making suggestions for improvements than most companies have employees.

Some consider Kodak to be a rather square place. It's true that Kodak people are not known for their flamboyance. In this sense they resemble Procter & Gamble people. They just get the job done, and they don't make a lot of noise tooting their horns.

In a 1976 article in *Money*, an accountant who had worked at Kodak for 15 years commented: "The competition to get jobs here is stiff, and the people they hire are the cream of the crop. They seem to promote the right people around here. The good ones get ahead. There's not as much politics as you might expect. I usually respect the people I work for. If my boss doesn't satisfy me, I can go above him."

Kodak's benevolence has been made possible by a lockhold on amateur film processing (85 percent of the United States market). That, in turn, has made the company a fair imitation of a perpetual moneymaking machine. But the times are changing. Japan's Fuji is beginning to give Kodak a run for its money—and mighty Eastman can no longer rest on past laurels.

The recession of 1981–82 caught up with the company in 1983. During the first six months of that year, more than 5,000 employees accepted either an early retirement plan or a buyout for quitting of a week's pay for every year of seniority.

The year-end merit raises for 85,000 others were deferred for six months. That was not all; another 2,700 were laid off altogether.

The magnitude of the cutbacks was unprecedented in Kodak's history, and it seriously dented "Father Yellow's" reputation. The *New York Times* quoted a middle manager still working at the company: "Kodak has always been one big happy family. Once you settled in a position, you felt at home. You tended to stay. But now some of that is gone. There definitely is some anxiety."

Whether the uncertainty will last remains to be seen. Kodak is clearly moving through a transitional phase. In 1984, the company told us it was actively seeking hundreds of people in various disciplines to support its entry into new businesses (telecommunications, magnetic media), but doubts have been expressed as to whether Kodak has the alertness or resilience to respond to new opportunities. "Has the world passed Kodak by?" was the question *Forbes* raised in a November 5, 1984, cover story which it concluded by noting that the company's chairman and president were both engineers who had spent decades inside Kodak's walls. *Forbes* writers Subrata N. Chakravarty and Ruth Simon said:

"Can the veterans who have spent all their professional lives at Kodak, absorbing its cautious, deliberate, technically oriented culture, and the arrogance born of years of competitive dominance, now learn how to scramble? Maybe, but the recent record is not reassuring."

Main employment centers   More than 60 percent of Kodak's 86,000 U.S. employees work in Rochester, the third-largest city in New York State, sometimes described as "the city without an image." (Phillip Horsely, an investment advisor and formerly a vice-president of the University of Rochester, described it as "a town of quiet money, which is why there is no Neiman-Marcus or Saks Fifth Avenue. Rochester really isn't the East Coast. It's more the heartland of America or like the Midwest.") Kodak has chemical facilities at Longview, Texas; Kingsport, Tennessee; Columbia, South Carolina, and Batesville, Arkansas. It has 125,000 employees worldwide.

Headquarters   Eastman Kodak Company
343 State Street
Rochester, NY 14650
724-357-4000

A.G. Edwards & Sons, Inc.

A. G. EDWARDS & SONS, INC.

A. G. Edwards is the largest stockbroker not headquartered on Wall Street. Employees: 4,580.

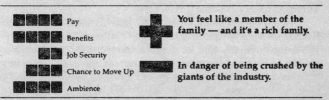

■■■■ Pay	✚ **You feel like a member of the family — and it's a rich family.**
■■■■ Benefits	
■■■ Job Security	
■■■ Chance to Move Up	■ **In danger of being crushed by the giants of the industry.**
■■■ Ambience	

Odessa, Texas; Huron, South Dakota; Lawton, Oklahoma; Claremont, New Hampshire; Dothan, Alabama; Hyannis, Massachusetts: those are all places where you might work if you were with this St. Louis-based brokerage house. Edwards is a stockbroker that has pushed into the boondocks, by either acquiring local outfits or starting its own branches from scratch. In 1982 alone, Edwards opened branches in such places as El Dorado, Kansas; Englewood, Colorado; Jackson Hole, Wyoming; Joplin, Missouri; and Mentor, Ohio. So now it boasts more than 250 offices in 43 states, where customers can come to watch the casino action on Wall Street or buy and sell shares or options or what have you, including A. G. Edwards, whose stock trades on the New York Stock Exchange.

Having 250 offices in the brokerage business *is* a big deal. Only seven other brokers, all but one headquartered in New York, have more branches than Edwards. Merrill Lynch, the leader of the pack, has more than 500.

Edwards is an old-fashioned stockbroker. Talking with Benjamin F. Edwards III, chairman and president, in his modest office at St. Louis headquarters, you wouldn't think you were in a brokerage house. He speaks quietly in a self-effacing manner. A radio turned to a classical music station plays in the background. If you ask how the market is doing,

115

he shrugs. He doesn't have a quote machine with a video screen. "I'm not important enough to have one of those," he says.

The great-grandson of the founder of the firm, Edwards makes it seem as if it were almost accidental that the company survived the crunch of the late 1960s and early 1970s when brokerage houses were dropping like flies. His father, he explained, had a heart attack in 1965, so he took a more active role in the firm earlier than had been expected. He was only 33 years old.

It so happened that Ben Edwards III spent his early days in the firm concentrating on the back-office area, where customer transactions and records are maintained—the unglamorous part of the business. As a result, the company developed a strong back-office operation, which it needed when trading picked up on the stock exchanges. A weak back office ruined many firms. They couldn't handle prosperity. Edwards could—and did.

Edwards also survived the doldrums of the 1970s, when trading dried up. Instead of mass layoffs, Edwards put people on four-day weeks. Ben Edwards also made a point of talking frankly to his employees, enlisting their help. When the firm began losing money in the mid-1970s, he asked employees to do what they could to reduce costs by 10 percent. They pitched in so vigorously that costs were chopped by 17 percent—and pilferage seemed to disappear. The company went into the black in two months. "I've never been disappointed in people when you take them into your confidence," Ben Edwards says.

There's a small-town family feeling here. Howard R. Posner left E. F. Hutton's New York office in 1981 to head the syndication department at Edwards. He describes Edwards as a place where there's "a real concern for people." He recalls that five months after he joined the firm, he lunched with Ben Edwards for 40 minutes. "Business," he said, "never came up once."

David M. Sisler, who played baseball for four major-league teams and whose father was Hall-of-Famer George Sisler, joined Edwards in 1963. He now directs the branch-office operations. "There's a feeling of sharing going on here," he says. The branch offices, he points out, look upon

St. Louis as "their Rock of Gibraltar. We give a damn about them."

Al Goldman, with Edwards since 1960, is in charge of short-term trading, and he talks about the "Mom's-apple-pie philosophy" of the place. "There's less politicking here and more teamwork. The individual who wants his own island of income wouldn't be good at A. G. Edwards."

There's an attitude at Edwards that you are supposed to be accomplishing something for the firm, not for yourself. This is one reason they are able to run a successful branch network. They put a great deal of emphasis on servicing those branches. "We kill our salesmen with kindness," says Goldman. He says that he learned early in his career about not getting a swelled head. He made a series of winning stock picks in the 1960s, and he began to regard himself as a genius. When the boom ended and his judgment was no longer infallible, Goldman learned some humility. As a result, he can say today, "I don't take myself seriously. It's good to get your ego down below your ankles."

Strewn around Goldman's office, on the floor and on his desk, are numerous market letters telling people what to buy and what to sell. Asked which letters he finds the most valuable, Goldman replies quickly: "None of them. I read them because I have to know what they are saying, what they are recommending. But I don't trust any of them. The only faith I have is in the market itself. When it starts to move up, I buy. This means that I may miss the very tops and the very lows, but I just try to go with the market. We don't think that we're smarter here than the market."

Edwards is also old-fashioned in that it hasn't built up a huge institutional customer base, doing trades for insurance companies, pension funds, and the like. Its focus is still the little guy. The typical Edwards customer trades in 100 to 400 shares at a time—and there are 250,000 customers on the books. Edwards does such a typical old-style brokerage business that commissions account for 60 percent of total revenues.

So this is a homey place, where teamwork is emphasized. And it has a lot of brokers. Every brokerage house naturally has a number of brokers, the customers' representatives, but Edwards has many more, relative to its size, than other houses. Of Merrill Lynch's 38,000 employees, for example, only 10,000 may be brokers. At Edwards, nearly half of the 4,580 employees are brokers. And they do pretty well, keeping 43 percent of the commissions they generate. The average Edwards broker makes upwards of $65,000 a year.

It's not only brokers and managers who make out well at Edwards. The company has a profit-sharing plan skewed in favor of low-income staffers. If your salary is below the Social Security base ($36,900), you're required, as a member of the plan, to withhold 1 percent of it annually—and the company then kicks in $2 for every $1 you save. Above that salary level, the company matches only one-for-one. In addition, the company makes discretionary contributions to the plan based on profits. If you were a $12,000-a-year employee in 1978 (the year the profit-sharing plan started), and if, heaven forbid, you had remained at that salary through 1983, your profit-sharing account at the start would have grown to $5,028, of which you had contributed only $720 (1 percent of your salary every year for four years). And that doesn't count the earnings on your money.

All Edwards employees may buy stock in the firm at 85 percent of the market value. It would not be a bad investment. Every dollar invested in Edwards at the start of 1975 was worth $30 at the start of 1983.

Edwards people tend to stay around for a long time. The average age of the 23 Edwards people on the board of directors in 1983 was 52—and they had an average of 19 years of experience with the company. Of the 4,300 employees on the payroll in mid-1983, 416 had been with the company 10 years or more. Considering that 10 years ago Edwards had only 1,200 employees, that's remarkable endurance.

Ben Edwards attributes this longevity to people being happy working on a team. "We decided ten years ago," he said, "that we were going to concentrate on the retail market and go after the individual customer in small cities across the country. We decided also that we were going to have fun."

Main employment centers   St. Louis and "Small Town," America.

Headquarters   A. G. Edwards & Sons, Inc.
One North Jefferson
St. Louis, MO 63103
414-289-3000

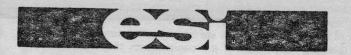

ELECTRO SCIENTIFIC INDUSTRIES, INC.

ESI makes laser trimming devices and testing equipment used by electronics manufacturers. U.S. employees: 750.

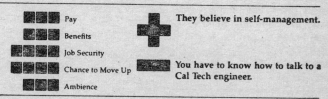

■■■■ Pay

■■■ Benefits

■■■■ Job Security

■■■■ Chance to Move Up

■■■ Ambience

+ They believe in self-management.

■■■ You have to know how to talk to a Cal Tech engineer.

ESI is one company that doesn't recruit M.B.A.'s. "We have not had good luck with M.B.A.'s," Chairman Douglas Strain says. "They have too many stereotypes. It annoys the people they are working with. It's easier to come to our people as an amateur." The top people at ESI are mechanical and electrical engineers.

We talked with Strain at the firm's Portland, Oregon, headquarters, in late 1983, shortly before ESI was to make its first public stock offering. Founded in 1953 by Strain and four other engineers, ESI has established itself as a leader in making instruments and systems that help other electronics manufacturers produce precision products. Their laser trimmers, for instance, are purchased by companies that make computer chips. Other ESI devices are used to test electronic transistors and resistors. In 1983, ESI derived 10 percent of its sales from Western Electric and 9 percent from IBM.

From its inception, ESI has also been high-tech in its managerial techniques. In his quiet, professorial manner, Strain challenges conventional ideas about management. "The Harvard Business School view is sterile," Strain said. "Their distinction between management and employee is far too sharp and not very productive. Lots of times management thinks that people have to be managed. But people manage

119

their own lives before they come to work in the morning and after they go home."

His theory leads him to think, "The real problem is the function of management. Most management gets in the way.

ESI Management Principles

1. To manage our business with the primary objective of making a contribution to society. Business can be one of the most effective vehicles through which man serves society. Thus, any service we perform should be oriented toward the public welfare, and any product we manufacture should be designed to be the best possible value in its class.

2. To recognize the dignity and personal worth of every individual. All employees should have the opportunity to share in the company's success, for each of them helps to make it possible. Every individual deserves job security in accordance with his performance on the job and personal satisfaction of being commended for a job well done. The objective is not simply to make the organization more efficient—although that will certainly be one result—but to emphasize beyond any possible doubt that human labor is not a commodity to be bought and sold in the marketplace.

3. To recognize our responsibility to our community. We are all indebted to those who developed and those who preserve our system of government for the freedom to carry on our business; to our schools and universities for pushing forward the frontiers of knowledge; and to our religious organizations for their moral training. We must vigorously support these institutions of our society if we wish to preserve our freedom and individual liberty.

4. To develop and encourage a better understanding of the nature of profit. Profit is the monetary measure of the contribution of the business to society. It is the difference between the cost of goods and services we produce and their value to society. It is our insurance that the business will continue to grow and flourish, meeting all of its obligations to customers, employees and the general public. It provides the stockholders with a fair return on capital and encourages further investment. Profit, in short, is not the proper *end* of business; it is merely the *means* that makes the achievement of the proper ends possible.

It's also a question of what is management. Is it a set of principles or is it a person? I consider a manager to be a person in a role. He or she should be like a lens, trying to help focus energy in a specific direction."

At ESI, Strain's theories have been translated into what is called "matrix structure" as opposed to the traditional pyramid structure of management.

An administrative committee, composed of those in charge of each division, operates by a "consensual or round-table method." Rather than vote on decisions or leave the final decision up to one person, the group tries to settle everything by consensus.

ESI employees we talked with seem to like the freedom implied by Strain's matrix structure. Tom Freeman, a product manager, explained, "You get to try a lot of things that you cannot do in a more structured company. I have been here nine years, and I am on my fifth job."

There is a drawback. "This is still a small company," Freeman says. "People have to be spread further than in a bigger one. At a company like Tek [Tektronix, ESI's Portland neighbor], there would be ten people doing what I do. You get a lot of responsibility here."

We visited ESI on a Friday morning. The headquarters is in a converted elementary school in a suburban area of Portland. Nearby are the modern, low-slung buildings where ESI's manufacturing and research facilities are located. Most of the employees, including corporate vice-presidents, were wearing blue jeans or other casual clothes as most employees take Friday afternoons off. With ESI's flex-time provisions, employees can work four 10-hour days, or four 8.8-hour days with a half-day on Friday, or five 8-hour days.

During the spring, groups of 12 to 15 ESI employees sit down with the company's president for what they call "Going Well/In the Way" meetings. As the title suggests, the gatherings are meant to help employees explain to the boss what they find good and bad.

The president systematically goes around the room and asks each employee, "What's going well, and what's in the way?" Another company official acts as a scribe and puts the comments on a blackboard. Donna Gelbach, a production employee, told us the meetings are "no holds barred."

In addition to these small meetings, the president meets with entire divisions of the company once every three quarters for what are called "Road Shows." At those sessions he announces the company's pretax profits for the quarter, 25 percent of which are put into the employee profit-sharing pool. Employees look forward to this event when they get a check for a quarter of their share, while the rest is put into their individual retirement or stock ownership accounts.

Main employment center   Portland.

Headquarters   Electro Scientific Industries, Inc.
13900 N.W. Science Park Drive
Portland, OR 97229
503-641-4141

WHERE EMPLOYEES OWN A LARGE PIECE OF THE COMPANY

Federal Express	People Express
Hallmark Cards	Publix Super
Linnton Plywood	Markets
Lowe's	Quad/Graphics

ERIE INSURANCE GROUP

Erie is the nation's twenty-first-largest auto insurer and the forty-ninth- largest property and casualty insurer. Employees: 1,870.

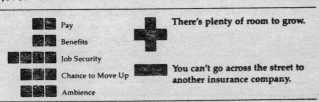

▨▨ Pay		**There's plenty of room to grow.**
▨▨ Benefits		
▨▨▨▨ Job Security		
▨▨▨ Chance to Move Up		**You can't go across the street to another insurance company.**
▨▨▨ Ambience		

The chairman of Erie Insurance has a door knocker on the *inside* of his door since it is never closed.

The door knocker is just one indication of the working atmosphere here. A couple of others: Everyone is on a first-name basis. Everyone—including the chairman and president—answers his or her own phone. And for many years, Erie has maintained a "hotline" to the chairman's office. Employees and policyholders are encouraged to use this direct line.

Erie believes in promotion from within. Tom Hagen, the president of Erie, started out as a file clerk. Half a dozen branch managers began in low-level jobs, and most middle-management people have come up through the ranks. Most stay to make a career with Erie. Keith Lane, Erie's enthusiastic communications director, told us, "When we hire an employee, we envision a long-term relationship."

The company has done better than most other insurance firms in advancing women, who make up 60 percent of the staff. In 1983, 40 percent of the supervisory staff were women, and the company had nine female officers. One, Maureen Dwyer, is vice-president of product and actuarial services. The Erie women managers have noted that when they attend meetings with other insurance company executives, they are often the only females in the room.

Thanks to a continuous expansion of its business, Erie has been able to offer many chances for people to advance. The company started in 1925 as an automobile insurer. Today, it also writes property/casualty coverage for homes and businesses, and it has a subsidiary that issues life insurance policies. The premiums collected by Erie companies have more than tripled since 1975, even though Erie operates only in Pennsylvania and five nearby states.

Much of the company's success appears to be based on superior service, as it does no advertising. In a survey of the major auto insurers taken several years ago, *Consumer Reports* rated Erie as one of only four to give its policyholders "much-better-than-average service." Erie claims to receive a dozen or so unsolicited "booster" letters a week from policyholders—something few insurers can claim.

Since 1975 Erie's employment rolls have increased by more than 40 percent. More than 200 were hired in 1982. Erie hasn't laid off a single person since its founding, a well-appreciated fact in an area plagued with high unemployment. A veteran newsman with the *Erie Morning News* told us, "This community is in debt to that company. Because of its rapid growth, Erie has offered a lot of opportunity for employment when jobs have been difficult to get and when many companies have pulled out."

The company's new $40 million headquarters building in downtown Erie elicited similar responses. Urban blight attacked Erie for many years, and the city was steadily losing jobs and population through the 1960s and early 1970s. In 1977, the old Erie Insurance building was landlocked in a neighborhood described by the *Erie Morning News* as a "combat zone" because of the prostitution and street crime. Instead of abandoning the city, Erie Insurance "made a gutsy decision to stay and fight for a total neighborhood-wide reclamation," according to a letter from a local nonprofit organization which nominated Erie for a national award for corporate leadership in urban development.

The Erie building at Perry Square—featuring a four-story atrium, light-filled offices, and quiet areas for reading and conversation—was opened on April 20, 1983. Five thousand people showed up, including Pennsylvania Governor

Dick Thornburgh. The dedication ceremonies were part of a week-long celebration which began with an open house for all Erie employees and their families. Erie's retirees were also invited to tour the building and have breakfast in the new cafeteria which seats 400 and may be the largest facility in the country operated by legally blind people. During workdays hot lunches are available for $1.50.

The city of Erie itself offers special attractions to those who like the life style of a small city. Located midway between Cleveland and Buffalo, it's a city of 285,000 people fronting 30 miles of Lake Erie shoreline. Presque Isle State Park, on a peninsula that extends nine miles into Lake Erie, gets more visitors each year than Yellowstone National Park.

The benefits are standard but not spectacular. It takes 10 years to get a three-week vacation, but the company does offer a profit-sharing bonus, based on its performance. Though not guaranteed, the bonus has been awarded every year since 1941. It's calculated at roughly a day's pay for each year's seniority, so a person who has been there five years gets a bonus equal to an extra week's salary.

People seem to know Erie is a good employer. It gets about 200 job applications a month. In 1983, it was looking for people with data processing and underwriting backgrounds.

Main employment centers   One thousand in Erie, 200 in Pittsburgh, and about 100 each in Harrisburg and Allentown, Pennsylvania, and Silver Spring, Maryland.

Headquarters   Erie Insurance Group
100 Erie Insurance Place
Erie, PA 16530
814-452-6831

EX**X**ON CORPORATION

EXXON CORPORATION

The biggest oil company in the world. U.S. employees: 74,000.

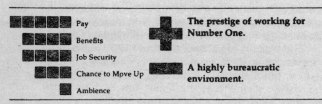

■■■■■ Pay	**+** **The prestige of working for Number One.**
■■■■ Benefits	
■■■■ Job Security	■ **A highly bureaucratic environment.**
■■■ Chance to Move Up	
■ Ambience	

Exxon is for people who have what Tom Wolfe called "the big-league complex." Wolfe was talking about the Big Apple, but Exxon is the Big Apple of Big Business. Number one on the Fortune 500, the largest industrial company in the world, Exxon has a long reach—44 refineries in 23 countries, 15,000 oil wells worldwide, subsidiaries in 80 countries. As one 20-year Exxon employee explained, "There's instant prestige when you say you work for Exxon."

Exxon has more to offer than prestige. Its remarkable management development program can be traced to former president Walter Teagle. In 1929 Teagle laid down the law that identifying and training a successor is the first priority of any manager. Today every Exxon manager must develop a systematic succession plan for all who report to him. It's all part of the company's view that the organization should, as much as possible, consist of interchangeable parts and not rely on exceptional personalities.

Exxon wants team players, but it insists that everyone be extremely well trained. Its management training program is one of the marvels of American business. *New York Times* reporter Anthony J. Parisi said: "Exxon likes to say its strength is its people. So does just about every other company. But few come close to matching Exxon's amazing attention to nurturing new leaders."

126

The process starts at Exxon's world headquarters in New York's Rockefeller Center. On Monday afternoons, Exxon's top management committee—composed of the company's chairman, president, and the six senior vice-presidents—meets to review the professional progress of the top 500 or so managers, as well as the pay of the next 3,000. The goal, according to Parisi, is "to spot talent early and nurture it."

Exxon doesn't rely on intuition or hit-and-miss methods to spot talent. It's incredibly methodical. Each of the company's professional and salaried employees is rated once a year. The company tries to make it as objective and impersonal as possible. Each person is evaluated by several superiors rather than just by his or her immediate supervisor.

The eight-page "appraisal review" form contains 33 different categories, from the quality of somebody's work to creativity and leadership. The review even includes an E.E.O. (equal employment opportunity) category, where Exxon employees are rated according to their "sensitivity to the needs of minorities, females, and other protected groups." In each category, supervisors rate employees from 1.0 for "exceptional" to 4.0 for "unsatisfactory."

Other firms evaluate employees regularly. What makes Exxon's system unique is that everyone is then compared with his or her peers. Supervisors send the results of the appraisal reviews to a departmental committee composed of senior managers. The committee prepares a list of all employees at the same level within the department and asks the supervisors to rank them from best to worst. This is done on a bell curve; if more than 10 percent are rated as "outstanding," the departmental committee reduces a few to the next category. Based on these detailed comparisons, Exxon establishes succession plans for each job in the firm. The management committee spends one full day a year reviewing the replacement schedules for all top managerial posts. As *Dun's Review* wrote, "Perhaps the company most totally committed to succession planning as a way of corporate life is Exxon."

Exxon employees seem to embrace the process. But it has its drawbacks. As one former employee told *Dun's Review*, "From the individual's viewpoint, the consensus approach at least guarantees that he will always be treated fairly. The only trouble is that no individual is indispensable under the system, and some people may find that unsettling."

With all the effort to seek out the best from within, it's no wonder Exxon rarely hires a manager from outside the firm. Most of the top people in Exxon started as engineers. The company takes great pains to "round off" managers and top technical people, especially the "high po's"—those considered to have the potential to go far. The ideal "Exxon man" serves the company in a variety of staff and line positions, and in a variety of locations, including overseas. Managers used to be transferred an average of once every three years. The pace has slowed recently for economic reasons.

Exxon rewards employees for loyalty. Most people who work here consider themselves "womb-to-tombers." The company believes in job security. It avoided layoffs during the recession of 1981–82 with its Special Program of Severance Allowance, or SPOSA (called "Disposal" by some more irreverent Exxon employees). SPOSA encouraged older employees to retire early. Those who did joined more than 23,000 "annuitants" (Exxonese for pensioners). The annuitants have their own glossy quarterly magazine called *Annuitant*, and there are nearly 140 Exxon Annuitant Clubs throughout the country. (The company contributes $25 per year to each club for each annuitant, spouse, or surviving spouse who is an active club member.) Exxon supplemented their pensions six times during the 1970s.

Exxon adopted one of the first pension plans in the United States, in 1903. During the 1930s, it didn't lay off one employee. It entered the depression with a worldwide work force of 49,898 and came out with 51,846. Exxon (then called Standard Oil of New Jersey) accomplished the feat largely because President Teagle introduced work-sharing. Teagle even took a six-month leave himself to promote the idea to other companies.

Everything about Exxon is writ large. Its immense size and scope boggle minds, including those of many people who work there. As one long-term employee explained, "By working for Exxon, you can be involved in the biggest and the best. But you're not alone. The nature and complexity of the company require tremendous coordination." That translates to committees, lots and lots of them. Exxon is highly structured; many would call it downright bureaucratic. There's a stuffiness about Exxon that won't go away.

On the plus side, Exxon employees like to think that they

are working for the Mr. Integrity of the oil industry. The company hands each new employee a pamphlet entitled "Ethics and Responsible Behavior." In plain language it says things such as: "We don't want liars for managers, whether they are lying in a mistaken effort to protect us or to make themselves look good," and "Falsification of books and records and any off-the-record bank accounts is strictly prohibited."

Just to make sure the point gets across, the company dispatches staffers to meet with each group of employees once a year to reiterate and explain the policy. Any hint of violation can doom an Exxon career, such as that of a Houston chemical plant supervisor who didn't report a $40 gift from an Exxon customer. The supervisor wasn't fired, but he doesn't expect ever to see another promotion. An Exxon executive caught bribing officials in Italy was not only fired, but the company also sued him to recover the money.

Exxon has more to sell prospective employees than prestige and integrity. The company makes sure to pay its people at least as well as, if not better than, any of its competitors. Some Exxon employees talk of the "golden handcuffs" by which they are bound. In other words, the pay and benefits are so good, they feel they cannot leave. The company offers few perks, aside from a 10 percent reduction in the price of Exxon gas and 15 percent off the price of TBA (tires, batteries, and accessories) from Exxon service stations. Instead of elaborate health spas or executive dining rooms, Exxon puts bucks into pay and benefits.

One especially generous benefit is a savings-and-investment program (though not unique to Exxon). An employee can set aside up to 6 percent of his or her income. That is matched, dollar for dollar, by the company. The company then invests the money in Exxon stock or a common stock portfolio or a fixed-income investment fund administered by Prudential Insurance. Employees with five years' service can withdraw funds or take out loans using their savings as collateral. Exxon instituted a stock purchase plan for employees in 1921, making it one of the first companies to do so.

To this day, Exxon has been resistant to unionization. For the most part, Exxon employees covered by union contracts are represented by local, independent unions rather than national ones.

Exxon has been at the forefront of many of the more

innovative employment practices. The company was one of the first to design and use aptitude tests and other behavioral indicators to determine the skills and potential of job applicants. When group dynamics and sensitivity training were the rage in the 1960s, many Exxon employees participated. Today, the company has a strong commitment to organizational development techniques, an outgrowth of the group dynamics movement.

Though the company likes to be on the cutting edge of such practices, Exxon can be terribly conservative in other areas. The headquarters of Exxon USA in Houston is located downtown, where many companies, including Shell, Gulf, and Tenneco, have formed van pools to reduce the nightmarish freeway traffic jams. But not Exxon. Van pools do, after all, cut into gasoline consumption.

Main employment centers Houston: 13,600; Baton Rouge/New Orleans: 5,000; Linden, New Jersey: 2,000; Carlinville, Illinois: 1,000; Gillette, Wyoming: 1,000; San Francisco/Los Angeles: 1,000. Eighty thousand people work overseas.

Headquarters   Exxon Corporation
1251 Avenue of the Americas
New York, NY 10020
212-333-1000

Exxon USA
800 Bell
Houston, TX 77001
713-656-3636

FEDERAL EXPRESS CORPORATION

The leading provider of overnight, door-to-door delivery of packages and letters. U.S. employees: 30,000.

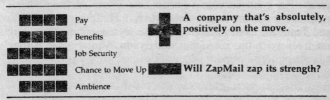

▰▰▰▰ Pay	✚ A company that's absolutely, positively on the move.
▰▰▰▱ Benefits	
▰▰▰▰ Job Security	
▰▰▰▰ Chance to Move Up	▰ Will ZapMail zap its strength?
▰▰▰▱ Ambience	

On December 11, 1984, the president, the executive vice-president, and the chief personnel officer of Federal Express spent more than an hour trying to decide whether a supervisor was right to have fired a courier in New York who had failed to report a vehicle accident.

It is rare in corporate America for the top officers of a multibillion-dollar company to spend any time contemplating the fate of a lower-level employee, let alone devote a full hour to such an issue. But that was only one of four employee grievances Federal's leaders heard that morning. They also considered cases brought by a Memphis cargo handler who had been terminated for not reporting to work for two days without informing his supervisor, a Los Angeles courier who had been let go for falsifying delivery records, and a Miami operations administrator who had received a warning letter for not filing expense reports on time.

That December morning was not unusual, either. The three top executives spend most Tuesday mornings listening to employee appeals. The meetings usually start at 8:00 in the morning and last until lunchtime. They hear between two and twelve cases a day. More often than not, they uphold lower management's decisions. But it is not uncommon for employees to win. In the case of the Los Angeles courier, for instance, he was reinstated after he showed that another courier had only been given a warning letter for the same infraction (forging signatures on delivered packages).

Why do the top officers of Federal Express spend so much time on what are essentially minor personnel grievances? We asked Jim Perkins, the senior vice-president of personnel and one of the participants in the weekly meetings. He said, "Most companies will say they are people-oriented and then just pay lip service to it. We want to make damned sure everybody here knows that it isn't just rhetoric." Perkins, incidentally, is black and worked his way up through the ranks. As a senior vice-president, he is one of the highest-ranking blacks in American business. Perkins added: "The president and chairman are dead serious about making sure employees are treated fairly. So they spend time on it. If they can spend three or four hours a week on GFT's [grievances], it is a good symbol."

The five-step grievance process that Perkins was referring to is called the Guaranteed Fair Treatment. It is but one method by which Federal Express tries to maintain, as the company founder and chairman Fred Smith told us, a work force of "committed people." He explained, "We are interested in making this a good place to work, where people are dealt with as human beings rather than as some number." Other policies include no layoffs; top wages; profit sharing; stock options to all managers; job posting; an open door to talk with managers at any time; paying up to $25,000 for productivity improvement suggestions, and offering unusual benefits such as the right to fly free on Federal Express planes and at reduced rates on other airlines.

No one who watches Federal Express employees in action would dispute that Smith has achieved a highly motivated work force, especially those who've seen Federal employees in action at the "Hub"—Federal Express's huge cargo transfer facility at the Memphis airport. Most packages sent via Federal go through the Hub. So a parcel going from New York to Los Angeles goes through Memphis, but more surprisingly, so does one from Houston to Dallas or from Chicago to Minneapolis. Next to Beale Street and Elvis Presley's Graceland mansion, Federal's Hub (with over 20 miles of conveyor belts) ranks as one of the favorite tourist sites in Memphis. Tours on Friday nights are booked months in advance. The show starts about 11:00 P.M., when visitors can look up and see jets converging on the Memphis airport from all four directions. Within two hours, Federal's fleet of 53 Boeing 727s and 11 DC-10s have landed, and a small army of 2,700 workers descends on the planes, unloads several hundred thousand small packages and letters, sorts them, and puts them on planes headed for their ultimate destinations. Federal employees like to call the scene "organized chaos." Yet by 3:00 A.M., the skies around Memphis once again are filled with jets loaded with packages that must be on someone's desk "absolutely, positively overnight."

After watching the frenetic scene one night, the president of a large Japanese electronics company remarked, "I didn't know Americans could work like that."

Louis Myers is typical of the 2,500 part-time employees who work at the Hub. A premed student at Memphis State, Myers has been working five years for Federal Express. A "Courier Pak" sorter, Myers is paid $9.75 an hour (the average Hub hourly worker receives about $9 an hour). "It's the best-paying part-time job in Memphis," Myers insists. Federal Express also pays for Myers's tuition—$725 a year—a benefit available to all part-time (and full-time) Federal Express employees. He has also flown free to Tampa, Florida, on vacation. Federal employees call it "jump seating" since they sit on an extra seat located behind the pilots in the cockpit. Myers expects to quit Federal Express when he finishes his premed studies.

Some Hub part-timers stick with Federal Express after school. We met Mike Williams, who at age 24 had already been with Federal for six years. After working his way through Memphis State at the Hub, Williams got hired as a ramp agent in Dallas. Two years later, he transferred to the Oakland, California, station as a ramp operations manager. Williams learned of the opening in Oakland through Federal Express's extensive job-posting program. Every Friday, the company posts on bulletin boards throughout the system a long list of all available positions. No job can be filled by an outsider unless no one within the company is interested and qualified.

Most Federal Express managers are young. Fred Smith, the president and chairman, was 40 in 1984; Jim Barksdale, the executive vice-president and chief operating officer, was 41; and 9 of the 11 senior vice-presidents were between 40 and 44 (the other two were 47 and 57). The average Federal Express manager was 34 while the average Federal Express employee was 29 (75 percent are under 35).

The company, after all, only recently celebrated its tenth anniversary. When Fred Smith launched the firm in the early 1970s, he literally created an industry. There was no overnight delivery service at the time. In less than 10 years, Federal Express had become a billion-dollar company, and other firms—Emery, Airborne, United Parcel Service, and the U.S. Postal Service—launched competing services. But by the end of 1984, Federal Express still dominated the industry with more than half the business, serving more than 40,000 communities. More than 300 cities had local Federal Express offices, and Federal's fleet of 10,000 radio-dispatched delivery vans could be seen scurrying from office building to office building in any business district in America. On one evening in mid-December 1984, Federal Express handled more than 500,000 parcels at the Hub. And the firm continued to grow at the mind-boggling rate of 20 percent to 50 percent a year. In 1984 more than 6,000 new employees were hired, bringing the employee total to over 30,000.

Because of the rapid growth, people at Federal Express like to speak of the firm as "entrepreneurial." They talk of a sense of adventure associated with a company that is changing so rapidly. People work hard at Federal Express and they're proud of it. As Jim Perkins told us, "Those who want a nice, quiet, green pasture won't like it here. It's green, but it sure isn't quiet."

The rocky launch of ZapMail was a major topic of conversation among Federal Express employees in late 1984. A two-hour electronic mail service, ZapMail lost over $100 million during the first year after its introduction in mid-1984. Far from being an academic issue, ZapMail had a direct impact on all employees' semiannual profit-sharing checks, distributed just before Christmas. For the first time employees were receiving less in 1984 (ranging between $50 and $300 per employee) than in the previous year. (In 1983, the payout ranged up to $1,100.) The company had made a concerted effort to explain the situation, as it does to explain other aspects of the firm's business. There's a barrage of newsletters and audio-video presentations at Federal, including an annual company-wide "Family Briefing." The 1984 briefing was a live, two-way video conference extravaganza between large gatherings of Federal employees and their families in Memphis, Atlanta, Philadelphia, Detroit, Sacramento, Toronto, and London. The Family Briefing was also telecast live to Federal employees who watched the show on large video screens in conference rooms at 240 Holiday Inn hotels across the country. Daniel Copp, the vice-president of corporate communications, proclaimed the meeting "the largest corporate video conference in history."

Another means of employee communications are "brown-bag lunches" at which Smith or one of the other top company officers regularly addresses groups of employees, often during lunch breaks in company cafeterias. Captain Don Jones attended one such lunchtime meeting in Memphis in early December 1984. Hired in 1972 as one of Federal Express's early pilots (there were over 500 pilots by the end of 1984), Jones was initially quite skeptical about the ZapMail project. After hearing founder Smith's presentation to a brown-bag meeting of pilots and listening to their responses to some very pointed questions, Captain Jones was convinced the company was on the right track with ZapMail. "It just may take a little longer than their original projections to break even," Jones explained.

As an old-timer at Federal Express, Jones feels he has every reason to place his faith in the company's management. Jones recalls that Smith assured the pilots of two things when he was hired: first, that they would never be furloughed; and second, that when the company started flying aircraft comparable to those of the major airlines, that they would be paid at the same rates as the commercial airline pilots. In 10 years, no Federal Express employee has been laid off even during hard times. And Jones and the other pilots are paid as much as the unionized pilots at Pan Am, TWA, United, or any other commercial carrier. (Federal Express pilots are not unionized, nor is any other group within the company.) For the DC-10 jumbo jet captains like Jones, that means an annual income of about $125,000 a year. Beginning Federal Express pilots earn about $40,000. "Fred has always given us a fair shake," Jones told us. "When he's said he is going to do something, he does it."

Newer employees we interviewed seemed to respect Federal's leaders. Angela Griffith works in Memphis as a customer service agent, answering calls from customers wishing to have a package delivered. The large, thickly carpeted room in which over 500 agents answer the phones was gaily decorated for Christmas when we were there. The wooden office furnishings seemed designed for maximum comfort. ("Ergonomic is a big word around here," one supervisor explained.) Griffith says that in the 14 months since she joined the firm, company president Fred Smith had twice stopped by her "pod" (work station) and asked her how things were going. She told us: "Our president makes a difference. He looks in on us. He's good at remembering names, and everybody calls him Fred. He's very people-oriented." From talking with several of her coworkers, it was clear Griffith's experience was not unique. Top executives at Federal Express make it a practice to be visible and accessible.

Janet Ashmore also answers phones in Memphis. She had a similar job as a directory assistance operator for AT&T. She took a small pay cut to join Federal Express because of what she perceived as the superior working conditions and the better opportunities for advancement. "After the breakup [of AT&T and the local phone companies], they no longer cared about the employees." Ashmore contrasted the loose, relaxed atmosphere at Federal Express with AT&T's: "[At AT&T] we were monitored constantly. They timed us on how many seconds we took per call. You had to sit in a certain way and wear your headphones in a particular way. You couldn't talk with anybody else, even when there were breaks between calls. You had to ask permission when you wanted to go to the bathroom. They even timed you when you went to the bathroom. If you were there more than three minutes, somebody would come in and get you."

At Federal Express, Ashmore says, "They do not count the number of calls you take. Quality is what's important. They only care how well you handle each of the calls." And there are no petty rules such as not being permitted to talk with other agents during breaks between calls. The agents can take advantage of "flex time"—if they arrive 10 minutes before the shift begins, they can leave 10 minutes early; they leave 10 minutes late if they arrive 10 minutes late. Dan Malone, another customer service agent we talked with, explained: "It's kind of a family atmosphere. Everybody is out to help you out. This is a people company."

That a number of employees we talked to referred to

Federal Express as a "people company" was not entirely surprising. One of the firm's slogans is "People/Service/Profit." In the employee handbook, the slogan is explained in these terms: "The People/Service/Profit philosophy of the company is based on the belief that motivated and conscientious employees will provide the necessary professional service to ensure profits and our continued growth." When we asked company executive vice-president Jim Barksdale to explain what's behind the PSP philosophy, he said simply, "Motivated people move faster." He then added, "You have to understand our business. Our people philosophy is not out of a spirit of altruism. You have fewer problems and make more money."

A graphic indication of the "people" orientation at Federal Express can be seen on any of their airplanes. Names like "Dusty," "Justin," and "Jennifer" are inscribed in large letters near the plane's nose. These are names of children of Federal employees. Before the company takes possession of a new plane, a lottery is held to pick which child is to have the plane named for him or her. In June 1983, Bridgette Patrice Gibson, the three-year-old daughter of an Atlanta courier, won the lottery to have her name painted on a brand-new Boeing 727. To mark the occasion, the company flew the Gibson family to Boeing's plant in Seattle. The parents and company officials, including Smith, did such a terrific job of coaching the girl that her daddy's company had bought her a plane that she acted beautifully during the entire ceremony. But, alas, when the festivities were over and people were leaving, the girl threw a tantrum: "I want to take my plane," she cried.

Main employment centers   10,000 work in the Memphis area. Over a third of Federal's work force, 11,400 employees, are couriers making deliveries throughout the United States.

Headquarters   Federal Express Corporation
P. O. Box 727
Memphis, TN 38194
901-369-3600

FISHER-PRICE TOYS

The world's largest producer of infant and preschool toys.
U.S. employees: 4,000.

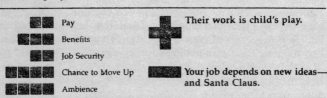

■■■ Pay	**Their work is child's play.**
■■■ Benefits	
■■ Job Security	✚
■■■■ Chance to Move Up	■■■ **Your job depends on new ideas—**
■■■■ Ambience	**and Santa Claus.**

Kathleen Alfano and Priscilla Hamlin think they have the best jobs at Fisher-Price Toys. They teach in the Fisher-Price Toys nursery. When designers come up with a new toy, they bring a prototype or a model into the nursery. Alfano and Hamlin, both certified teachers, estimate that they observe the nursery's children play with up to 500 toys a year in different stages of development.

According to Alfano, Fisher-Price is the only toy company with an on-site nursery school. It reflects the firm's commitment to quality. "I'm very proud to work here," Alfano says. "A lot of effort goes into making a quality toy at Fisher-Price Toys. If there are any questions raised about the safety or play value of these toys, the designers and engineers act on it immediately."

The nursery is housed in the Fisher-Price research and development building, where about one hundred designers, artists, and engineers also work. The Fisher-Price Toys campus in East Aurora, New York, also houses the three-story corporate headquarters and a toy factory. Children aged two months to nine years attend the nursery twice a week. When we stopped by in late 1984, Alfano and Hamlin were in the midst of testing production models of a bubble mower—a plastic lawn mower that spews out bubbles when a child pushes it. Based on the reactions of the nursery's children,

Hamlin thinks Fisher-Price has a winner: "The kids love it. The bubbles offer an element of surprise."

The idea for the bubble mower originated with Larry Nagode and a group of other toy designers as they met informally after work at the Roycroft Inn in East Aurora. A 20-minute drive from Buffalo, East Aurora is a quiet village of 7,000. It was the hometown of Millard Fillmore and of Elbert Hubbard, whose *Message to Garcia* is one of the most widely published pamphlets in history (80 million copies). Nagode believes the small-town atmosphere helps Fisher-Price foster a creative environment. It's certainly quite a contrast from his previous employer, Ideal Toy, headquartered in the Queens section of New York City: "There it seemed like a life-and-death struggle getting to work every day. You had to be careful just walking from the parking lot to the factory. Here you don't even have to bother locking your car."

Though the bubble mower was his idea, Nagode refuses to take credit for it. He explains that at Fisher-Price toys are created by teams composed of a dozen designers, engineers, and marketing people. They meet regularly from the time the toy is conceived until it is in stores. He says, "Everybody on the team has a sense of ownership. Everybody becomes attached to that toy." Not so at Ideal. After toy designers came up with their concepts, others within the organization took over. "Rarely would the marketing or engineering people ever check back with us to tell us of changes they were making in our designs," Nagode said. "The next time we saw it was when the toy appeared in the catalog."

To Nagode, "the sense of ownership" is what helps Fisher-Price create high-quality toys. Virtually everyone we talked with at Fisher-Price—production-line workers, designers, middle managers, and executives—spoke with pride about the firm's reputation. A 1983 Gallup Poll of mothers, for instance, rated Fisher-Price first in consumer preference, brand awareness, and product satisfaction. An estimated 84 percent of homes with young children have at least one Fisher-Price toy. Founded in 1930, Fisher-Price now makes 200 different toys (60 new ones a year) and sells about 70 million a year. "Everybody strives for quality here," Nagode told us. "Nobody wants to be the first to blow it."

Denise Bowen-Fishback was a marketing department representative on the bubble mower team. Now a marketing manager, Bowen-Fishback started here five years ago as a personnel recruiter after spending a year with Procter & Gamble as a sales representative. She says her rapid movement up the ranks has been typical of many people in the company. She feels that "you can have an impact on things here." As an example, she said that not long after she joined the company, she suggested offering baby blocks to any customer who bought two Fisher-Price toys. To her amazement, the idea was implemented, as was another idea she had for a sales rebate.

Bowen-Fishback also finds top managers to be remarkably accessible. "It seems very unusual for someone as low on the totem pole as I to know the president of the company and to have him know me." She says Bruce Sampsell, Fisher-Price's president, usually has lunch in the employee cafeteria along with everybody else. The architecture of the home office also adds to the visibility of the top officers. Anita Dahlberg, a secretary in the headquarters, explained: "Lots of time you hear about a company having an open-door policy. But here it is true. There aren't any doors." Sampsell's office, for instance, has only a low partition to separate it from other offices.

It's not just professional and white-collar employees who talk of the approachability of Fisher-Price managers. So do production-line workers at the plants in East Aurora and Holland (a nearby village). "I feel they bend over backwards and deal fairly with us," Patricia Anger, an hourly worker since 1969 at the East Aurora facility, told us. She likes the clean working conditions, the absence of time clocks, and the giving of regular raises "without an argument." (Production workers were getting $6.82 an hour in early 1985.)

Several coworkers talked of how the company's managers nearly always seem to bend the rules to take care of personal concerns. A 15-year veteran, Lynn Pautler, for instance, told us, "Communication here is really good. You can go to anybody. Everybody feels free to talk to the big bosses. Everyone is on a first-name basis." Alice Bush, who has worked in the Holland plant since 1971, explained how the firm let her take time off to go to Florida on a vacation with her husband after he retired.

Because the toy business is so cyclical—two-thirds of the sales come during the Christmas season—layoffs are a normal part of life for production workers. The number laid off varies from year to year, depending on the work load, and most workers are recalled. At the Holland plant, for example, employment dropped in 1984 from a peak of about 600 in July to a low of about 450 in December.

The Holland plant was doing better than anticipated that year, so the layoffs were not as extensive as in previous years. This caused an unusual problem: a number of the longtime workers wanted to be laid off during the week between Christmas and New Year's, but plant manager Bruce Inglis told them he couldn't let them off because of the increased orders. Nearly 50 employees signed a "Speak Up," a written form used by individual workers to express a grievance. After meeting with workers who had signed the Speak Up, Inglis agreed to make arrangements to hire temporarily some part-timers and others who had been laid off earlier. "I figure it cost us about $4,000 more," Inglis told us. "But it was money well spent." Inglis was especially happy because the day we visited the plant he had received a Christmas card signed by the same workers with the inscription: "Consider this a Speak Up. Merry Christmas."

The management's flexibility extends beyond reacting to personal concerns. Production-line workers are expected to be able to work on the various machines in the plant. According to Alice Bush, "We are trained in all departments, so we can do anything in the plant. Every day you change machines every couple of hours. They try to eliminate boredom."

Several times during the work day, an employee circulates through the plant with a tray of Gatorade. They used to offer glasses of plain water or lemonade, but Gatorade became the beverage of choice after Quaker Oats bought Stokely–Van Camp, the maker of Gatorade, in 1983. Quaker is also Fisher-Price's parent, having acquired the toy company in 1969. By all accounts, the relationship with Quaker is a good one. Quaker has provided capital for the company's dramatic growth in recent years, but left the firm's management alone. Almost the only exception is Bruce Sampsell, moved from vice-president of research and development of Quaker's grocery products to become Fisher-Price's president in 1983.

Quaker did not disturb Fisher-Price's noteworthy profit-sharing plan. The company sets aside 22 percent of its pretax profits for profit sharing. Employees can receive an amount up to 20 percent of their annual salary from this fund. In the last five years, the bonus has ranged between 9.9 percent and 17.4 percent. Part of this annual bonus is distributed on Fisher-Price's profit-sharing day, traditionally held in mid-December. We were in East Aurora on profit-sharing day in 1984. The firm rented East Aurora's only movie theater for the day, and employees from headquarters and all the upstate plants arrived in shifts to be addressed by Sampsell and to see an audiovisual demonstration of the new toy line. After the presentation, they received a check equal to 6.1 percent of their annual salary (the rest was to be put either into a deferred pension plan or distributed in March 1985).

When the workers returned to their plants and offices, they were handed 17-pound frozen turkeys—another tradition that Quaker has not tampered with.

Main employment centers   About 3,000 work in East Aurora, Holland, or Medina, New York. Another 830 work in Murray, Kentucky. About 1,500 work in border plants in Mexico, and about 1,000 work in Europe.

Headquarters   Fisher-Price Toys
636 Girard Avenue
East Aurora, NY 14052
716-687-3000

H. B. FULLER COMPANY

Fuller is one of the world's largest makers of glues, adhesives, and sealants. U.S. employees: 1,765.

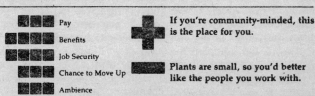

■■■ Pay		If you're community-minded, this is the place for you.
■■■■ Benefits		
■■■ Job Security		Plants are small, so you'd better like the people you work with.
■■■■ Chance to Move Up		
■■■ Ambience		

When most companies begin construction of a major new facility, they have what's called a ground-breaking ceremony. With cameras popping, company officials scoop token shovelfuls of dirt. When, in 1981, Fuller started building its new corporate headquarters and technical laboratory near St. Paul, it was called a "ground planting." Employees and officials spread seeds of wild flowers and prairie grasses on the site that will eventually become a 95-acre nature preserve. Fuller's concern for the environment has won plaudits from the Sierra Club—a group that rarely has kind words to say about any chemical company.

Fuller is decidedly *not* just another big chemical company. Its "good guy" image extends to the progressive role it plays in three dozen communities around the country where it makes glues and sealants.

Fuller encourages its people to participate in voluntary activities. An Outstanding Volunteer Award is given annually. At Christmastime, through what's called the Fuller-Up Program, employees collect toys and food for distribution to the poor. And the company itself donates 5 percent of its pretax profits to community involvement programs and charity. (The average, among big companies, is 1 percent.) In 1984, that represented nearly $750,000—and the disposition is decided by employees. Each plant elects a local community affairs council to disburse a proportional amount of the total within its area. For the past few years, the chairpersons of the local councils (who meet yearly in St. Paul) have decided to put a special emphasis on battered women and child abuse. The company's Rape and Sexual Assault Legal Advocate Program in Minneapolis has been praised throughout the country. It stations a legal advocate at the courthouse to work with rape victims who decide to prosecute their rapists.

Fuller's social consciousness is nothing new. It can be traced to its longtime chairman, Elmer Andersen, former governor of Minnesota. (Dave Durenberger was Fuller's corporate counsel until elected to the U.S. Senate in 1980.) Elmer's son, Tony, who is the current president, has continued and expanded the company's community affairs program. The Andersen family no longer owns the firm, as its shares were publicly traded for the first time in 1968, but it still has the feeling of a family-owned enterprise. Tony Andersen is a highly approachable, down-to-earth man who often goes out for lunch at a local McDonald's. The executive offices share an unpretentious building with a Fuller glue factory in an industrial area of St. Paul.

Andersen keeps the family touch alive by making it a point to pay regular visits to each of the 41 domestic plants in 35 different communities throughout the country. A typical Fuller factory employs approximately 30 people, about half of whom are in manufacturing; the rest are salespeople, office workers, and about a half-dozen chemical or mechanical engineers. During his local visits, Andersen meets with employees, selected at random. Managers meet with him separately.

Once a year, Andersen makes himself available to everyone in the company through what's called "The President's Hot-Line." Anybody can call him on that day on a special toll-free number to complain about their supervisors or make suggestions for improving their products or talk about anything else on their minds. He usually gets between 40 and 50 calls. In 1983, they included people telling him things like: "I've got an asshole for a boss"; "My office manager procrastinates"; "Don't trap the muskrats. It's inhumane." The last caller works at a plant located near a pond. The company decided not to set the traps.

It's not surprising that a company concerned about welfare in the community would also pride itself on the benefits it provides employees. It was one of the first companies to publish a manual spelling out the company's responsibilities to its employees. It offers an unusual approach to potential layoffs and cutbacks. The company pledges that any reductions at a particular plant will affect equally everyone who has been working for the company for at least two years. When the vacuum-cleaning division had to reduce hours in 1982, it meant that everyone, including the vice-president of the division, was cut back to a four-day work week. The company's manual also guarantees a 32-hour week for anyone with two years' seniority, unless the entire company reports a loss for the year (which has never happened).

Among many benefits, Fuller grants $1,500 to cover adoption costs and gives employees the day off on their birthdays. Retired employees have the first shot at part-time openings and special projects. Fuller also extends a special bonus vacation every five years starting on an employee's tenth anniversary with the company. That is, on the tenth, fifteenth, twentieth, and every fifth year thereafter, a person gets an extra two weeks off with pay that year, plus $800 to spend on a vacation.

Most local Fuller managers have come up through the ranks (many from the sales side of the business). The company policy of promotion from within includes a nationwide posting of all professional job openings. Hiring is done through both local offices and the national headquarters.

When considering outside applicants, Fuller looks closely at someone's ability to get along with others. "We're not interested in the driven professional or a whiz kid, someone who is all numbers and thinks only of bottom-line results," explained Lars Carlson, director of public affairs. "We're more interested in somebody who's concerned about the process of getting there."

Main employment centers Except for a concentration of people in Minnesota, employment is spread among the small plants in 20 different states.

Headquarters H. B. Fuller Company
2400 Energy Park Drive
St. Paul, MN 55108
612-645-3401

GENERAL 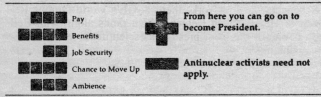 ELECTRIC

GENERAL ELECTRIC COMPANY

GE makes light bulbs, turbine generators, jet engines, TV sets (in America, yet), robots, dishwashers, nuclear reactors—and thousands of other industrial and consumer products. U.S. employees: 245,000.

■■■ Pay	✚ From here you can go on to become President.
■■■■ Benefits	
■■ Job Security	
■■■ Chance to Move Up	■■ Antinuclear activists need not apply.
■■■ Ambience	

General Electric is regarded so highly as a training ground that other corporations frequently find their leaders within the GE walls. So if you can't reach the top at GE, you might at another company. Ex-GE people have gone on to head a slew of other companies. Among them are David Packard (Hewlett-Packard), Hicks Waldron (Avon), Robert Frederick (RCA), Stanely Gault (Rubbermaid), Thomas Vanderslice (GTE), Alva Way (Travelers), George DeLucca (Sterling Vineyards), Sandra L. Kurtzig (ASK), Richard Gralton (Savin), Thomas Albani (Sunbeam), and James Worsham (Douglas Aircraft).

And it's not only GE engineers who benefit from this extraordinary in-house training. The company has a distinguished number of alumni who were trained in advertising and public relations at GE—and then went on to find glory in other settings. Among these alumni are the novelist Kurt Vonnegut; ad agency leaders Carl Ally, Henry Schachte, and Al Ries; and Richard Q. Kress, who rose to become president of Norelco Consumer Products. Indeed, there are so many graduates of the GE communications school that they meet every other year in an alumni gathering. At one of these sessions, a GE graduate said, "There are three great experiences available on earth—the Roman Catholic Church, the Mafia, and General Electric."

Education is a major activity at GE. The company maintains one of the finest management development schools in the country at a 50-acre estate in Crotonville, New York. More than 5,000 GE people attend classes there every year. If an employee wants to go for a master's degree in engineering he or she can do it through joint programs GE conducts with 24 universities.

During any year, about 50 percent of all GE employees are enrolled in some kind of company-paid education program, whether it's a tuition-refunded college course of study or a skills-improvement class conducted at a GE facility. And at Schenectady, New York, there is GE's world-famous Research & Development Center, which ranks along with Bell Labs as one of the most prestigious scientific research facilities maintained by a private company. Some 2,200 people work at the center, half of them scientists. In 1983, a typical year, they received 640 patents.

All these benefits do not go to only white males, either. In recent years, GE has made a special effort to recruit minorities and women. It was selected by *Black Enterprise* as one of the 10 best coroporations for blacks to work for. At the start of 1983, minorities accounted for 11.3 percent of GE's United States work force. In 1983, one out of every five engineers hired was a woman. One out of every four GE employees is a woman. In 1982, GE hired away Joyce Hergenhan from New York's Consolidated Edison and installed her as a vice-president in charge of corporate public relations.

About one-third of GE's work force is represented by unions who had to fight their way into GE, which always felt that it knew what was good for employees. There's still some of that "Papa knows best" attitude at GE, but labor-management antagonism has diminished.

GE somehow manages to maintain a spirit and momentum that you don't expect to find in a big, sprawling company with 365 plants in 26 countries and more than 340,000 people on the payroll around the world. GE is the third-largest private employer of American workers, exceeded only by General Motors and Sears, Roebuck. And it is determined to avoid the tendency of big companies to become bureaucratic and lazy, content to rest on past laurels.

When John F. Welch, Jr., a chemical engineer, became chief executive officer in 1981, he was only 45 years old. He's the youngest chief executive officer in GE's history—

and he's also the first Ph.D. to head the company. Welch immediately imparted a sense of urgency to the company. He issued a pronunciamento that GE will be first or second in all the 250 businesses in which it competes—or else it will quit the business. Recently he said, "We want GE to be a place where the bias is toward action—a high-spirited, world-class enterprise that uses the resources of a large company but moves with the agility of the youngest and smallest." That's why GE decided in 1983 to stop making toasters and other small houseware products.

GE fosters agility by decentralizing operations and pushing responsibility down into the ranks. Welch says, "If you pick the right people and give them opportunity to spread their wings—and put compensation as a carrier behind them—you almost don't have to manage them." One of the persons picked by Welch was James A. Meehan. Only 41 years old in 1983, he's a key manager in GE's drive to become the leader in robotics. Speaking to a *Business Week* reporter about GE's work style, Meehan said: "You get a sense that you own the business. What that means is that you're going to spend a lot less time worrying about whose toes you're going to tread on and much more time worrying about how you're going to move that business forward."

GE is the original Boy Scout company. It conducts its business in a wholesome manner. What other company can boast of having once had a future President of the United States as its spokesman? He was Ronald Reagan, as earnest and "gee whiz" a guy as any General Electric engineer. GE people are not known for their sartorial splendor. They're not flashy. They tend to be straitlaced engineers devoted to getting the job done. And they're smart. Some 15,000 people at GE have technical degrees. And 1,750 of them hold Ph.D.'s. GE has received 50,000 patents, more than any other company.

In 1983, a sharp-eyed writer for the *Berkshire Eagle* in Pittsfield, Massachusetts (a major GE plant city), noted that if the three-piece suit is back, "you'd never know it" from the General Electric annual report, which featured pictures of 50 male executives, not one of them wearing a vest, all wearing four-in-hands, none showing "a wisp of whisker on a corporate lip, chin, or jowl"—and all 100 corporate ears visible, free of all hair.

GE is virtually a founding member of what's called

"smokestack America," the type of industry that some observers predict is on the way out. GE is not about to give up. One of its top group executive vice-presidents, James A. Baker, delivered this message to a group of Chicago engineering executives in 1981: "U.S. business faces a threefold choice in the eighties: automate, emigrate, or evaporate."

In its wrenching effort to automate, GE is working closely with union leaders and employees to ease the readjustment, offering liberal severance benefits and special retraining programs for displaced workers. In 1983, for example, it announced that it was modernizing its lighting business, which will mean the closing of six plants in northern Ohio, including the Cuyahoga lamp facility at Nela Park in Cleveland. *Crain's Cleveland Business*, a weekly paper, interviewed a number of the women workers at the plant (the employee force is 80 percent female) and was so astounded by the praise for GE that it labeled the event "one of the most humane plant closings this area has witnessed." GE gave the employees advance notice of nearly two years, offered job counseling, possible transfer to other GE facilities, retraining for other jobs, and benefits that included continuation of medical and life insurance for all employees with 25 years of service at Nela Park.

One worker, 56-year-old Tulip Karavolos, told reporter Leah Ward: "Why should I be bitter? It's done us good to work for GE all these years. I've never been laid off in fourteen years."

Main employment centers   GE has the most national presence of any manufacturer in the United States, operating 230 plants in 34 states and Puerto Rico. Only several hundred people work at corporate headquarters in Fairfield. International operations are headquartered in the old GE building on Lexington Avenue in New York City. Some 100,000 are employed overseas. The largest GE plants are Schenectady, New York (motors, generators, turbines), 19,000 employees; Louisville (major appliances), 14,000; Evendale, Ohio (jet engines), 14,000; and Lynn, Massachusetts (turbines, generators), 12,000.

Headquarters   General Electric Company
3135 Easton Turnpike
Fairfield, CT 06431
203-373-2000

‏ General Mills, Inc.

GENERAL MILLS, INC.

A large food company that also runs restaurants, makes toys and clothes, and operates some specialized retail stores. U.S. employees: 71,000.

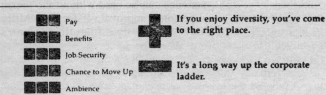

▚▚ Pay	**If you enjoy diversity, you've come to the right place.**
▚▚▚ Benefits	
▚▚▚ Job Security	
▚▚▚ Chance to Move Up	**It's a long way up the corporate ladder.**
▚▚▚ Ambience	

Ask somebody waiting on tables at a Red Lobster or sewing the alligator on an Izod sport shirt for whom they work, and they probably won't say General Mills, let alone tell you they are members of General Mills's "family." Most employees of General Mills's 60-plus subsidiaries identify strictly with their immediate business. And that's precisely how the folks running General Mills want it. It's part of their idea of how an ideal corporate family should operate.

Family is the name of General Mills's employee magazine. The company sponsors periodic studies of social issues called "American Family Reports" and introduces the company to outsiders with a document entitled "From Our Family to Yours." General Mills even has a corporate mother figure, Betty Crocker, whose test kitchens are located in the basement of General Mills's headquarters in the Minneapolis suburb of Golden Valley. Where else would the ideal American family live?

General Mills certainly does not have a conventional, close-knit family. It has doubled in size in the past decade to more than 80,000 members worldwide, working in five entirely different fields. The largest group produces and markets consumer foods—Cheerios, Bisquick, Gorton's fish sticks, among various other brands. An increasing number work in restaurants—Red Lobster, York Steak House, Good Earth.

Still others dream up and sell toys for children under the Parker Brothers (Monopoly, NERF) name. And a relative handful design clothes or shoes with the Izod/Lacoste, Ship 'n Shore, or Foot-Joy labels, or sell camping gear at Eddie Bauer stores or wallpaper at Wallpapers To Go shops.

The company believes in a decentralized management structure (an operating principle since the company was formed from a merger of several flour mills in the mid-1920s). There are, however, a number of policies that apply throughout the corporation. For instance, nobody with more than 15 years' experience can be fired without the president of General Mills's personal approval. If General Mills decides to sell a subsidiary, which it does from time to time, the buyer has to agree to retain the same employee benefits package for a period of not less than five years.

Perhaps the most notable corporate policy involves General Mills's executive compensation incentive plan, a bonus of up to 20 percent of regular salary. A brand product manager in the food division is eligible. For a new M.B.A. graduate, it would typically take only three or four years to reach that level. Each executive sets his or her goals for the year in several areas, including financial performance, long-term strategy, and manpower development.

Several years ago, the company introduced affirmative action as part of the goalsetting. *Savvy,* a women's magazine, was sufficiently impressed by the fact that nearly one-quarter (currently more than one-quarter) of the professional and managerial staff is now female that it named General Mills one of the best places for a woman to work. A high-ranking officer is Jane Evans, president of Monet Jewelers, a more than $100-million-a-year manufacturer and marketer of better fashion jewelery. She is one of the top-ranked women in all of corporate America.

In 1981, General Mills added another area to the incentive plan, "external involvement." At the beginning of the year, each manager must state his or her plans to get involved in the community. These typically include volunteer activities such as the United Way or the Red Cross. Not everyone liked the idea, explained executive vice-president Paul Parker. He cited one longtime executive who resisted the idea at first but eventually decided to help a local volunteer group that worked with the aged. "Now he's always coming around trying to get everyone else to contribute or do something for the aged," said Parker. "Sometimes you can barely get him to talk about anything else."

Parker works in the executive suite of the home office. General Mills people usually refer to the headquarters as MGO (Minneapolis general office) or simply GO (general office). A mile away, about 600 scientists and technicians work at the company's main research laboratories. General Mills's Golden Valley "campus" occupies 148 acres and includes ponds and an apple orchard. Large sculptures, parts of the company's art collection, sit on the grounds.

The collection is so large that it employs its own curator to oversee, 1,100 original pieces of art. The paintings range from traditional landscapes and portraits to abstract collages. Newcomers can pick a work of art for their own office from a large trove in the basement of the building.

Everything has been done to make the place seem homey. There's a barbershop and variety store, and an employee cafeteria where hot meals cost $2; in the summer, people can take their trays outside to a patio and enjoy watching the Canada geese on the pond. During the winter a pickup truck goes around the parking lot to jump-start cars whose batteries have lost their charge from the Minnesota cold.

This comfortable working environment complements the sometimes frenetic pace at the 10-story Bell Tower, attached to the executive office building. The marketing staff for the consumer foods operations work in Bell Tower (named for a former company president). Most of the people work on a team devoted to a specific General Mills brand. The cereals, called the "Big G" group, would have distinct teams working on Cheerios, Wheaties, Trix, Kix, Nature Valley Granola, and so on. The teams work on all facets of the product, from the technical questions involved in its production, to advertising campaigns, to distribution.

Ken Powell, who has an M.B.A. from Stanford, became a product manager on Yoplait yogurt in 1982 and a product manager in the Betty Crocker division two years later. In five years at General Mills, Powell has already worked on Big G cereals, Betty Crocker cake mixes, Yoplait, and now Betty Crocker frostings and toppings. He echoed sentiments of several others at Bell Tower: "I really like the depth of support here. You're able to talk with people from many different areas." He believes even the newest employee is listened to, because nobody can be sure whose idea is going to succeed in the marketplace.

Ken and other marketing specialists frequently call upon research technicians like Verne Weiss. A chemical engineer, Weiss has been with General Mills for more than 25 years and is currently responsible for packaging research and development. "This is not a high-tech company. But it's challenging for a scientist anyway because of the constant interaction with the marketing people. It's interesting trying to work on problems that directly relate to people."

Dave Tolmie, a former Betty Crocker product manager, summarized the working atmosphere in Bell Tower by saying, "Teamwork is the name of the game. We do not have one-man or one-woman projects around here. You have to recognize that a lot of people contributed to the finished product. We may have some stars around here, but they don't flaunt their status."

Many in the business world consider General Mills's brand manager system as a great training ground. It's tough to get a job there in the first place. General Mills interviews extensively on college campuses (2,900 personal interviews in 1984). Before someone is hired, he or she typically goes to Minneapolis for two more days of interviewing (or to Florida for the restaurants, New York for fashion, Boston and Cincinnati for toys).

Much may be invested in people who are hired, but General Mills is not reluctant to push them out the door, either. Jack Frost, senior vice-president of personnel, explained that people can move up quickly at General Mills. But those managers who don't seem to have much chance to rise higher are told so early. "We encourage movement of people out of the company if it looks like they cannot be promoted. We don't tell them they have to leave, but we try to be real honest with them about their chances."

Frost says General Mills offers opportunity for the aggressive person who wants to get ahead in the business world. Except in the high-growth areas such as restaurants and toys, where the company does a lot of outside recruiting, promotion from within is the rule.

Main employment centers   Minneapolis (headquarters and research): 3,500; Buffalo, New York, Chicago, Illinois, and Lodi, California (flour mills and food production plants); New York City (fashions); Beverly, Massachusetts (Parker Brothers toys); and Cincinnati, Ohio (Kenner Products toys). Another 9,000 work overseas. In early 1985, General Mills announced plans to sell both its fashion and its toy business.

Headquarters General Mills, Inc.
9200 Wayzata Boulevard
Minneapolis, MN 55440
612-540-2311

BEST EMPLOYEE FITNESS CENTERS
ROLM
Springs
Tenneco

GOLDMAN SACHS & CO.

Goldman Sachs is a major investment banking and brokerage firm. U.S. employees: 4,000.

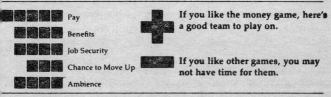

	Pay
	Benefits
	Job Security
	Chance to Move Up
	Ambience

+ If you like the money game, here's a good team to play on.

If you like other games, you may not have time for them.

Goldman Sachs is the Dallas Cowboys of investment banking. "This is a very competitive business, very much like professional football," George E. Doty, a Goldman Sachs limited partner, explained to us at the firm's Wall Street headquarters. "The other players play their positions very well, so when you come aboard you will be taxed to become an accepted member of the organization. But you know you are playing on the best team."

Many others see Goldman Sachs as the best team. *Financial World* magazine named Goldman Wall Street's "best broker" for eight straight years. *Institutional Investor* selected Goldman Sachs analysts for 26 positions on its All-American research team.

Goldman's game is money—big money. Investment bankers operate like a familiar stockbroker, such as Merrill Lynch or E.F. Hutton. But while those firms count among their clients ordinary people who may be investing only a few hundred or a few thousand dollars, investment banking firms get involved only when the amounts of money are huge. Like its competitors—Salomon Brothers, Morgan Stanley, Lazard Freres, Lehman Brothers Kuhn Loeb, among others—most of Goldman Sachs's clients are large corporations (Sears, Ford, Xerox, AT&T have long been Goldman clients) or governmental bodies (the State of New York and Dade County, Florida, among others).

The investment banking game is played in the various stock and bond markets or in board rooms across the country. Dozens of Goldman Sachs employees work in large trading rooms behind video monitors, sometimes with a phone in each hand, ready to buy or sell. *Forbes* estimated that Goldman Sachs traders account for fully 5 percent of the daily volume on the New York Stock Exchange, and 25 percent of trades of 10,000 or more shares. Other Goldman professionals give advice based on research compiled by the firm's team of analysts. Or they help make deals. A Goldman adviser was at his side when Gordon Getty, reputed to be the richest man in America, sat down for hard bargaining over selling his Getty Oil stock to Texaco to create the biggest corporate merger in U.S. history.

Life inside many of the Wall Street firms reflect the high stakes involved in the business. It's dog-eat-dog free enterprise at its most intense. People who devote their working lives to trying to get small advantages for their clients are expected to operate the same way when their own careers are involved. Job hopping between firms is common. It's the kind of atmosphere that puts strains on elementary human civility.

In the midst of this jungle, Goldman stands out as a different kind of place, *New York* magazine put it best when it headlined a piece about Goldman, "Nice Guys Finish First." The article quotes a competitor as saying, "It's the class act on Wall Street. What's also amazing is that nearly everyone there is nice." Or, as *Forbes* expressed it, "Goldman has achieved this eminence with a minimum of infighting that afflicts most Wall Street firms. And when did you last hear of a Goldman partner leaving for greener fields elsewhere? Indeed, this unusual harmony is a major reason for the firm's unparalleled success."

Part of the reason for this harmony can be traced to Goldman's leader, John Weinberg, chairman of the firm's Management Committee since 1976.

He takes a dim view of internal politics. "We try to make it unattractive," Weinberg explained. "We reward the guys well for working within groups. Those who work well within those activities achieve favor. The financial incentive is to do it together."

When Goldman's chairman talks of financial incentives you can bet he's talking big bucks. A beginning professional, straight from graduate school, *starts* at $55,000 a year ($45,000 salary and $10,000 bonus). It is not uncommon for professional staffers to be making in excess of $100,000 after several years with Goldman Sachs. Goldman Sachs is a partnership (the only remaining partnership among the top 10 investment bankers). Some of the 81 partners are said to earn over a million a year.

But the firm also is generous to those who are not partners, including the clerical and office nonprofessional staff. In 1984, the entire staff received a Christmas bonus equal to 23 percent of their annual salary. That Christmas bonus was in addition to an already substantial salary. The clerical staff is paid between 20 and 25 percent more than the average paid clerical workers in corporate offices in Manhattan, and Goldman's office staff gets 15 percent more money than others in the investment banking industry, according to Michael H. Merrill, a personnel vice-president.

On top of the salary and bonuses, Goldman employees also share in the profits. In recent years, the partners have set aside the equivalent of 15 percent of an employee's salary and bonus into his or her profit-sharing retirement account. The employee can match the company's contribution with nontaxable income.

The firm can afford to pay these hefty salaries, bonuses, and benefits. In 1984, the Goldman team was a big winner in the real-life game of money. *The Economist* estimated that Goldman Sachs's profits for fiscal 1983 were over $400 million before taxes. That was no mean trick considering that Goldman had only an estimated $363 million in capital to begin the year. So, the firm made more than a dollar for every dollar it had to play with. That put Goldman at the very top of the securities industry, far ahead of the return achieved by Citicorp, Phibro-Salomon, Merrill Lynch, or J.P.Morgan. (In comparison with Goldman's more than 100 percent return on capital for the year, the average for the securities industry was about 20 percent.)

By one other standard, Goldman stood at the top of the heap. It ranked as Wall Street's leading deal maker in 1983. For helping various corporations buy or sell other businesses, and float huge offerings of securities, Goldman in 1983, earned $22 million in fees. In 1983, Goldman Sachs helped complete 75 corporate mergers, including 35 transactions in which the purchase price was over $100 million. The *Wall Street Journal* stated in December 1982 that "so far this year, and for the past five years, Goldman Sachs is believed to have served as an adviser in more merger and acquisition transactions than any other firm on Wall Street. And on deals involving more than $100 million there's no doubt that it stands supreme."

A closer look at Goldman Sachs's involvement in mergers and acquisitions says a lot about the type of company it is. Some people call Goldman Sachs "the pacifist" in the sometimes brutal battles over control of a company. The firm has a policy of not representing any company that is trying to take over someone who doesn't want to be bought.

So, in 1982, no one was surprised when, during the widely publicized takeover battle involving Bendix, Allied, and Martin Marietta, Goldman Sachs stayed on the sidelines, even though at least one of the companies involved asked the firm to represent it. Goldman Sachs preferred that year to take an active part in the $4 billion deal between Connecticut General and INA (producing CIGNA) and the $582 million merger of Morton-Norwich and Thiokol. In both cases Goldman Sachs represented both sides of the deal. Fifteen Goldman Sachs professional employees worked six months to earn the firm a cool $5 million in fees for the CIGNA deal.

Besides shying away from acting as the aggressor, Goldman Sachs professionals involved in such deals stay out of the limelight. There are no Tony Dorsett-type superstars on the Goldman Sachs team, unlike several of their competitors: Lazard Freres's Felix Rohatyn, or Morgan Stanley's Eric Gleacher, for example. That's intentional. Former cochairman John Whitehead told us, "We try to recruit people who will be good team players. We're not looking for erratic superstars." Chairman John Weinberg, added, "We don't like big egos here. We have superstar talent, but they are not out to publicize themselves."

Goldman Sachs recruits its team players largely from the most prestigious business schools. Richard L. Menschel, the firm's partner in charge of institutional sales, read off a list of where his associates attended graduate school: 25 came from Harvard; Columbia, 27; University of Chicago, 16; Penn's

Wharton School, 18; Stanford, 12; New York University, 12; and Brigham Young, 9. Whitehead estimated that half of all employees have advanced degrees. "We may have more M.B.A.'s than General Motors."

The vast majority of Goldman Sachs professional employees are hired directly out of business schools and stay with the firm for their entire careers. The company believes in promotion from within. Those who don't make partner are well compensated, and about 650 have been named vice-presidents. Turnover is about 5 percent among professionals and 10 percent overall—half the industry average.

Goldman had one ugly incident to live down—and indeed it may have spurred the firm to outdo competitors in the minority recruitment area. In 1970, a Goldman recruiter at Stanford graduate business school allegedly told James E. Cofield, Jr., a black who was in the graduating class, "that his application couldn't be given further consideration because of the negative view held by a senior partner regarding blacks." Cofield sued the firm and received an out-of-court settlement. Stanford banned Goldman from recruiting at the graduate business school for a year. But the firm is certainly back in favor today. One of the firm's partners is a member of the school's advisory council, and in 1984 Goldman was the single largest recruiter of Stanford M.B.A.'s. Cofield considers the case over, too. "It was some time ago," Cofield told us. "I am sure Goldman Sachs has prospered since then, and I know I have prospered." In 1970, less than 10 percent of all employees were minorities; today, the figure is between 18 and 20 percent, though no blacks or women are partners.

Competition to get into the firm is intense. Of the nearly 4,000 applicants for professional positions in 1983, only 100 were hired. It's common for successful candidates to be interviewed by as many as a dozen people in the firm.

Once hired, a Goldman Sachs professional is expected to pick a specialty and stick with it. There's very little movement between departments. The company wants its professionals to know their positions better than anybody else in the business.

Goldman Sachs also expects people to work hard. "We do not coddle people around here," Doty explained. The nature of the business is fluid, and it's clearly not a place where strict office hours are observed. Doty, who recently retired as the partner in charge of administration, said he didn't even know what the regular office hours were. He just knew that almost any time of day or night people were working. Another employee told us that "sixteen-hour days are common." As one Goldman partner told *Institutional Investor*: "Why do I work until 2:30 in the morning and then come back for a breakfast at 8:00 almost every day? Because I own a piece of this. We've built this, and I feel a tremendous commitment to seeing it continue."

The company avoids frills. "It is not a play firm," explained Merrill. "It's not a place where there is a lot of partying. Nor will you see the limousines lined up in front like at some of the other Wall Street firms. We don't have a company plane or even a company car."

On the other hand, people can expect an informal, collegial (a big word at Goldman Sachs) atmosphere. Partners practice an open-door policy, and the chairman has regular question-and-answer sessions with groups of employees. After one month with Goldman Sachs, an employee who previously worked for J.P.Morgan said he had made one great discovery: "That my first name is Frank."

Main employment centers   About 3,000 work in New York, in the company's new $150-million, 29-story building in the middle of the financial district. Smaller offices are in 11 other cities in the United States and four cities overseas.

Headquarters   Goldman Sachs & Co.
85 Broad Street
New York, NY 10004
212-902-1000

W. L. GORE & ASSOCIATES, INC.

Gore makes a synthetic fiber called Gore-tex, used in camping equipment, among dozens of other products. U.S. employees: 3,000.

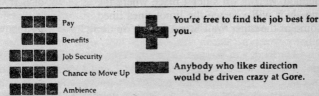

■■■ Pay	**+** You're free to find the job best for you.
■■■ Benefits	
■■■■ Job Security	
■■■■ Chance to Move Up	■ Anybody who likes direction would be driven crazy at Gore.
■■■ Ambience	

Who says Silicon Valley has a monopoly on unstructured working environments? Certainly not this Delaware-based firm. Compared with Gore, most Silicon Valley companies are about as egalitarian as the U.S. Marine Corps.

In some ways Gore looks like another high-tech success story. Bill Gore, a research chemist, worked on a task force at Du Pont that sought uses of polytetrafluoroethylene, or PTFE, more commonly known as Teflon. By tinkering with the substance in his basement at night, he discovered other uses for it that Du Pont wasn't interested in pursuing. So Gore and his wife, Vieve, founded this company in 1958, initially to make insulated electrical cable wires and continue their experimentation.

A few years later, Gore's son, Bob, found a way to stretch PTFE into a fabric. That led to Gore-tex, a breathable yet waterproof fabric. Gore-tex has turned into a gold mine. It is used in everything from camping gear and space suits to artificial arteries and industrial filters. The company's sales exploded to more than $150 million by 1983; and there are now 30 Gore plants, from Delaware to Arizona, and from Scotland to Japan.

Other tinkerers have discovered gold in their garages or basements. What makes Gore special is a unique manage-

161

ment style—or as *Inc.* magazine put it, its "system of un-management." Gore is a company without titles, hierarchy, or any of the conventional structures associated with enterprises of its size. It has turned most forms of corporate life on their heads.

If you apply to work here, you may receive a letter that gives you fair warning of what to expect: "If you are a person who needs to be told what to do and how to do it, Dr. Gore says, you will have trouble adjusting. . . . An associate has to find his own place to a high degree. There's no job description, no slot to fit yourself into. You have to learn what you can do."

Jack Dougherty discovered that the letter was more than a mere word of caution. He told *Inc.* that when he showed up for his first day of work at Gore, Bill Gore shook his hand and said, "Why don't you look around and find something you'd like to do." The startled 23-year-old business school graduate then spent the next several weeks wandering around between various plants in the company until he found himself excited about the people turning Gore-tex into fabics for parkas and camping gear. Once committed, Dougherty put on his jeans to work on the production line. (Gore laminates the Gore-tex to fabric and sells it by the yard to camping gear manufacturers.) That was 1976. By 1982, Doughtery was in charge of all advertising and marketing of Gore-tex fabrics.

Bill Gore calls this system the "lattice organization," in contrast to the pyramid organization typical of most companies. Instead of people relating to others within a hierarchy, each person in a lattice can interact directly with every other person. Gore explains that a lattice has several attributes, including:

"No fixed or assigned authority;

"Sponsors, not bosses;

"Natural leadership defined by followership;

"Person-to-person communication;

"Objectives set by those who must 'make them happen';

"Tasks and functions organized through commitments."

Gore applied his lattice theory from the outset. But he discovered that once his original plant reached about 200 people, the direct, person-to-person system began to break down. He realized he didn't even know everyone else's name anymore. Rather than throw out his theory, Gore decided to build

The Lattice Organization

Bill Gore sums up the governing principles of his company with these four thoughts:

Everyone will:

1. Try to be fair. Sincerely strive to be fair with each other, our suppliers, our customers, and all persons with whom we carry out transactions.

2. Allow, help, and encourage his associates to grow in knowledge, skill, scope of responsibility, and range of activities.

3. Make his own commitments—and keep them.

4. Consult with his associates before taking actions that might be "below the waterline" and cause serious damage to the enterprise.

---

another plant. Today, no Gore facility has more than 150 to 200 people. Though that requires substantial outlays of capital, Gore "associates" (no one is an "employee" at Gore) insist that their productivity more than makes up for the added expenses.

Most of Gore's plants are located near the company's headquarters on the outskirts of Newark (pronounced New Ark), home of the University of Delaware. Adjacent to the small corporate headquarters building is a Gore plant where a mostly female work force is putting together the company's original product, electrical cable wires. Assembly-line associates have a good view of the rolling farmland surrounding the plant, since the building is lined with windows.

How about practical issues like pay? There are compensation teams that review wage levels. Since each associate has a "sponsor" instead of a "boss," the sponsor acts as advocate on the associate's behalf. It is common for associates to have their wage scales reviewed twice a year.

Entry-level pay is "in the middle" for comparable jobs, according to Sally Gore, daughter-in-law of the founder and an associate with responsibility for professional recruiting. "We do not feel we need to be the highest paid. We never try to steal people away from other companies with salary. We want them to come here because of the opportunities for growth and the unique work environment."

The company does, however, offer two lucrative profit-sharing plans to all associates. Twice a year, Gore distributes about 15 percent of the company's profits among all associates. In addition, Gore buys company stock equivalent to 15 percent of an associate's annual income and places it in a retirement fund called ASOP (Associates' Stock Ownership Plan). The Gore family and the employees own 90 percent of the privately held stock. In the past decade the value of Gore stock has increased dramatically, as has the size of each associate's nest egg.

Main employment centers   Most of Gore's plants are near its Newark headquarters. Several medical-products plants are in the Flagstaff, Arizona, area. Nearly 1,000 work overseas.

Headquarters   W. L. Gore & Associates, Inc.
555 Paper Mill Road
P.O. Box 9329
Newark, DE 19711
302-738-4880

Hallmark

HALLMARK CARDS, INC.

Hallmark is the world's largest greeting card company. U.S. employees: 12,000.

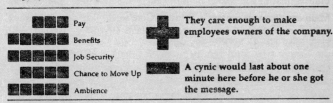

■■■ Pay	✚	They care enough to make employees owners of the company.
■■■■■ Benefits		
■■■■ Job Security		
■■■ Chance to Move Up	▬	A cynic would last about one minute here before he or she got the message.
■■■■■ Ambience		

Twenty-fifth anniversaries are big occasions at Hallmark. After all, this company is in the sentiment business. An employee can invite any and all of his or her friends from throughout the company to share the anniversary cake and coffee (provided by the company, of course), and the guests are let off work to go. It's not uncommon for 200 people to attend these gatherings, and as many as 1,000 have been known to show up.

If he is in Kansas City, Donald Hall makes it a point to go to twenty-fifth-anniversary celebrations, whether the employee is a vice-president, an artist, or a production-line worker. He waits his turn in the receiving line, just like the dozens, or hundreds, of others. Hallmark's chairman makes it seem perfectly ordinary, and most Hallmarkers take his presence in stride. They're used to seeing him in the company cafeteria carrying his own tray. But it is certainly not typical of presidents of firms the size of Hallmark (1984 sales exceeded $1.5 billion, with 19,000 employees worldwide). And it certainly is not typical of the richest people in America (Hall personally owns a majority of Hallmark's stock; *Forbes* estimated his wealth to be in excess of $400 million).

Few would claim that Hallmark is an ordinary company. Don Hall's father, Joyce Clyde Hall (known to everyone as "Mr. J. C."), launched an entirely new industry when he

165

started Hallmark in 1910. For people in Kansas City, he also became widely known as the best employer in town.

Any list of Hallmark benefits justifies that reputation: adoption assistance of up to $1,000; interest-free loans of up to $1,000 for unexpected emergencies; free refreshments during breaks; a physical-fitness building at the corporate headquarters; automatic low-interest $2,500-a-year college loans for children of employees, with no payback until after graduation.

Perhaps the best benefit is profit-sharing. Each year Hallmark sets aside a percentage of corporate profits and puts it into an employee fund. Much of the money is invested in Hallmark stock, so that the employees own about one-third of the shares (the Hall family owns the rest). In 1983, the company put $32 million into the fund—equivalent to about 11 percent of each employee's annual salary. When employees retire or leave the company, they can withdraw their personal account from the fund. Many have retired with thousands of dollars in profit-sharing money alone.

The company also provides free indoor parking for the more than 6,000 employees working in the headquarters complex in Crown Center in downtown Kansas City. But don't expect to see any Cadillacs parked in the lot. There's a strong bias against ostentation here. Mr. J. C. drove a 1963 Buick to the office until shortly before he died in 1982 at the age of 91.

Employees don't, however, recite their benefits when they talk about Hallmark being a great place to work. They say Hallmark is like "a family," and they speak of "how people care for each other." (Corny is a concept that doesn't seem to exist here.) They talk with pride about what it means to become a "Hallmarker." Just being hired by the company isn't enough to make someone a Hallmarker. Employees have to internalize Hallmark's sense of quality. It may be hard to define what makes a card a Hallmark card, but press operators will refuse to print cards they think don't meet Hallmark's standards. They may disagree with the content or tone of the message, or think the artwork doesn't look right. Whatever the reason, they can expect to be patted on the back rather than reprimanded, even if their objections cost time and money. True Hallmarkers care about their product.

Hallmark hires more commercial artists than any other firm in the country. The 600 artists working in Kansas City create about 13,000 card designs a year. Though this output is immense, artists we talked with insist they have no quotas. Ellen Sloan has been designing cards at Hallmark for the past 11 years. A graduate of the prestigious Rhode Island School of Design, Sloan said that when she first came to Hallmark there was a stigma attached to doing card designs. But she thinks that opinions have changed in recent years and many now consider it an art form.

An easterner, Sloan did not find Kansas City to be the cultural backwater she expected. The Nelson-Atkins Museum of Art is superb (partly thanks to gifts from Hallmark), and the company brings internationally famed artists such as Mark English and Karl Heldt to spend months at a time with the staff. Sloan has been sent to London, Santa Fe, and San Francisco, where she visited art exhibits with groups of four or five other Hallmark artists. She said Hallmark routinely sends artists on such trips "not as a reward, but strictly for stimulation. Sometimes they'll have someone who has temporarily been a lackluster performer go on one of those visits just to get him on track again."

According to Sloan, "Hallmark not only lets you grow creatively, they are hungry for it, almost insistent on it. It's the only bourgeois commercial art job I know where you can be this creative and yet have security."

Hallmarkers certainly have job security. For one thing, no one can be fired unless two corporate officers (the top two dozen people in the firm) agree to the termination. The company also doesn't believe in layoffs. During the recession of 1981–82, Hallmark's business was off. Several hundred agreed to a company offer to take voluntary time off without pay but without losing benefits. About 600 others (mostly production workers) were loaned to other departments to do work that otherwise would not have been done (such as repainting) or to work in the community. A group of a dozen spent seven months weatherizing 75 homes in a neighborhood near the headquarters. We talked with Manuel Meneses, a production worker, who was made a supervisor at a skating rink in the Crown Center, a complex of hotels and shops adjacent to Hallmark's buildings that is owned by the company. Meneses said he was paid his regular salary while working in the rink.

J. D. Goodwin, the plant manager of the production

center in Kansas City, estimated the company spent about $10 million on surplus labor in the last year. But, he said, "Our attitude is that when we have a downturn, it's the managers who have a problem. It shouldn't be an employee problem."

Main employment centers   About 11,000 work in Kansas City or in additional production plants in Topeka, Lawrence, and Leavenworth, Kansas, or the distribution center in Liberty, Missouri. Another 740 work in the Enfield, Connecticut, warehouse.

Headquarters   Hallmark Cards, Inc.
2501 McGee
Kansas City, MO 64108
816-274-5111

H. J. HEINZ COMPANY

H. J. Heinz, the world's number-one ketchup maker, ranks as one of the nation's 10 largest food processors. Employees: 28,000.

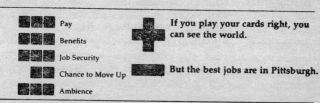

People like working for H. J. Heinz. Whether you talk to them in Pittsburgh, where the company was born and is still headquartered, or in England, where H. J. Heinz is a power-house and has been around for so long that people are sur-prised to learn that the company is American, or in Tracy, California, in the San Joaquin Valley, where Heinz processes more than 500,000 tons of tomatoes a year, you sense a feel-ing of belonging.

This is not a fly-by-night company. It dates to 1869. The founder's name is still on the door. Descendants of Henry J. Heinz still own huge chunks of stock. At the same time, there's no question that today H. J. Heinz is a professionally managed corporation. It's looking for the same marketing whizzes that Procter & Gamble recruits.

Heinz doesn't show the paternalism you see at S. C. Johnson and Hallmark. But it does have special characteris-tics—caring about how it makes its product and caring about the people who work for it—that go back far in the com-pany's history. In 1906, when reformers were trying to get a pure food and drug law through Congress, most of the leaders of the food industry bitterly opposed the legislation. Heinz was for it—and at Heinz today this stance is still cited as an example of why the company is different (and better) than competitors.

Heinz is more than ketchup and baked beans. Or even pickles. Or even the "57 Varieties" which served as the company's symbol for many years. It has expanded into a bunch of new businesses, mostly by acquiring other companies and bringing them into the family. Star-Kist tuna is a Heinz operation. So are Ore-Ida frozen potatoes, Weight Watchers, Foodways, Gagliardi Brothers (Steak-umms), and the Hubinger corn refining company, whose own history can be traced back to Keokuk, Iowa, in 1881. Heinz makes wine (Stanley) in Australia, baby food (Plada) and candy (Sperlari) in Italy, Bismarck herring and rollmops (Nadler) in Germany. It also operates Burger King restaurants in Puerto Rico.

Some people on the East and West Coasts might consider Heinz's headquarters city, Pittsburgh, a disadvantage. But they may not have visited there recently. Brian Ruder, who grew up in the New York metropolitan area and who was a marketing manager at Heinz, pointed out to us that Pittsburgh "has undergone a complete rejuvenation and renaissance. It's now more white-collar-oriented than blue-collar, it's the third-largest headquarters location of Fortune 500 companies, and it has a growing crowd of up-and-coming, highly educated executives who do a fair amount of socializing."

Ruder graduated from the Amos Tuck business school at Dartmouth and was given early responsiblity by Heinz. He said that three and one-half years after his graduation he was running a $250 million business as product manager on Heinz ketchup. He was only 29 in 1983. Heinz, reports Ruder, has these things going for it:

• The company is "driven by the spoken word rather than the written word." Senior managers would rather make decisions by talking to you than by reacting to memos.

• Heinz is much less formal than General Foods, Procter & Gamble, or General Mills. There's a unity of purpose in the ranks.

• People relate on a first-name basis. And you know you are not going to be stabbed in the back.

• The executives are young.

• You can move up fast because Heinz is gaining momentum, adding companies, and bringing out new products, yet it runs on a very lean staff. So while you may be able to advance quickly, this means you will also have to work very hard.

• Heinz is still in the process of changing from what it was—a lethargic company making products that were easy to make—to an aggressive one making products that consumers want to buy. (As an example of the old Heinz, Ruder cited the company's experience in the early 1970s when it reformulated its entire soup line to the point where it claimed its product had higher quality than Campbell's. The trouble was that consumers still preferred Campbell's. Consumers, said Ruder, were not interested in buying the better product.) Ruder left Heinz at the end of 1983 to become a new product development manager at PepsiCo in Purchase, New York, but he left singing the praises of Heinz.

A Heinz manager can move around within this growing family, including to posts in Europe. Heinz is perhaps the most international of all U.S. food companies. Anthony J. F. O'Reilly, one of the greatest rugby players Ireland ever produced, became chief executive officer in 1979 when he was 43 years old.

Charles B. Berger, a native of Scranton, Pennsylvania, graduated from Princeton and the Harvard Business School before joining Heinz in 1964 as a product marketing manager in Pittsburgh. In 1970, he was posted to London to become marketing director for Heinz's British operations. Less than two years later he went off to Italy to head up Plasmon, the Heinz affiliate in that country. He's the only American ever to hold that post. In 1978, back in the United States, Heinz bought the Weight Watchers business—and Berger was brought home to run it. He's based at Weight Watchers headquarters on Long Island.

Heinz bought Ore-Ida Foods in Boise, Idaho, in 1965. Within four years the top nine executives at Ore-Ida were recruits from other Heinz units. I. E. "Ike" Lynch is an Idaho native (born in Pocatello, reared in Burley, and schooled at the College of Idaho) who joined Ore-Ida in 1967. He was posted to Ore-Ida's Ontario, Oregon, facility as quality control manager—and he moved four years later to become manager of the Ore-Ida plant in Greenville, Michigan. In 1976, he was promoted to plant manager at the Heinz "mother plant" in Pittsburgh, staying only a year before being transferred back to Ore-Ida in Boise as general manager/manufacturing for vegetable products. Two years later he was on the move again—to Keokuk, Iowa, where he joined newly acquired

Hubinger. Three years later, in 1981, he was named president and chief executive officer of Hubinger. He was 36 years old. The peripatetic Lynch moved right off the Heinz reservation in 1983, joining Ultra Systems in Irvine, California. He was succeeded by Bruce Brown, who came to Hubinger in 1977 from Central Soya when he was 35 years old.

At the Tracy plant in northern California the Heinz workers are represented by the Teamsters union. In 1983 they were working on a contract that set the entry-level wage at $7.82 an hour, rising to a top, for a lead mechanic, of $12.42 an hour. It's the same contract operative at other plants in California where the Teamsters are the bargaining agent.

However, the big advantage of working for Heinz in Tracy is that you have a much greater chance of year-round employment. Heinz doesn't can seasonal fruits like peaches and pears. It makes prodigious amounts of ketchup, but it has found a way of evaporating the water and making a paste that can be stored aseptically in giant containers; it can— and does—ship this paste in tank cars to other Heinz plants. So ketchup can be made all year long. From June 20 to October 5, tomato-harvesting time, the Tracy plant goes full blast, 24 hours a day, seven days a week. But then the work evens out.

You become a full-time employee at Heinz-Tracy after working there for 1,400 hours. At its peak, the plant employs 550 people. Some 400 of them work 12 months of the year. Turnover is low. There's a company picnic once a year. And at Christmastime every Heinz employee everywhere in the world gets a gift—the same one. In 1982 it was a stadium blanket.

About 100 salaried people also work at the Tracy complex, which serves as Heinz's western regional headquarters. Western regional manager J. Ogden Perry, Jr., holds a meeting of his six top managers every morning at 9 A.M., six days a week. Perry is a hard-driving, chain-smoking manager who began his Heinz career 23 years ago as an hourly employee at Salem, New Jersey, where there was once a tomato-processing plant. He moved later to the Heinz plant in Muscatine, Iowa, and he came to Tracy in 1976. He cares a lot about his work. He was having lunch in a downtown Tracy restaurant in the summer of 1983 when the lights began to flicker. With just a few words of apology, he bolted, rushing to get back to the plant in case there had been an outage (there wasn't).

Charles E. Bailey, Heinz's regional manager for West Coast agriculture (he buys $42 million of tomatoes a year from California farmers), has been with Heinz for 17 years, but he spent the previous 15 years with Libby, McNeil & Libby in Chicago. He and his wife are West Coast natives and they wanted to get back. Libby refused to transfer him, and so he transferred to Heinz, which sent him to Tracy. The difference between the two companies is marked, according to Bailey. Libby never seemed to know what it was doing. "Heinz is first-class all the way. They know what they are doing."

The people orientation at Heinz is impressive. You can see that the company takes the time and space in its publications to salute rank-and-filers, not just managers. H. J. Heinz is the only big company we know of that regularly uses its communications to shareholders to tell them about the people who are working for Heinz, including personal details of their lives. It's a family-oriented company. In one of its annual reports to shareholders, people who work for the company, on all levels and in many locations, were featured. In another annual report, employees were depicted in their off-the-job pursuits. In still another, a bunch of employees were allowed to speak out on matters of personal concern.

Then, in 1981, Heinz held a worldwide poetry contest for employees. More than 300 employees around the world submitted more than 700 poems. Outside judges selected 10 prize winners—and Heinz printed all of them in its 1982 annual report, illustrating them with works done by 10 of the world's great artists; each was specially commissioned. Here is one of the prizewinning poems:

WHITHER

I am still waiting . . .
What for—I don't know;
So, how will anybody else.
However,
　　　　I guess
　　　　It will soon be over
Then, I'll start waiting again.
Wondering
　　　　What I'll be doing
　　　　Whom I'll be with

> to share the uncertainty,
> Expounding the myth—
> And continue wondering . . .
> Where am I headed?

The poetess is Toyer Jappie, a sales clerk with Heinz's Australian company. No company that prints poetry in its annual report can be all that bad.

Main employment centers   Pittsburgh: 3,000; Boise: 1,500; Muscatine: Iowa, 1,200. Some 15,000 work overseas.

Headquarters   H. J. Heinz Company
600 Grant Street
Pittsburgh, PA 15129
412-237-5757

WHERE TRANSFERRING IS PART OF LIFE

Du Pont	IBM
Exxon	Westin Hotels

Hewitt Associates

HEWITT ASSOCIATES

Hewitt Associates is a consultant that designs compensation-and-benefits programs for companies. Employees: 1,050.

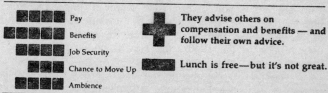

■■■■ Pay	✚ **They advise others on compensation and benefits — and follow their own advice.**
■■■■■ Benefits	
■■■ Job Security	**Lunch is free—but it's not great.**
■■■ Chance to Move Up	
■■■ Ambience	

It was an unusual letter. Word got out that we were looking for companies considered outstanding places to work. Back came this reply from Linda Menees, a secretary in the Rowayton, Connecticut, office of Hewitt Associates: "Have I got a company for you! . . . Every Hewitt associate takes pride in the work they do, from the partners to the personnel in the mailroom. . . . As a secretary, I can state that I have never felt or been treated differently than even a partner. Everyone here is entitled to his or her opinion and the right to be heard. . . . If a mistake is made, it's everyone's mistake. If there is any management here, well, you just don't feel it. You are your own manager. Rarely does anyone ever need monitoring. We all try to be responsible people." Perhaps the most impressive aspect of the letter was that not once did it make any reference to "employees." It only talked about "people" and "associates."

If any company should be a good place to work, it ought to be Hewitt Associates, whose basic business is to help other companies become better employers. It's akin to being a doctor's doctor. Hewitt is a consulting firm specializing in designing compensation-and-benefits programs. In working with companies to set up these programs, it likens its role to educator, catalyst, facilitator." Hewitt was the leader in introducing flexible compensation-and-benefits programs, sometimes called "cafeteria benefits" in that they allow employees to tailor benefits to their individual needs. With 1982 revenues of $75 million from its clients, Hewitt ranked second in its field. The largest consultant in employee benefits is Towers, Perrin, Forster & Crosby.

Being sensitive to the care and feeding of employees in general, Hewitt has worked at establishing an easygoing style that encourages people to be open and stretch themselves. The Hewitt headquarters in Lincolnshire, Illinois, is secluded in a woodsy area right off the Chicago-Milwaukee toll road. Offices are not elaborate. Everyone seems to know everyone else by first name. Everyone eats in the same cafeteria—and lunch (while not marvelous) is free. In a set of principles dating back to the 1940s, the Hewitt philosophy was expressed, in part, as follows:

"We try to remember to demonstrate that every job is important and each individual, in carrying out his function well, is an important contributor. . . .

"We believe most people have capabilities beyond those they are called on to demonstrate in their jobs. . . .

"Associates are given the opportunity to participate in the determination of their own jobs, direction of progress, and areas of interest and regional location. . . ."

Christine A. Seltz joined Hewitt in 1973 fresh out of Skidmore College. She says she's grateful to the company because she really didn't know what she wanted to do when she got out of college—and at Hewitt they allowed her to find her place. That place is writing reports and booklets. Hewitt places a great deal of emphasis on communication skills because it often has to help clients present benefit programs to employers. In 1983, Hewitt had 85 associates with more than 10 years of service—and 67 of them had jobs created specifically for them.

Getting hired at Hewitt is not easy. In its 1984 fiscal year (Hewitt works on a year ending September 30), the firm interviewed 2,361 professional people—and hired 170. Here's how the new hires have broken down by professional areas:

	1982	1983	1984
Actuarial	24	13	36
Account Management	16	2	20
Compensation	6	4	10

	1982	1983	1984
Communication	5	2	9
Systems	37	16	66
Legal	5	4	10
Research	2	1	3
Investment Services	1	1	1
Other	1	1	15
TOTAL:	97	44	170

(Systems has to do with computers and data processing operations. Actuaries are people traditionally hired by insurance companies—they are trained in the analysis of data related to deaths and injuries over time.)

Peter E. Friedes, the young (he was 43 in 1984), low-keyed chief executive of Hewitt, says, "Obviously we look for those who are bright, hardworking, and ambitious. But we're also looking for something else—an indication that the person will be a team player with the firm. We're not looking for individual egoists."

Hewitt functions as an extension of the client's staff, so it places a premium on people who can work together *and* work well with the client. It tries not to foster competition among its own people. Turnover at Hewitt is less than 10 percent a year (low by consulting industry standards).

Most consultants are secretive about their business, and being privately owned, they need not disclose anything. Hewitt has the refreshing attitude that the people who work for the firm "have a right to know anything about Hewitt Associates that might be useful to them in their judgments about the organization and their future in it." So Hewitt clues its people in to what's going on through frequent reports, highlighted by an annual gathering where the associates are told how the firm did and who made partner and how much money, on the average, the partners make. In 1982, for example, the average compensation of partners was $166,000, higher than the average at the Big Eight accounting firms. It takes, on the average, five to seven years to make partner—and in 1984, a bumper year for Hewitt, 15 associates made partner, bringing the total number of partners to 112—more than 10 percent of the staff). It was the largest new partner "class" in Hewitt's history. To celebrate the good year, Hewitt awarded its first-ever cash bonus—3 percent of pay to all associates, even those who'd joined only a month earlier. The cash award was on top of the company's maximum contribution to deferred profit-sharing plans in which all associates are enrolled.

There are no titles at Hewitt Associates. The only gradation is partnership. There are no vice-presidents or associate managers or senior or junior consultants.

As you might expect, the benefits package here is very good, as is the compensation. Hewitt pays what it calls "highly competitive salaries" at all levels, and during your first three years here, you are reviewed at least every nine months. The benefits include a profit-sharing plan that vests fully after five years (meaning you can take it all with you if you leave) and adds 10 percent to your pay; flexible credits of up to $1,500 to cover medical costs not covered by insurance and other expenses, such as unreimbursed educational courses.

The company has never had a layoff—even during difficult times in the early 1960s. In 1961, partners took a pay cut to keep everyone on the payroll—and paychecks were distributed according to need.

Main employment centers   About 670 people work in the 48-acre Lincolnshire headquarters. The four other main offices are in Rowayton, Connecticut, on Long Island Sound; Newport Beach, California, on the Pacific Ocean; The Woodlands, Texas, near Houston; and Toronto, Canada.

Headquarters   Hewitt Associates
100 Half Day Road
Lincolnshire, IL 60015
312-295-5000

HEWLETT-PACKARD COMPANY

A premier electronics company that makes computers, calculators, and various precision instruments for computation and for the measurement and analysis of various phenomena. U.S. employees: 56,000.

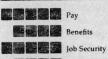

Pay

Benefits

Job Security

Chance to Move Up

Ambience

You get a chance to work with a lot of brainy people who are not stuck on themselves.

You may be handicapped here if you don't have a degree in electrical engineering — or if you're female.

When Queen Elizabeth visited the United States in 1983, she went to only one company: Hewlett-Packard in sunny Palo Alto, California, hard by the Stanford University campus. It wasn't surprising that she should do this. H-P makes all the "best" lists—and for good reason. It's a model of how a company can grow, prosper, and still retain a personal feeling in its operations.

You can sense that H-P people feel good about themselves and their jobs just by a casual visit to a facility. The atmosphere is friendly, informal, and low-pressure. The cafeteria, where you can get a very respectable lunch for less than $3, is filled with employees from all levels. No one is wearing a jacket. The conversation is animated. There's laughter. You could be in a university dining room.

The high regard employees have for the company has been confirmed in surveys. In 1979, H-P hired an outside firm, International Survey Research Corp., to interview 7,966 employees and get their views on various company practices. The results were embarrassingly favorable to the company. Indeed, John Stanek, president of the research company, wrote to Hewlett-Packard to say: "The positive view employees have toward Hewlett-Packard and, specifically, their feeling of belonging and willingness to recommend the company as a good place to work, places H-P in the upper one-

179

half of 1 percent of the more than 1,000 U.S. organizations studied in the past quarter century."

That's what you call high praise. Even H-P blushed.

You pick up these feelings of happiness when you talk to H-P people. Mary Anne Easley, who moved to the company from Levi Strauss in 1982, was struck by the sensitivity employees showed toward waste and misuse of materials or excessive spending. "I've never experienced that in another company," Easley said. Katherine Nutter, who worked at Bechtel before coming to H-P, said that what impressed her most was the sense of humor, even irreverence, displayed by people high up in management ranks.

There is a lot of playfulness at Hewlett-Packard. It's common to see, as you walk about, clumps of employees celebrating someone's birthday or another occasion. The company provides free refreshments twice a day. There are informal beer busts in the afternoons to mark an event.

Cofounder David Packard served three years as deputy director of defense in the Nixon administration. When he returned, happily, to H-P, he was asked what his biggest accomplishment in Washington, D.C., had been. He thought for a moment and replied, "I gave up smoking."

As we were walking around the H-P engineering systems plant in Cupertino, California, we saw posted on a bulletin board an NCR advertisement for one of its computers. The ad cited the efficiencies this computer brought to office workstations. H-P hardware had already done that (at least H-P thought so), and an employee had therefore penciled in the sarcastic comment, "Thank you, NCR." But alongside this comment another H-P employee had scrawled, "Wait a minute, think about this. For NCR and its users, this *is* a breakthrough."

H-P has institutionalized a way of working. Units are kept small. There are no time clocks. You can work any eight-hour shift you want, beginning at 6:00 A.M., 7:00 A.M. or 8:00 A.M. The typical H-P office layout is a network of open partitions. Everyone is accessible. There's an H-P management practice called MBWA, which stands for "management by wandering around." Executive vice-president John Doyle explained: "It's not enough to sit and wait for people to come to see you with their problems and ideas— they probably wouldn't in many cases. The managers had better get off their chairs and go and get in touch with people." H-P practices are codified in a document called "The H-P Way." The keynote is Bill Hewlett's dictum: "Men and women want to do a good job, a creative job, and if they are provided the proper environment, they will do so."

The Hewlett-Packard practices grew up with the company. They were not imposed. Frank Cavier, one of the company's earliest employees, once told how someone in the 1950s offered Hewlett and Packard $10 million to sell out. They turned down the offer. "They probably won't say why," said Cavier, "but it's my interpretation they felt this would expose the employees to a bunch of strangers—strangers whose interest was primarily financial." Cavier also recalled once looking at a plant with the idea of buying it. The plant had a plush executive suite. The office and laboratory areas were air-conditioned, but not the manufacturing areas. "The point is," he said, "this would not happen at H-P because—while we have not always had air conditioning—it is inconceivable that H-P would put it in the front office but not in the shops."

Jon Wood, who went to work for H-P as a machinist in its Avondale, Pennsylvania, plant, said, "I thought: these people are putting me on. Why, there's not a shop in the world where someone isn't bad-mouthing the management. So it bothered me that no one was really saying anything really bad about H-P. I still can't say I really understand why it works, but it does."

Hewlett-Packard has a superior pay-and-benefits package. The lowest-level employee, a production worker with no previous experience, earns $900 a month. In general, the company makes a conscious effort to pay more than other companies. Here's the formula it uses:

• Take the five to 10 leading companies in the nation—and H-P salaries will be about equal to the levels in those firms.

• Take 10 to 20 companies that are similar to H-P—and the salaries at H-P will be 5 to 10 percent higher.

• Take a broad-based group of 30 companies—and H-P salaries will range from 10 to 15 percent higher.

There's a cash profit-sharing plan under which the company distributes to employees 12 percent of pretax profits. Payouts are made in June and December. In recent years the plan has augmented salaries by about 7 percent. The company picks up 100 percent of the premiums for medical and dental insurance. If you wish, you may sock away up to 10 percent of your salary for the purchase of H-P stock—and for every $3 you put up, the company will kick in a dollar. There's also a new 401K pension plan that enables employees to save pretax dollars, with the company providing a one-for-three match.

But good pay and a good working environment are not all that H-P employees enjoy. Hewlett-Packard also maintains recreation areas for employees—and their families—who want to get away from it all and spend some time in a relaxing outdoor environment. The initial impetus was to find a site that could accommodate the annual company picnic for employees in Northern California. That's why Little Basin Park in the Santa Cruz Mountains was acquired in 1962. Now the picnic is an H-P tradition, and the company has 10 different recreation areas, including three in Colorado, one in the Pocono Mountains of Pennyslvania, a beach villa in Malaysia, a lake resort in Scotland, and a ski-chalet complex in the German Alps. H-P employees anywhere in the world may make reservations to stay, at a modest cost, at any of these places for a limited number of days.

One of the unwritten policies at H-P is never to lay off people. When you come to work here, the philosophy is that "we are offering you a permanent job: you do your work well and we will provide the employment." The story goes that the company had an opportunity to land an important military contract during World War II. To do so, it would have had to bring in 12 new employees. Hewlett asked a manager, "When the contract is finished, will we have work for those twelve people?" The manager said, "No." Hewlett said, "Don't take the contract." In 1901–71, when the company's order rates declined, rather than lay off employees, H-P chose not to work one day in 10, and everyone—from Hewlett to the newest employee—took a 10 percent pay cut.

Of course Hewlett-Packard is not perfect. Although the company is proud of its equal employment opportunity record, you do not find too many women in the ranks of upper management. And it is decidedly an engineer's company. It has yet to place a black or a Hispanic on its board of directors. A woman, Shirley M. Hufstedler, joined the board in 1982.

The HP Way

Hewlett-Packard held a management meeting in 1975, and the participants developed this list of concepts as central to the way the company works:
- Belief in people; freedom
- Respect and dignity; individual self-esteem
- Recognition; sense of achievement; participation
- Security; permanence; development of people
- Insurance; personal worry protection
- Share benefits and responsibility; help each other
- Management by objectives (rather than by directive); decentralization
- Informality; first names; open communication
- A chance to learn by making mistakes
- Training and education; counseling
- Performance and enthusiasm

Getting into H-P is not easy. Applications pour in at a rate of 4,000 a month. The company recruits heavily on college campuses and is usually able, because of its reputation, to get the "cream of the crop." In recent years, only IBM has recruited more MIT graduates. One good way is to look for a summer internship there while you are in college. Once people do join H-P, they tend to stay unless they want to start up a company of their own—and many of them have done that. There are H-P satellites all over Silicon Valley.

Of the 82,000 persons on the payroll at the end of 1984, 26,000 worked overseas. H-P has manufacturing facilities in Brazil, Britain, France, West Germany, Japan, Malaysia, Singapore, Korea, Canada, Puerto Rico, and Mexico.

Main employment centers   Hewlett-Packard facilities are scattered across the United States. The biggest employment concentration is still in Northern California, where some 22,000 people work. Next is Colorado, where H-P employs more than 8,000. Here's the lineup of manufacturing facilities in the United States:

California: Palo Alto, Cupertino, Rohnert Park, San Jose, Mountain View, Roseville, San Diego, Santa Clara, Santa Rosa, and Sunnyvale; Colorado: Colorado Springs, Fort Collins, Greeley, Loveland; Idaho: Boise; Massachusetts: Andover, Watham; New Jersey: Rockaway;

Oregon: Corvallis, McMinnville; Pennsylvania; Avondale; Washington: Marysville, Spokane.

Headquarters   Hewlett-Packard Company
3000 Hanover Street
Palo Alto, CA 94304
415-857-1501

COMPANIES WITH COUNTRY CLUBS

Du Pont
IBM
3M

 **Inland Steel**

INLAND STEEL COMPANY

Inland Steel is the nation's fourth-largest steel producer. Employees: 29,000.

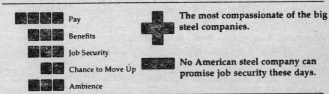

Pay	The most compassionate of the big steel companies.
Benefits	
Job Security	
Chance to Move Up	No American steel company can promise job security these days.
Ambience	

A well-callused hand shot up. Its owner doffed his red baseball cap and said to the speaker: "I can't get any straight stuff. If I phoned you, would you answer my calls?" The speaker, Tom Katsahnias, manufacturing vice-president of Inland Steel, replied: "Sure, try me." An assistant handed the worker a card with Katsahnias's telephone number. Ninety minutes and 44 questions later, Katsahnias ended the third "employee forum" he conducted in 1984, but he lingered another thirty minutes to take other questions and comments from a line of hourly employees and their spouses that snaked almost to the door of the grade school auditorium.

With dismal conditions prevailing in the steel industry in 1984, Inland felt it was important to have its managers report directly to the work force. So it scheduled a series of these forums in communities with a heavy concentration of Inland employees. The meetings were held in churches, schools, and other public buildings. The workers were encouraged to bring along their families—and ask any questions they had on their minds.

At the same time, Inland was holding a series of training sessions for its salaried, supervisory, and managerial people, drilling home, sentence by sentence, the essence of a new corporate philosophy statement: "Our people are our most im-

185

portant resource, and will be treated with dignity and respect." It was a reaffirmation of beliefs long held at Inland.

This is not the kind of ambience associated with the steel industry, but then Inland is not your typical big steel company. And it is big, ranking as the nation's fourth-largest steel producer, but it prides itself on being the maverick of the industry. It does not walk in lockstep with the rest of the major steel producers. Founded by a Jewish family, the Blocks of Chicago, Inland has managed to go its own way; witness these corporate landmarks:

• It was the last company to be organized by the steelworkers union, because its labor practices were so good.

• It was one of the first companies in the industry, or in America, to adopt an eight-hour workday.

• It was the first steel company to have a pension plan (1920).

• It was a nondiscriminatory employer in the 1930s. After World War II, when the Illinois legislature was considering a Fair Employment Practices Commission, Inland was one of the two companies that supported the act.

• It was the last major producer to "downsize" its salaried force during the 1981–84 steel recession, exhausting natural attrition first before hiring outside consultants to determine how to make further reductions as objectively as possible.

These progressive actions still characterize Inland Steel today. The company is the largest industrial employer in the Chicago metropolitan area, and more than one-third of its Chicago-area work force is composed of minority-group members. Of the 29,000 people on its payroll at the end of 1984, 17 percent were black and another 17 percent were Hispanic. Minority penetration extends to management ranks, too. Nearly 6 percent of Inland's officials and managers are black and 5 percent are Hispanic. It's one of the largest minority representations of any Chicago company.

The company has also been making a special effort to recruit women. Over the past seven years 25 percent of its management trainees have been women.

Employee turnover at Inland is low. It runs about 4 percent a year in the salaried ranks—lowest in the steel industry. Inland has hardly ever instituted an across-the-board layoff of salaried personnel. In 1982, a rough year for the steel industry, the company offered an attractive early-retirement package to 972 eligible employees; 472 accepted.

Inland's Indiana Harbor Works in East Chicago, Indiana, just outside of Chicago on the shores of Lake Michigan, is the largest steel mill in the country, employing some 22,000 workers. It's one of the series of mills stretching from South Chicago to Gary, including plants of U.S. Steel and Bethlehem Steel. You don't make any more money working in an Inland mill than you do at any other. They all operate under industry-wide contracts signed with the United Steelworkers of America. In 1983, the average hourly wage was $23.50, which put the steel industry 95 percent above the United States' manufacturing average. However, Inland has long been regarded as the employer of choice along the Lake Michigan waterway. While other steel companies have been closing facilities, Inland has been keeping its furnaces going. There has been no general strike in the steel industry since 1959, when all the companies were struck. However, the sign of worker dissatisfaction comes in the form of wildcat strikes. Inland Steel has not been hit by a wildcat strike since 1968.

There's upward mobility at Inland, even from plant to management ranks. About 40 percent of the company's managers have come up from noncollege, hourly ranks. Inland also maintains a tuition reimbursement program to enable employees to continue their schooling during their off-hours. The company has more University of Chicago M.B.A.'s than any other Chicago company—some 200 of them—and nine out of 10 earned their degrees by going to night school while working at Inland.

Inland Steel has also been unique in the steel industry in that it has long recruited on college campuses. It has been visiting colleges since 1938. Other steel companies have visited college campuses but none for as long as Inland. It now goes to 80 colleges every year, looking for some 200 recruits, 50 percent of whom are engineers, 25 percent business majors, 25 percent liberal arts majors. Inland is rare in the steel industry for seeking out liberal arts majors and hiring them for sales positions. Deans steer their best candidates to Inland. As a result, Inland tends to get good people, the "cream of the crop."

Inland offers a full range of benefits for its work force, including a pension plan and the ability to buy Inland's stock at a 10 percent discount. Benefits at Inland account for 40 percent of compensation. For salaried people, there is a thrift plan under which employees can salt away anywhere from 1 percent to 15 percent of their pay into tax-deferred funds. And on the first 5 percent employees elect to save, Inland matches the contribution dollar for dollar.

Main employment centers   The Indiana Harbor Works at East Chicago, Indiana, employs 19,000 people who need to work different shifts (the mill never closes down). There are also two small construction material plants in Milwaukee. Some 8,800 people make up the salaried force —5,000 so-called exempt employees (higher echelons) and 3,800 nonexempt (clerks, secretaries). Most of these work in the Chicago area. Inland's main office is in the Chicago Loop. Inland's subsidiary, Joseph T. Ryerson & Son, operates steel service sales centers across the country.

Headquarters   Inland Steel Company
30 West Monroe Street
Chicago, IL 60603
312-346-0300

INTEL CORPORATION

Intel is one of the leading developers and makers of the microelectronic products that are at the heart of the computer revolution: the microprocessor, memory chips, and computer systems. U.S. employees: 16,000.

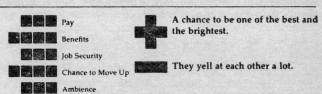

■■■ Pay	A chance to be one of the best and the brightest.
■■■■ Benefits	
■■■ Job Security	
■■■■ Chance to Move Up	They yell at each other a lot.
■■■ Ambience	

If you want to work in a tough, demanding environment where you are constantly being pushed to your limits, Intel is the place for you. In the words of its own employees, Intel is a "driven company."

One of the premier whiz outfits in California's Silicon Valley, south of San Francisco, Intel was founded in 1968 by refugees from Fairchild Camera & Instrument. They made an immediate breakthrough with a powerful memory chip and followed up quickly with another: the development of the microprocessor, which is, in effect, the brains of the computer placed on a silicon chip measuring one-eighth by one-sixth of an inch. The microprocessor has found its way into more than 100,000 products, including personal computers, automatic teller machines, and Boeing's new 767 jetliner.

Many companies make microprocessor and memory chips today. Intel ranks fourth in chip production behind Texas Instruments, National Semiconductor, and Motorola. That doesn't bother Intel—too much. What would bother Intel would be to fail to make the next breakthrough. Intel prides itself on being on the cutting edge of technology. People there are somewhat demonic in their determination to crack through frontier after frontier.

It's not just the engineers and computer scientists who are revved up at Intel. The nervous energy of the place seems to spill over into all areas, so that even someone who's turning out catalog copy is pumped up.

Intel's an intense place with few of the trappings of big business. There are no dress codes. The president of the company walks around with an open shirt showing a gold chain around his neck. You won't find any mahogany-lined offices. There's no executive dining room—everyone eats in the cafeteria. And there are no reserved parking places for the top executives. At the same time, you won't find "flex-time" or job-sharing at Intel. There are no time clocks, but you are expected to arrive at 8:00 A.M. The company wants you there, not for the bureaucratic reason of enforcing mindless discipline but because it's anxious to have all the brains present knocking heads with other brains.

In a *Harvard Business Review* interview, Dr. Robert N. Noyce, cofounder of Intel, explained: "It is another way of saying to people that they're valuable to us. How can we do our work if they're not here? Intel is the only place I've ever worked where an 8:00 A.M. meeting starts at 8:00 A.M."

So Intel is not for everyone. In general, it's for high achievers who don't mind being measured, because at Intel you are always being measured—by your peers and your managers. Asked once whether scientists objected to this handling, Noyce said no. "High achievers love to be measured, when you come down to it, because otherwise they can't prove to themselves that they are achieving."

Noyce also gave this nugget of the Intel philosophy: "We've had people come in who have never had an honest review of their work. We get senior managers who come in, and we say, 'Okay, in your six-month review, or your annual review, here are the things you did poorly, here are the things you did well.' A lot of these people have never heard that they ever did anything poorly. It's the new culture of our schools, you know, no grades. Everybody passes. We just don't believe in that."

People who come to Intel after having worked at other companies describe it as "culture shock," which is an apt term because employees at Intel have an opportunity to attend classes in "Intel Culture." One course is designed to instruct employees on how to get the most out of meetings. There are a lot of meetings at Intel, but they are not supposed to be time-wasters. It's a place where "constructive confrontation" takes place, where arguing and fighting are encouraged—and it's entirely appropriate at Intel for lower-level people to challenge top-management executives. Here are snippets of our interviews with Intel employees:

"Seniority has no place at Intel."

"It's all right to make a mistake here but you're in trouble if you make the same mistake twice."

"The worst thing you can do around here is hide a problem."

"You have to know how to take flak from your peers."

"No one tells you how to do your job."

"You can't survive here if you sit around like a wallflower. After a year or so you'll just be swept out."

"What's important at Intel is your contribution to the working group."

"It's the kind of company where you go out after work and find yourself talking about work."

Given this kind of intensity, you might expect turnover to be high—surprisingly, it's not. Intel's annual turnover rate, about 10 percent, is one-half the industry average. However, that doesn't mean Intel hasn't lost bright people who start their own companies—that's an old Silicon Valley pattern. And some have left because they didn't like working in a pressure cooker. *Fortune* once found a former Intel executive who reported that the management reviews there (and everyone has to submit to these) are "run with an unsparing search for truth that bruises the performer with verbal brutality, even ridicule, not out of sadism but to test his case." This former executive added the comment: "There are no sissies at Intel."

An Intel manager, David House, who runs the company's microcomputer group, describes the Intel style as one of "snake-biting," meaning that Intel people constantly look for "snakes" or problems to solve. "When a good, solid problem is discovered," said House, "we study the daylights out of it. How big is it? What color is it? How much does it weigh? Everybody studies, looks, jabbers about the problem and admires it, like putting it on a pedestal. Finally somebody breaks the code, grabs it and stomps it to death. Everybody cheers."

In 1983, Andrew Grove, the feisty president of Intel, told *Wall Street Journal* reporter Marilyn Chase: "Sure, we expect a great deal of people. But if you're competitive, a tough race is a turn-on; an easy race is a bore. And by any standards, we're in a tough race."

It's not everybody's ideal working environment, but those who remain at Intel appear to love it. And they come right out and say it. Melissa Rey, who does advertising and public relations for Intel, gushes, "I love my job." Intel has an above-average wage-and-benefits package. It's not at the very top of the scale, but it does have some unusual features, including a sabbatical program and stock options for 60 percent of the professionals or a total of 5,000 people. But pay and benefits are not the prime motivators for Intel people. They are there for other reasons. For one thing, to get ahead: in a typical year 30 percent of the people at Intel are promoted.

The company has rewarded employees during hard times. Toward the end of 1982, the economic recession brought industry-wide price-cutting and sharp declines in profits. Intel chose not to lay off people. Instead, it put into effect salary cuts that were graduated by income. If you were earning as little as $750 a month, you didn't have to take any cuts; the deepest cut, 10 percent, was taken by employees making more than $2,750 a month. A year later, after sales and profits were on the upswing, Intel rewarded its people by rescinding the pay cuts and giving bonuses of two weeks' pay to employees on the payroll before January 1982 and one week's pay to those hired in 1982.

Intel introduced a sabbatical program in 1981. If you work at Intel for seven years, you are then eligible for eight weeks off, with full pay, on top of your regular three-week vacation. You may also, at that time, apply for six months off, with pay, for public service, teaching, or exceptional educational opportunities. Intel was a little worried that many employees might take their sabbaticals and not return. In the first year 302 employees took sabbaticals. Six did not return.

They're a masochistic bunch.

Because it has been such a successful company, Intel has become a bigger and bigger employer. In 1972, it had a payroll of 1,000 persons. Today, it's up to 26,000. Intel has a very young staff. The average age of the top officers of the company is a little over 40. The company has been recruiting heavily on campuses. It hired 1,000 college graduates in 1983: electrical engineers, computer scientists, physicists, chemists, business administration majors.

It looks for people who want to "work smart." There's always this monkey on its back. As Noyce says, "There is no resting on your laurels, because you will get wiped out next year if you sit back."

A company with quite different style, IBM is both Intel's largest customer and largest stockholder. IBM bought into Intel in 1983, acquiring 15 percent of the company's stock—quite a testimony to Intel, where only 10 percent of the work force wears neckties.

Main employment centers   San Francisco Bay Area, 6,500; Portland, Oregon, 4,000; Phoenix, 3,000; Albuquerque, 800. Another 10,000 work overseas.

Headquarters   Intel Corporation
3065 Bowers Avenue
Santa Clara, CA 95051
408-987-8080

INTERNATIONAL BUSINESS MACHINES CORPORATION

IBM is the world's largest computer and office equipment company. U.S. employees: 220,000.

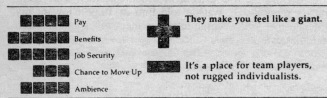

- Pay
- Benefits
- Job Security
- Chance to Move Up
- Ambience

They make you feel like a giant.

It's a place for team players, not rugged individualists.

If you work for IBM, you're working for a company that makes more profit after taxes than any other company in the world. You're also working for the company that's the acknowledged leader of the industry of the future. That IBMers wear these "titles" with a minimum of arrogance reflects an extraordinary culture that goes back to the company's founder.

Thomas J. Watson created an environment where employees could take pride in their work and thereby identify their interests with IBM's. Some ways in which he accomplished this feat were recalled recently by Peter Drucker in a profile of Watson in *Esquire*. Watson, he pointed out, started job enrichment in the 1920s. In the 1930s he invented what the Japanese later came to call "quality circles." Watson, 50 years ago, abolished the position of foreman. Supervisors became "managers"; and their function was "to make sure that workers had the tools and information they needed, and to help them when they found themselves in trouble." Watson blurred the distinction between blue collar and white collar. He had the idea, as Drucker put it, "that the individual worker should have the biggest job possible rather than the smallest one." In 1958, IBM abolished hourly wages, putting everyone on a salary.

Needless to say, IBM has never been unionized. And no

194

one can recall IBMers walking off their jobs in protest. Why should they when the company virtually guarantees lifetime employment, another concept mistakenly credited to the Japanese? Watson laid down his "no layoff" policy in the darkest days of the depression.

Perhaps his most signal achievement was to foster at IBM a culture in which people felt good about what they were doing. It was tantamount to empowering workers. Watson was particularly intent, Drucker recalls, in building this confidence in salespersons because he himself had been a "drummer" and suffered from the low esteem in which salesmen were held. Drucker reports that Watson told him in 1939, "I want my IBM salesmen to be people to whom their wives and children can look up. I don't want their mothers to feel that they have to apologize for them or have to dissimulate when they are asked what their son is doing." Drucker added that he had the feeling then that Watson was talking about his own mother. Watson ran IBM from 1914 to 1956, when the reins were taken by his son, Thomas J. Watson, Jr., who retired as chief executive officer in 1971. The younger Watson, who served on the IBM board of directors until April 1984, once said: "Our early emphasis on human relations was not motivated by altruism but by the simple belief that if we respected our people and helped them respect themselves the company would make the most profit."

Regardless of the motivation, few companies of any size can match IBM's benefits. They include high wages, generous pension, health, and dental insurance for employees and their families, health classes and physical examinations, a wide range of employee assistance programs, adoption assistance (up to $1,000), and recreation facilities at most major IBM locations including IBM country clubs at Poughkeepsie, Sands Point, and Endicott, New York, which employees can join for $5 a year.

IBM has never laid off anyone for economic reasons. The closest it came to such a move was during the recessions of 1974–75 and 1981–82, when IBM encouraged people to accept early retirement.

Employees get more than benefits and job security from IBM. The company instills a distinct set of beliefs. The Watsons preached that the company was based on three "cornerstones":

1. *Respect for the individual*. Caring about the dignity and rights of each person in the organization, and not just when it is convenient or expedient to do so.

2. *Customer service*. Giving the best customer service of any company in the world. Not some of the time, but all of the time.

3. *Excellence*. Believing that all jobs and projects should be performed in a superior way.

IBM, more than any other big company, has institutionalized its beliefs the way a church does. They are expounded in numerous IBM internal publications to ensure that employees know what's expected of them. And they are reflected in codes of behavior, still in force even though the Watsons are no longer around. The Watsons insisted that salespersons wear dark business suits and white shirts; that's no longer a strict regulation but most IBM salesmen continue to dress that way. The Watsons wouldn't permit drinking, on or off the job; today IBM policy prohibits the serving of alcoholic beverages on company premises or as part of meetings held to conduct company business.

Everyone at IBM is appraised at least once a year. Working with your manager, you develop a Performance Plan for the year, which sets goals. You're reviewed in 12 months to see how you have met those goals. People who sell IBM equipment have quotas—and they are held to them. If a customer returns an IBM machine that he bought, IBM forces the salesperson who sold the equipment to return the commission. IBM maintains a "100 Percent Club" for people who meet or exceed sales quotas. If you want to get ahead, you'd better be a member.

The result is a company filled with ardent believers. (If you're not ardent, you may not be comfortable.) Susan Chace, a perceptive reporter for the *Wall Street Journal*, profiled IBM in 1982, concluding that the IBM culture "is so pervasive that, as one nine-year (former) employee put it, 'leaving the company was like emigrating.'"

Indeed, IBM is a world unto itself. One of the 10 largest industrial corporations in America, with a work force exceeded by only three other firms (GM, Ford, and GE), IBM has employees in almost every city of any size and in lots of smaller ones. The company has long had a reputation for transferring its people around. A longstanding joke among employees is that their company's initials really stand for "I've Been Moved."

The transferring has decreased somewhat in recent years, for a variety of reasons: there are more dual-career families, IBM itself is more decentralized than before, and relocation costs are high. The company currently relocates 3 percent of its employees a year, down from 5 percent 10 years ago. And there is now a guideline which specifies that employees will not be transferred more than once in two years or more than three times in 10 years. Still, with 3 percent transferred every year, 6,000 IBMers in the United States pack their bags annually.

IBM maintains a company-wide open-door policy. And managers are expected to treat employees fairly. "The easiest way to get fired around here is for a supervisor to be capricious or unfair in dealing with subordinates," Edward Krieg, director of management development, told us during our visit to the corporate headquarters in Armonk, New York, a suburb of New York City. If you're not satisfied with your treatment, you have the right, as an IBMer, to appeal all the way up to the head of the company, including a personal interview with the chairman if that is "appropriate."

Those who don't abide by "Business Conduct Guidelines," a 30-page code of business ethics, don't last long. "If anybody does anything that's the least bit shady, the heavens descend on them from their supervisors on down," Krieg explained. "People see we have a basic set of beliefs and we adhere to them."

IBM expects its people to spend their careers with the company. According to Krieg, IBM is looking for "people with a very positive self-image, who are willing to have their talents tested. People who can enjoy collegiality of interests with others. People who are stimulated by their peers." He claimed that though the company is "competitive, it is not dog-eat-dog."

Like any good church, IBM has powerful training programs. Its management development program began in 1956 when the younger Watson told one of his managers, Tom Clemmons: "Our business is outrunning our supply of top managers, and I want you to solve the problem. There'll be enough money to do it right. You will report directly to me."

Classes began the following year at the Sleepy Hollow Country Club near Tarrytown, New York; two years later they shifted to the 205-acre Solomon Guggenheim estate at Sands Point, New York. They were taught by some of the most distinguished teachers in the academic world; IBM spared no expense in the education of its own people. It still doesn't. It invests $500 million a year on employee education and training. Management training is now conducted at a spectacular Management Development Center that was completed in 1979. It sits on 26 acres of the corporate headquarters site at Armonk. Designed by Eliot Noyes Associates, the center, in IBM's own words, "might pass for a monastic retreat—until you find yourself in its busy classrooms. Despite all the natural scenic competition, fieldstone commands the site. Some 6,700 tons of it were hauled in from abandoned stone walls of the farmsteads that once dotted the surrounding countryside."

Secrecy is one of IBM's hallmarks. It spends great amounts of money making sure its research is kept from potential competitors, and it vigorously sues any ex-IBMer it suspects of having betrayed one of its processes. Partly because of this obsession, many have remarked that there's something terribly in-groupish about IBMers. IBMers tend to socialize with each other rather than with outsiders. Because of these tendencies, some have compared joining IBM with joining a religious order or going into the military. (One long-time IBM watcher told *Time*, "If you understand the Marines, you can understand IBM.") You must be willing to give up some of your individual identity to survive. On the other hand, because of its position in the industry, IBM is a great source of information. It answers 35,000 press inquiries annually.

Of the 220,000 IBMers in the United States, some 19,000 are black. And a minority of these black employees (less than 10 percent) belong to an IBM Black Workers Alliance. *Black Enterprise*, a magazine reaching black managers in business, reported in 1983 on a case involving Richard Hudson, a leader in the black group at IBM and a veteran of 17 years with the company. Hudson was fired by IBM after he distributed a confidential IBM document on wage guidelines in an effort to determine whether the company was discriminating against black employees. Hudson appealed his dismissal to the National Labor Relations Board, which sided

Climbing the Ladder at IBM

John F. Akers was designated chief executive officer of IBM in September 1984. *Forbes* charted his 24-year progress in the company as follows:

July 1960: Hired as sales trainee, salary $6,500.

February 1962: Marketing representative, $15,000.

April 1967: Marketing manager, $40,000.

July 1968: Assistant district manager, $45,000.

May 1969: Branch manager, $60,000.

March 1971: Administrative assistant to the president, $55,000.

April 1972: Director of distribution/media industries data processing division, $65,000.

January 1973: Vice-president and regional manager, data processing division, western region, $75,000.

April 1974: President of data processing division, $150,000.

July 1976: Vice-president of the corporation, $200,000.

August 1976: Vice-president and assistant group executive/plans and controls, data processing product group, $200,000.

April 1978: Vice-president and group executive, data processing marketing group, $250,000.

October 1981: Vice-president and group executive, information systems and communications group, $335,000.

May 1982: Senior vice-president and group executive, information systems and communication group, $375,000.

February 1983: President and director, $600,311.

September 1984: Named chief executive officer, effective February 1, 1985, $750,000.

---

with the company in a 2-to-1 decision (Howard Jenkins, the only black on the board, dissented). The NLRB majority decision conceded that "by denying the very information needed to discuss wages, a company like IBM muzzles employees who seek to engage in concerted activity for mutual aid or protection." But it concluded that IBM's "legitimate" business need for secrecy in these matters outweighed the workers' right to know. In another discrimination case brought by the Equal Employment Opportunity Commission on behalf of black professionals and managers at IBM's data processing facilities in Maryland, federal Judge Norman P. Ramsey ruled in 1984 in favor of IBM, declaring that the company had in place a nondiscriminatory system that "is the standard for its industry and for private business nationwide."

Main employment centers   IBM has large concentrations of employees throughout the United States, with the largest single concentrations in New York State (65,000), followed by California (18,000), Texas (13,000), and Florida (9,000). Another 135,000 work overseas.

Headquarters   International Business Machines Corporation
Armonk, NY 10504
914-765-1900

THE BEST EMPLOYEE PARTIES

| Advanced Micro Devices | Apple Computer Leo Burnett Hewlett-Packard | Odetics Tandem Computers Time Inc. |

Johnson & Johnson

JOHNSON & JOHNSON

Johnson & Johnson is the largest health-care company in the United States. U.S. employees: 35,000.

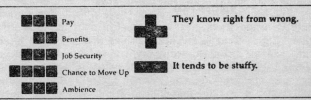

Pay	
Benefits	
Job Security	
Chance to Move Up	
Ambience	

They know right from wrong.

It tends to be stuffy.

People who join J&J find themselves working for a conservative company but one with a strong concern for its employees and the communities where they live. The company's decision to keep its headquarters in New Brunswick, New Jersey, rather than move to a sterile suburban location—a decision made in 1978 when it approved plans for a new $50 million headquarters complex—was the catalyst in a redevelopment program that is bringing life back to a city that lost much of its population and business after World War II.

Johnson & Johnson was founded in New Brunswick in 1886. The deterioration of the city, home of Rutgers University, was reflected in a grim set of statistics. In 1943, the city collected $1.8 million in taxes from the central business district; in 1976, only $300,000 was collected from the same area. It was an erosion suffered by many urban centers across the country as people fled to the suburbs. J&J chose to remain and fight. It was a turning point in the revitalization of New Brunswick. J&J's new I. M. Pei-designed headquarters opened in the spring of 1983.

So J&J is a company that cares. What else would you expect from the maker of Band-Aids? At the same time, it's not a company of backslappers. They take themselves rather seriously at J&J—and it's a more formal place than ones you will find in, say, the "high-tech" field.

It doesn't pay the top money in its industry, nor does it have the best benefits package. But you are always conscious, when you are working at J&J, that it has high standards and will not compromise its principles, which are expressed in a document called "Our Credo." J&J sets great store by this credo. Prospective employees are told about it. A copy is given to all new recruits. And it is an unusual document in that it puts in last place responsibility to "our stockholders"—after employees and customers. Many other companies, where stockholders always come first, would consider this rank heresy.

The credo served the company well in the Tylenol crisis in 1982, when seven persons in the Chicago area died after taking Extra-Strength Tylenol capsules that had been laced with cyanide. J&J acted decisively, without regard to cost, in pulling back from the shelves of every store in the country all packages of Extra-Strength Tylenol capsules. J&J did this even though it was sure that the tampering did not originate in its factories. It never hesitated for a second—and its actions were universally applauded.

The way J&J emerged from this crisis is indicative of its reputation among consumers. Many wiseacres on Madison Avenue predicted flatly that the Tylenol brand was finished, and they recommended that J&J reintroduce the same product under a different name. J&J rejected that advice, packed Tylenol in tamper-resistant packages, and in a matter of months was well on its way to recapturing the dominant share of the analgesic market.

It's a comeback that says something about the way J&J is regarded. James Burke, chairman of J&J, told us shortly after the incident that he believes that those companies that do well in the marketplace have in common a strong ethical code of conduct. When we mentioned some companies that appear to be successful sans ethical code, he said, "Well, a couple of exceptions might prove the rule. And aside from that, I believe their lack of ethics will eventually catch up to them."

Burke disclosed in a 1981 *Fortune* interview what J&J's special character is. The company had brought out a cold remedy for children, Arrestin, which failed miserably. Here's Burke's explanation for the failure: "Johnson & Johnson stands for gentleness. When the baby is sick, a mother wants something strong, and Johnson & Johnson doesn't say strong."

So if you're looking for a gentle company, here it is. It is, in fact, a gentle giant, with annual sales of more than $5 billion. One way it tries to overcome the disadvantages of its large size is by decentralization. The J&J family comprises 160 different companies—and each runs on its own head of steam. This self-determination is reflected in the fact that each of these companies has its own board of directors that sets policy, makes plans, and checks on performance. There's probably not another company in the United States organized in this fashion; the result is that an employee can still have the feeling of working in a small company rather than one that is, in fact, one of the largest corporations in the nation. The largest Johnson & Johnson company, J&J Products, has 6,300 employees; the smallest, Technicare in Belgium, has 7 employees. Measured by the number of people on its payroll, J&J would rank as the fifty-first-largest company in the United States. Its employee population has nearly doubled in the past decade. One advantage of this decentralization is more rapid advancement. Surveys taken by J&J indicate that its people are promoted "about three and a half years sooner than at companies we measure ourselves against."

J&J plants, some organized by the Amalgamated Textile Workers, can be found in more than a dozen states, but two-thirds of its 35,000 U.S. employees work in New Jersey. Nearly half the total work force is female, and women hold 11.5 percent of the management positions in the company. J&J is one of the few big companies whose board of directors includes two women. Minority-group members make up 20.4 percent of the J&J work force and they held 9.4 percent of the management positions in 1983.

J&J employees are covered by both medical and dental insurance—and you can insure your spouse and children for a modest cost: $7 a month if your earnings are under $10,000 a year, $9 a month if they are over $15,000. The coverage pays for 70 percent of psychiatric care—up to 52 visits a year. However, J&J does not offer a profit-sharing plan, and it wasn't until 1982 that it adopted a savings plan open to all salaried people and most hourly employees. The plan enables employees to save up to 6 percent of their pay, with the company matching every dollar with 50 cents of its own.

Johnson & Johnson's "Live for Life" program is one of the best employee health plans in American business. Em-

Our Credo

We believe our first responsibility is to the doctors, nurses and patients, to mothers and all others who use our products and services. In meeting their needs everything we do must be of high quality. We must constantly strive to reduce our costs in order to maintain reasonable prices. Customers' orders must be serviced promptly and accurately. Our suppliers and distributors must have an opportunity to make a fair profit.

We are responsible to our employees, the men and women who work with us throughout the world. Everyone must be considered as an individual. We must respect their dignity and recognize their merit. They must have a sense of security in their jobs. Compensation must be fair and adequate, and working conditions clean, orderly and safe. Employees must feel free to make suggestions and complaints. There must be equal opportunity for employment, development and advancement for those qualified. We must provide competent management, and their actions must be just and ethical.

We are responsible to the communities in which we live and work and to the world community as well. We must be good citizens —support good works and charities and bear our fair share of taxes. We must encourage civic improvements and better health and education. We must maintain in good order the property we are privileged to use, protecting the environment and natural resources.

Our final responsibility is to our stockholders. Business must make a sound profit. We must experiment with new ideas. Research must be carried on, innovative programs developed and mistakes paid for. New equipment must be purchased, new facilities provided and new products launched. Reserves must be created to provide for adverse times. When we operate according to these principles, the stockholders should realize a fair return.

ployees have available to them a large fitness center where they can work out—but it's much more than that. It's a comprehensive program in which enrollees undergo a physical examination at the start and then have professionals guide them in a physical fitness regimen, whether the goal is losing weight, building up muscles, or engaging in other supervised activities to improve their health. It includes such areas as eating the right foods and cutting out dangerous habits such as smoking. When the program began at McNeil Labs, 30 percent of the staff smoked; now less than 20 percent do. Many companies install fancy gymnasiums at the headquarters location—and forget about the rest of the company. At J&J, toward the end of 1984, "Live for Life" programs were operating at 42 separate locations of 16 J&J companies.

Main employment centers   New Brunswick, 12,000; Philadelphia, 3,000; Cleveland, 2,000; Of J&J's 75,000 employees, more than half work overseas.

Headquarters   Johnson & Johnson Products
One Johnson & Johnson Plaza
New Brunswick, NJ 08933
201-524-0400

S. C. JOHNSON & SON, INC.

A leading maker of household products. U.S. employees: 3,500.

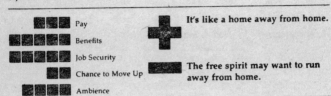

Pay	It's like a home away from home.
Benefits	
Job Security	
Chance to Move Up	The free spirit may want to run away from home.
Ambience	

Bernice Adams, a black woman born and raised in Arkansas, moved with her family to Racine, Wisconsin, in 1963. Asking neighbors and friends about likely places to get a job, she found that the unanimous choice for the best place to work in Racine was Johnson Wax. So she applied—and kept on applying. It took her 15 years before she was finally hired in 1978. Now she works the overnight shift at Waxdale, the company's production facility.

Was it worth the wait? (She did work, in the interim, at a government agency.) She certainly thinks so. She describes Johnson Wax as the kind of place where "you're allowed to give your opinion." Bernice Adams—and just about everyone else in Racine—gives high marks to S. C. Johnson, a company unique in American industry.

It's one of the last of the big privately owned companies in the country. It's still headed by a direct descendant of the founder. And it takes care of its people—all of them, wherever they are—in a close, familial way. Paternalistic? Yes. But when we put this question to one Johnson employee, he said, "If this is paternalism, I love it."

Once you're hired at Johnson, it's for life. You can be dismissed, of course, for poor performance. And the company may ask employees to pull in their belts during hard times—in 1982, for example, a wage freeze was in effect. But you know your job is secure. Johnson Wax has never had a layoff. After all, you don't throw anybody out of your family.

To be able to do that, you have to be successful at what you do. And Johnson Wax is. Since the company is private, financial figures need not be disclosed. But Johnson people don't argue with estimates placing sales volume at more than $2 billion a year, which would rank the company among the 200 largest industrial manufacturers in the nation.

Originally a parquet floor manufacturer (the company was founded in 1886), it made an easy transition to floor wax and then to furniture polish (Pledge, Jubilee) and from there to a host of other household and personal care products, including Raid insecticides, Off! insect repellent, Edge shaving gel, Glade air freshener, Agree shampoo, Shout soil and stain remover, Big Wally foam cleaner, and Soft Sense skin lotion, among others.

Many big companies that outgrow their original missions in life become uncomfortable with their original names and search for nondescript identity umbrellas: ITT, TRW, United Technologies, IC Industries. But the people here seem quite comfortable with the old "Johnson Wax" identity. Although the company is incorporated as S. C. Johnson & Son (S. C. Johnson stands for the founder, Samuel C. Johnson), Johnson Wax appears on all the company's printed materials, and the switchboard operators answer incoming calls with "Johnson Wax." It's like an old shoe that you become attached to. The weekly company paper is always running snippets of nostalgia such as: "Do you remember when the Johnson's Wax men's glee club took first place in the Chicago competition?" Answer: 1950.

The visibility of Johnson management is an important plus for many people here. Richard Chay, marketing research director, previously worked at the Shulton toiletries company, which is not as large as S. C. Johnson, and he says that while he sees the top people all the time in Racine, at Shulton he was "seven layers removed" from the top—and he rarely, if ever, saw the leaders. Not so at Johnson. Every summer there's a picnic at which Chairman Samuel C. Johnson (great-grandson of the founder) and his family greet the employees and their families. Every 18 months the top managers, including Sam Johnson, meet with all employees for a face-to-face question-and-answer session. You get the feeling that this is a company that wants its employees to know what's going on. There's probably more communication here than in most publicly owned companies.

Johnson pays its people well—the average factory wage in 1983 was $12 an hour—and has a benefits program difficult to match. Some of the benefits flow from an employee-directed organization, the Johnson Mutual Benefit Association (JMBA), which was formed in 1922. The JMBA administers the recreation programs and provides various other benefits, including the prescription-drug program.

Employees are wrapped in various security blankets. For example, flash your JMBA card at a local pharmacy and any prescription will be filled for $1.50. The company pays the entire cost of your medical and dental premiums. It recently adopted a new flexible health plan that deposits $300 in your account at the beginning of the year, these funds to be used to pay charges not covered; any money left over at the end of the year is paid to you in cash. (This is an incentive for staying healthy.)

Jim Piper, an engineer at Johnson Wax, died of cancer at age 40 in 1979. He left a wife and three children. The death benefits were significant, encompassing the following: separation pay based on 14 years' service, profit-sharing cash payouts, basic life insurance at 125 percent of Jim's salary, supplemental life insurance of three times his salary, return of contributions to a deferred profit-sharing plan plus interest— and, important for his widow and children, continuation of medical, vision, prescription-drug, and dental insurance.

The recreational facilities available to Johnson people are centered in Armstrong Park, a 147-acre park six miles from corporate headquarters in Racine. The park is open only to Johnson families. It has softball fields, tennis courts, jogging trails, golf driving ranges, picnic areas, and a new recreation center building that's wondrous to behold if you are athletically minded. This 50,000-square-foot building, completed in 1979, is a multipurpose facility that houses a gymnasium big enough to hold two full basketball courts and four volleyball courts, racquetball and squash courts, an archery shooting room, a fully equipped exercise room, and various other rooms that can be used for both social and business meetings.

Beyond Racine, there are resorts made available to Johnson employees. For 32 years, the company has maintained the

Lighthouse Resort in Northern Wisconsin as a vacation place for Johnson families. It has 17 units for rent by the week. In 1983, a three-bedroom cottage was being rented for $85 a week. In addition, the company has now set aside resort facilities in eight different parts of the country to serve Johnson people who are not based in Racine. They range from Cape Cod to Lake Tahoe.

But insurance and family resorts are not the only ways the company shows employees it cares. It has had a profit-sharing plan since 1917. Today, it maintains both a cash profit-sharing plan and a deferred profit-sharing program. Roger Mulhollen, vice-president of corporate personnel, explained in 1980 what this means to individual employees: "In the United States, a typical Johnson factory employee will receive the equivalent in profit-sharing payments of about six weeks of base pay this year. This payout is based on the previous fiscal year's results and is divided into two payments—June and December. Employees of overseas Johnson companies could receive about the same amount. However, in a very few Johnson companies overseas, which have had exceptional profit years, long-service office and factory employees will get profit-sharing equal to as much as twenty weeks' base pay."

Johnson Wax, it should be noted here, is one of the few companies to export its profit-sharing plan. All of its companies overseas have such plans, which is rarely the case with other multinationals. And it's a significant export. Johnson does 60 percent of its business outside the United States.

Johnson also exports the idea of having its employees surrounded by comfortable, striking facilities. Its buildings overseas tend to be attractive places, as do the offices and factories at headquarters in Racine. Three of the buildings at Racine are registered as historic landmarks. The main office was designed by Frank Lloyd Wright and went up in 1939. An open structure with no partitions locking people into cubicles, it looks as if it were built yesterday.

A spectacular example of how Johnson considers all its employees—everywhere in the world—part of one family occurred in 1984 after Samuel Johnson attended the profit-sharing meeting at the company's British plant at Frimley Green, 40 miles outside of London. Chatting with employees, he found some of them concerned about their future and wondering how they fit into this big American company. It happened that 1984 was the 70th anniversary of the British subsidiary (it was the company's first overseas unit), and so Samuel Johnson hit upon a happy way to mark it. He closed the plant for a week, chartered a Boeing 747 jet, and flew the entire British work force—480 people—to the United States. They went first to Racine, where they were put up in hotels, toured the company's facilities, shopped, and were feted at a company banquet. On one night employees in Racine picked up the British guests and brought them to their homes for dinner. Before flying back to Britain, the Johnson employees spent two days in New York City sightseeing. The company staked all of them to dinner at the World Trade Center.

You could catch the flavor of S.C.Johnson best if you were able to sneak into the annual profit-sharing meeting and party held at the recreation center just before Christmas. Just about all the employees in Racine attend. Samuel Johnson presides and delivers a message that is extremely personal in nature. Here are excerpts from the 1982 address:

"This is a season when families do get together and our family is beginning to assemble. Gene [his wife] is here today with her Uncle Ed Powers and Aunt Vickie and a brace of cousins. A few weeks ago I was with our grandson, Odinn Johnson, and I was quizzing him a little about Christmas. I asked, 'What did the three men bring as presents to the young Jesus?' He thought for a minute and said, 'Gold, Frankenstein, and mermaids.'

"Speaking of the future, you might wonder what the next generation of Johnsons is doing. Starting with the youngest, Win just got married to a musician and she is the business manager of the band. . . .

"Helen, who still works with Foote, Cone & Belding in Chicago, has been promoted to account executive on Peter Pan peanut butter, and you can imagine what kind of peanut butter we eat around the house.

"Curt, our oldest, is finishing his master's in business administration at Northwestern University. When a next generation of the family joins the company, you will be the first to hear about it. I hope it will not be in the too distant future. . . ."

And that's before some 2,000 assembled people—all part of the family.

Main employment centers   Racine, on the shores of Lake Michigan, where 2,500 people work. Another 1,000 work in U.S. field offices. Eighty-five hundred work overseas.

Headquarters   S.C. Johnson & Son, Inc.
1525 Howe Street
Racine, WI 53403
414-631-2000

SCANLON (SHARE THE WEALTH) PLAN COMPANIES

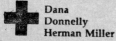
Dana
Donnelly
Herman Miller

KNIGHT-RIDDER NEWSPAPERS, INC.

Knight-Ridder delivers more newspapers to the homes of America than anybody else. Employees: 22,000.

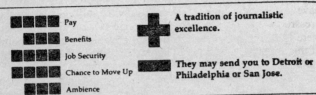

Every Christmas Eve when he was general manager of the *Miami Herald*, Alvah Chapman used to go to the pressroom and visit with the troops as they brought out the Christmas edition. "You have to believe that people are important to get out of the sack at two or three in the morning," Chapman told us when thinking back on the tradition.

Chapman went on to become the president of Knight-Ridder Newspapers, one of the largest newspaper chains in the country (29 dailies). There he has promulgated what he calls "visible management"—sort of an extension of his Christmas Eve expeditions. All Knight-Ridder publications now have what are called "management coffee breaks" with the publisher. Each publisher regularly meets with groups of 20 to 25 rank-and-file employees for an hour and a half over coffee. Employees can send in questions in advance. ("Some are real zingers," says Chapman.) And the only ground rule during the meeting is that personalities of specific supervisors cannot be discussed.

Another element of Knight-Ridder's visible management is the year-end management meeting. A large hall is rented so that the entire staff of the publication can attend. Management spells out what has happened during the year and tries to answer any questions presented from the floor.

"If we are a good place to work, and I hope we are, it's because we select good people and share the maximum amount of information with them," explained Chapman.

Many journalists consider Knight-Ridder to be the premier place to work in a field with few desirable workplaces. Knight-Ridder has cultivated a human touch in its managers. Part of this character can be traced to Byron Harless, an industrial psychologist and Chapman's personnel troubleshooter since 1970. When labor problems have developed at local papers, Harless has moved there and spent months getting to know the people and listening to their problems. He claims to have spent every night for several months during 1980 in the pressroom of the *Detroit Free Press*, where the pressmen were breaking in a new $50 million printing plant. The point of this exercise was to get to appreciate the problems faced by the pressroom force.

One place where managers learn the company's approach is the Knight-Ridder Training Institute. Every year several hundred Knight-Ridder managers or trainees come to Miami to take seminars and courses. Knight-Ridder is the only newspaper chain with such a program.

The chain has developed such a good reputation for training good managers that when other publishers seek to fill high-level jobs, Knight-Ridder people are often at the top of the list. For an opening as the publisher of a daily newspaper in Texas, seven of the 10 final candidates were from Knight-Ridder. None of the Knight-Ridder candidates accepted the job. The chain is proud of holding its people. Some Knight-Ridder executives have gone on to other positions, though. Most notable of the defectors was Al Neuharth, president of the competing Gannett newspaper chain. Another former Knight-Ridder official was Derick Daniels, the former president of Playboy Enterprises.

The papers are fiercely independent when it comes to editorial policy, and the small corporate office in Miami makes no attempt to dictate in that area. But the chain has a tradition of journalistic excellence, having won 28 Pulitzer prizes—more than any other newspaper organization except for the *New York Times*. In 1982, both the *Miami Herald* and the *Fort Wayne News-Sentinel* won the prestigious award. For the chain's flagship Miami paper, it was the third Pulitzer in four years.

The *Herald* typifies the teamwork, even family spirit, that Knight-Ridder executives try to foster in their other publications. Its new editor in 1983 was Heath Meriwether, who at 41 was one of the youngest editors of a metropolitan daily in the country. It's a Knight-Ridder tradition to take a chance on young people. Meriwether is homegrown, having started as a reporter for the paper.

The *Herald* is different from most of the other major Knight-Ridder newspapers in that it is nonunion. (Sixty percent of the chain's work force belong to unions.) From the employee cafeteria in downtown Miami, people have a spectacular view of Biscayne Bay and Miami Beach. Many of the people who work on the paper are related. Dick Capen, the *Herald's* publisher, says, "There are lots of children, nieces, and nephews working here. The manager of our Palm Beach edition had a grandfather and father who were with the *Herald*."

When Capen came to the Knight-Ridder organization several years ago from the Copley newspapers in California, he was amazed at "how there is absolutely no politics or backbiting in Knight-Ridder newspapers." This unusual behavior appears to be a tradition that goes back to how the Knight brothers ran their organization before their merger with the Ridders in 1974. After the two combined, Chapman says, "we worked hard to keep politics out of Knight-Ridder. We decided to avoid creating a situation that made people be identified as a Knight man or as a Ridder man. We wanted them to be Knight-Ridder men."

Main employment centers   Twelve hundred work for one of the chain's six largest newspapers: *Philadelphia Inquirer* and *Philadelphia Daily News*; *Miami Herald*; *Detroit Free Press*; *San Jose Mercury and News*; or *Charlotte Observer and News*. The chain also owns the *Aberdeen American News*, *Akron Beacon Journal*, *Boca Raton News*, *Boulder Daily Camera*, *Bradenton Herald*, *Columbus Ledger*, *Columbus Enquirer*, *Duluth News-Tribune & Herald*, *Fort Wayne News-Sentinel*, *Gary Post-Tribune*, *Grand Forks Herald*, *Lexington Herald-Leader*, *Journal of Commerce*, *Long Beach Press-Telegram*, *Macon Telegraph and News*, *Milledgeville Union-Recorder*, *Pasadena Star-News*, *St. Paul Pioneer & Dispatch*, *State College Centre Daily Times*, *Tallahassee Democrat*, and *Wichita Eagle-Beacon*. In addition, Knight-Ridder owns five TV stations, the largest of which, WKRN-TV in Nashville has 120 employees.

Headquarters   Knight-Ridder Newspapers, Inc.
One Herald Plaza
Miami, FL 33101
305-350-2650

KOLLMORGEN

KOLLMORGEN CORPORATION

Kollmorgen makes sophisticated electro-optical instruments, electric motors and controls, and printed electronic circuit boards. U.S. employees: 5,000.

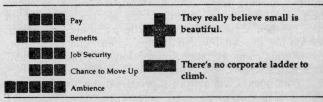

■■■ Pay	✚ They really believe small is beautiful.
■■■ Benefits	
■■■ Job Security	
■■■ Chance to Move Up	■■ There's no corporate ladder to climb.
■■■■ Ambience	

Robert Swiggett makes one of the most unusual commutes in New York. His two commuting partners meet in the morning at a beach club in suburban Huntington, on Long Island's north shore. They walk down to the dock to board Swiggett's 29-foot power boat. Their destination: Kollmorgen's corporate headquarters in Stamford, Connecticut, a 45-minute voyage across Long Island Sound.

When they arrive, the three men walk across a lawn, up a flight of stairs of an unpretentious two-story building, and into a large room. Only six other people, including two secretaries, share the room. Their desks are arranged in a semicircle around a common conference area with one table and several chairs. Kollmorgen is a high-tech conglomerate, with 16 different divisions and subsidiaries throughout the United States and Europe, 1983 sales of a quarter of a billion dollars, and 4,500 employees. Yet that one large room constitutes the entirety of Kollmorgen's home office.

Kollmorgen doesn't just say it is decentralized. It calls its organization "productized." Each of the company's products —which range from submarine periscopes and photographic light meters to industrial high-torque motors and computer circuit boards—has its own product manager. The manager has almost total control over the making and selling of that item. If the product makes a profit (defined in terms of pretax

215

return on net assets, or RONA), everybody who worked on that product gets a bonus. Kollmorgen's policy is to pay out up to 33 percent of its pretax profits in bonuses. In a good year Kollmorgen employees can receive bonuses of from 25 percent to 50 percent of their base salary. When business is off for that product, no bonuses.

Kollmorgen believes that "Small is Beautiful." Whenever one of its divisions becomes so successful that it has more than a couple of hundred employees, it usually splits into two or more new divisions. Those who had helped build the former division are given "second paychecks" to reward them for their success. "Since we believe that divisions which get too big lose vitality, family atmosphere, and easy, informal internal communication, we recently split two large divisions into six new ones," Swiggett once explained.

What makes Kollmorgen especially distinctive is the autonomy of new divisions. Many corporations typically employ group vice-presidents who oversee new divisions. But each Kollmorgen division has the same standing, with its own president and board of directors. Decisions are made by consensus rather than by majority vote. The board is composed mostly of the president's peers, rather than his superiors within the company. That's why there's little activity in the Stamford office.

What's behind this unusual corporate structure? Swiggett regularly visits plants and meets with supervisors and managers in all-day "Kolture meetings." He preaches a libertarian philosophy. "We apply the free market internally," Swiggett says. Kollmorgen's three main tenets are:

1. People are basically honest and good.
2. People like to play in a game, to play hard, and to bet on the score of that game. Employees are referred to as "partners" since they participate in the company's profit-sharing.
3. Economies of scale are usually offset by inefficiencies of scale.

At Kollmorgen's Photocircuits Division plant in Glen Cove, Long Island, we found that employees were extremely fond of how ideas worked in practice. The plant has recently adopted a system that institutionalizes Swiggett's philosophy of employees as partners. It's called the "reverse review." It means that in addition to the normal annual performance review that all assembly-line workers receive from their supervisors, employees also get to evaluate their supervisors. According to Louis Pagano, who works on the circuit board line, "The reverse review helps dispel the fear people have of supervisors. We see them as just having a different role."

Sue Schwartz, who also works at the circuit board assembly plant, told us: "Everybody feels a part of the team here because we all share in the profits." Schwartz found the egalitarian atmosphere at Kollmorgen a great contrast with Bulova Watch, where she worked for eight years: "Everybody there was Mr. This or Mrs. That. If a vice-president went through the plant, you practically had to stand up and salute."

A co-worker, Barbara Brown, had a similar experience at North American Philips, which has a nearby electronic assembly plant, roughly the same size as the Photocircuits facility, where Brown found "a great gulf between management and employees. They almost never would sit in the same room with us."

That's certainly not the case at Kollmorgen. Each month managers and employees hold "People Meetings" to discuss the state of the business and give employees the opportunity to talk about any issues that concern them. Brown likes the fact that the managers level with everyone. "If we don't get something, we are given a reason. There's a feeling that you count here, that you mean something."

Rich Giddens, who works at Kollmorgen's Multiwire Division plant, also in Glen Cove, likes the meetings and the Kollmorgen environment because "I have some of the rabble-rouser in me. Here you can say what's on your mind and it won't cost you. You won't have to worry about what you say affecting how you do tomorrow."

Rick Savior, who works with Giddens, added simply, "We operate more as a team than as boss and subordinates."

Jay Smith talked of how the company fosters "a spirit of ownership. We have a feeling that you are a part of what's happening."

An important part of what's happening is socializing. Each plant has a social activities committee. At the Photocircuits plant, the social activities committee, composed of a cross section of employees, had a budget in 1983 of $25,000 to be used as it saw fit. The funds were primarily used to sponsor monthly outings. In the previous year busloads of employees had spent days in Atlantic City, Great Gorge, and a "Cruise to Nowhere"—a day-long ocean cruise. "Not only do we work hard together, but we play hard together," explained Smith.

Kollmorgen did not come to its philosophy and organizational structure as a result of some business school management courses. It happened only after the company had tried an entirely opposite approach in the late 1960s involving central control and computerized accounting. But the new system didn't work. "The computer system worked beautifully but company performance, if anything, got worse!" explained Swiggett. "Foremen were preoccupied with printouts instead of people. Managers spent time worrying about internal systems instead of our customers."

In desperation, Kollmorgen sent the System 360 back to IBM and substituted its productized approach with product teams that typically had about 50 people in them. The result was that between 1970 and 1982, the company's sales doubled every four years, and Swiggett can take a boat to a quiet office instead of managing the small details of a growing conglomerate.

Main employment centers   Long Island and Newburgh, New York; Radford, Virginia; Northampton, Massachusetts.

Headquarters   Kollmorgen Corporation.
66 Gate House Road
Stamford, CT 06902
203-327-7222

LEVI STRAUSS & CO.

Levi Strauss is the world's largest clothing maker. U.S. employees: 27,000.

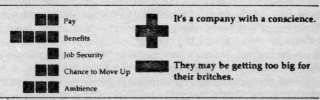

■■ Pay	**It's a company with a conscience.**
■■■ Benefits	
■ Job Security	
■■ Chance to Move Up	■■■ **They may be getting too big for their britches.**
■■■ Ambience	

There are many reasons for beating a path to this San Francisco-based company. To begin with, it's the largest clothing maker in the world. That's how far the jeans revolution carried this company. Today, Levi's produces much more than jeans—shirts, slacks, jackets, suits, hats, active wear, children's clothes, women's apparel.

As a result, Levi's employs a lot of people: 39,000 across the world, 27,000 in the United States. So there are career opportunities at various levels and in various locations. Levi's has also been a sensational performer. In 1970, sales were $325 million. Ten years later they were pushing $3 billion.

Another attraction is working for a company whose name is one of the best-known—and most admired—in the panoply of American products and brand names. Levi's blue jeans are, in fact, known around the world, making them one of the most widely counterfeited products.

Still another lure, if you're thinking about a headquarters position, is the company's home base in San Francisco, which rates on most counts as one of the most livable cities in the country. And San Francisco is more than just an address for Levi Strauss. The company was born here in 1850. Its history is intertwined with the history of San Francisco and the history of the West.

219

Those are all good reasons, but the one that may surpass all others in importance is Levi Strauss's conduct as a socially responsible corporation. This has always been a decent company to work for, whether you were a manager or a sewing machine operator. In addition, it has been extremely generous in supporting the social and cultural needs of the communities where its facilities are located. Caring for people is a legacy from the founding German-Jewish family, whose members remain active in the company.

However—and it's a big however—these glittering reasons lost a little of their luster in 1984 when sales went into reverse, profits went straight downhill—and the company closed 20 plants across the country, eliminating 5,000 people from its payroll. It was a sobering time that left many people inside the company shaky and uncertain about the future.

No company likes to go around boasting that it's good at closing plants. It's a painful experience. But if there's a way to relieve that pain, Levi's is probably a good model. They put together an exemplary termination package for employees ticketed for separation because of a plant shutdown. Everyone was given a minimum notice of 13 weeks (or 13 weeks' pay if the closing was done instantly); their health insurance was maintained for an additional three to six months; severance was paid at the rate of one week's pay for each year of service; and an outplacement office was set up to help them find new jobs (including the opportunity to transfer to another plant that was hiring—not many were). In at least two plants employees were so pleased with this treatment that they broke into applause when the termination package was announced. And at the Memphis plant 539 employees who were about to be rendered jobless actually signed a letter thanking the company "for the Package you put together for us," adding: "We are proud to have been a part of the Levi Strauss family."

The feelings were not so warm in the San Francisco home office, where the managerial and sales ranks were also shrunk. Levi's used to be a close-knit company with a strong family feeling. The explosive growth of the 1970s brought an influx of new people—and the transition was bumpy. The place became more bureaucratic, top management became more removed from the lower ranks and, as the business faltered, a strong sense developed inside Levi's that the company had lost its direction; namely, it didn't have a strong handle on what it was doing. The disenchantment among older employees was especially pronounced. Their resentment at the changes in the company was heightened in 1984 with the implementation of a new employee rating system, Objective Judgment Quotient, to help top management evaluate the performance of managers. Levi's managerial, professional, and technical people were given forms on which they were asked to list people who could appropriately evaluate their performance in such areas as productivity, problem-solving, creativity, leadership, and interpersonal relations. They could name as few as four and as many as nine colleagues. The OJQ was supposed to provide Levi's management with additional information that would be useful in deciding such questions as whom to promote and whom to terminate. Some employees quickly dubbed OJQ as the "screw-your-buddy" system. One employee interviewed by Paul Shinoff, veteran labor writer for the *San Francisco Examiner*, said: "It's a cover-your-ass move. If anyone challenges being laid off, they want an airtight way of avoiding such challenges."

OJQ was not a move characteristic of the old Levi's. In the old days they didn't have to go through such gyrations to evaluate employees. But those old days, to which many oldtimers look back with fondness, are never going to return. This *is* a new Levi's. The question is: Can Levi's hang on to the values it grew up with, now that it's a big company confronted with serious business problems? And will it continue to be a caring company?

One strong link with the tradition of caring is the continuing family influence. Although Levi Strauss & Co. is now a publicly owned company whose shares are traded on the New York Stock Exchange, direct descendants of Levi Strauss (yes, there *was* a Levi Strauss) still own 47 percent of all the stock. When Robert T. Grohman became chief executive officer in late 1981, it was the first time in the company's history that a nonmember of the family had occupied that position. He held it for more than two years, after which 41-year-old Robert D. Haas, took over the reins. He is the great-grand nephew of the founder. He once told us that he thinks it's proper for a company to serve as a "moral compass" for employees.

The policies and practices in place here do represent considerably more than window dressing. When the company passed the $1 billion sales mark in 1975, it gave out more than $2 million worth of stock and cash to employees as rewards. When it passed the $2 billion level in 1979, employees were once again presented with cash awards. In 1982, it extended the profit-sharing long available to headquarters staffers to field workers.

Levi Strauss was one of the first companies to place women and minorities on its board of directors. And there are few companies in the industry—or in the country, for that matter—with an equal employment record that can match Levi's. At the end of 1982, 50.4 percent of all domestic employees were minority-group members, and they made up 18 percent of the officials and managers, 29.5 percent of the professionals, and 36.5 percent of the technicians. Women constitute 77.5 percent of the company's work force, and they hold 31.6 percent of the "officials and managers" positions, 51.1 percent of the professional jobs, and 40 percent of the technical jobs.

Levi Strauss has a pension plan, a profit-sharing plan, and a stock investment and savings plan. It has long been a leader in the hiring of the handicapped. It keeps in close touch with—and looks after—retirees.

Many other progressive companies have similar programs. But Levi Strauss is unique in having a "Social Benefits Program," designed to encourage its employees to be active in community and educational activities outside the company. Under this program, if you are active in a community organization for at least a year, you may ask the Levi Strauss Foundation for a $500 contribution to that group. If you serve on the board of a nonprofit organization, Levi Strauss will back your efforts by giving that organization a grant of $500 (if it has a budget up to $100,000) or $1,000 (for budgets between $100,000 and $1 million), or $1,500 (for budgets over $1 million).

In the early 1970s, as the company's sales started to head for the stratosphere, Levi Strauss outgrew its old quarters at 98 Battery Street in San Francisco and spread out into several downtown buildings. In the interests of efficiency, the company decided to consolidate by moving in 1973 into a new skyscraper at 2 Embarcadero Center. Since the company was the largest tenant in the structure, its name went up outside.

The move did not quite fit this humanistic company. It meant going up and down elevators. It was the cold world of modern business—steel and glass.

Such things wouldn't have bothered most companies, but it definitely bothered Levi's. So even though the lease had another 13 years to run, Levi's elected to move into its own headquarters complex on a 8.2-acre site at the foot of Telegraph Hill, near San Francisco Bay. Opened in 1982, it has already been saluted as one of the most spectacular corporate homes in America. It consists of a series of low-slung, red brick buildings that look as if they are steps leading down from Telegraph Hill. None of the buildings is higher than seven stories. The buildings are placed in a setting of green lawns, a huge open plaza, streams, waterfalls, and wild flowers.

It has all the appearances of a sunny California university campus—and before long it was, in fact, dubbed "Levi Strauss University." The building interiors have been described as having "the trappings of a workers' paradise." There are skylights and open balconies. Each floor has two or three miniplazas equipped with couches, tables, chairs, and kitchenettes (to make coffee or microwave frozen dinners). If you've had a particularly bad day, you may retire to a Quiet Room where you can bang on the walls or chant mantras. Or you can repair to a 7,000-square-foot exercise facility. One typical Levi's touch: as a courtesy to residents living in the hills above Levi's Plaza, the window blinds facing west are drawn every day at 4 P.M. to keep any glare from interfering with the residents' view of the bay.

The move to Levi's Plaza cost the company something like $25 million, and it came in a year of great sales difficulty. But the company went ahead with the move because, as Walter A. Haas, Jr., father of Robert and longtime chief executive officer of the company, put it, "There's a feeling of isolation in a high rise."

Main employment centers Of Levi Strauss's 39,000 employees, 12,000 work overseas. Some 1,700 work in the headquarters complex in San Francisco. The remaining 25,300 work in 45 manufacturing facilities and 8 distribution centers spread across the United States, primarily in the Southwest and the South. The largest number of employees work in Texas plants. Levi's is the largest employer in Amarillo, Texas; Albuquerque, New Mexico; and several other cities. It's a major employer in Knoxville, Tennessee, where it has a huge sewing plant. About half of Levi's factory work force is unionized. The company has never opposed unions.

Headquarters   Levi Strauss & Co.
1155 Battery Street
San Francisco, CA 94120
415-544-6000

THE MOST BEAUTIFUL COMPANY HEADQUARTERS

Cummins	Johnson Wax	Physio-Control
Engine	Levi Strauss	ROLM
Deere	Northwestern	Weyerhaeuser
Hallmark	Mutual Life	
Cards		

Liebert

LIEBERT CORPORATION

Liebert makes air-conditioning and power supply systems for computer rooms. U.S. employees: 1,750.

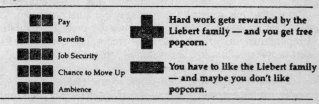

■■■ Pay	**Hard work gets rewarded by the Liebert family — and you get free popcorn.**
■■■ Benefits	
■■■ Job Security	
■■■ Chance to Move Up	**You have to like the Liebert family — and maybe you don't like popcorn.**
■■■ Ambience	

Every Friday at Liebert's main plant in Columbus, Ohio, associates (they're never called employees) can be seen walking through the halls with red-and-white-striped boxes full of popcorn. A large, glass-enclosed popcorn dispenser, much like the ones at movie theaters, is set up outside the company cafeteria to provide free popcorn all day long.

The popcorn is but one of many unusual perks that go with being an associate at Liebert. The company also operates gas pumps exclusively for its associates. The cost averages 15 cents to 22 cents per gallon below the retail price. No need to pay cash or offer a credit card, either; it's deducted from your payroll checks.

Then there's the monthly "Associates' Lunch," held in the company cafeteria, called "The Rathskeller," decorated Tudor-style with wooden chairs, a fake fireplace, and soft lighting. The cafeteria sits between the factory area and the executive offices at the front of the huge, modern, warehouselike building located in a new industrial park in Columbus. A typical lunch includes beef tips with noodles, green beans, salad, and dessert for only a dollar. Drinks are free. And the company owns a 40-acre site with a lake in nearby Delaware, Ohio, where associates and their families can go fishing, hiking, camping, or picnicking.

If you think such benefits sound paternalistic, you're

right. Liebert is run by the Liebert family. Though the company went public in 1981, the Lieberts still own 75 percent of the stock, and three of them serve as company officers. But, as secretary Lynette Langfitt told us, "It's a very nice family to work for."

Ralph Liebert bought a small refrigeration franchise in 1946 with a loan of $600. A refrigeration mechanic, Liebert developed the world's first large industrial heat pump and later pioneered in making freeze-dried foods and coffee. It was not until the mid-1960s, though, that Liebert created a product that has become the company's mainstay: a computer room air conditioner. Such units must be precise, regulating temperatures to within one degree. According to *Forbes*, Liebert dominated that market, supplying more than a third of all such systems by 1983.

When Liebert first sold stock to the public in 1981, it loudly trumpeted the productivity of its associates, claiming that sales per associate were double the computer industry average of $50,000 per person. The company attributes its productivity to incentive and profit-sharing programs.

Liebert associates participate in a quarterly plus-performance incentive system. Not strictly a profit-sharing plan, it is based on shipments compared with costs. In 1984, each associate received a quarterly check worth a total of 195 hours (5 weeks) of extra pay for improvements in productivity.

Liebert also believes in profit-sharing. In 1983, the company put slightly more than $1.35 million into the profit-sharing pool. It was split among all the associates, according to their base pay, and held in individual accounts until they left the company. The profit-sharing trust fund is administered by a committee of six hourly and four management associates.

Main employment centers   About 1,500 in Columbus, 250 total in Fremont, California. Another 175 in Ireland. Of the total, there are 1,081 hourly production workers, 481 office workers, 62 in R&D, 60 engineers, and 93 in sales.

Headquarters   Liebert Corporation
P.O. Box 29186
1050 Dearborn Drive
Columbus, OH 21986
614-888-0246

LINNTON PLYWOOD ASSOCIATION

The Linnton co-op makes plywood used for construction and furniture. U.S. employees: 205, including 189 worker-members.

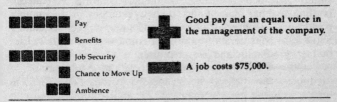

Pay
Benefits
Job Security
Chance to Move Up
Ambience

Good pay and an equal voice in the management of the company.

A job costs $75,000.

"This is sort of like a mom-and-pop operation, except there are one hundred eighty-nine pops."

Linnton Plywood's general manager was trying to explain what it's like to work for a cooperative. It's clear Linnton is not the usual sort of enterprise even before you walk into the mill. A bright red sign, easily visible from the highway, proclaims: "Linnton Plywood Assocation—Worker Owned." The mill occupies 25 acres of prime industrial real estate on the scenic Willamette River 15 minutes north of downtown Portland, Oregon. Dozens of tied logs can be seen floating in the river on one side of the mill. On the other side sit tall stacks of finished plywood sheets.

While an increasing number of companies are adopting various forms of employee ownership (often as a last resort to stave off bankruptcy), Linnton has been owned and controlled by its work force since its inception in 1951. According to Robert Kerr, a Portland attorney specializing in cooperative law, "Linnton is one of the most successful" of the 18 plywood co-ops in Washington and Oregon, all of which were formed between the late 1930s and 1955. They produce about 20 percent of the nation's plywood. Linnton produces approximately eight million board feet of four-by-eight-foot Douglas fir plywood a month. Its annual sales are about $20 million. Kerr attributes Linnton's success to its "care in selecting members and the willingness of its members to work it as a classic cooperative."

Linnton has always run according to strict democratic principles. Each member-worker owns one, and only one, share of stock. Only those who work at the mill can own stock. Everyone, from the general manager to the newest mill worker, is paid at the same hourly rate. All have the opportunity to work the same number of hours a week. When business slows down, all are cut back equally. Pay is called "Advance on Profits." Each quarter, profits are split according to how many hours each worker put in during that period. In a good year, the average Linnton worker earns over $50,000—considerably more than employees of mills owned by Georgia-Pacific and Weyerhaeuser.

Once a year the membership elects a nine-member board of directors to make basic business decisions. The board in turn selects the general manager, the mill foreman, and two shift superintendents. If the workers don't like the management, they can vote them out. That's not just theory. Six of the nine directors were voted out of office in 1982, after the company had its first red-ink year in its history.

In keeping with the company's egalitarian rules, all jobs in the mill are bid and determined by seniority. The mill's supervisors can discipline members who violate work rules, but workers can appeal to the board of directors. Smoking in restricted areas can bring an automatic three-day suspension. Other infractions (like habitual absenteeism, abusive language toward another worker-owner, or refusal to carry out a work order) can result in increasingly severe punishments: from warning slips to three-day, two-week, and one-year suspensions. The one-year sanction must be authorized by a two-thirds vote of the entire membership. At least one member accused of egregious behavior was suspended for a year. No one has ever been expelled altogether.

Dick Hall worked as a plugger (removing knots from plywood sheets) before being named Linnton's general manager in March 1982. He held a variety of jobs in the mill, but no other white-collar jobs, during the 15 years he has been with the company. An accountant by training, Hall was previously regional manager of Napa Genuine Auto Parts in Portland. He thoroughly investigated Linnton with local banks and Dun & Bradstreet before buying into the company. He discovered it had held its own as a commercial enterprise, and was considered a good investment.

At the time Hall joined Linnton, a share in the association cost $27,000. Today it costs about $75,000 to work there. Since the number of shares (and hence member-workers) has not increased since the founding of the company, he had to purchase his share from a member who was retiring or quitting. In mid-1983, about 10 members were willing to sell their jobs/shares at Linnton. The buyer and the seller work out price and financing arrangements. Thus, the buyer may have to put only a small amount down and pay off the balance from his earnings at the mill over a specified period of time. Their agreement must be approved by the board of directors. Someone who buys a share must also pass a physical and work for two weeks on a probationary basis before the board votes on accepting him.

According to Hall, most Linnton workers consider their jobs primarily an investment. Those who initially pay only part of the share can usually earn enough to pay off their investment within a few years. Few previously worked in wood mills, though most had blue-collar jobs. Only about 10 percent are college graduates, while 75 percent completed high school. The typical worker joins the company at about age 30, and the average age of those working there is 48. All are male, and all are white. Many are related to each other. Four are brothers.

Linnton's worker-owners generally prefer the egalitarian setup to working under the typical hierarchy of most companies. They can speak their minds without fearing for their jobs. They feel like their own boss. There's mutual supervision rather than a management group to oversee the work. They do not tolerate loafing, from either themselves or their co-workers. Anyone not pulling his own weight is seen as taking money from everyone else's pocket. Studies done by outsiders support the claim that such co-ops exhibit higher productivity than their absentee-stockholder-owned counterparts. One study in the 1960s indicated that co-ops produced 170 square feet of plywood per man-hour as opposed to 130 square feet for conventional firms. A similar study in the mid-1970s showed co-op workers producing nearly one-and-a-half times as much as their counterparts.

At the same time, Linnton offers few side benefits, unlike the large corporate wood products manufacturers. There's a flat two weeks' paid vacation and a conventional group health insurance plan. There are no provisions for extra sick days or holidays. Most members bring their own lunches in brown bags, as the company has no cafeteria. But Linnton has its own gas pump where employees can fill up their cars and vans at wholesale cost.

One great advantage to working for Linnton is the freedom to take extended personal leaves. Some take off several months a year. The foreman can approve any leave of less than 30 days, but the board of directors must okay longer periods. Hall says no requests have ever been turned down. To fill in while the member is gone (and to handle business upturns), Linnton hires temporary workers who are not stockholders. There are normally no more than 20 such temporaries on the payroll. Their hourly salary is similar to that of the association members (a figure Linnton will not disclose), but they do not receive quarterly profit-sharing bonuses.

All this is not to say that Linnton worker-owners consider their mill to be a utopia. For one thing, the work itself is boring manual labor. "The work is very monotonous, very repetitious," explained Hall. Most men make sure the wood keeps going through the system by standing in front of a machine all day. Most of the jobs are solitary in the sense that workers spend little time interacting with anybody else.

Though working relationships are generally amiable, there is little camaraderie off the job. It's not the sort of place where everybody goes to the local tavern after work or where there's a constant round of parties. People tend to clock in and clock out and go home alone. Only about 20 percent attend the annual company picnic, according to Hall.

But few Linnton members would trade their jobs at Linnton for another job. "Where else can you make good money and be your own boss?" Hall asked. "We're just a group of blue-collar fellows trying to make a living from our investment."

Main employment center   Portland.

Headquarters   Linnton Plywood Association
10504 NW St. Helens Road
Portland, OR 97231
503-286-3672

LOS ANGELES DODGERS

The Dodgers own one professional major-league baseball team and six minor-league clubs. U.S. employees: 950.

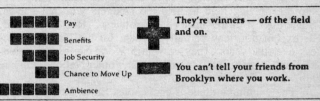

■■■■ Pay	➕ They're winners — off the field and on.
■■■ Benefits	
■■ Job Security	
■■ Chance to Move Up	■ You can't tell your friends from Brooklyn where you work.
■■■■ Ambience	

Most people in baseball agree that Dodgertown, in Vero Beach, Florida, is the best spring-training facility in the game. It symbolizes what Dodger employees cite as a principal reason they like the club: "The Dodgers are a first-class organization." Players, front-office people, and even ushers told us that again and again. Dodgertown is also where generation after generation of players acquire the spirit of Dodger Blue.

First opened in 1948, Dodgertown was the first (and is still one of the few) training camps where players from the major and minor leagues practice together. As its name implies, Dodgertown is a little baseball village. Streets such as Duke Snider Road, Jackie Robinson Avenue, Sandy Koufax Lane, and Roy Campanella Drive weave through the 450-acre site. Training coaches include former Dodger greats such as Koufax and Campanella. Off-hours, the players have use of an Olympic-sized pool, two basketball, six tennis, and two shuffleboard courts, and both a 9-hole and an 18-hole golf course (the latter is called Dodger Pines Country Club).

Camaraderie develops among the players at Dodgertown. "When you are together like that, the young players get to see the major leaguers. It means a lot to those guys," Bill Russell, the team's shortstop, told us. We talked with him during batting practice, shortly before a game between the Dodgers and the Montreal Expos at Dodger Stadium in the summer of

1983. Russell was once in their place, having first gone to Dodgertown in 1967 while a minor leaguer himself. He was promoted to the Dodgers in 1969 and as of 1984 had been with the team longer than any player then on the roster.

Russell says the only significant change in the last 16 years has been the much higher salaries players now receive. "What has not changed is the family feeling of the Dodgers," he said. "They go out of their way to make everybody feel like part of the organization."

The Dodger shortstop believes that the team spirit spills onto the playing field to help the Dodgers win ball games. "Sometimes it makes up for lack of talent," Russell claimed. His explanation may partially account for the Dodgers' success over the years. They've won 5 World Series championships and 20 pennants—more than any other National League club.

The winning attitude is contagious. Steve Sax, 25 and in his fourth year in the big leagues, told us, "Everyone expects us to win—the fans, the organization, everyone. It just isn't part of the script to lose. Winning is the Dodger tradition."

Like the majority of Dodgers, Sax and Russell have never played for another professional ball club, something increasingly rare in the major leagues. The Dodgers prefer to find and develop their own talent. Other clubs rely on "The Bureau," a scouting pool that provides tips about promising young players. But the Dodgers employ their own crew of 24 full-time and 22 part-time scouts to comb the United States and Latin America for potential big leaguers. *Forbes* estimated the Dodgers spend about $3 million annually on this operation, which nets only about three new major-league players a year. That's a million dollars per player. But the club believes it is worth the price, since bidding for free agents can cost as much if not more.

Partly because the Dodgers have such a good farm-club system, the club doesn't keep older players around when capable younger ones are in the wings. When some of these older players have been traded—Steve Garvey, Ron Cey, and Davey Lopes, for instance—they've issued bitter statements to the press. It's hard to accept being kicked out of the family. These trades have had little impact on the morale of the remaining Dodgers.

One testimony to the Dodgers' commitment to their own

scouting is a large ledger book hidden in a locked cabinet at Dodger Stadium. The book is the property of Al Campanis, the Dodgers' player-personnel chief. In it, Campanis has written in the team's starting players for the opening game of the season for the next five years. Campanis himself played briefly for the Brooklyn Dodgers in 1943. He became a scout in 1950.

Among those who seem happiest with the Dodgers are players who spent time with other teams. Outfielder Ken Landreaux played with the California Angels and the Minnesota Twins before being traded to the Dodgers in 1981. "I have been treated better here. The Dodgers treat the players more like human beings," he told us. ''I felt the difference as soon as I got here. With the Twins, you are just like another piece of property that they can use or abuse. With the Angels you're like something they could maneuver with."

Relief pitcher Pat Zachry, formerly with the Cincinnati Reds and the New York Mets, thinks the Dodgers take care of little things for the players better than he has ever seen before. "The travel arrangements and the facilities are better than those at other clubs," he said. He likes the fact that "throughout the year they take care of our families. When we are on the road, they have get-togethers where the families can go with the kids. That's important for a ballplayer." During spring training, the club hosts other events for the whole family, including a Christmas party with a Santa Claus and imported snow, and barbecues.

The 160 ballplayers make up only part of the Dodger family. There's minimal turnover among the 225 front-office executives and staff, including secretaries. Many, like Bill Schweppe, head of minor-league operations, have been with the club since its days in Brooklyn. (The team's name comes from the nickname of that borough's residents, who were known as "trolley dodgers.") "When we moved from Brooklyn in 1958, more than 50 percent came along, including ticket sellers, ground crew, and secretaries," Schweppe said.

Schweppe contrasts the loyalty among Dodger employees with that of other major-league clubs: "We have a feeling of security here in a business that's very insecure. We have a family-type relaxed atmosphere despite it being such a competitive business."

Other clubs have absentee owners or new owners every

few years. But the Dodgers have been owned by the O'Malley family since 1950; Walter O'Malley brought the club west from Brooklyn. His son Peter, a graduate of the University of Pennsylvania's Wharton business school, started full-time work with the team in 1962 as director of Dodgertown. He began running the club in 1970.

Ken Hasemann, the club's controller and 23-year Dodger veteran, says many of the employees appreciate that "Mr. O'Malley makes a point to get to know everybody," and that his door is always open for employees to talk with him. After the Dodgers won the World Series in 1981, O'Malley took all the department heads and their spouses to Hawaii. Front-office employees also have a profit-sharing plan.

Even the part-time employees—the ushers, ticket sellers, and security guards—speak of being part of the Dodger family. We talked with usher Greg Rigaldo, whose post is outside the Dodgers' locker room. A 30-year veteran of the post office, Rigaldo has been impressed with how the club is so "well run" and how "the Dodgers take care of their people." It's difficult to get a job as an usher at Dodger Stadium. Their base pay is $7.25 an hour, and they are unionized. It helps to be recommended by someone who already works there. Not surprisingly, "lots of people are related to each other here," as Rigaldo told us. "It's sort of like the movie studios that way."

Once on board, ushers adhere to a rigid dress code. Men's hair must be cut above their collar, they must be clean-shaven and cannot chew gum on the job. The team provides them with a powder-blue jacket, blue trousers, a Dodgers necktie, and a straw hat. "I know we're better than ushers at other stadiums," Rigaldo asserted. "I've seen them on TV."

Nick Cardona, Jr., was working as an usher near the Dodgers' dugout the evening we were there. In his early twenties, Cardona has been ushering for the past five years. He insists that "this job is not for everybody. You have to like baseball." Cardona clearly does. The ushers have their own softball team; they play the security guards at the stadium once a year. The team also throws an annual party for them in the dugout. The main attraction is three six-foot-long submarine sandwiches. "It's the Dodgers' way of saying thank you," Cardona said. The team also gives ushers and other employees the same gifts (Dodger caps, jackets, bats, and so on) that are handed out to the fans during the dozen or so giveaway games each year.

Many players find Dodger Stadium one of the club's principal attractions. The team spent $1 million to landscape the stadium, planting olive and palm trees in the parking lots and a Japanese garden in center field. Fans seem to like it, too. The team leads both leagues in attendance almost every year. With 27,000 season-ticket holders, it's the only team to have had more than three million fans in a year—and it's done it five times, in 1978, 1980, 1982, 1983, and 1984. In 1982, only 6 of the 26 major-league teams were estimated to have made any profit at all. None made more than $1.5 million that year. Except for the Dodgers, that is. They are estimated to have cleared a cool $7 million.

Tommy Lasorda has been the Dodgers' manager since 1977. He succeeded Walter Alston, who ran the club from the dugout for 23 years—a major league record. Lasorda has been with the Dodger organization for 36 years, 11 years as a minor league pitcher, 5 years as a scout, 7 years as a minor league manager, and 4 as a Dodger coach. One of baseball's most colorful personalities and prone to hyperbole, Lasorda has often told sports writers of his great love for the Dodger organization. It was no different when we talked with him before the Expos game.

"The Dodgers are the best company to work for in the world, not just in America," he asserted. Why? " 'Cause it's an organization with a heart. The people who run it make those of us who work for them feel very much a part of it. They make us feel appreciated." He cited the incident of how the Dodgers gave a job to former Dodger catcher Roy Campanella after he was paralyzed by an auto accident.

Another not-so-well known example occurred several years ago after ex-Dodger pitcher Don Newcombe had pawned his 1955 World Series ring at a shop in downtown Los Angeles. Newcombe was an alcoholic at the time. When Peter O'Malley heard about the ring, he went to the pawnshop himself and redeemed it. He then went to Newcombe's house and handed the former pitcher the ring, saying it was a present for his son when the boy turned 18. O'Malley later gave Newcombe a job as director of community relations.

Lasorda says his devotion to the Dodgers will extend beyond his retirement. "I used to tell my wife that when I die,

I want it written on my tombstone that Dodger Stadium was his address, but every ball park was his home."

According to Lasorda, when O'Malley heard of that, he had a plaque printed with Lasorda's preferred epitaph and a heart painted in Dodger blue. "When I accepted it, I told Mr. O'Malley, 'I want to go on working for the Dodgers even when I am dead and gone.' Mr. O'Malley said, 'I can understand your feelings, Tommy, but how are you going to work for the Dodgers when you are dead?' I told him, 'Mr. O'Malley, when I die, I want the Dodgers' schedule put on this tombstone. When people are in the cemetery visiting their loved ones, they will say, 'Let's go to Lasorda's grave and find out if the Dodgers are home or away.'"

Main employment centers   Los Angeles and Vero Beach, Florida (Dodgertown). The minor-league clubs are in Albuquerque, New Mexico; San Antonio, Texas; Bakersfield, California; Vero Beach Florida; Great Falls, Idaho; and Bradenton, Florida.

Headquarters   Los Angeles Dodgers
Dodger Stadium
1000 Elysian Park Avenue
Los Angeles, CA 90012
213-224-1500

MOST UNUSUAL MANAGEMENT STYLES

Gore
Kollmorgen

People Express
Quad/Graphics

LOWE'S COMPANIES, INC.

The nation's biggest lumber and hardware supply retailer.
U.S. employees: 8,700.

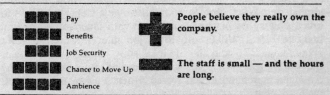

■■■□ Pay	✚	**People believe they really own the company.**
■■■■□ Benefits		
■■■□ Job Security		
■■■■ Chance to Move Up	▬	**The staff is small — and the hours are long.**
■■■■ Ambience		

Lots of people in the mountains around North Wilkesboro, North Carolina, had heard about Lowe's, even if they'd never been inside one of its stores. Lowe's is where people got rich, so the rumor went. Stories circulated of janitors retiring with a million or secretaries with several hundred thousand dollars in the bank.

Flake Johnson had "heard of all these Lowe's people making millions." At the time, about a dozen years ago, Johnson was living on a chicken farm in the Appalachian foothills and engaged in moonshining, making illegal alcohol. When his partner had a brush with the authorities because of their still, Johnson decided he "wanted to make it rich without any risk." He has been at Lowe's since 1972, working as a maintenance supervisor in the corporate office.

Johnson's motivation for joining Lowe's is typical. The stories about Lowe's profit-sharing plan are true. A $125-a-week warehouseman retired in 1975 with $660,000; a truck driver, with $413,000; and two store managers, with $3 million each. Those joining Lowe's today, however, shouldn't expect such huge payouts from the company's profit-sharing plan. Yet Lowe's still has one of the most successful, large-scale profit-sharing plans in the United States. As Johnson says, "I do not think I will get rich, but I think I will have a good savings account when I leave."

There was nothing unusual about the first Lowe's hardware store when it opened its doors for business in North Wilkesboro in 1946. But when he bought out the original owner 10 years later, Carl Buchan had a vision of creating a chain of hardware stores. He saw the stores selling their wares at a disount if they bought directly from manufacturers rather than from wholesalers. By 1960, there were 13 Lowe's stores selling hardware, home appliances, and lumber at discount prices.

Buchan also had his own ideas about how his store should be owned. Bob Strickland, Lowe's chairman, likes to tell the story of his first encounter with Buchan. Strickland went to North Wilkesboro for a job interview in 1957. He accompanied Buchan and the local store manager on a tour of the warehouse. When the group reached the area where the damaged merchandise was stored, Buchan asked the manager, "What is that?"

"It's damaged merchandise, sir."

"Look at it more closely and tell me what you see," continued Lowe's owner.

"Well, that's a damaged water pump, and a dented refrigerator, and windows with broken glass," replied the manager.

"That's not what I see when I look over there. What I see is money—my money—because I paid for it. And before the year is out, we're going to have a plan whereby part of that will belong to you and the other employees. Then when you look you'll see money, too, and you'll take better care of your money than you're doing now, and consequently you'll take better care of my money."

Buchan had instituted only the first part of his plan when he died in his sleep in 1960 at the age of 44. But his will specified that Lowe's employees, through a profit-sharing plan and trust, had the option of buying all his stock. The plan wound up with about half the shares of Lowe's stock, which meant, in turn, that Lowe's employees were the major beneficiaries as Lowe's went through a phenomenal expansion during the 1960s and 1970s and the value of Lowe's stock skyrocketed.

By 1984, Lowe's was operating 250 stores. Most are in small towns in North Carolina or nearby states, though Lowe's stores can be found in 19 states—from Pennsylvania to Florida, and from Illinois to Texas. Lowe's sold more than a billion dollars' worth of goods for the first time in 1982. The employees, through the original profit-sharing trust and an Employee Stock Ownership Plan (ESOP) that replaced it in 1978, now hold approximately 25 percent of all the company's stock. And this proportion goes up every year as the company makes an annual contribution to each employee's account to buy more stock. That contribution has ranged in recent years from 12 to 15 percent of an employee's pay; Lowe's employees put up nothing. As with most ESOPs, employees can cash in their accounts only when they leave the company. Those who leave before retirement must have been there 15 years to get 100 percent of their account.

The Lowe's ESOP served as a model for ESOPs now being created all over the country because of changes in the tax laws. Lowe's chairman, Strickland, is positively evangelical on the subject. He insists that profit-sharing made the company successful, helping to motivate people. He cites figures showing that Lowe's sales ($164,154) and profits ($5,806) per employee are more than double those of the three biggest retailers (Sears, K mart, and J. C. Penney). Strickland has testified several times before congressional committees considering laws favoring ESOPs. He told us, "What is more Republican than making people capitalists? And what is more Democratic than sharing the wealth?"

Discussions with Lowe's employees support Strickland's view that the ESOP makes them feel like part owners of the business. Hence Lowe's employees have an unusual degree of commitment to the success of the enterprise. Bill Harris, a purchasing agent, explained, "We work under a management but we are part owners. So everything doesn't come from the top down. A lot comes from the bottom up. I try to give my best. The better the company does, the more money that goes in my little kitty."

Linda Blackburn is a corporate buyer. Like others we talked to at Lowe's, she finds the underlying feeling of ownership conducive to people speaking their minds. "I feel I have a lot of opportunity to say what I like and dislike," she told us. "I will not be chastised or held back for what I say."

Blackburn started working for Lowe's 15 years ago in the costing department. When she decided she did not want to be a secretary all her life, she asked to become a buyer. Though the company had never had any women buyers before (and there are still no female store managers), she was given the job. But she felt she deserved it. "You have to pay your dues around here for a while. Everything around here is not a gimme. You got to earn everything you get."

Blackburn works in the corporate office on the outskirts of North Wilkesboro (population 3,260). Despite its size, two other companies have their headquarters there: Holly Farms Poultry (along with a big chicken slaughterhouse) and American Drew Furniture (and its chair factory). The town also boasts Smithey's Department Store, Dunn's Gun Store, Lowe's Bible Bookstore and Music Center, and Lowe's Fur and Herbs Store (no connection). The outside of the Lowe's corporate offices looks like any Lowe's store. There are no windows. Executive offices tend toward the spartan. They don't believe in spending money for appearances at Lowe's. Many feel such expenditures come out of their own pockets.

Virtually everybody starts at the bottom at Lowe's. New salespeople must go through a training period of about a month in a store's warehouse where they learn all the items the store carries. Inventory control is almost an obsession at Lowe's. New salespeople learn how to type sales orders into the computer. Lowe's has been heavily computerized since the early 1960s, and it still is much more highly computerized than almost any other retail establishment. Every sales transaction—even someone buying a handful of nails—is put into the computer. Each Lowe's store has a minicomputer and several terminals linked to a big mainframe in North Wilkesboro.

Once the salespeople hit the sales floor, they have to hustle. Their income comes strictly from commissions on sales. The rate varies according to the item sold (between about 1 and 10 percent). How much each person makes depends on what he or she (a growing number are women) sells. A typical salesperson makes $18,000 to $20,000 a year, but some make as much as $80,000 to $90,000 a year.

The Lowe's system favors the aggressive. Those who do well become master sales managers, supervising other salespeople. The next step is often assistant store manager, overseeing sales to professional home builders, who account for nearly half of Lowe's sales. If people show enough promise, they can become store managers. The process can take as little as four years or more than a dozen.

Rising young store executives frequently move between

Lowe's stores, especially when they are promoted to master sales manager or store manager. Larry Stone, manager of the Lowe's store in North Wilkesboro, moved from the Lowe's store in Hickory and then to Raleigh before assuming his current position. He especially appreciates the sense of being his own boss, despite Lowe's size: "It's like running your own store with somebody backing you. As a store manager, I am really allowed to wheel and deal."

Store managers have an unusual amount of autonomy. They are free to set the sale price of any item in the store. Like their sales staff, their pay is also based largely on the profits of their store. Some of them make sizable incomes, even larger than that of company vice-presidents. Several made more than $100,000 in 1982.

Lowe's maintains a rah-rah atmosphere to keep the troops selling more nails and boards. There are lots of contests, slogans ("Bust a Billion"), and T-shirts ("Make It with a Lowe's Stud"). Until a few years ago, Lowe's had an annual hootenanny that was also its company-wide sales meeting. They were pretty wild affairs, according to all reports. Strickland said these meetings were "like a gathering of the clans." But Lowe's has grown and is no longer a North Carolina company run strictly by men from the Appalachian towns around North Wilkesboro. The 1982 annual sales meeting was held in Orlando, Florida, with merely a representative from each store attending rather than everyone descending on North Wilkesboro, as in the "good ol' days."

The Appalachian flavor still permeates Lowe's, nevertheless. On their birthdays, corporate staffers get a free lunch in the cafeteria. On Thanksgiving, everyone gets a turkey; on Christmas, a ham. For the annual picnic, employees have a "pig picking"—a pig roasted on a stick.

Main employment centers   Stores in 19 states in the Southeast.

Headquarters   Lowe's Companies, Inc.
Highway 268 East
Box 1111
North Wilkesboro, NC 28656
919-667-3111

⟨M⟩ MARION

MARION LABORATORIES, INC.

Marion manufactures and sells drugs prescribed for coronary problems, major burns, and gastrointestinal disorders. U.S. employees: 2,000.

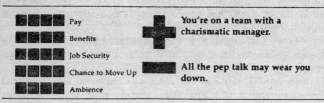

Pay ■■■■□

Benefits ■■■■□

Job Security ■■■■□

Chance to Move Up ■■■■□

Ambience ■■■■□

✚ You're on a team with a charismatic manager.

▬ All the pep talk may wear you down.

The baseball season is not complete in Kansas City without Marion Associates Appreciation Night. That's the game at Royals Stadium in late summer when all of Marion's employees (referred to as "associates") and their spouses or guests fill up the left-field bleachers. Twenty-five hundred strong, they wear a baseball cap or T-shirt with a big M on it as they root loudly for the home team. Top executives of the company go up and down the aisles handing out free drinks and other refreshments.

In the midst of the crowd, a short, balding gentleman invariably finds himself besieged with autograph seekers wanting his name inscribed on their programs. The center of attention is not a retired baseball great. It's Ewing M. Kauffman, chairman of Marion, who also happens to be the owner of the Kansas City Royals ball club.

Kauffman founded the company in 1950 using his own middle name as the company name. Operating out of his home in Kansas City, Kauffman sold drugs and vitamins manufactured by others. Even today Marion does no basic research. It makes drugs under license from other pharmaceutical firms, mostly foreign. Marion ushers the drugs through the Federal Drug Administration approval process and then manufactures and promotes them to private doctors in the United States.

A supersalesman, Kauffman is known by everybody at Marion as "Mr. K." One of his first associates, Jean Sperry, recalled his first encounter with his boss-to-be: "He was such a dynamic guy. He could sell you on anything. At that time, Eli Lilly was the largest pharmaceutical company in the world, but if Mr. K had told me that his company, Marion Laboratories, was just as big as Lilly, I wouldn't have doubted him one bit."

Kauffman's charisma still seems to inspire the company. Associates look forward to his speech at the quarterly "Marion on the Move" meetings. "He makes you want to work for him," an associate reported after one meeting.

The entire company attends the Marion on the Move meetings. During the summer meeting, the company announces the profit-sharing bonus for the year. In 1982, all Marion associates were given a bonus check equal to 40 hours' pay.

These meetings are also used to present other awards. In 1983, for instance, Kauffman gave a production worker 100 shares of Marion stock (worth $8,000) for 10 years of perfect attendance. Kauffman also hands out the Marion Spirit Suggestion awards, given to associates who have come up with money-saving ideas. In 1982, Kauffman handed out stock worth $15,000, $12,000, and $7,000 to three associates. Each year the person who offers the best suggestion receives a week-long, all-expenses-paid trip for two to any city in the world, plus an extra week of vacation.

The bonus checks and suggestion awards are only part of Marion's attraction. For one thing, Marion's generous benefits rank in the top 20 percent of the high-paying pharmaceutical industry, according to an independent survey. In 1984, it became the first in its industry to offer a prepaid legal service plan. That year, Marion also opened a health and fitness center near its main plant. More than half the associates regularly attend the center's fitness classes, participate on one of the numerous sports teams, or use professional weight-training facilities. From the beginning, Kauffman has insisted that "those associates who produce shall share in the results." Marion has a wide variety of profit-sharing and incentive plans. Its profit-sharing retirement trust has made a number of

Marion's Foundations for an Uncommon Company

Our Relationships: We should treat others as we would be treated—with dignity, respect, integrity, and honesty. This applies to: associates and their families; customers (consumers, health care providers, wholesalers); stockholders; suppliers; financial community and general public.

Those who produce should share in the results.

Each Marion associate has the right to:
- Be treated as an individual
- Be rewarded for performance
- Know what is expected on the job and where we stand in relation to that expectation
- Get problems resolved and be heard
- A safe and healthy workplace
- Share in the growth of the company through personal and career growth

We earn these through our high productivity and commitment to quality in all that we do.

Marion associates millionaires upon retirement. In fact, the company put a limit of $1.5 million as the maximum that any associate's fund could have upon retirement. About a dozen have retired with the maximum amount. (Kauffman himself owns about 24 percent of the stock, worth $150 million in late 1983.)

Marion also gives each associate stock options. After being with Marion for one year, an associate can purchase up to 100 shares of Marion stock at any time during the next 10 years at the price it sold for on the date of his or her first anniversary with the company. Because the value of Marion stock has shot up more than 1,000 percent in the past 10 years, many Marion associates have made a bundle on their options.

Marion associates take an understandable interest in how the company's stock is faring on Wall Street. A sign displaying Marion's current stock-market price is prominently displayed on the receptionist's desk at all company facilities. The company is proud of this interest. In the 1982 annual report, the company wrote, "An employee of a company thinks and performs differently than someone who has ownership, or an equity interest, in the company's operations. One of the reasons for Marion's continued strong performance and high productivity is that its associates participate as part-owners of the company."

Stock options are normally reserved only for top corporate executives in most companies. As a consequence, Michie Slaughter, vice-president of personnel, says, "We have to educate the average person what a stock option is. Many do not know what stocks are, let alone the meaning of a stock option."

Some of this education takes place in the five two-hour orientation sessions held during the first month of employment. All new employees attend these sessions, regardless of their position in the company. One of the meetings is held at night so that the employee's spouse can attend. The company wants to make sure that people understand what it means to belong to the "Marion family."

Though the company talks about itself as a "family," Marion does not hire relatives of employees. Many production workers come from small towns or farms south of Kansas City. They work at the company's plant in the 159-acre Marion Park in the southeast corner of Kansas City, where all of Marion's drugs are produced.

Marion makes a point of not hiring sales representatives from other drug firms. "We prefer to train our own people so they learn our own style of sales," says Jim Mason, director of personnel. Though a few salespeople are hired directly from college, most have had previous work experience, preferably as pharmacists, nurses, or science teachers.

Competition for jobs at Marion is intense: 15,000 applications were received in 1982, of which 5,000 were for sales jobs alone. Those hired can expect considerable job security, as Marion has never laid off anyone due to lack of work in its 34-year history.

The company hired additional people in mid-1982 for the launching of a new drug, Cardizem, for treatment of angina and other heart conditions. When final FDA approval was delayed for several months, Marion reassigned dozens of people to other positions within the company or to various maintenance jobs that otherwise would have gone undone. Cathy Vogel, a manufacturing technician who was sent to several different areas, reported: "I love it, I really do. It's given me an opportunity to learn more about the company and meeting people has been the greatest part about it. It's fun."

Marion's commitment to job security has not been at the expense of growth and profitability. The company has more than doubled its sales since 1980, to $226 million in fiscal 1984, and its profits per share of stock have grown 50 percent each year since 1982. The firm's growth has meant lots of opportunities within the company. Each year for the past five years, one out of five associates has been promoted or taken a career development transfer.

Marion associates work shortened hours on Fridays during the summer. It's a program called "uncommon days." Instead of the usual 7:00 A.M. to 3:30 P.M. workday, plant employees work from 6:00 to 12:15.

"We call it 'uncommon days' because we call ourselves an 'uncommon company,'" explained Michie Slaughter. "We try to make sure working for Marion is not the same as working for a typical corporation."

Main employment centers   1,450 of Marion's employees work in Kansas City, including 900 production workers and 300 engaged in research and development.

Headquarters   Marion Laboratories, Inc.
9221 Ward Parkway
P.O. Box 8480
Kansas City, MO 64114
816-966-5000

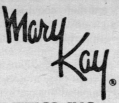

MARY KAY COSMETICS, INC.

Mary Kay sells its own brand of cosmetics through "Beauty Shows" held in the homes of prospective customers. Employees: 1,400, and an independent sales force of nearly 200,000 "Beauty Consultants."

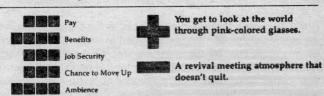

■■■□ Pay	**+** You get to look at the world through pink-colored glasses.
■■■■ Benefits	
■■■□ Job Security	A revival meeting atmosphere that doesn't quit.
■■■□ Chance to Move Up	
■■■□ Ambience	

"Driving a pink Cadillac down the street is more than fun—it's a happening. Why not have it happen to you?"

The quote is from *Applause*, the newsletter for Mary Kay's huge army of independent saleswomen. The Cadillacs —painted a distinctive soft shade called "Mary Kay pink"— and other prizes such as mink coats and diamond rings are handed out to top sellers at the Mary Kay Seminar. Over 20,000 women descend on the Dallas Convention Center each year for this unique blend of Academy Awards night, Miss America pageant, and old-fashioned revival meeting. In 1981 the theme was "Dreams Can Come True." At one point, the stage boasted a four-story-high castle as knights and ladies danced to the theme song of *Camelot*.

The growing fleet of pink Cadillacs illustrates the astonishing success of Mary Kay. The number of full-time employees doubled between 1980 and 1983, as did the number of Mary Kay Beauty Consultants (who are considered independent contractors rather than employees). Yet the company retains Chairman Mary Kay Ash's unique imprint, as distinctive as the pink Cadillacs.

On their birthdays, all Mary Kay employees receive a

birthday card and a voucher for a free lunch for two. During Secretary's Week, all secretaries get flowers. And when people join the company, they meet with Mary Kay herself during their first month.

It's all part of what Mary Kay calls the "personal touch." After 25 years with various door-to-door sales outfits, she felt men invariably discriminated against her simply because she was a woman. So, in 1963, she founded Mary Kay Cosmetics as her "dream company," one "that would be based on the golden rule and offer women unlimited opportunities." To a remarkable extent, Mary Kay has succeeded in doing just that, at least so far as the full-time employees in the Dallas headquarters and manufacturing facility are concerned.

Bob Eckelcamp has worked as a data processing professional for several different companies in the Dallas area over the past dozen years. When he applied to work for Mary Kay, he was impressed by the extensive interview process. "Mary Kay is a very female-oriented company," he said. "When I was interviewed, there were a number of warm and personal questions. Not intimate, but personal. I thought it was the strangest series of interviews I had ever gone through. They were primarily interested in whether I'd fit into the family."

Not everyone fits into the Mary Kay family. Because it's run by a woman, male chauvinists need not apply. Few do. The male executives are carefully screened to determine their ability to work with women as peers. Ironically, most of the company's vice-presidents are men, including company president Richard Rogers, Mary Kay's son.

There's little room for those who like executive trappings. Everyone eats in the same cafeteria; no titles appear on office doors; and there's a written open-door policy. As Gail Daniel, a corporate purchasing buyer, reports, "There's a Mary Kay attitude that there are no lower people. Everybody is treated the same." No one is called Mr., Mrs., or Ms.; Tom Howell, who works in the consultant relations department, says, "I worked here thirty days before I knew Mary Kay even had a last name."

The employee cafeteria sits on the second floor of the manufacturing facility, located a few blocks from the corporate headquarters in Dallas. A pink shuttle bus (driven by a woman) takes employees from the corporate office to the other building. The company partly subsidizes the lunches (a hot meal costs less than $3). Again, there's the female touch. Each table has a white tablecloth and a vase of flowers.

Mary Kay makes all its cosmetics in the Dallas plant. The company gives each production-line worker three sets of work clothes a year. Women get a bright red jump suit as well as reddish outfits with printed blouses and slacks. Men wear blue trousers and shirts and matching baseball caps. Virtually all manufacturing employees work a four-day week of 10-hour days. The factory is air-conditioned, unlike several perfume plants in which perfumier Tom Pampinello worked on the East Coast. One day a year, Pampinello and all other white-collar manufacturing employees work on the production lines. "It gives them an idea of what it's like for us all the time," says machine operator Frances Spencer.

The corners of all Mary Kay buildings are rounded. Mary Kay doesn't like sharp edges; she believes that rounded corners indicate more of a people orientation. The eight-story headquarters building, with its gold-tinted windows, literally glitters in the hot Dallas sun. Live plants adorn virtually every office and desk in the place. A full-time landscaping staff of a dozen people works in a hydroculture greenhouse at the manufacturing building. About once a week, one of the staff shows up in each employee's office to water the plants and polish the leaves.

The headquarters exudes what Mary Kay calls "a living room atmosphere." There are lots of sofas. Those who work in individual offices pick their own furnishings and works of art. Mary Kay's office has a beige rug with a border of pink flowers, a large sofa with pink pillows, and several dozen beautiful porcelain figurines in a mirrored cabinet. A sign on her desk reads, "Thank you for not smoking." (Drinking is not permitted at any Mary Kay function.)

In the spring, all employees get together for the annual employees' meeting. Mary Kay and her son, company president Richard Rogers, report on the company's financial performance and other items of interest. Held at the Dallas Convention Center, the employees' gathering has the evangelical atmosphere of the annual Mary Kay Seminar for the sales force.

Mary Kay is definitely not a place for someone who'd be embarrassed by the fervor of such a meeting. The emotionalism associated with motivating a huge sales force carries over into all aspects of the company. Employees say the enthusiasm over Mary Kay, their products, and the company's success is genuine, not hype. They claim the spirit of the place invariably catches them up almost as soon as they enter the facility every morning. Yet it's clearly not the sort of environment for someone who prefers solitary work or simply doesn't want to be part of a high-spirited group effort.

Few of Mary Kay's regular employees previously worked as part of the independent sales force of beauty consultants. Successful Mary Kay saleswomen earn too much money. In 1982, for instance, more Mary Kay saleswomen earned over $50,000 than women with any other company in the United States. According to *Advertising Age*, the 3,391 Mary Kay sales directors (a notch above the beauty consultants) earned an average of $25,000 annually, plus a rental car. The 31 national sales directors earned an average of $75,000. (By contrast, the comparable people in Avon's sales force earned $15,000 and $50,000 a year.) The top Mary Kay saleswomen earn about $250,000 a year.

There is a darker shade of pink for many of those at the lowest levels of the sales force. About 80 percent of the beauty consultants leave and are replaced annually, though *Business Week* says the rate is lower than that of competitors like Avon. Because the turnover is so high, the average consultant sells only $3,600 worth of cosmetics a year (of which she keeps $1,800). Reasons these consultants drop out vary from lack of interest to an aversion to the constant pressure to produce.

In late 1983, a former consultant, Liz Bailey of Smyrna, Georgia, described her two-year stint as a Mary Kay consultant as a "nightmare." She told a *Wall Street Journal* reporter that she left Mary Kay when her sales director called her while she was in the hospital recovering from surgery. The director was asking her to place another order for cosmetics.

"That's when I quit," Bailey said. "Really, I thought it all stunk. I hate being pushed."

Turnover is no problem among regular employees at the Dallas headquarters, however. Mary Kay employees—as opposed to those in the sales force—qualify for benefits comparable to those of many large corporations. But there's the Mary Kay twist for some of them. Over the past 15 years, the company has put a generous 13 percent of the payroll into a profit-sharing plan, which employees normally receive when they retire. Christmas bonuses, equal to between 1 and 5 percent of an employee's annual salary, are given each year. On an employee's fifth anniversary with the company, she or he is given 20 shares of stock; on the tenth, 80 shares; on the fifteenth, 120 shares. In late 1983, 100 shares of Mary Kay stock were worth $1,600.

College tuition is reimbursed on a sliding scale: 100 percent if the employee gets an A or a B; 75 percent if a C. The company also provides college and high school classes at the manufacturing plant. Mary Marco, a manufacturing supervisor, received her G.E.D. diploma at the age of 55 in early 1983. She had joined Mary Kay as a machine operator 11 years earlier after raising her family.

Though Marco is proud of her degree and her advancement at the company, it is Mary Kay's "personal touch" that has earned her loyalty. She learned in early 1983 that her brother had terminal cancer. Though he was not an employee of the company, Mary Kay herself sent him a letter and included a poem. According to Marco, "He treasures that letter. I thank God I am working for such a woman."

Main employment centers   Dallas, plus regional distribution centers in Los Angeles; Atlanta; Itasca, Illinois; and South Plainfield, New Jersey.

Headquarters   Mary Kay Cosmetics, Inc.
8787 Stemmons Freeway
Dallas, TX 75247
214-630-8787

THE MAYTAG COMPANY

THE MAYTAG COMPANY

Maytag makes washing machines, dryers, dishwashers, and other major appliances. U.S. employees: 4,700.

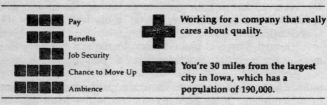

▓▓▓▓ Pay	**Working for a company that really cares about quality.**
▓▓▓ Benefits	
▓▓ Job Security	
▓▓▓▓▓ Chance to Move Up	**You're 30 miles from the largest city in Iowa, which has a population of 190,000.**
▓▓▓▓ Ambience	

Harvey Jackson works in the machine shop at Maytag's plant in Newton, Iowa. Several years ago, while taking a vacation in the Bahamas, he went into a local boutique to buy a gift for his wife. As he was talking with the saleslady, he discovered she had a new Maytag washer that didn't work. Concerned about his company's reputation, Jackson reported the problem machine to people in Newton. Within a matter of days, Maytag had sent a replacement machine to the hotel. The defective machine was returned to Iowa and put in the "boneyard," where quality control experts examined it carefully to find out what had gone wrong.

The incident indicates how Maytag has instilled a commitment to high-quality merchandise in its work force. It is an unending source of pride for those who work there that Maytag machines rank at the top in industry comparisons for durability and dependability. The average Maytag washer is said to last 14 years without problems. The company plays on this reputation in its famous "Old Lonely" TV ads featuring a Maytag repairman who never has any work to do. As Jackson told us, "We're proud we make the Cadillac of washing machines."

Jackson is an unabashed Maytag booster. He says, "The company is very good to employees in terms of being fair. We have had a good understanding with the company." By "we"

Jackson means the union; he is vice-president of the United Auto Workers Local 997, which represents production-line workers at the Newton headquarters.

Not many companies could expect union officials to evidence such enthusiasm. But Maytag doesn't pretend to be an ordinary company. It pays its people well for producing the best. "Maytag wages are higher than those paid by its competitors," according to *Fortune*. (Maytag customers also pay a premium, about $75 more for a washing machine.) The company's benefit package—pension plan, life, dental, and health insurance—is one of the most generous in the appliance industry. It's no wonder jobs at Maytag are hard to get; turnover is extremely low.

The high wages reflect an incentive system that has been in effect at Maytag for generations. Most assembly-line workers are paid extra for producing above established rates. According to the union, it's not unusual for someone working eight hours to get paid for 11 hours of work. That means many are regularly earning over $10 an hour.

It goes without saying that the incentive system doesn't mean Maytag only wants its workers to produce parts as quickly as possible. There's a quality control force of nearly 200 workers who constantly inspect parts. It's said to be common for other workers to reject items saying, "It's not Maytag quality."

Maytag's suggestion plan also plays an important role in its relentless drive to maintain quality. Called "work simplification," the plan went into effect in 1947 and has been hailed as a model throughout the country. It goes far beyond suggestion boxes. Each employee must attend a training session, while supervisors attend eight two-hour conferences. Ideas must be presented on a two-page form that details the suggestion along with an estimate of how much money and time it could save the company. The employee then shows the form to his or her foreman, and the two of them try to improve the suggestion before submission.

For accepted suggestions, employees are given one-half of the savings from their ideas over the first six months of implementation, up to a maximum award of $7,500. During 1983, 1,629 workers (94 percent of those eligible) offered 4,745 suggestions. That was an average of 3.2 suggestions per employee. Some of these ideas were implemented, resulting in payouts of $169,410.

Supervisors are not paid for their cost reduction ideas but are honored at a year-end banquet. Maytag estimated that supervisors' suggestions in 1982 saved the company over $4.5 million—an average of $26,637 per supervisor. For ten of the past 11 years since 1972, Maytag won top honors from the National Association of Suggestion Systems.

During the early months of the year when appliance demand decreases, the company often cuts back its work force. Most are recalled within a matter of weeks.

Most employees live in Newton or in nearby small towns or farms. With a population of 15,000, Newton sits among the rolling cornfields of the Midwest, about 30 miles east of Des Moines. The Maytag family of Newton founded the firm in 1893 to manufacture farm equipment. It introduced its first clothes washer, a wooden tub model, in 1907. Not long after, Maytag brought out its wringer washer, which was its exclusive product until after the Second World War. (The last wringer washer was made in 1983.) In 1949 Maytag began making automatic washers, followed by clothes dryers, dishwashers, and other appliances.

The Maytags have dominated the social life of the small town for years. The family donated a 50-acre estate, complete with swimming pools and other recreation facilities, to the town several years ago. The brother of a former company president runs the Maytag Blue Cheese company, located near Newton.

The family ran Maytag until the first nonfamily member was appointed president in 1962. The current president, Daniel J. Krumm, was brought up in Newton. Few managers have worked anywhere else. Many start with Maytag as trainees straight out of college. Manufacturing managers tend to have worked their way up through the ranks. Nine of the ten foremen in the machine shop, for instance, first worked on the shop floor, and the department's supervisor also started at the bottom.

Main employment centers   Twenty-six thousand work in the Newton facility, and another 400 in various field service offices across the United States. Maytag also owns Hardwick Stove, with 850 employees in Cleveland, Tennessee; and Jenn-Air (electric grill ranges), with 750 employees in Indianapolis, Indiana.

Headquarters   The Maytag Company
Newton, IA 50208
515-792-7000

McCORMICK

McCORMICK & COMPANY, INC.

McCormick is the largest spice maker in the world. U.S. employees: 6,800.

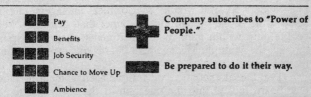

■■ Pay	✚ Company subscribes to "Power of People."
■■ Benefits	
■■■ Job Security	
■■■ Chance to Move Up	■■ Be prepared to do it their way.
■■ Ambience	

"Labor is not a commodity to be bought, sold, or exchanged in the market place. The great working force of any business is a collection of individual human beings, all with individual rights and individual problems worthy of consideration."

No, those aren't the words of a labor organizer. They were written 35 years ago by industrialist Charles P. McCormick in his book with an equally unlikely title, *The Power of People.*

Charles McCormick's legacy continues in the form of "Multiple Management" boards that operate throughout the spice and seasonings company founded by his uncle. Each of the 15 boards functions like a junior board of directors for the company's major operating divisions. They parallel the divisional boards composed of the key functional executives within each part of the company. While the divisional boards concentrate on basic administrative questions, the Multiple Management boards analyze and offer solutions to a wide variety of nuts-and-bolts problems. New ideas are hashed over and worked out.

"We're not sure whether Multiple Management is more of a management tool or a way to develop and train our new people," McCormick president Hillsman Wilson told us. "In either case, it's very much part of what makes McCormick tick."

Wilson considers himself a product of the Multiple Management system. He knew nothing about the spice business when he was hired as a one-man legal department in the early 1950s. "I came in as a lawyer. But when I sat in the Multiple Management board meetings and worked on projects with people from accounting, sales, and all the other departments, I began to get a real appreciation of the whole business."

Wilson's board activities also gave him visibility within the company, which he thinks helped him move up the corporate ladder. Several young McCormick managers cite the same value in the system today. Rather than getting to know people only within their own departments, they are exposed through the Multiple Management boards to a cross section of the company.

Two recent examples of Multiple Management in action: One board looked into the question of the "office of the future." After much discussion, it recommended that the company buy equipment that combined word and data processing. The board also drew up a questionnaire with 400 questions for the 50 competing computer makers and then narrowed the field to six possible computers. What made the process work was getting maximum input from the people most directly affected by computerization.

Another example: A Multiple Management board helped decide whether the company should enter the Mexican food market and, if so, how the new products should be marketed. The result was Tio Sancho, "the Mexican restaurant you take home," which began appearing on grocery shelves in 1982.

When Charles McCormick first introduced Multiple Management in 1932, the boards immediately attacked some basic employee concerns. Time clocks were eliminated in the factories, and today McCormick's hourly employees don't clock in except when working overtime. They also established a buddy system, now called a "sponsorship" program, whereby a new employee is introduced to others throughout the company by an old hand.

One of the early boards came up with the idea of erecting an Old English tea room and museum for salesmen, customers, and visitors. "Ye Olde McCormick Tea House" is still used by visitors to McCormick's original plant on Light

Street, near Baltimore's waterfront. The corporate head-quarters has moved to a 10-story building in the northern suburb of Hunt Valley, where the company has also built six large, clean-looking factories.

Though the corporate setting has changed, the company's leaders still cite Charles McCormick's *The Power of People*, and they continue to hand it to new employees. In the book, McCormick described what happened after he took over the company in 1932 on the death of his uncle, who founded the firm in 1889. The son of Protestant missionaries, McCormick immediately raised wages 10 percent and reduced hours from 56 to 45 per week. He told workers that the company could survive only if they improved their productivity. Such moves obviously raised more than a few eyebrows in depression-era America. But they worked. Productivity increased, and the company went from the red to the black within a year.

Charles McCormick was also one of the first employers to introduce profit-sharing and medical and life insurance plans. The profit-sharing plan is available to all employees (with the exception of one unionized plant in California). McCormick's benefit plans today also include dental coverage.

Another of Charles McCormick's legacies is calling people by their first names. President Hillsman Wilson, for instance, is called "Hilly" by everyone.

This informality is reflected in a give-and-take of ideas. Multiple Management boards and other management groups are frequently the scenes of table-pounding sessions. They call the process "harmonious clash of ideas," and it's encouraged. The boards must, however, cast a three-fourths majority vote before a proposal is recommended to the divisional board. According to Charles McCormick, this voting "tends to tone down some of the wilder ideas."

McCormick's participative management system has apparently helped the company to remain largely nonunion. None of the company's plants on the East Coast is unionized. Some plants in California that were part of Schilling (purchased by McCormick in 1947) did have union contracts. Hourly employees at the packing plant in Salinas, however, voted to decertify the ILWU (International Longshoremen's and Warehousemen's Union) in 1982. Only one plant in California is still unionized.

Working for McCormick is highly desirable, especially in the Baltimore area, so getting hired can be difficult. Salaried employees can expect up to 40 hours of interviews, including a session with an industrial psychologist. They're looking for people who can work well in a group environment. "We're interested in team players, not individual stars," explained Wilson.

For a number of years, McCormick has proclaimed one Saturday each year to be a "Charity Day" to spur employees to contribute to the United Way. Instead of being paid for work on "C Day," employees donate their pay at time and a half to charity. The company matches their earnings dollar for dollar. According to Wilson, more than 90 percent of the employees participate.

Main employment centers   Baltimore and Hunt Valley, Maryland (2,400 employees); Gilroy and Salinas, California (1,400 employees). McCormick has about two dozen other plants scattered throughout the country. Some 1,500 work overseas.

Headquarters   McCormick & Company, Inc.
11350 McCormick Road
Hunt Valley, MD 21031
301-667-7301

MERLE NORMAN®

MERLE NORMAN COSMETICS

Merle Norman makes its own brand of cosmetics in Los Angeles and sells them through 2,500 privately owned Merle Norman studios in the United States and Canada. U.S. employees: 1,000.

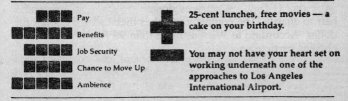

■■■	Pay	✚	**25-cent lunches, free movies — a cake on your birthday.**
■■■■■	Benefits		
■■■	Job Security	■■	**You may not have your heart set on working underneath one of the approaches to Los Angeles International Airport.**
■■■	Chance to Move Up		
■■■■■	Ambience		

Merle Norman has to have the most unusual company picnic of any firm in America. The picnic is held during the summer in a park in the San Gabriel Mountains north of Los Angeles. To get there, employees ride in style—in a procession of Rolls-Royces, Dusenbergs, Pierce Arrows, Packards, an Hispano-Suiza, an Isotta-Fraschini, and other antique or classic automobiles owned by company chairman J. B. Nethercutt.

Since Nethercutt keeps the cars in perfect running order, the processions zips past newer cars on the highway, much to the astonishment of other L.A. freeway drivers and to the considerable amusement of Merle Norman employees. Once at the park, the employees are treated to a gourmet luncheon prepared by French chef Yvon Hunckler, formerly the chef of the Beverly Hills Hotel and the Hotel de Paris in Monte Carlo.

Gourmet meals are no novelty for the folks at Merle Norman. Chef Yvon prepares a seven-course lunch daily for employees of the California cosmetics firm. In his book, *Dining at San Sylmar* (where the company's container factory is located), Chef Yvon declared, "At San Sylmar a sandwich is to food what a handshake is to love." Menus for the plant workers typically include such entrees as prime rib, trout amandine, and barbecued spareribs. The cost: 25 cents. There is no charge, however, for snacks and beverages spread out in the company dining room during morning and afternoon breaks. In the morning, employees can choose from a variety of muffins, pastries, and croissants, and in the afternoon they can pick from an assortment of pies or cakes, doughnuts, cookies, or ice cream. (The company does not, alas, have any physical-fitness facilities.)

The 25-cent lunch and the free break-time snacks are only two of the many perks available to all Merle Norman employees. Some others: gasoline at cost from company-run pumps; an employee store that sells Merle Norman cosmetics at cost; a free professional "beauty makeover" for female employees; and dental work by staff dentists provided at about one-tenth the usual fee (employees are paid while they are at the dentist).

In case they lack for entertainment, the company sponsors an Employee Night every other Saturday at the San Sylmar facility. First-run movies are shown for employees (who may bring up to six friends) in the lush Cameo Theater. After the movie, employees and their guests can make their own ice cream sundaes (also free of charge). They can then take a tour of the Merle Norman Classic Beauty Collection. A window in the employee dining room looks directly onto the collection's Grand Salon, built to look like the luxurious auto showrooms of the early 1920s, which displays the star attractions of Nethercutt's collection of 157 classic and antique automobiles. The Salon has shiny green Italian marble floors with 36-foot marble columns from Zaire rising to a handcrafted ceiling painted with 24-karat gold leaf. Light comes from chandeliers made from 1,500 prisms hand-cut from Bavarian crystal.

Among the more notable cars that may be sitting in the Grand Salon are Rudolph Valentino's 1923 Avions Voisin and silent-screen comedian Fatty Arbuckle's flaming red 1923 McFarlan Knickerbocker Cabriolet. Nethercutt also has a complete set of the Rolls-Royce Phantom series, including a 1956 model previously owned by the sheik of Kuwait and a 1913 version with a mink floor.

Employees may also want to browse among one of the world's largest sets of player pianos, musical watches, and orchestrions (such as the Popper Gladiator, a 12-foot-high, 14-foot-wide piece that contains a piano, mandolin, xylophone, bells, pipes, and drums). Carmine Coppola recently used the collection's "Mighty Wurlitzer" theater organ (with

2,463 pipes and 35 ranks) to score the epic silent film *Napoleon.*

Surrounding employees with beauty is an important ingredient in the cosmetics business, according to Nethercutt, whom everyone calls "J.B." He also considers the nearly 1,000 Merle Norman employees to be part of his "family." He and company president Gary Hollister go to great lengths to get to know employees individually. Nethercutt keeps track of everyone's birthday and, when possible, makes a point of seeking out people to wish them well on that day. The chef also makes a special cake and everyone sings "Happy Birthday" in the dining room as the cake is presented at lunchtime.

At Christmastime, the company provides a special turkey luncheon. The company's executives serve the buffet-style meal. Nethercutt and Hollister usually dish out the salad at the first table. Employees also get a check for an extra week's salary as a Christmas bonus.

The family feeling seems to rub off almost immediately on new employees. Poucette Duggan, hired as a secretary in 1983 after having worked at a small bank in Florida, told us: "When I came here, I did not know anyone in the Los Angeles area, but I got a sense of belonging immediately after coming here. I felt like I was part of a family."

The perks and the family feeling have resulted in a company with negligible turnover ("Usually only when somebody's spouse has to move away from the area," according to Rae Wisely, vice-president of personnel). Even more impressive are the statistics of perfect attendance. In 1983, for instance, 72 employees did not miss one minute of work because of absenteeism or tardiness. That's more than one-tenth of all hourly employees! Twenty-one of the 72 worked more than 5 years and 8 more than 10 years without missing time. To recognize those who achieve perfect attendance, the company offers gifts:

One year: a gold engraved watch;
Two years: either an Atari video game, a Farberware cookware set, or Oneida stainless flatware;
Three years: either a Toshiba personal stereo or a Panasonic portable TV;
Four years: either a Sunbeam or a Cuisinart food processor;

Five years: a Nikon 35mm camera;

Six years: a Panasonic AM/FM stereo eight-track cassette player with two-way speakers;

Seven years: an RCA 19-inch color TV;

Eight years: a Panasonic microwave oven;

Nine years: a specially designed ring;

Ten years: a two-week, all-expense-paid trip to Hawaii for two (in 1983, three employees and their spouses took the trip);

Fifteen years: a two-week, all-expense-paid trip to anywhere in the world for employee plus spouse, relative, or friend.

Most of the people working at Merle Norman are women. But relative newcomer Duggan insists they are not second-class citizens. She reports that her first day on the job a man came up to her and introduced himself as "Gary" and told her he was happy she had joined the company. Only after he left did she find out that "Gary" was company president Gary Hollister. "At the bank in Florida, there were only fifty employees. But the men, even if they were tellers, were 'Mr. So-and-So,' while the women, even if they were a vice-president, were on a first-name basis." The equality of the sexes extends beyond how people are referred to, according to Duggan. "There are so many women here in higher positions. There's more of a chance for a woman."

Merle Norman has made it a point to provide women with opportunity. Nethercutt insists that "we've probably put more women in business than any other corporation in the world." Nearly 95 percent of the 2,500 Merle Norman studios are owned by women. Many are in small towns, and the bulk of the studios are located in the South, Southwest, and Midwest. Some of the studio owners do quite well. One in Dallas owns a dozen studios and grosses more than a million dollars a year. Since the establishments are privately owned, the studio owners and the people they hire to help sell the cosmetics ("beauty advisors") are not technically Merle Norman employees, unlike those in the Los Angeles area who make the products.

New studio owners come to Merle Norman's Los Angeles headquarters for a two-week training period (the company pays for their hotel). Once a year all studio owners hold a convention at which new products are introduced. Some compare the emotional outpouring at the event to the annual Mary Kay Cosmetics convention in Dallas, but company president Hollister insists, "Ours isn't quite as flashy; Mr. Nethercutt doesn't descend from the ceiling like Mary Kay."

The company has grown tremendously since 1978, the first year it began advertising its products in national women's magazines. It was founded in 1931 by Nethercutt's aunt, Merle Norman, who cooked up her own complexion potions on an old-fashioned kitchen stove in her home in Santa Monica. When she started selling the product, she asked her nephew to help her. He helped launch the distinctive method of sales, through independently owned studios. Most of its competitors sell cosmetics either through drugstores or department stores (Revlon, Max Factor) or through a force of independent saleswomen (Avon, Mary Kay).

For its first 47 years, Merle Norman relied only on word-of-mouth to advertise its products. In 1978, Hollister launched an advertising campaign. He recalls putting up ads of all the major cosmetics companies on the wall of his office. After blocking out the name of the manufacturer, he asked various Merle Norman executives to identify the maker with the ad. They couldn't. He used the experiment to generate a distinctive ad campaign, in which the same woman is shown "before" and "after" using Merle Norman cosmetics. Sales have shot up from $30 million in 1978 to over $90 million in 1983. (Retail sales would be double those figures.)

The increased sales have meant more hiring, about 90 new employees in 1983. Pay for most positions is higher than at other cosmetics companies in the Los Angeles area, according to people who've worked at other places.

But Merle Norman makes it clear the company is not for everyone. Mel Baker, vice-president of manufacturing, who has worked at four other cosmetics companies, said, "Merle Norman is not for someone who wants to be a superstar. It is not for people who are highly emotional, high-pressure types, where you can expect a lot of yelling and screaming. This is not a company where you must innovate or perish."

Terri Erspamer, who has been with the company for 16 years, added that "Merle Norman is not a place for a free spirit. You must be able to adapt to a certain structure. Sloppiness is not tolerated." Production workers are given beige or blue uniforms, and office personnel are expected to adhere to a dress code. For men, that means a suit, tie, and no beards; for women, dresses, or pants only if part of a pantsuit.

Most people at Merle Norman do not expect the company to change greatly despite its recent growth. In fact, Hollister says that he and other company executives are committed to "Mr. Nethercutt's philosophy of wanting to make this one of the nicest places to work. He feels the employees make the best product when they like where they work." So, Hollister said, "Hopefully, you will be able to come back here in twenty-five years and you will see no change in the family atmosphere or working relationships. There may be a few more buildings, but that's about the only difference you'd see."

Main employment centers   The cosmetics are made at the Los Angeles headquarters (located directly under a runway approach to Los Angeles International Airport). Of the 650 working there, about 300 are production workers, with many of the rest involved in support of the studios. About 300 more work at the container manufacturing facility at San Sylmar in the San Fernando Valley about 25 miles from downtown Los Angeles. Some 50 more work at a manufacturing facility in Saugus, California. Another 50 work at a distribution center in Memphis, Tennessee.

Headquarters   Merle Norman Cosmetics
9130 Bellanca Avenue
Los Angeles, CA 90045
213-641-3000
Public tours of the Merle Norman Classic Beauty Collection are free and given daily at San Sylmar. Advance reservations are required as there is a waiting list. Call 818-367-2251 for reservations.

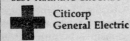

BEST TRAINING GROUNDS—FOR OTHERS

Citicorp	IBM
General Electric	Procter & Gamble

◣ herman miller

HERMAN MILLER, INC.

Herman Miller makes office furniture. U.S. employees: 3,500.

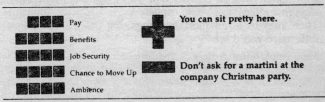

Pay	**+** You can sit pretty here.
Benefits	
Job Security	
Chance to Move Up	Don't ask for a martini at the
Ambience	company Christmas party.

Herman Miller specializes in improving the work environment with well-designed office furniture. It should be no surprise, then, that Herman Miller provides a superior working place for its employees.

Take, for instance, the company's seating plant in Holland, Michigan. The *AIA Journal*, published by the American Institute of Architects, devoted a feature story to it in 1982. Entitled "A Splendid Workplace," the AIA article said the seating plant's "interior is colorful, cheerful and seems of manageable size." Eye-level windows surround the plant, as does an acrylic clerestory that bathes the entire factory in natural light. Though people are engaged in a conventional manufacturing process, the plant was designed and built with the individual worker in mind. "Democratic daylighting" is what the *AIA Journal* called it.

This is exactly what Herman Miller has been doing for years in workplaces throughout the country. The company introduced the open office (called the "action office") to America in the late 1960s. Workspaces divided by shoulder-level dividers is a Herman Miller concept that has become a standard feature throughout corporate America. It beats closed-door offices. The *Minneapolis Tribune* once summed up neatly Herman Miller's contribution to the way Americans live inside apartments, offices, and homes: "This tiny company, since the late 1930s, has done more to revolutionize the way Americans live, what they sit on, what kind of space they work in, and how their functional surroundings look like than any other design group. The reason is the company's incorruptible honesty of design and its ability to inspire some of this country's greatest designers."

Not just another furniture company, Herman Miller has consistently been an innovator, with such prominent interior designers as Gilbert Rohde, Robert L. Propst, Gene Nelson, and Charles Eames. The well-known Eames and Ergon chairs came from Herman Miller.

Some of the country's best interior designers therefore work at Herman Miller's research lab in Ann Arbor, Michigan. The company spends 3.5 percent of total sales on research and development, a figure unheard of in the industry. The lab has two unusual restrictions: it won't work on any defense industry-related projects, and it won't be "involved in any projects which in relation to human environmental design are meaningless and worthless." Not many furniture companies can make that statement.

The vast majority of employees work at manufacturing furniture, mostly in plants in and around Zeeland, Michigan. A rustic area near Lake Michigan, Zeeland attracts many people who like small-town living.

But a surprising number of those who start on the shop floor are college graduates. They are attracted by Herman Miller's rapid growth. Sales went from $40 million in 1974 to $400 million in 1984. Others are drawn by an unusual management style.

Long before participatory management became a fad in business circles, Herman Miller was pioneering in labor and management cooperation. Based on the program developed by labor leader Joseph Scanlon, the company's plan is similar to the productivity plans at Dana and Donnelly Mirrors. It allows workers to share in productivity gains.

Company founder D.J. De Pree adopted the Scanlon Plan in 1950. De Pree (who named the company after his father-in-law) decided he needed to change his attitude after attending the funeral of an employee. He discovered that the deceased factory worker had been an accomplished poet, though "I had looked upon him as one who was good at fixing machinery and motors." A deeply religious man, De Pree sensed he had to do something to consider the employee as a whole person. "We had been very heartless about some things and still were. We might have said to someone in the factory, 'We don't have enough work, so don't come back on Monday.'"

The Scanlon Plan offered an alternative to the piecework system that the company had used to that point. The program has been revised several times since 1950, most recently in 1982. Today, all Herman Miller employees participate in a "Scanlon Information Meeting" once a month to discuss ways of improving their performance. Monthly bonuses, based on meeting goals set in areas like on-time shipments, inventory control, and customer service, have averaged 11 percent of salary over the past 10 years. The company also has profit-sharing and stock-ownership plans for all employees. Just over 40 percent of Herman Miller employees own stock in their own name. The company also offers a host of generous benefits including child care assistance, $1,500 for adoption aid, and a career bonus paid in cash each December to all with at least five years' service. The bonus ranges from $100 to $1,000 and is based on length of service (someone with 15 years, for instance, receives about $500). The company even has a new vice-president for people, Michele Hunt, who's in charge of human resources, the Scanlon Plan, health and wellness, and business literacy.

De Pree's son, Max, is now the company's president. He inherited some of his father's strong moral convictions. Annual stockholder meetings begin with a prayer. Alcohol is strictly forbidden at all company functions. De Pree likes to expound on his philosophy of management. In a speech he gave in 1982, he stated that "in addition to all of their ratios and goals and parameters and bottom lines, it is fundamental that corporations have a concept of persons. In our company this begins with an understanding of the diversity of people's gifts. Understanding the diversity of our gifts enables us to begin taking the crucial step of trusting each other."

Because of his emphasis on trust, De Pree emphasizes "roving leadership" as opposed to hierarchical leadership, and "covenantal relationships" instead of legal or "contractual" ones. He defines a covenantal relationship as "one which is based on shared commitment to ideas, to issues, to values, to goals, and to management processes. Words such as love, warmth, personal chemistry are certainly pertinent. They fill deep needs and they enable work to have meaning and to be fulfilling. Covenantal relationships enable corporations to be hospitable to the unusual person and to unusual ideas."

People who work at Herman Miller expect that sort of homily. Moral uprightness is part of the atmosphere. You get some sense of what it's like to work here by looking at the company's 1983 annual report wherein various Miller people sound off on how they feel:

Andy McGregor, director of product marketing at Zeeland headquarters: "Politics can be a positive force; coalitions for good causes are extremely political. If people see you take on something that may not be 'smart' politically, they may also see you with conviction. I choose to believe that in this corporation there are still quite a few people who are here because of such convictions. To retreat from the political arena is to . . . leave control to others who may not hold these values. I think I've experienced negatives from being outspoken. But it's a question of whether you want to stay with your convictions, and your convictions should be more important than this company is. . . . If you're only going to do it when it's convenient, that's what I call situation ethic. I don't buy it."

Rusty Ridgely, production supervisor at the Roswell, Georgia, plant: "I was with a very well-known firm before this, a national company, and it was very cold and hard and businesslike and bottom-line oriented. When I came to Herman Miller, it was just a tremendous change. I guess it fits me, and I know that fitting me is not one of the company's goals, but the company fits me and I fit the company because of the way I feel about things like that."

Alan Colley, professional services manager in Dallas: "When I came to Herman Miller I felt an obligation to speak my mind on topics that I felt were important. It's gotten me into a lot of trouble emotionally, you know, you put a heavy emotional commitment into the kind of thing because it's your company."

Martha Bel, who retired from the company in 1983 after 24 years: "My husband has often made the comment, 'People ask "Where do you work?" and I'll say "Herman Miller," and off we go into a discussion about the company'—he'll say, 'They only asked you where you worked, you don't have to sell them the company.'"

Herman Miller has grown exponentially in the past few years. In 1976 the company had 500 employees; today there are more than seven times that number. Once a week, the company posts a listing of job openings, and most managerial positions are filled from within the ranks. The compensation manager, for instance, originally worked as a sewer in the plant, while the new vice-president of health/science division is a psychologist who started in the sales department.

Prospects look good for the industry, too, as some project that office workers will increase at a rate of 22 percent per year over the next decade. Herman Miller hopes that many of them will be sitting at Herman Miller desks on Herman Miller chairs behind Herman Miller partitions.

Main employment centers About 2,500 work in Zeeland, Holland, or Grandville, Michigan; another 200 in Roswell, Georgia, Grand Prairie, Texas, and Irvine, California. The company has a sales force of more than 200 in offices throughout the country.

Headquarters   Herman Miller, Inc.
Zeeland, MI 49464
616-772-3300

MINNESOTA MINING & MANUFACTURING COMPANY

3M makes 45,000 different products, from Scotch tape and video cassettes to orthopedic casts to reflective coatings for street signs. U.S. employees: 52,000.

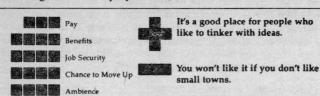

▪▪▪▫ Pay		
▪▪▪▪▪ Benefits	➕	It's a good place for people who like to tinker with ideas.
▪▪▪▫ Job Security		
▪▪▪▫ Chance to Move Up	▪▪▪	You won't like it if you don't like small towns.
▪▪▪▫ Ambience		

Art Fry found it annoying when the bookmarks fell out of his hymnal during services at his church in North St. Paul, Minnesota. It would be better, he thought, if he could put in a piece of paper that would adhere to the pages yet be removable to mark other pages.

Several years later, little yellow message pads called Post-It note pads began proliferating in offices throughout the United States. The slips of paper had the remarkable quality of sticking to a page, yet they could be taken off without leaving a trace.

The story of how Art Fry translated his idea of an adhesive bookmark into Post-It goes far toward explaining why 3M is such a superlative employer.

Forbes once said that 3M's secret lies in its "ability to nurture creativity." Indeed, inventors like Art Fry are the very backbone of 3M. Nearly 4,000 scientists, engineers, and inventors (some with no more than a high school diploma) work in 3M's research labs. The company spends more than $300 million a year on research and development.

Every year hundreds of new products pour out of 3M's labs and into the marketplace. It is a company goal that one-quarter of the company's annual sales must come from products that did not exist five years before. One observer pointed out that you can't talk with a janitor at 3M without the conversation turning to the subject of new 3M products.

3M's 45,000 products cut across virtually every industry: from recording tapes and video cassettes for home entertainment, to surgical masks and orthopedic casts for hospital care, to photocopies and absorbent materials to soak up oil spills, to 3M's best-known product: Scotch transparent tape.

Two sayings typify 3M research. One is "Never kill an idea, just deflect it." The other, called the Eleventh Commandment: "Thou shalt not kill a new product idea." The burden is on those who want to stop research since the company has often found an application for many a seemingly off-the-wall idea.

No one told Art Fry he was crazy when he first mentioned his adhesive bookmark idea in 1973. But he didn't get much support for it, either. A research chemist working in the adhesive division of 3M's huge labs at the St. Paul headquarters, Fry was expected to tinker with his ideas. The company allows its researchers about one day a week to dabble with their own pet projects. It took Fry almost a year of dabbling to create a prototype of his removable bookmark.

But 3M doesn't believe that inventors should be stuck in the research labs for the rest of their lives. 3M encourages them to get involved in marketing their own ideas. Since 3M's inception, employees have been told that scientists must be sales-oriented and salespersons must be science-oriented.

An inventor who cannot sell an idea within his own division is free to sell it elsewhere within the company. If he finds a taker, both he and his potential product move in with the new sponsor. 3Mers with new project ideas are also free to recruit marketing professionals from other parts of the company to work on the project.

It took Fry several months after he had created his prototype to convince enough people in his own division that his idea was sufficiently marketable and form a team of about a dozen researchers and sales specialists. Critics didn't see why people would want to spend many times the cost of scratch paper to buy Fry's version of the same product. But they weren't about to violate 3M's injunction against killing ideas.

As the idea developed, Fry spent increasing amounts of

time considering the sales potential of the idea. Fry told us that during the early stages he kept a detailed log of each person who took samples of his adhesive note pads: "I made my initial sales projections based on how often they came back for more."

After literally years of figuring out the best ways to manufacture the pads (a complicated process requiring precisely the right kinds of paper and adhesive) and market testing, Post-It note pads began appearing in stores across the country. The product sells at an estimated rate of $40 million a year, and hundreds of 3Mers are employed making or selling it. (3M won't disclose precise sales or employment figures on any of its products for competitive reasons.)

Art Fry is still working in the lab—by choice. Successful scientists like Fry who prefer to stay in the lab receive promotions in a system parallel to that for managers, and profit-sharing related to the performance of their division, as do managers. The amount can equal a bonus of 10 to 40 percent in addition to their regular base pay. But they receive no royalty from their discoveries, because 3Mers believe that the success of an individual product is the result of a team effort rather than one person. Fry has also received prestigious company-wide awards, including the coveted Carlton Award, an honor given annually to the best scientists at 3M. In the lobby of 3M's St. Paul headquarters is a display devoted to Carlton Award winners.

Some especially successful products have created entire divisions, often headed by the inventors who came up with the original idea. Lewis Lehr, 3M's current chairman, is a case in point. A chemical engineer, Lehr helped create some of 3M's original health care products—surgical drapes and hypoallergenic adhesive tape. He became increasingly interested in the administrative side of the business and was made the first head of the newly created medical products division in 1962.

Fluid movement within the company is a 3M hallmark. The company's structure is considered to be more "biological" than a traditional organizational chart. When a new product develops enough sales, a new division is created (3M has 40 divisions).

3M is decentralized physically, too. About 52,000 of 3M's 87,000 employees are located in the United States. But 3M has insisted on acting small. Only 5 of the 91 U.S. plants (in 35 different states) have more than 1,000 employees. Median plant size is 115 people. 3M locates its plants largely in small-town America, in such places as Honeoye, New York; Wahpeton, North Dakota; Cynthiana, Kentucky; and Prairie du Chien, Wisconsin. The largest U.S. plant is in Hutchinson, Minnesota, population 8,000. Harry Heltzer, a former 3M chairman, once explained that 3M preferred locating its plants in semirural communities. "People in small communities have a great interest in their jobs, maybe because there are not many other diversions."

Don't look at 3M if you've spent most of your working career elsewhere. Promotion from within is gospel. Managers are virtually never hired from outside. Executive recruiters also have difficulty getting 3M managers to leave the company. One New York headhunter told *Fortune*: "I've never been successful in getting anyone from 3M. Generally, one out of three times you call a candidate you can get him interested enough to meet you and maybe half of that time to meet the client. Most of the time I don't get any reaction at all from a 3Mer."

For someone just entering the labor market, 3M has much to recommend it. There's no junior executive training program; it's on-the-job experience from day one. Most 3Mers like it that way, it seems. Over 4,000 employees have been with 3M for more than 25 years.

Though 3M appears to be a veritable mecca for bright inventors and aggressive salespeople, assembly-line workers praise it, too. Worker participation is institutionalized at 3M. The company has "quality circles," where production workers meet regularly to discuss ways of improving their work. The method, first adopted in one of 3M's Japanese plants in 1971, was introduced in a U.S. plant in 1978. By 1982 more than 350 quality circles had been organized at about 100 different 3M plants throughout the world.

Not surprisingly, 3M has a long record as an excellent corporate citizen. 3M's ride-sharing program is a model for other companies throughout the nation. 3M spends a lot of money on pollution control through its "Pollution Prevention Pays" program.

But chinks have appeared in the 3M armor. Watergate besmirched the company's image. In 1974 newspapers carried stories that the company had a secret slush fund for political candidates. Of the quarter-million dollars in cash that was in the fund, nearly $30,000 found its way into President Nixon's 1972 campaign. Top 3M executives resigned; employee morale plummeted. One employee even declined to give a speech about 3M to a church group after the scandal was revealed. The pastor tried to dissuade him, saying that no one was perfect. But, the employee replied, "I always thought 3M *was* perfect."

3M's headquarters, the 3M Center in St. Paul, is located on a plot of 400 acres that is often referred to as a campus because of its universitylike atmosphere. A few miles away is the Tartan Club, a country club exclusively for the use of 3Mers. Membership costs $4 a year.

Main employment centers   Twenty-two thousand 3M employees work in Minnesota. The next-largest concentration is in Southern California, where about 5,000 work. Between 1,000 and 2,000 work in these midwestern states: Wisconsin, South Dakota, Iowa, Missouri, and Illinois.

Headquarters   Minnesota Mining & Manufacturing Company
3M Center
St. Paul, MN 55144
612-733-1110

MOOG INC.

MOOG INC.

Moog (rhymes with rogue) makes electrohydraulic control products—such as servovalves to guide missiles—for the aerospace industry. It's also a machine tool maker. Employees: 3,100.

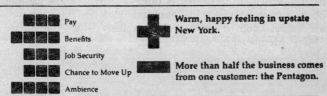

▪▪▪ Pay	**+** Warm, happy feeling in upstate New York.
▪▪▪ Benefits	
▪▪▪ Job Security	
▪▪▪ Chance to Move Up	**More than half the business comes from one customer: the Pentagon.**
▪▪▪ Ambience	

One summer evening in 1981, Bill Moog rode one of his four motorcycles to the company's main office in East Aurora, New York. Later on, as he was leaving to drive home, he was spotted by a group of Moog production workers who were taking a break outdoors. They stood and gave him a loud burst of cheers and applause.

This story was recounted by reporter Don O'Hara when he profiled William C. Moog and the company bearing his name in the Sunday magazine of the *Buffalo News*. O'Hara also interviewed some Moog retirees. Joseph J. Schmitt, who was a retired tool designer, told him, "I never had a day when I didn't want to go to work at Moog." Another retiree, Tillie Weiber, who was a subassembler, said, "I've worked at more places than you can count on both hands—and Moog was best of all."

Moog seems to inspire such comments. When you join this young company, based outside Buffalo, you receive an employee handbook that starts off as follows: "Our philosophy at Moog is a simple one. We believe in the people who work for us. We believe work can be a more rewarding and satisfying experience for everyone in an atmosphere of mutual trust and confidence."

It's a nice introduction—and Moog is a company that practices what it preaches. Time clocks have been eliminated.

The company relies on each employee to report his or her performance. No time studies are conducted. There are no scheduled coffee breaks or prescribed times for rest periods. Moog does not have guards or locked offices. And even though the company does 56 percent of its business with the Pentagon, security-surveillance activities are carried out only when required by government regulations.

Moog does not have floor inspectors to check every product. Employees are expected to check their own work. There are, however, random quality-control checks. It's just that you don't have people standing over you. Everyone works on a salaried basis. There's profit-sharing. In fact, there are two profit-sharing plans—one for the great bulk of employees, one for managers. The management profit-sharing plan doesn't come into play until after the employee plan is paid out.

Moog, as a matter of policy, establishes "salary rates above the community averages." The company maintains one of the few machine shops in the country with piped-in music, air conditioning, and tile floors. Twice a year all employees are invited to attend a meeting with management where they may ask any questions they want.

Moog has liberal benefits, giving employees a wide range of options to tailor a program appropriate to their needs and desires. Moog also has a unique sabbatical benefit. When an employee reaches his or her tenth anniversary with the company, he or she is credited with an additional seven-week vacation benefit (on top of the three weeks for which he or she is already eligible). Another seven-week vacation benefit is awarded on each subsequent fifth-year anniversary (fifteenth, twentieth, twenty-fifth, etc.). If you don't want to take the time off, you can take payment instead.

Moog was founded in 1951 by Bill Moog, who had invented a new kind of valve while he was an engineer at Cornell Aeronautical Laboratories. The laboratory tried to license the production rights to several manufacturers but none was interested. So Moog left to form his own company to make the valve. From the very start he was committed to having a company where people "would be much more effectively motivated in an environment of trust, respect, positive rewards, and reinforcement than in an environment of coercion, punishment, and threats."

The philosophy seems to have worked. Moog has grown to the point where sales exceed $200 million a year and the employee force numbers more than 3,000. Moreover, it seems to be a happy work force. The satisfaction is reflected in Moog's incredibly low turnover. In 1982, it was 1 percent. Even though the company is only a little over 30 years old, in 1983 it had 200 employees with more than 25 years of service. Between September 1, 1981, and December 31, 1983, 6 employees celebrated 30-year anniversaries, 76 25-year anniversaries, 196 20-year anniversaries, 50 15-year anniversaries, 363 10-year anniversaries, and 383 5-year anniversaries.

The low turnover explains why it's difficult to get hired at Moog. The company gets 15,000 job applications a year; it hires 250. Temporary summer jobs are filled by children of employees.

Moog has never had a work stoppage. And in 1983, it had its first layoffs in 11 years. Of the 44 people who were let go, 21 were rehired before the year was out, and the company went through elaborate outplacement efforts to help the laid-off employees find new jobs.

Bill Moog is an engineer. But in 1966, Joe C. Green joined the company from General Motors as vice-president for human resources. He is an articulate proponent of the working style at Moog, describing the difference between General Motors and Moog as one of "180 degrees." Green sees Moog as an organization dedicated to creating an environment where "human dignity and individual worth" are valued. He once developed the following laundry list of Moog features as testimony to this dedication:

Mutual trust and respect
No time clocks
No labor unions
No scheduled breaks
No bells and whistles
Employees report own time
No assembly lines
Cross training—OJT
Job enrichment and
    enlargement
Responsibility for own
    inspection

New-hire orientation
Preretirement planning
Tough hiring requirements
Employees as human beings
Employees want to do a good
    job
100 percent educational
    assistance
Employee meetings regularly
Affirmative action plan
Grievance procedures
Tile floors

Air-conditioned factories
Best equipment and tools
Above-average pay rates
Probationary periods
Reduction procedure
Family security package
Vacation-extended plan
Profit-sharing
Employee stock purchase plan
Job security
Overtime equalization
Personal time
Supervisory style
Dual ladder concept
Supervisor training
Technical training center
Professional organizations
Seminars
Communications program
Employee handbook—policy guidelines
Job posting
Counseling/documentation
Supervisor manual
Social and recreation programs
Employee committees—safety and others
Buildings designed with human amenities
Civic responsibility
Community relations
Good housekeeping
All employees salaried

Main employment centers   East Aurora, Elma, and Orchard Park—all suburbs of Buffalo.

Headquarters   Moog Inc.
East Aurora, NY 14052
716-652-2000

The Morgan Bank

J. P. MORGAN & CO. INCORPORATED

The fifth-largest U.S. bank in terms of deposits and assets. U.S. employees: 12,965.

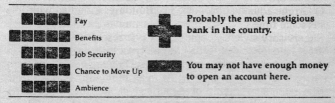

■■■■ Pay		
■■■■■ Benefits	**+**	**Probably the most prestigious bank in the country.**
■■■■ Job Security		
■■■■ Chance to Move Up	■■	**You may not have enough money to open an account here.**
■■■■ Ambience		

Morgan runs the class act of the banking industry. As the president of a competing bank once told *Fortune*, "They've made it their business to get the best people, they treat them very well, they develop them very well, they have them in depth—and it shows.".

It shows in the bank's statistics. In 1984, for instance, Morgan made $41,507 in *profits* for each employee, more than double the average of other large banks. Morgan also ranked first in return on assets, while having the lowest percentage of bad loans.

Morgan demonstrates that it is the elite of the elite in other obvious ways. It is not your typical neighborhood bank. You can't open a checking account with Morgan Guaranty Trust unless you can keep a $5,000 no-interest minimum balance (with penalties if it dips below).

The well-to-do customers rarely pop in to cash a check at the Morgan bank located at the corner of Wall and Broad streets, across from the New York Stock Exchange. There are no tellers' cages, only bank officers sitting in leather chairs behind their wooden desks. Above the main banking room hangs a two-ton chandelier with 1,900 crystal pieces. The building's cornerstone contains a copper box with the will of founder J. Pierpont Morgan. Morgan, whose very name is synonymous with wealth and power, bequeathed one year's salary to each member of his staff upon his death in 1913.

Morgan employees today don't expect such patrician generosity, but they do get a free lunch. Literally. Every day Morgan serves a free lunch to approximately 6,000 employees who work in the 38-story skyscraper at 15 Broad Street. The fare ranges from a top-rate corporate cafeteria for most of the troops, to an excellent, buffet-style spread for the junior executives, to a four-star, multicourse repast for top executives and their guests. No alcohol is served, but a waiter offers cigars from a silver platter at the conclusion of the executive luncheon. The bank spends $8 million a year on the noontime perk.

Don't plan on stopping by for lunch if you're on Wall Street, though. Security is extremely tight. You have to flash an employee ID card or have a specific appointment with someone even to get into the Morgan building. As one of the most tangible symbols of American capitalism, Wall Street has found itself a target of terrorist bombers in the past. Thirty people were killed in 1920 from a bomb planted on the street outside Morgan Bank's headquarters, and one Morgan executive was slain and two others severely injured in 1975 when Puerto Rican nationalists blew up the Fraunces Tavern five blocks south on Broad Street.

Those who possess the Morgan ID card, however, enter a world that offers some of the best working conditions in America. Tasteful art adorns the complex. A large percentage of the people work in spacious rooms behind large wooden desks. Though dozens may work together in the same room, the overall impression is that of a library reading room. The thickly carpeted floors seem to muffle sound.

The quiet, restrained atmosphere is intentional. As Morgan's chairman, Lewis T. Preston, once explained to the *New York Times*, "We spend an extraordinary amount of time just worrying about the environment and the people in it." Or, to quote J. P. Morgan, son of the founder, the aim of the firm is "doing only a first-class business, and that in a first-class way."

Morgan stresses "relationship banking," meaning they want their people to develop long-term working ties with the bank's customers. And Morgan is very picky about whom it relates to. Aside from a handful of wealthy individuals, Morgan deals primarily with very large corporations or governments. Of the 100 largest corporations in the world, 96 are Morgan clients. While other banks are busy trying to set up offices throughout the country to be close to the companies, Morgan often expects its clients to come to them. With operations centralized in New York, Morgan keeps its lines of communication short. Morgan people get to know each other and their clients extremely well.

Besides working together in the New York headquarters, many Morgan people know each other from the company's unparalleled management training program. It lasts six months (just three months for those with an M.B.A.) and exposes people to all phases of Morgan's operations. The training classes are relatively small, about 50 people per session. Since 1965, more than 2,000 professional employees—about 15 percent of the entire company and more than half the officers—have gone through the program.

People don't come to Morgan for training and then move on to greener pastures. Morgan's pasture is as green as any in the entire banking industry. Reflecting on Morgan's ability to hold on to its people, *Euromoney* magazine recently said, "There are perhaps more lifetime employees in Morgan than at any other bank, so strong is the house ethic." Morgan trains and cultivates a special kind of banker, and it wants things done the Morgan way or not at all.

It almost goes without saying that Morgan pays well. When compared with other large banks, Morgan salaries are at or near the top for most positions, though not as high as they are at some investment banking houses, like Goldman Sachs.

Morgan was one of the first banks to institute a profit-sharing plan for all its employees. It is still one of the most generous in the industry, according to Allan H. MacNeill, an assistant vice-president and secretary of the committee that administers the deferred profit-sharing plan. Morgan's current plan, begun in 1959, gives those with two years or less at the bank an annual cash payment of up to 6 percent of their salary. Those with more than two years' service receive a profit-sharing contribution that can reach up to 15 percent of their salary. They can elect either to receive all or part of it in cash or have it invested in any of six funds. The bank has made the maximum contributions of 6 percent and 15 percent to the profit-sharing plan each year since 1965. Employees can borrow up to 50 percent of the money they have deferred, up to $50,000. They have five years to pay it back. Junior and senior executives at Morgan also qualify for additional bonus and incentive plans including stock options for the top 200 to 300 officers.

Unlike banks that urge their employees to develop an expertise and stick with it forever, Morgan encourages its people to move around. Employees typically rotate jobs every three to five years. Most professionals at the bank can expect to be offered an overseas assignment at some point in their career. Morgan has banking offices in 22 countries, from London to Tokyo to Buenos Aires.

There's an undeniable snobbishness associated with working for Morgan. The *Wall Street Journal* carried an item recently about a Morgan telephone directory that had the following admonition to employees, "Avoid saying 'hello.' This elsewhere pleasant and familiar greeting is out of place in the world of business." The directory suggested instead to "identify yourself, such as 'bookkeeping department, Miss Smith speaking.'"

But it is wrong to infer, as many people do, that only certifiable blue bloods from Ivy League schools work there. "That blue-blood image may have been true in the 1930s or 1940s," says one personnel executive. "But it just isn't so today." Morgan takes great pains to recruit its people from colleges throughout the United States. It does not insist that all of its professional recruits have M.B.A.'s, and only about half of the 200 or so to whom it annually offers jobs come from business schools.

That does not mean Morgan has become plebeian, any more than has Harvard, Yale, or Princeton because they routinely admit students not born into the upper crust of society. Being hired by Morgan provides a sense of having made it, of having been accepted into the elite. High standards are expected. People are supposed to be competent, to work hard, to be part of a great team. Since one has "made it," he or she should take the time to cultivate a personal life. Workaholics are not encouraged; vacations are considered important.

Linda Scheuplein, Morgan vice-president and Mount Holyoke graduate, who previously worked at Citicorp and the accounting firm of Price Waterhouse, expressed the Morgan attitude well: "Morgan stands for quality, not for mass volume or being trendy. Everybody is very proud of working here. We are convinced this is the very best bank in the world. Morgan is where it's at in terms of banking."

Main employment centers   Aside from the headquarters on Wall Street, several hundred Morgan employees work in midtown Manhattan offices. Other offices are located throughout the world.

Headquarters   J. P. Morgan & Co. Incorporated
23 Wall Street
New York, NY 10015
212-483-2323

MOST STRONGLY UNIONIZED

Anheuser-Busch	Cummins Engine	General Electric
	Dana	Inland Steel
	Deere	Maytag

NISSAN MOTOR MANUFACTURING CORPORATION U.S.A.

Nissan manufactures small trucks in the United States. U.S. employees: 2,000.

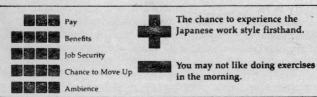

Pay

Benefits

Job Security

Chance to Move Up

Ambience

The chance to experience the Japanese work style firsthand.

You may not like doing exercises in the morning.

A year after he started working for Nissan, Ken Herndon sold his '76 Chevy station wagon and started driving a brand-new Nissan Stanza sedan. It was not just company loyalty that caused Herndon to switch to the Japanese car. Any Nissan employee with 12 months' service qualifies for a leasing program. The $160 a month the company deducts from Herndon's paycheck also takes care of maintenance, tax, license, and insurance costs. "All I have to do is put gas in it," explained Herndon, who works as an assembly-line technician.

At General Motors, Ford, and Chrysler, only top managers are entitled to such leasing deals. But executive perks run counter to Nissan's philosophy of "participative management." Besides making small trucks at its new $660 million plant outside the rural central Tennessee town of Smyrna, Nissan intends to make the plant a showpiece of Japanese-style management—with a few distinctively American twists.

Like their Japanese counterparts, some of Nissan's Tennessee workers begin their day with morning exercises followed by small group ("team") meetings. But the calisthenics are optional, and there's no singing of the company song as is common in Japan. Nearly everybody wears the company uniform to work. Assembly-line workers sport dark blue slacks and caps with light blue shirts. "Nissan" in block letters is sewn above one shirt pocket and the worker's first name is stenciled on the other. Office employees have their own company wardrobe, including dark blue blazers and white shirts and blouses with the Nissan logo written on the sleeve. The company provides employees with three changes of work clothes at no expense and stresses that wearing them is strictly voluntary. Nissan decided against constructing apartment complexes near the plant as it has done in Japan to house workers and their families.

Unlike some Japanese companies that have built plants in the United States (such as Honda's factory in Ohio), Nissan's facility is run entirely by Americans, with two exceptions—the vice-president of quality assurance and a vice-president of finance. Marvin Runyon, the American president of the subsidiary, worked for Ford for 37 years. He started as an assembly-line worker in Dallas and retired as vice-president for body and assembly operations. The only perk reserved for Runyon is the right to lease Nissan's luxury model, "The President," which looks much like an expensive Mercedes but is not for sale in the United States.

Runyon usually lunches in one of the two large employee cafeterias (there is no executive dining room) with other workers. When in the plant, he wears the blue work clothes with "Marvin" inscribed over the right pocket. Everybody calls him and the other managers by their first names. Runyon has lunch with all new employees in small groups, and he conducts company-wide meetings at least every four months.

More than 150,000 people applied for the initial 2,000 openings at the plant. The state of Tennessee helped screen applicants and agreed to put up $7 million for a preemployment training program. The state's classes range from welding and machine shop to hydraulics and electronics. Prospective employees took the classes in the evenings or on weekends for a period of at least six weeks before being interviewed by as many as a half-dozen people at Nissan. With so many people to choose from, Nissan could afford to be extremely selective, placing much emphasis on verbal skills and ability to work with others.

Once on board, employees continue learning skills for their jobs at the plant's $4 million training center. It's run by Larry Seltz, a 22-year Ford veteran. Seltz emphasizes cross-training, another Japanese technique whereby assembly-line workers are taught a variety of jobs and skills. For instance, a person operating a resistance welding machine at Nissan learns how to change the welding tips when they become corroded, or make other minor adjustments in the equipment. Seltz said that at Ford the machine operator would have to wait for a skilled craftsman to make such changes. "We have found the people enjoy the whole job," Seltz says.

Before the first truck came off the line in June 1983, Nissan's training and screening procedures had come under fire from the United Auto Workers union. One UAW official called it "brainwashing," and the union has vowed to organize workers at the plant despite the strong objections of Nissan's Runyon, who contends that working conditions "absolutely cannot be improved on." The UAW's president. Owen Bieber, countered, "History proved Henry Ford wrong and history will likewise prove Marvin Runyon wrong."

Judging from interviews conducted at the plant in mid-1983, Runyon and Nissan were winning the battle hands down. Nonsupervisory employees can best be described as having a love affair with Nissan. For one thing, a sizable percentage (383 employees to be exact) had been sent to Nissan's plants in Japan, where they worked on the line for at least six weeks to pick up the Japanese way firsthand.

Lonnie Blittle, who formerly worked for J. C. Penney and General Electric, was hired to work on the assembly line in the paint shop. What impressed him most about the Japanese plant was "the teamwork. Nobody is ever yelling at anybody. It was a team effort. Everybody is constantly improving themselves on a daily basis. They are good at what they do."

Blittle also found remarkable the quality of communications in the plant. "Nobody seemed to be in the dark. Everybody knew what was going on. Nothing was ever hid back. There was none of the hush-hush atmosphere with management behind closed doors and everybody else waiting until they drop the boom on us. They are right down pitching in, not standing around with their hands on their hips."

This feature of the Japanese system appears to have been exported directly to Tennessee. Ken Herndon's previous job was at Du Pont's Dacron plant in Old Hickory, from which he was laid off in 1981. "Du Pont had a supervisor for everything," Herndon explained. "Here you don't have so many people telling you what to do. There are only five levels between me and the president of the company." (By contrast, the typical U.S. auto maker has 12 levels of supervision between the line worker and the company president.)

Herndon said that at Nissan "the managers are out on the floor. They are not in separate offices. At other places I've worked, they will sneak around and try to catch you doing something wrong. Or a supervisor is so scared to death when the manager shows up that he runs around and makes everybody clean things up. But here, he is just one of us." Supervisors have desks on the plant floor in areas reserved for breaks.

Kathy Thomas also appreciates the teamwork: "It makes you feel that you are not a peon with everybody standing over you and shoving you around."

Thomas previously was employed as a construction worker for the company that built the Nissan plant. Before that she had worked as a secretary. Her job with Nissan is on the assembly line in the body area of the plant. She especially likes the fact that Nissan appears to be concerned "about you as a whole person."

On the Thursday night before she came to work, the company sponsored a family orientation program at the plant. Thomas brought her two young daughters to the presentation that included refreshments and slides about Nissan in Japan and the United States. The company also gave everyone a set of drinking glasses with *Nissan* printed on them. The day before Thomas came to work, four different people called her to welcome her to the company.

The emphasis on physical fitness at Nissan extends beyond the morning calisthenics routine. Ping-Pong tables and basketball hoops are scattered throughout the 78-acre plant. Baseball diamonds and volleyball courts are located just outside. Many employees play quick games during the lunch or morning and afternoon break periods. Nissan has also constructed an employee activity center with Nautilus weight-training equipment; a full-sized swimming pool is located in a recreation park at the plant site.

Nissan's base wage rate for entry-level assembly workers was $9.80 to $11.40 an hour in late 1984 — about average for the industry. But Nissan's employees also receive a $1.35-an-hour bonus for each hour they are on the line. It is a unique plan for the auto industry and appears to be aimed at reducing the problem of absenteeism that plagues other car manufacturers. The bonus checks, which amount to more than a thousand dollars, are paid twice a year, at the beginning of June and the beginning of December.

The company also has a Pay for Versatility program. In other words, the more different jobs a person can perform in his or her area, the more that employee gets paid. The company provides training during working hours for those interested in picking up new skills.

The company was producing about 10,000 trucks a month by the end of 1984 and had plans to begin building Nissan Sentra passenger cars in the spring of 1985. In June 1985 Nissan expects to add an extra shift and another thousand employees to the rolls. It contends its wages are comparable to other U.S. car makers. The policy of paying competitive wages presents Nissan with a real challenge, since labor costs in the U.S. auto industry are 60 percent to 80 percent higher than the cost of labor in Japan.

Part of the solution, Nissan feels, lies in automation. The plant has 228 robots, more than any Nissan plant in Japan, which means that Nissan employs about two-thirds as many workers as a comparably sized older American auto plant.

But the bottom line depends upon the productivity of Nissan's workers. According to Seltz: "Our efficiencies are going to come in other ways than pay, particularly in how we structure the jobs. It will not be at the expense of the worker."

Peter Laarman, a spokesman for the UAW in Detroit, agrees that Nissan's wages and benefits are comparable to those of UAW members in Ford, GM, and Chrylser: "Nissan did not set up its plant in Tennessee to save a nickel in labor costs." He contends, though, that Nissan workers need to unionize for their own "dignity." He told us: "Even though Nissan offers lots of employee goodies, these things are not a matter of right and enforceable nor the result of the workers' decision to achieve them through struggle. Rather they are at the discretion of the employer. And he who gives it can take it away."

So the UAW's Laarman thinks the honeymoon between Nissan and its workers is only temporary: "Nissan is a good place to work, but it would be better with a union."

Main employment center   Smyrna.

Headquarters   Nissan Motor Manufacturing Corporation U.S.A.
Smyrna, TN 37167
615-459-1400

nordstrom

NORDSTROM INC.

Nordstrom operates 39 fashion specialty stores in the western part of the United States. Employees: 13,500.

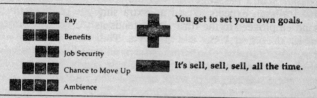

Pay	■■ ■		You get to set your own goals.
Benefits	■■ ■		
Job Security	■		
Chance to Move Up	■■ ■		It's sell, sell, sell, all the time.
Ambience	■■■ ■		

How would you like to work for a company that continually posts reminders? Reminders such as these:

"Make a daily 'to do' list."

"What is the best use of my time now?"

"List goals, set priorities."

That's the way Nordstrom is. You might have a conversation with a manager during the course of a day, and he or she might say to you, "By the way, what are your goals for today?" If you don't like to work in a "gung-ho" atmosphere where people are always revved up, this is not the place for you. But Nordstrom does clearly have something terrific going for it—and it has a lot to do with those simple reminders.

It's not that Nordstrom treats employees like children who need to be nagged all the time. If that were the case, it would be resented—and ignored. But Nordstrom has working for it a strong employee spirit, one that flows from an operating style in which employees are encouraged to take charge of their jobs and treat their customers like gods and goddesses.

Constant reinforcement goes on at Nordstrom through various pats on the back. The most prestigious is the Pacesetter Award, given to people who have exceeded the goals they set by a considerable margin. In 1982, 95 new employees were admitted to the Pacesetters Club, bringing the grand total

289

to 1,501 over the 14 years it has been in operation. As a Pacesetter, you're given a certificate, a new business card that says "Pacesetter" on it, and you and a guest are invited to a lavish evening of dining, dancing, and entertainment. In addition, for the following year, Pacesetters enjoy a 33 percent discount on all Nordstrom merchandise (the standard employee discount is 20 percent).

At Nordstrom, the customer *is* always right. Many stores say that, but few practice it. Nordstrom does. The salespersons you meet in Nordstrom stores will knock themselves out for you. If you're in a Nordstrom and you're in a rush to catch a plane, you'd be surprised to find that the salesperson might drop everything and drive you to the airport. After you buy something at Nordstrom, you will very likely receive a thank-you card in the mail from the salesperson. If you buy a suit for $300 and next week see that the price of that very same suit has been knocked down to $200, you might feel cheated; if you complained to a Nordstrom person, you might be handed $100 on the spot. They carry this "customer is always right" policy to the extreme. If a customer comes in and says he bought tire chains at Nordstrom and wants a refund, he gets one promptly with no ifs, ands, or buts—even though Nordstrom has never stocked tire chains. All these examples were cited by Nordstrom salespersons we talked to in Seattle.

The Harvard Business School once did a case history on Nordstrom, talking to employees who had worked elsewhere. Here are some snippets from those interviews:

"When I used to work at I. Magnin, I didn't know the people on the second floor. Here we get to meet everyone."

"I think the company takes pride in the people that work for them. For instance, it's a small thing, I know, but everyone was invited to the Christmas party, not just department store managers and buyers."

"You feel you are in business for yourself. They give you quality merchandise, a good selection, advertising and promotion, and they produce the traffic for you. So all we have to do is go out and sell."

One big reason Nordstrom people seem to be happy in their work is that they are given a good deal of authority. You know that common scene in department stores—a salesperson looking for a manager to approve something, a refund or a return or a customer's personal check. That doesn't happen at Nordstrom (at least it's not supposed to). The salesperson has the authority to make those decisions on the spot. In most department and specialty stores, the buyers work in separate offices, sometimes not even in the same building where the store is located. At Nordstrom they work on the floor so that they can stay in touch with the customer. They even try to sell the stuff they have ordered. And while Nordstrom does have secretaries, executives, including the top people in the company, answer their own phones.

The Nordstrom philosophy is to have ideas come from the bottom up. People at all levels are urged to make their own decisions. There are not a bunch of tight rules to follow. The Nordstroms, descendants of a Swedish immigrant who opened a shoe store in Seattle in 1901, own 57 percent of the stock—and they are very visible in the company. In early 1983, there were 11 Nordstroms working there. The company has no formal organizational chart. The top management is known as "the five," consisting of three Nordstroms—referred to widely in the company as "Mr. Bruce," "Mr. John," and "Mr. Jim"—and John McMillan, a brother-in-law; and a close family friend, Robert E. Bender. Store managers are told that if they have any problems, they should ring up "one of the five" or "talk to any one of us who picks up the phone."

Young, enthusiastic people thrive at Nordstrom. Tom Bosch came to work at Nordstrom's Seattle store as a stock boy. In 1982, he was named manager of Nordstrom's first store in Northern California; he was 29 years old. Betsy Sanders had a B.A. in German and an M.A. in secondary education when she became a salesperson in Seattle in 1971. She's now one of the company's nine officers, in charge of the Nordstrom push into California. She was 37 years old in 1983. When Nordstrom opened its Fashion Valley store in San Diego in 1981, Jamie Baugh was placed in charge as manager. She was 28 years old, a veteran of eight years at Nordstrom. She said at the time in an interview in the *San Diego Tribune*: "It's amazing to me at times when I drive in and see this huge building I'm in charge of. I pay all the bills. I'm basically in charge of the operational end. The Nordstroms let you run your own deal. I'm the kind of person who loves freedom. You give me freedom and I'll give 100 percent."

In addition to freedom and recognition, Nordstrom people are paid well. The salespersons are virtually all on a commission basis. And it is quite ordinary at Nordstrom for a salesperson to be making $25,000 a year. All promotions come from within, so you get a chance to move up.

Another reason you get a chance to move up is that Nordstrom is in an expansionist mode. Its style of operation has succeeded so well that it's one of the fastest-growing retailers in America. Its sales of $100 million in 1972 grew to $600 million in 1982. And its return on sales is certainly one of the best in the industry. It consistently brings home 5 percent of sales in aftertax profits—almost unheard of in the retail industry. Nordstrom entered California's Orange County market in 1982 at about the same time Neiman-Marcus did. Each opened with the same size store, and although Neiman-Marcus is a much better-known name and is backed by the resources of one of the nation's largest store chains (Carter Hawley Hale), Nordstrom outsold the Dallas retailer by a large margin.

It pays to treat customers—and employees—well.

Main employment centers   13,500 people in Washington, Oregon, California, Montana, Utah, and Alaska.

Headquarters   Nordstrom Inc.
1501 Fifth Avenue
Seattle, WA 98101
206-628-2111

NORTHROP

NORTHROP CORPORATION

Northrop makes fighter and attack aircraft and weapons systems for the military. Employees: 37,000.

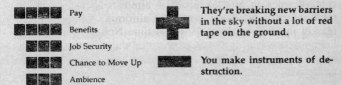

■■■□ Pay		They're breaking new barriers in the sky without a lot of red tape on the ground.
■■■□ Benefits		
■■□□ Job Security		
■■■□ Chance to Move Up	■■□□	You make instruments of destruction.
■■□□ Ambience		

"Northrop is a good place to work" reads a large sign at El Segundo and Crenshaw Avenues, not far from Los Angeles International Airport. It's a recruiting slogan the big military contractor has been using for over 40 years. And to listen to Northrop employees who have worked at other aerospace firms in Southern California, the slogan is true.

Because 94 percent of Northrop's business involves weapons systems, those who have serious doubts about the military need not apply. Larry Littrell, corporate director of industrial relations, says that there has been an occasional resignation by individuals who developed moral qualms about building weapons of mass destruction. "Someone would have to come to grips with the defense issue to work here," he says. You also have to be a U.S. citizen.

We met with hourly employees at Northrop's huge fighter aircraft manufacturing facility in El Segundo in late 1984. They work in small groups on two assembly lines that extend the length of the building—2,100 feet, the equivalent of seven football fields. Along one line, workers are constructing F-5 tactical fighters; along the other, F/A-18 Hornet attack fighters. Overhead are huge banners with slogans like "Build It As If You Were Going to Fly It," "Put Yourself in the Pilot's Seat," and "Our Nation Needs This Product."

Dion DeBois has worked on the F-5 line for three years.

He finds the atmosphere more relaxed than at Douglas Aircraft, where he worked for 15 years. "You couldn't go to the bathroom without asking the supervisor there," DeBois asserted. DeBois cited the picnics and other social events: "In all my years at Douglas, we never had events where hourly and salaried people mixed together."

Others claimed Northrop's relative informality can be traced at least in part to the absence of unions. Northrop is the only large aerospace firm in Southern California that is not unionized. Charles Caples, a 10-year Northrop veteran now on the F/A-18 line, used to work for Rohr and General Dynamics, two other large defense contractors. Being nonunion means more job flexibility. According to Caples, "In a union job, you have to drill holes, and that's all you can do. But here you can paint, seal, or drill holes, depending on what's needed."

Not having a union hasn't hurt workers' pocketbooks. Northrop's wages and benefits are comparable to those at unionized firms. Rates for structural mechanics like Caples start at $7.50 and peak at $12 an hour. Benefits include a year-end holiday—a full week off with pay in addition to vacations—and the company picks up the entire tab for medical, dental, and life insurance as well as all retirement contributions. The Northrop Savings Plan is open to all employees. The company makes a contribution for any money an employee sets aside, up to 8 percent of his or her income. Twenty-one percent of all company stock is held by the plan. Employees and retirees, through the Savings Plan and in their own names, own about one-third of Northrop's stock.

George Kosearas, who also works on the F/A-18 line, thinks the Team Hornet program is "one of the greatest programs at Northrop." Visitors can see evidence of this quality control program throughout the El Segundo plant. Every 10 yards or so are poster boards with group photos of the employees who work in each area identifying them as part of either a "Team Hornet" or a "Can-Do Team" (for the F-5 workers). Kosearas says the teams meet twice a week to identify problems and improve their productivity. Some of the team photo boards have awards on them indicating that a team has won an ongoing internal competition for quality. (Others outside the company have noted Northrop's attention to quality. In June 1984, the *New York Times* reported that smaller defense contractors "single out the Northrop Corporation . . . as the most active contractor in pushing for cost and quality reforms over the years.")

There's also an entrepreneurial flavor to Northrop—a quality distinctly lacking in an industry almost totally dependent on one customer: the Pentagon. It's a characteristic infused into the company by founder Jack Northrop, one of aviation's pioneers (he designed the Lockheed Vega Amelia Earhart flew solo across the Atlantic). Carl Constanten, a mechanical design engineer on the F-5, says he was attracted to Northrop in 1973 "because it was the most entrepreneurial aircraft company. It approaches business differently from the others." Instead of simply developing plans based on specifications drawn up by the Pentagon, Constanten claims Northrop "looks at what the market needs. Then it tries to convince the government to do it. We try to keep from having a knee-jerk response to the government."

The F-5, the most widely used supersonic fighter in the world, was originally designed in that fashion, according to Constanten. And more recently, Northrop has invested hundreds of millions of dollars in an advanced supersonic fighter called the F-20 Tigershark. Alas, as of early 1985, Northrop had been unable to sell even one F-20 (more than 3,500 F-5s have been sold). Northrop's inability to sell the F-20, which all observers claim to be an excellent machine, has been blamed on the Reagan administration, which has not seen fit to support this entrepreneurial effort. (The F-20 story has been featured on CBS's "60 Minutes," on ABC's "Nightline," and in the *Atlantic Monthly*.) The Northrop employees we interviewed sounded convinced that eventually they would be able to sell the F-20, and were pleased to be working for a company that was doing projects with its own money rather than using the taxpayers'.

Other middle managers we talked to pointed with pride to the fact that their company buys rather than leases its own buildings and equipment, unlike most other defense contractors. Northrop does, however, make periodic cutbacks. But because the company has a number of contracts and prefers to move people to different jobs rather than lay them off, Northrop has for the most part avoided the mass layoffs that are characteristic of an industry dependent on the whims of one big customer. In early 1985 Northrop was very much in a state of expansion, advertising widely for new engineers and other professional employees. Its sales doubled in the previous three years to reach $3.26 billion in 1983, and its employment rose from 28,000 to over 40,000 worldwide. It was a primary beneficiary of the huge military buildup instituted by President Reagan. Northrop has the prime contract for the supersecret Stealth bomber system, and is a major contractor for the MX missile.

Even though the company has expanded rapidly, it does not seem to have lost its personal touch. For one thing, many people at the company seem to be related to one another. "One of the first questions they ask you is, 'Who works here from your family?'" Leo Pedroza, who works on the F-5 line, told us. And there are a lot of people like Norm Henry, whose wife, daughter, and daughter-in-law all work at Northrop, and whose son used to work there.

Henry has been working on various missile systems in Northrop's electronic division since the mid-1950s, and he says it hasn't changed. He describes Northrop as a "friendly, down-to-earth place where you do not have to call people Mr. So-and-So." It goes beyond the custom of managers being called by their first names (founder Northrop was always called "Jack"). As an attempt to further reduce distinctions, the company recently changed the photo IDs worn by all employees (such photo IDs are commonly worn throughout the defense industry). The security badges used to be shaped and colored according to employee's positions, so that it was possible to determine someone's rank from a distance. But now the only obvious markings are the number of stars on the badges, based on security clearance rather than job title. Thus, an hourly employee can have a badge with more stars on it than a vice-president.

Alec Uzemeck noticed another aspect of Northrop's personal touch when he first joined the firm after stints with Memorex, ITT, and North American Rockwell. "When you walk in the door, you don't get a list with the Ten Commandments on it," Uzemeck said. Now a facilities manager in the electronics division, Uzemeck added: "Things are stated positively. You learn procedures on how to *do*, not how not to do them." He considers Northrop to have a "much more positive atmosphere." He and others we interviewed explained that they have the sense that people accomplish things through the informal network of contacts they build up with others rather than through a hierarchical chain of command. "Within management, everything seems to be up for negotiation," Uzemeck explained. "Things don't come down from on high."

Uzemeck is also impressed with the lack of political infighting: "People don't seem to fight here over territorial prerogatives. There does not seem to be much politics here." He contrasted that with his work at North American on the Apollo project, where "it was like a bunch of used car salesmen fighting for position."

The firm also seems committed to promoting almost exclusively from within its own ranks. Of the 30 top officers, for instance, all except three have been with the firm at least five years. And many—such as 45-year-old Gene Hauser, now vice-president and general manager of the electronics division—started at the bottom. Jack Northrop's successor was Tom Jones, who took over in 1959 and has run the firm since then. In 1983, Jones was paid $1.2 million.

Main employment centers   Two-thirds of the work force is in Southern California. Some 3,600 work in Chicago on electronic countermeasures; 1,500 in Boston on gyroscopes; and 600 in Kansas City, with its Wilcox subsidiary, which makes aircraft landing systems and navigation aids. Another 2,300 work overseas, mostly maintaining and servicing Northrop-built aircraft.

Headquarters   Northrop Corporation
1800 Century Park East
Los Angeles, CA 90067
213-553-6262

Northwestern Mutual Life

NORTHWESTERN MUTUAL LIFE INSURANCE COMPANY

The tenth-largest life insurance company in the United States. Employees: 2,385.

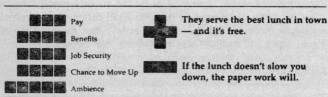

Pay

Benefits

Job Security

Chance to Move Up

Ambience

They serve the best lunch in town — and it's free.

If the lunch doesn't slow you down, the paper work will.

Northwestern boasts a four-star employee cafeteria. Literally. In a citywide survey of 45 lunchtime eating establishments, *Milwaukee Magazine* awarded NML's employee cafeteria the highest ranking, saying: "The food is excellent. Classic get-fat breakfasts—sweet rolls and doughnuts are made on the premises daily, and are still warm if you get there by 7 A.M. Lunches always feature two hot entrees and a wide selection of sandwiches and salads." The magazine noted sadly that you have to work for Northwestern to eat there, but that if you work for the city's largest employer, lunch is on the house.

A free, four-star lunch is only one of the reasons many people invariably point to Northwestern as the best insurance company to work for. "The Quiet Company" has led the way with innovations such as flex-time hours and job redefinitions to reduce the drudgery of the overwhelming paperload associated with the business (NML receives about 15,000 pieces of mail a day).

Located a block from Lake Michigan in downtown Milwaukee, Northwestern's headquarters looks more like a museum than a place of business. Classic Greek Corinthian columns line the exterior of the building. Ornate gold light fixtures hang from a sculpted white Italian marble ceiling in the cavernous lobby. An intricately carved wooden spiral staircase leads to the upper floors where chandeliers and stained-glass windows grace lobby areas. Every day, company guides lead school tours throughout the building to see some of the more than 1,300 paintings (including works of nearly 100 Wisconsin artists), photographs (Karsh's famous "bulldog" photo of Winston Churchill, for example), and art pieces (such as a seventeenth-century French tapestry).

Bill Hanson felt the place looked like a mausoleum when he went there to apply for a job as a baker in the cafeteria. "I thought they were going to bury me in this place," he recalled. "But the woman in the personnel office was extremely friendly, as were all the other people I met there. It wasn't long before I felt like I was part of the Northwestern family."

"Family" is how many Northwesterners describe their company. It's an attitude that starts at the top. "I look at this place as a family," NML president Don Schuenke explained to us. " I don't know all of the people on a first-name basis, but I know most of them."

Company officers often eat lunch in the cafeteria with the rest of the troops. Partitions topped with plants separate tables, reducing the institutional ambience of the cafeteria. Windows on one side overlook Lake Michigan; on the other is a six-story atrium with tropical plants. Rather than prices, the daily menu reports how many calories each item contains. The benefit costs the company about $3 million a year, or $4 per employee per day. Employees say their noontime perk is well known around Milwaukee. When they tell people where they work, the invariable response is, "Northwestern, that's the company with the free lunch, isn't it?"

According to life insurance studies, Northwesterners earn their free lunch. Year after year, *Best's Review* rates NML first among the 71 largest life insurance companies on a variety of technical criteria. Northwestern performs well largely because of the productivity of its work force. When compared with competitors, NML ranks number one, with just over three home-office employees per $100 million of life insurance in force, about half the industry average. Executive vice-president Don Mundt estimated that if Northwestern were to add as many people as the second-most-efficient life insurer, it would have to pay an extra $17 million in salaries alone (equivalent to another thousand employees).

What is the secret to NML's high level of productivity?

Besides the free lunch, Northwesterners refer to two other tangible features. In 1973, NML became one of the first major companies to institute flex-time. The workday is seven and a half hours (excluding a half-hour for lunch). Most employees arrive between 7 A.M. and 9 A.M. and leave between 3 P.M. and 5 P.M. One employee remarked that the variable working hours are a "real boon to the working mother." Sandra Hughes-Ball, who works in the adminitrative services central records department, told the company magazine: "I love it. I get home in time to pick up my son from school—and to watch my soap operas."

More recently, Northwestern has redefined many jobs in the home office, where most are engaged in clerical work such as processing applications or responding to claims. In the new business department, for instance, 64 distinct job descriptions were reduced to 6. To make it possible for the same people to handle more tasks, they have gone through an extensive retraining process, lasting nearly two years.

Kathy Mandella has been with NML for five years. Before the reorganization, she spent all day in front of a computer terminal updating a few items on each application form. The form was then sent to someone else who added information on a few more items. Mandella's title is now service representative, and she handles each application entirely by herself, including making phone calls to agents.

When asked her reaction to the change, Mandella replied, "I think it is great. At first everybody had a scary feeling. But it's more interesting than just punching numbers on the screen. We are doing more than before, but I think it's beneficial to us because we are learning more about the underwriting aspects of the job. Now we can read the attending physician's statement. We never even looked at that before. There's a better opportunity to move up to underwriting."

Northwestern preaches and practices promotion from within. Job openings are posted on a central bulletin board outside the cafeteria. Employees frequently move between departments. Marge Winter, for instance, started working for NML in 1969 as a messenger, delivering mail to various departments on roller skates. She convinced her boss that she was underutilized and was trained as a data-processing programmer. After working for four years as a programmer, she became a data-processing trainer. From there she became a supervisor in the new business department.

"They're not afraid to take a chance on someone," Winter said. "They let me move from training to becoming a supervisor in an entirely unrelated part of the business." All the while, Winter took college courses fully paid for by NML. In 1983 she received her college degree. The company also offers dozens of in-house training courses on subjects ranging from raising teenage children to speed reading (President Schuenke said he'd taken that one twice).

Large numbers of NMLers participate in dozens of clubs, ranging from fishing and running (the NML Striders) to an NML chorus. It's common for top company officers to be part of such groups, further accentuating the "family" atmosphere. Many retirees, some with 40-plus years at NML, continue participating in the clubs, though they do not have to pay the dues. Retired employees also get together for a dinner just before Thanksgiving.

Not everyone fits in at Northwestern. "People who want a nine-to-five routine don't like it here," explained Paul Johnson, a specialist in policy benefits. The company conducts intensive interviews with prospective employees. It's common for someone to be recalled two or three times for separate interviews before being hired.

Northwestern pays well. Using surveys of pay scales of the largest insurers, NML makes a point to pay its people in the top 10 percent for comparable jobs. Turnover is small, especially considering that most of the jobs are clerical—about 4 percent a year.

About half of Northwestern's home-office staff belong to the Office and Professional Employees Union. It dates to the depression era when "management wasn't as enlightened," according to executive vicepresident Don Mundt. He pointed out, however, that Northwestern didn't lay off anyone during that period.

Today, the union has generally amicable relations with the company and negotiates a contract covering all nonmanagement staff, including those who do not wish to join the open shop union. "We have good faith bargaining," explained union member Mike Barriere. "The company does not lose sight that the union represents part of the family." Grievances are rare, and the company's president told us he is personally aware of any grievance that is filed.

Much of the camaraderie apparent at Northwestern's home office is shared by the company's 4,000 field agents located throughout the country. Though not technically Northwestern employees, almost all field agents sell only NML insurance. Every July, they pay their own way to the agents' annual convention in Milwaukee. Staffers from the home office also attend a big agents' rally held at the Milwaukee Convention Center, which has featured such entertainers as Bob Hope, Bob Newhart, Melissa Manchester, and Neil Sedaka.

The agents' meetings have a reputation for being extremely highspirited, part of "the ol' Northwestern religion." A national underwriter who attended one said, "This is not a convention. This is a revival."

Main employment center   Milwaukee.

Headquarters   Northwestern Mutual Life Insurance Company
720 East Wisconsin Avenue
Milwaukee, WI 53202
414-271-1444

nucor corporation

NUCOR CORPORATION

The nation's tenth-largest steel manufacturer, Nucor also makes steel joists and steel decking for nonresidential construction and steel grinding balls for mining. U.S. employees: 3,700.

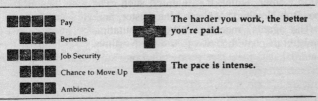

▮▮▮▮ Pay	✚	The harder you work, the better you're paid.
▮▮▮ Benefits		
▮▮▮▮ Job Security	▮▮▮	The pace is intense.
▮▮▮ Chance to Move Up		
▮▮▮ Ambience		

Nucor built its first steel mill in 1969 at Darlington, South Carolina. Since then the company has erected three other steel mills and four joist plants in equally obscure towns in rural areas of Indiana, Nebraska, Texas, Alabama, and Utah. "We prefer rural areas because the work ethic is stronger," explained John Savage, Nucor's manager of personnel services. "Working for us is hard work. Many people in rural areas are used to working all day during the growing season. They can handle working in one of our steel mills."

Hard work is the name of the game at Nucor. We visited Nucor's Vulcraft joist plant near Brigham City, Utah. The long, gray warehouselike building sits in a grain-farming valley located between the scenic Wasatch Mountain Range and the Great Salt Lake. Jerry Stephens works as a rigger at the northern Utah facility. "I am running all day long," Stephens told us. "It gets hot and you get tired. My wife doesn't like it because sometimes I come home and fall asleep right away."

But Stephens relishes the fast pace. "It's the best-paying job in the state from what I've seen," he said. He estimated his 1983 income at nearly $30,000, comparable to the average earnings of Nucor production workers elsewhere in the country. *Fortune* estimated in 1981 that Nucor's workers earned about $5,000 more than unionized steelworkers at firms like U.S. Steel, probably the most highly paid blue-collar workers in America. Unlike members of the United Steelworkers union, Nucor's employees (all nonunion) have relatively low hourly wages. Much of a Nucor worker's income comes from productivity bonuses.

Every production worker is assigned to a work crew, which has certain goals. If they exceed the target, they get paid accordingly. No allowance is made for equipment breakdowns, and anyone who is late for work (even because of illness) loses his bonus for that day.

Stephens works on a crew of 16. The crew makes joists from start to finish, from cutting the rods and beams to putting them into place and welding them together. The crew is expected to complete two tons' worth of joists per hour. If they word hard, they can produce more than twice that amount. Thus, Stephens, whose base pay is about $7 an hour, would make $14 an hour if his crew produced four tons per hour. Production records for each day are posted on a blackboard in the plant. Workers are paid weekly, and their productivity bonuses are included in each paycheck. Stephens said he always made at least $10 an hour during 1983, sometimes as much as $20 an hour.

The productivity incentives affect how people work together. Rod Zilles, a maintenance technician in the Brigham City plant, explained what happens when one of the machines stops working: "When something goes down, people ask me how they can help. Nobody sits around. Every minute you are down, it's like dollars out of your back pocket. So everybody really hustles."

Zilles contrasts the attitude at Nucor with what he found at Thiokol, a big weapons manufacturer where he previously worked: "At Thiokol, guys didn't care whether the machines were down. They said it did not matter whether we accomplished anything because it was a government contract anyway." Zilles prefers the "teamwork atmosphere" at Nucor.

The teamwork philosophy extends to its very minimal supervisory ranks. There are no more than three levels separating a production-line worker and the president of the company. In some of the large steel companies, there are as many as 12 levels.

Nucor can be hard on people who do not work up to speed, because each worker's weekly income is based on how well his crew performs. The company does little screening and minimal training. How someone performs on the job is watched closely, especially during the first three months. Loafers get weeded out quickly.

The steelworkers union has made several unsuccessful attempts to organize workers at the Darlington mill. Harry Pigg, a regional representative of the USW, told the *New York Times* that he thinks Nucor's low base pay, high incentive plan is "a system that abuses workers, burns them up. It's like a carrot with a mule." Lloyd McBride, the USW president, added, "The history of management is that when they have a free rein, they become greedy. I don't think Nucor is an exception."

Once an employee has been with Nucor for three months, he or she is virtually assured of a job for life, as long as he or she continues to perform. Nucor has never laid off anyone in its history. When times are tough in the steel business, as was true for much of 1981 and 1982, production workers can be cut back to four- or three-day weeks. Similarly, rather than hiring more workers during especially busy periods, Nucor goes to six-day weeks. Bonuses for the sixth day are based on time-and-a-half pay.

Nucor offers one especially good benefit to all employees with at least two years' service. Each of their children is entitled to a $1,400-a-year college scholarship. This benefit is especially appreciated at the Nucor mills in Utah where the work force is largely Mormon, as Mormons tend to have large families.

Ken Iverson, Nucor's president, said he was troubled in 1974 when he discovered that bonuses were paying as much as 100 percent of base wages, but he decided to stick with the system and expand variations of it to all employees of the company. He insists the company's productivity makes it worthwhile. *Fortune* stated that in 1981 Nucor took less than four man-hours to produce a ton of steel, as opposed to five in similar Japanese plants and more than six in comparable U.S. mills.

This competitive edge meant that in less than three years after Nucor opened a steel mill in Plymouth, Utah, it had cut the Japanese share of California's market for steel rods and bars from 50 percent to 10 percent, according to the *Wall Street Journal*. The *Journal* also reported that the efficient Plymouth mill produced as much steel with 300 workers as it took 1,100 workers at a now-closed-down Bethlehem Steel plant in Los Angeles.

Nucor's mania for productivity affects all aspects of company life. It has perhaps the most spartan corporate office of any Fortune 500 company. Located in a residential area of Charlotte, North Carolina, Nucor shares the fourth floor of a small office building with an insurance agency. Aside from Iverson and John Savage, there are only 14 other people, including 5 secretaries and 4 accountants. The company does not believe in perks. Iverson and other Nucor officials have no company car, and they fly coach class. They do have an executive dining room—a Chinese restaurant in a shopping center across the street.

Main employment centers   Steel mills (300 to 500 employees each): Darlington, South Carolina; Norfolk, Nebraska; Jewett, Texas; Plymouth, Utah. Steel joist fabrication plants (200 to 400 employees each): Florence, South Carolina; Norfolk, Nebraska; Fort Payne, Alabama; Grapeland, Texas; Saint Joe, Indiana; Brigham City, Utah.

Headquarters   Nucor Corporation
4425 Randolph Road
Charlotte, NC 28211
704-366-7000

Odetics inc.

ODETICS, INC.

Odetics makes robots and spaceborne tape recorders. U.S. employees: 430.

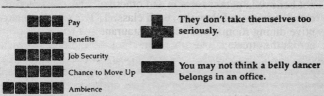

■■■ Pay		**They don't take themselves too seriously.**
■■■ Benefits		
■■■■ Job Security		
■■■■ Chance to Move Up		**You may not think a belly dancer belongs in an office.**
■■■■■ Ambience		

If there is a company in America that can truly be said to have an anticorporate corporate culture, it is Odetics. Joel Slutzky, the company's chairman, delights in breaking virtually every unspoken rule of how corporate executives are supposed to behave.

Take the day in 1981 when Odetics' stock was first sold to the public. No formal ribbon-cutting ceremonies for Odetics. Slutzky and the other five members of the board of directors showed up at the office in T-shirts that read: "Thank you, Paine Webber."

The offbeat approach continued when Slutzky penned the management's first annual report to stockholders. "Frankly, we're lousy at quarter-to-quarter managing . . . ," he wrote. "I believe we made some management mistakes. . . . The model changeover probably cost us in the neighborhood of $200,000. Better planning could have cut that in half."

Slutzky also teaches a course entitled "Industry 101" or "How to Start Your Own Business and Grow Gray Hair." Open to all employees, it explains in 12 sessions the ins and outs of setting up a corporation.

Does Slutzky worry that some of his employees may go off and form their own businesses? Not at all. He proudly points to one "graduate" of Industry 101 who now runs his own machine shop (and does business with Odetics) and two

307

others who operate their own electronics firm. "Not many decide to leave Odetics, but if they do, we want them to succeed," he says.

Whatever else may be said of Odetics' unusual style, the company has an enviable record of keeping people. In an industry where job-hopping is a way of life, Odetics has the lowest employee turnover of any electronics firm in California's Orange County, according to *The Executive of Orange County.* "Associates" (the firm junked the term "employee" in 1984) talk of the company as "the family," and even recruitment brochures talk of becoming part of "The Odetics Family."

The company has its own Fun Committee, which launched "Project Girth," where for every pound an employee lost, a dollar would be sent to his or her favorite charity. Then there was the "Guess the Stock Price on March 31" contest. The winner got a free lunch at the Hoagie Bar in Santa Ana.

Odetics may be the only corporation in America with its own repertory theater company. During the summer, the company rents the South Coast Repertory Theater, the largest performance space in Orange County. One year they performed *You're a Good Man, Charlie Brown*; the next year, Neil Simon's *The Good Doctor.*

But don't expect Odetics to put on a show there every year for the rest of the century. Slutzky says, "I prefer things that are spontaneous. Things I hate the most are the routine, expected things like an annual company picnic. I think it's important for there to be an element of humor, laughter. It adds to the company. It's one more thing that makes you want to get up in the morning and go to work."

One thing's for sure. Odetics' employees don't always know what to expect when they get there. The company's Spaceborne division, for instance, worked many long hours to try to get one of their recorders to pass a crucial test of the ability of the recorder to withstand extremely low temperatures. The morning after the machine finally passed the test, a mariachi band paraded through the plant, followed by some girls from the local Baskin-Robbins franchise offering free ice cream so that the employees could do their own coldness tests.

Nor do outsiders know what to expect when they go to Odetics. More than one customer for the company's space recorders has been surprised when entering the plant's conference room. Above the table is an exact replica of the space shuttle *Columbia*—made out of Budweiser beer cans.

It's not all fun and games at Odetics, though. The company makes extremely sophisticated devices: spaceborne tape recorders, time-lapse video recorders (used in retail stores to observe customers), and courtroom audio recorders. The company dominates the space recorder market, making more than 70 percent of the total for U.S., French, Italian, and Japanese space agencies. In early 1983, the company announced a 370-pound, six-legged robot or "functionoid." During a demonstration, the robot lifted a small pickup truck and walked across the room with it.

When Odetics faced a downturn in its video recorder business in 1983, it managed to keep all of its people aboard through attrition and transfer to other divisions. In 1982, the company opened its Odexercise Center, offering aerobic dance classes, exercise machines, and health-training programs. A full-time fitness coordinator supervises the facility, which is open to all employees from 6 A.M. to 7 P.M. In early 1985, Odetics added a swimming pool and volleyball courts.

Everyone at Odetics, including top management, is on a first-name basis. No managers have assigned parking places. There's one reserved parking spot, for the person selected as "Associate of the Month." Several Odetics buildings are within sight of Disneyland. From the front door of the small headquarters building you can see the Matterhorn, located just across a freeway.

Those who work at Odetics can expect a great deal of personal freedom. Hanging plants adorn the machine shop. Virtually everybody decorates his or her individual workspace with family pictures or other mementos. One secretary had two male pinups above her typewriter. There's a birthday album at the Spaceborne plant, where everybody's picture appears on his or her birthdate on a huge calendar hung along a wall.

It's a place where hard work and fun go hand in hand. But sometimes it gets a little out of hand. One Friday afternoon, a time when people often knock off early for an on-site beer bust, one employee decided to invite a belly dancer to entertain the troops. So over the plant's PA system blared some Middle Eastern music as a beautiful young dancer made her way around the premises.

It seemed a good time was had by all—until Monday morning. Into the plant manager's office marched a group of irate associates. The belly dancing had taken place on Good Friday.

Main employment center   Orange County, California

Headquarters   Odetics, Inc.
1515 South Manchester Avenue
Anaheim, CA 92802
818-774-5000

THE OLGA COMPANY

Olga makes fine-quality undergarments for women. U.S. employees: 1,800.

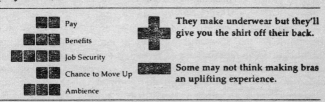

■■■ Pay	✚ They make underwear but they'll give you the shirt off their back.
■■■ Benefits	
■■■■ Job Security	
■■ Chance to Move Up	■■■ Some may not think making bras an uplifting experience.
■■■ Ambience	

Regular readers of *Vogue, Glamour, Harper's Bazaar,* and other high-fashion magazines may recognize the name, if not the face, of Olga. Ads for this company's bras and lingerie all carry the slogan, "Behind every Olga there really is an Olga," with a small inset photo of the company's cofounder, Olga Erteszek.

The ads don't tell the remarkable story of the woman behind the face. Olga and Jan Erteszek started the company in Los Angeles more than 40 years ago with an investment of $10. The $10 represented the Erteszeks' net worth when they arrived in California after fleeing their native Poland at the outset of World War II. The couple spent $5 for a sewing machine and the balance for some fabric. Olga designed some garter belts. A buyer at the Bullocks-Wilshire department store liked Olga's designs, and the Erteszeks were on their way.

Jan ran the company while his wife designed their increasingly large line of intimate apparel. But the company didn't adopt the typical employment patterns of most garment manufacturers. In fact, to this day Olga doesn't call its workers "employees"; they are "associates." It's all part of the Erteszeks' business philosophy. Jan goes around the country these days lecturing at various universities on such topics as

"A New Style of Corporate Life: Christian Values and the Free Enterprise System."

According to Erteszek, "The traditional view is that the only investor is one who supplies capital. But others invest talent, administrative skills, know-how. Some even invest their total lives in some business institution. To the extent that they are all investors, they must participate in the fortunes of the company. The concept of a 'hired hand,' of labor as a commodity, is obsolete and incongruent with Christian teachings as they pertain to the dignity of man. It is the total man which becomes a member of a company; it is the total man who must be served by the company."

Unusual words for the chairman of a $60-million-plus corporation, let alone the head of a garment manufacturing firm. For Olga's associates, Erteszek's theories are more than just words. The Erteszeks instituted a generous profit-sharing plan in 1954. In recent years, the company has set aside between 20 and 25 percent of its *pretax* profits for associates. That is one of the highest profit-sharing rates for any corporation of Olga's size in the country. In 1981, for instance, Olga put up more than $1 million of the company's $5 million in profits. It goes without saying that all associates qualify for the plan.

Although Olga makes it clear that associates should share in the company's fortunes, Erteszek also lets them know they must share in the more difficult times. In 1982, for instance, the company found itself overstocked. While other companies suffering from the recession simply laid off employees, Olga enrolled in an obscure state program called "Workshare," designed to reduce unemployment. Without the plan, Olga would have had to lay off 20 percent of its people. Instead, Olga cut back to four-day weeks, and the state helped make up the difference for the fifth day. Olga did not have to lay off anyone.

Olga production-line workers, most of them women, do not belong to any union. The company pays them slightly higher than union scale.

Those around Olga talk about the company's "family feeling" and sense of "community." Jan Erteszek talks about the "commonwealth." Olga's "Creative Meeting" helps foster this sense. The company's designers had used this technique for years to brainstorm new design ideas. Then, in the early

1970s, Jan Erteszek applied it throughout the company. At first, he asked 12 to 18 members of the cutting department to come to his office and tell him how they would run the company if they had his job. More recently, small groups of associates meet once a week for six weeks, for about an hour per session. Most associates participate in such Creative Meetings two or three times a year.

In addition to discussing ways of improving their own jobs, they talk about what else they would like to see their company doing. One group of sewing-machine operators, for instance, urged Olga to offer classes in basic English for associates who had immigrated to the United States from Latin America or Asia. Now the company gives hour-long classes at the end of the workday, with half the hour on company time.

In mid-1984, Warnaco, a large clothing conglomerate, purchased Olga for $28 million. But according to Jeff Paul, Olga's executive vice-president, nothing much has changed as a result: "It's the same people, the same products, and the same policies as before."

Olga's corporate offices are contained in a plain, one-story brick building in a warehouse district of a Los Angeles suburb. A tipoff that Olga is involved in something more glamorous than its electronics assembly and beer distribution neighbors is the huge sign outside the headquarters that reads: "Olga: the first lady of under fashion." Visitors who enter the small waiting room are greeted with full-size color photos of models displaying the latest Olga lingerie, brassieres, and panties. The visitors' passes are pink.

Main employment centers   Nearly three-quarters of Olga's 1,800 employees work in manufacturing. Six of Olga's plants are located in Van Nuys. Three other plants are in nearby Ventura County, and one other is across the California border in Mexicali. Olga also employs 60 sales representatives in regional sales offices spread throughout the country. The sales force sells Olga's apparel directly to major department and specialty stores.

Headquarters   The Olga Company
7900 Haskell Avenue
Van Nuys, CA 91405
818-782-7568

JCPenney

J. C. PENNEY COMPANY

J. C. Penney is the third-largest general merchandise store chain in the United States, following Sears and K mart. Employees: 163,000.

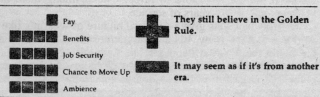

▪ Pay	**They still believe in the Golden Rule.**
▪▪▪▪ Benefits	
▪▪▪▪ Job Security	
▪▪▪▪ Chance to Move Up	**It may seem as if it's from another era.**
▪▪▪▪ Ambience	

Oscar Chavez is a computer scientist who works for J. C. Penney's regional office in Dallas. Legally blind because of a birth defect, he was passed over by 15 companies before Penney hired him in 1982. By sitting close to a screen and through the use of special spectacles, he can read the characters on a computer terminal if white letters are displayed against a gray background. When he reached Penney's, he couldn't read an IBM terminal with black characters. Penney's asked IBM what it could do. After working for seven weeks, the computer maker came up with a modification that increases character size by 33 percent and intensity by 50 percent—and displays the characters in white. Chavez can now use the terminal with no difficulty, and IBM has "a new product that opens up our field to other visually handicapped persons."

The Chavez story ran in a 1982 issue of the company newspaper, *J. C. Penney Today*. The same issue carried these items:

• During the 1982 Christmas season Penney employees in Dallas raised money by collecting recipes from other Penney people and publishing them as a cookbook which sold for $4.50; all proceeds went to the Salvation Army. Gerry Miller, a computer programmer, helped put the cookbook together. One of the recipes came from her mother, Marilynn Bell, a

314

25-year veteran of Penney's in Fayetteville, Arkansas.

• The J. C. Penney store in Laurel, Montana, was 53 years old in 1982. For the previous 25 years it had had the same manager, Pat Mullaney. The store held a Twenty-fifth-Anniversary Sale to honor him.

• Susie Walker retired from the Northgate Mall store in Chattanooga, Tennessee. She originally came to work one week to see if she liked it. She stayed for 39 years.

• Irene Mezek, Angelina DeAngeles, and Bessie Nickas work in the Penney store in Price, Utah. Among them they have a total of 114 years of service.

These snippets give a postcard picture of what it's like to work at J. C. Penney. It's a family atmosphere. Relatives are not only permitted at Penney's, they are encouraged to come and work where their father, mother, brother, or sister worked —or still works. If two Penney associates marry, it's not necessary for one to resign as it is in some other companies.

William R. Howell, who became chief executive officer of Penney in 1983, is the son of a Penney store manager. Robert Gill, the vice-chairman, is also the son of a former Penney executive—and he has two children working at Penney's. Donald V. Seibert, whom Howell succeeded, told the top managers of the company in 1983: "We're very proud of our two-generation and three-generation Penney families. We emphasize our family relationships more than other companies I observe. We see one another socially. We like each other."

J. C. Penney has many attributes that appear to be downright corny. They go back to James Cash Penney, the son of a Baptist minister, who founded this retailing business in 1902 on the concept of the Golden Rule ("Do unto others as you would expect them to do unto you"). He believed in it so much that he named his first store, in Kemmerer, Wyoming, "The Golden Rule."

The Penney name went up on the stores in 1913, at which time the company adopted a code of conduct pledging to subject every policy to this test: "Does it square with what is right and just?" Penney people still quote those maxims to you. This is a company whose leaders are not afraid to say: "People join our company with the expectation that they will retire from our company. And it's our commitment to do our best to make that possible."

Some people whom we interviewed at other companies described Penney as "square," a relic from yesterday. Penney people themselves have recognized that their stores do not have the dashing, glamorous image that a Neiman-Marcus or Bloomingdale's has. But Penney hasn't stood still, the way W. T. Grant and Montgomery Ward did. Over the past few years Penney has completely modernized more than 100 of its department stores in shopping centers—and by the end of this decade it plans to have upgraded the merchandise and the look of all its stores. It expects to slug it out, fashionwise, with the established department stores.

Penney's people are never referred to as employees. That's another part of the heritage from James Cash Penney. If you work here, you're known as an "associate." Mr. Penney called his store managers "partners," and every year these partners gathered to initiate new partners in what was at first called an "obligation ceremony" and later an "affirmation ceremony." That, believe it or not, still goes on today.

The affirmation ceremonies are now normally held every four to five years—and today they take place in various locations. In 1980, for example, they were held in 15 different cities at which 1,000 Penney management associates were "affirmed." During the ceremony a pledge is given to the founding principles of the company, and at the conclusion each newly affirmed associate receives an HCSC pin, standing for Honor, Confidence, Service, Cooperation.

Mr. Penney once said: "I will have no man work for me who has not the capacity to become a partner. Any man whom I employ must understand that as soon as he has proved his ability, he will become a partner in one or another store. I will give him an interest and he shall pay for it out of his earnings."

As old-fashioned as they may seem, these ideas still infuse the J. C. Penney Company. It wasn't until 1962 that anyone at Penney's had a base salary higher than $10,000 a year; managers earned bonuses tied directly to store profits. Penney still tries to give its associates a piece of the action. Many Penney managers continue to receive a substantial portion of their income from profit-sharing incentive compensation. In 1984, the company instituted a bonus plan for all of its non-commission sales associates in all stores. In addition, Penney people are encouraged to deposit up to 16 percent of their earnings in a savings and investment plan, and the company matches up to 6 percent of that contribution. Nearly half of all Penney employees participate in this program. And the company's largest shareholder, with 16 percent of all the outstanding stock, is the employee savings and profit-sharing plan.

The benefits package in place at Penney's may be the best in the retail industry. In addition to the savings and profit-sharing program, there's a pension plan for all associates, no-cost life insurance, medical and dental insurance (requiring a monthly payment by associates), three weeks' vacation after five years, and 15 percent off all Penney merchandise. Most notable is that anyone who works 20 hours a week is eligible for the benefits—a marked contrast with the practice at many retail organizations, which is to avoid paying benefits to part-timers.

These benevolent policies tend to keep associates working for Penney's during their entire careers. They become quite attached to the place. James Cash Penney died in 1971, at age 95: His executive secretary, Virginia Mowry, had come to Penney's only a few years earlier from a career in personnel, but she had become so imbued with the heritage of the company that she stayed on to become its archivist. Although retired, she was still there in 1985 as a part-time historical consultant.

Happy Penney people are the best proof that the original ideas of James Cash Penney have staying power. Marie Fogel, manager of operations and personnel at the Corte Madera store north of San Francisco, started at Penney's in 1965. She needs little prompting to begin talking about the caring atmosphere. "It's often forgotten," she told us, "that at other companies you're just a number. The very fact that we call employees associates shows we care."

Fogel related that when the manager of her store, Tony Munoz, had to have a heart bypass operation, many associates volunteered to give blood, and a daily report on his condition was posted to keep people from constantly calling the hospital.

Many stores hire part-timers but do not extend corporate benefits to them. At Penney's, Fogel pointed out, if you work 20 hours a week for 13 consecutive weeks, you're eligible for benefits. The pay is certainly not lavish. In 1983 new employees were paid $3.65 an hour. You moved to $3.80 an hour after three months. But Fogel pointed out that when people, especially teenagers, choose J. C. Penney as a place to work, "I think they really do like the family atmosphere. They remember shopping there with their parents."

Penney's, as you might expect, promotes from within. Most of its senior managers have never worked for another company. To prepare people for advancement, it runs an intensive in-house training program. Ex-chairman Seibert once said: "In many companies, when someone is promoted into a senior position, two or three people resign and go somewhere else. It's expected. I've had people tell me they're amazed it doesn't happen here. But there really is no cause for such amazement. Such actions are not in our heritage. They are foreign to our culture."

The bulk of training goes on in the stores themselves. Large stores have as many as 100 training programs, with all sales associates attending at least one session a year. Penney also operates training centers at Schamburg, Illinois; Buena Park, California; Atlanta; and Dallas. More than 4,500 associates went through those centers in 1982—and that doesn't count the 21,000 associates who attended one-day sales workshops.

Penney hires between 500 and 1,000 management trainees a year. They train for 26 weeks under the supervision of a general merchandise manager, rotating among all departments in the store. Penney recruits from 200 colleges and universities, including business schools. Among the places it draws from are Villanova, Brigham Young, City University of New York (the Baruch School of Business), New York University, Cornell, the University of Florida, the University of Illinois, California State University, the University of Colorado, and the University of Washington. It does not regard the Ivy League schools as especially fertile places for candidates.

Penney's work force is dominated by women (77 percent of the total), but few have made it to the highest management rungs. In 1984, only one of Penney's 43 officers was a woman. Nevertheless, Penney's now claims that 44 percent of its officials, managers, and professionals are women, as are about half the people in management training today. In 1983, 69 J.C.Penney stores (out of 1,600) had women managers.

Main employment centers   Penney operates more than 2,000 stores (including some 360 Thrift drug stores). It's one of the few retailers with a presence in all 50 states. Some 5,000 people work at Penney headquarters in New York—a 45-story building that the company owns. There's not enough room, so Penney occupies 10 floors of another building at 1633 Broadway. Penney employs 4,400 persons in Europe, where it has a store operation in Belgium, and it has 1,300 employees in Puerto Rico.

Headquarters   J. C. Penney Company
1301 Avenue of the Americas
New York, NY 10019
212-957-4321

PEOPLExpress

PEOPLE EXPRESS AIRLINES, INC.

People Express is a new airline using Newark International Airport as a hub to offer low-price fares reaching 29 cities in 16 states—and London. Employees: 4,000.

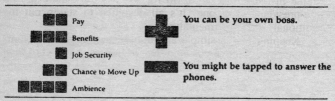

▌▌ Pay		**You can be your own boss.**
▌▌▌ Benefits	✚	
▌ Job Security		
▌▌ Chance to Move Up		**You might be tapped to answer the phones.**
▌▌▌ Ambience		

How would you like to work in a company where there are no secretaries? Well, here it is. At People Express, everyone is a manager. In January 1985, when the airline was nearly four years old, the employee force broke down as follows:

> 2,700 customer service managers
> 1,000 flight managers
> 200 team managers
> 55 maintenance managers
> 9 general managers
> 7 managing officers

In addition, there were some 2,000 people working part-time on an hourly scale, mostly answering telephones to take flight reservations.

People Express has had a meteoric growth since it began flying in April 1981, offering the cheapest fares in the sky. It had 730 people on the full-time payroll in June 1982. Six months later, it had 1,200. It went into 1985 with a complement of 4,000. And it still had the "help wanted" sign out, such was its rapid ascent. As it kept adding new routes, it became not just the fastest-growing airline but the fastest-growing company in the history of American business. Its sales reached $600 million in 1984. No enterprise had ever reached that level in so short a time.

In the midst of this explosive growth, People Express went to great pains to maintain its simple organizational structure, one that emphasizes self-management and eschews hierarchies. A word that's taboo at People Express is "supervisor." Just as there are no secretaries (everyone does his or her own letters), there are no supervisors in this company—at least none so designated. People Express may be unique in the corporate world for another trait: there are no vice-presidents, not one. It's all designed to stamp out the traditional "we/they" mentality.

Keeping things simple and unbureaucratic as an organization grows is not easy—and People Express has had to treat those growing pains. Originally, there were no team managers; the company was small enough to allow quick communication from the bottom to the top. In 1983, it layered in the new level of team manager. As the airline continued its breakneck expansion, the structure was revamped again in 1984 with the creation of operating teams consisting of 200 to 300 people each. The teams were organized around aircraft. At the start of 1985 there were three 737 groups, six 727 groups, and one 747 group.

Although its name sounds as if it had been coined by Marxist revolutionaries, People Express Airlines is really an exemplar of rugged individualism. It was started in 1981 by refugees from Texas International Airlines who, in the words of one of them, decided "there must be a better way to run a company." People Express offers basic air transportation at rock-bottom prices, what it calls an "honest fare." It offers no-frills service. You pay extra for baggage. There's no free coffee aboard. You can call for reservations, but People Express does not have any sales counters, not even at airports. You pay for tickets in flight.

The revolutionary aspect of People Express is not its discount fares, however, but its style of working. It seeks to maintain an environment in which employees are free to move around and grow. There's a great emphasis on training. There are no rigid job slots. People are encouraged to look for the work they like best to do. The pilot who flies you from Washington to New York may be working the next day in headquarters on marketing. The flight attendant who collects your fare on board may be working in scheduling the following week. In 1985, the company's chief financial officer, Bob McAdoo, was still doing weekly stints as a flight attendant. People Express believes that, ideally, every person working in the airline should be familiar with every job in the company. Someone quipped, "Yes, but I hope this doesn't mean that my flight attendant will be fixing the planes tomorrow." No chance—People Express contracts out its maintenance work. Needless to say, no employee is represented by a trade union.

People Express has some strong ideas on what work should be like. Here they are:

"The work to be performed must be meaningful, with reasonably attainable objectives that are consistent with our overall corporate objectives.

"The work must be challenging and must create a learning opportunity for the individuals involved. While certain aspects may be routine, the total work package must be varied enough to provide mental stimulus for personal growth.

"The work must provide some built-in feedback. The people performing the task need to be able to discern how well they are meeting their objectives, and the work should therefore have built-in checkpoints and standards for self-measurement."

There is a messianic quality to People Express that Donald C. Burr, founder and charismatic leader, does nothing to dispel when he holds orientation meetings for newcomers and tells them that one of the objectives of this company is to "make a better world." It's not exactly a message for Wall Street.

Starting salaries at People Express are not high, nor do they ascend to the stratosphere as you go up the organizational ladder. In 1983, they were hiring people as reservations clerks for as little as $5 an hour. A second-year pilot was making $36,000, well under what other airlines were paying. But one of the egalitarian features of People Express is a very compressed and simplified salary structure; there's not a huge gap between the top and the bottom—and everyone within each level makes exactly the same salary. In 1985, for example, the base pay capped after five years as follows:

Customer service manager: $26,000
 Customer service team manager (level one): $33,200
 Customer service team manager (level two): $37,200

Maintenance manager (level one): $35,700
 Maintenance manager (level two): $50,300
 Maintenance manager team manager: $59,000

Flight manager (first officer, flight engineer): $48,500
 Flight manager (captain): $56,250
 Flight manager team manager: $63,500

Managing officer
General manager $63,500
President and chairman

That's the entire *salary* picture at People Express.

But it's not the whole compensation picture. There are attractive stock and profit-sharing programs that tie your contribution to the overall performance of the company, and these are skewed so that if People does well, managers at upper levels will benefit more than those in lower levels. It's mandatory at People Express for all employees to be stockholders; you must hold a minimum of 100 shares, and you can acquire this stock in various ways—repay a company low-interest loan with payroll deductions over five years, contribute to a deferred profit-sharing plan (with People matching every one of your dollars with 25 cents), or exercise stock options (made available to all employees). One-third of People's stock is held by employees. Profit-sharing bonuses are paid out quarterly, based on the airline's performance over the previous four quarters—and the formula here takes into account your level in the company and your years of service. For example, the maximum payout would be made if the company achieved the incredible result of a 20 percent pretax return on sales. In that unlikely event, however, a flight manager (a pilot) who had been with People for 10 years would double his salary for that quarter; a customer service manager with 10 years' experience would get a payout equivalent to 55 percent of his or her salary. People holds an employee-stockholders meeting every three months. They call it a "financial party."

People Express hires one out of every hundred persons who apply for a job. It looks for high-energy people, risk-takers rather than security-seekers. And it's an awfully young-looking crew—in the cockpits as well as in the aisles of the planes. Only a couple of pilots are in their forties. The average age of employees is in the late twenties or early thirties.

That's the way it was when the airline began. Burr left Texas International to start People Express when he was 39 years old—and at that age he was the "old man" of the founding bunch. Among the founders were Melrose K. Dawsey, who was 31; Lori L. Dubose, who was 27; Donald E. Hoydu, who was 38; McAdoo, who was 36; Harold J. Pareti, who was 32. All came from Texas International.

By having people work at different jobs, People Express makes efficient use of its employees. It also seems to have a highly motivated work force. All of which might help to explain why it was one of the few airlines to make money in 1982.

The airline business is risky. You take your chances when you go to work there. But People Express at least seems to be willing to let its employees in on the decision-making—and on the sharing of the rewards.

Up to a point, that is. The self-management concept was never extended to part-timers taking reservations over the phone—and that led in 1983 to a bitter labor flap. Some 650 reservation clerks were phased out of their jobs in favor of college students. The clerks rendered jobless protested that they had been exploited by People Express. They pointed out that they were paid low wages ($5 an hour) without any benefits because they were part-timers. They said that they had expected to be upgraded to customer service managers (flight attendants). They also claimed their ranks were 85 percent minority and female.

People Express rejected these claims but conceded that it had made a mess of the telephone reservations sector. The company explained that its original idea was to have full-timers—the flight attendants—take reservations when they were on the ground. But the airline grew so quickly that it couldn't hire enough qualified customer service managers in time to put this plan into operation, so it resorted to part-timers hired off the street. And it gave them contracts that made it clear that this was only temporary work for a specific period, usually three months. The airline admitted, however, that the longer people did work in such a post, the more expectations were raised that they would graduate to full-time employment. The unspoken code words here were: "The Newark people hired as temps did not have the ability to be customer service managers for People Express." So the airline allowed their contracts to expire and replaced the workers with students from Rutgers, Seton Hall, and Fairleigh Dickinson—part-timers who, as students, were not looking for full-time employment. The airline also said that 40 percent of its new part-time force was minority, which it maintained was a higher percentage than obtained in the previous crew.

It was a sad episode for an airline that prides itself on the "involvement of all its people in the management of the company." That obviously doesn't apply to the underclass of telephone reservation agents.

The use of college students to answer the phones didn't work either, and by 1985 People was contracting the reservations function to an outside supplier, First Data Resources, which had been operating a reservations system for the airline in Omaha. First Data was planning to employ 1,200 persons in a new People Express reservations center in Jacksonville, Florida. And similar centers were being planned for Los Angeles and Pittsburgh. So the people who answer the phone when you call People Express may not be employees of the airline.

Main employment center   Newark International Airport.

Headquarters   People Express Airlines, Inc.
North Terminal
Newark International Airport
Newark, NJ 07114
201-961-2931

PHYSIO CONTROL

PHYSIO-CONTROL CORPORATION

Physio-Control makes medical electronic products, including defibrillator/monitors (used to treat heart attack victims) and dialysis equipment (used to treat patients with failed kidneys), and noninvasive blood pressure products. Employees: 1,100.

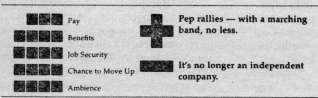

■■□□ Pay	➕ Pep rallies — with a marching band, no less.
■■■■ Benefits	
■■■■ Job Security	
■■■□ Chance to Move Up	■■□□ It's no longer an independent company.
■■■■ Ambience	

Is it possible for a company to retain its special characteristics after it has been absorbed by a much larger corporation? Physio-Control, based in bucolic Redmond, Washington, northeast of Seattle, has managed to do that. A maker of electronic medical instruments, Physio-Control was acquired in May 1980 by Eli Lilly, one of the giants of the pharmaceutical industry. Yet if you visited the 25-acre campus that's home to Physio-Control, you would see very little evidence of Lilly. Its name is not on the door or any of the buildings, and printed materials do not identify Physio-Control as a Lilly subsidiary.

However, you might guess there's a connection when you see Eli Lilly's annual report casually resting on a table in the reception area. (Eli Lilly? "Oh, yes, they own us.") And it may be that Physio-Control will change in the future, although W. Hunter Simpson, the charismatic, chainsmoking ex-IBMer who has been the driving force behind Physio-Control, says: "ninety-eight percent of the people here will probably never know we're part of Lilly."

Simpson joined the company in 1966 when it was still a research laboratory with four employees. He left a cushy job as Pacific Northwest manager of IBM to head a tiny, underfinanced enterprise that had never made any money. But it did have a product—a defibrillator/monitor, a device that delivers an electrical shock to the heart; for a person in cardiac arrest, it can literally be a lifesaver.

Under Hunter Simpson's prodding, Physio-Control went from sales of $42,000 in 1966 to $41.5 million in 1979. When Lilly bought the company in 1980, an investor who had put in $25,000 in the 1960s could have cashed in for $3.5 million.

But what Simpson also built over those years—and this is still in place—is a way of working that makes Physio-Control an open, nourishing environment. There's an infectious spirit operating here. Because Simpson thinks it's "degrading" to call anyone an employee, the people who work at Physio-Control are called "team members." The employee benefits booklet that everyone gets is called the "Team Handbook." All the publications issued by the company refer only to "team members." People are told upon joining Physio-Control that "belief in personal integrity" is "a basic corporate philosophy."

That philosophy manifests itself in various ways. The physical setting itself is uplifting—open, light, airy structures placed unobtrusively in a wooded glen. It's the opposite of grimy. Physio-Control instituted a four-day work week in 1971, and most team members still work 10 hours a day, Mondays through Thursdays. To keep the assembly line going, there's a crew of "weekend warriors" who work three-day shifts, Fridays through Sundays. The company subsidizes a bus service that leaves downtown Seattle at 6:15 A.M. and gets to Redmond at 6:45 A.M., returning at the end of the day. There are no time clocks at Physio, nor are there many written rules. Team members are advised that when in doubt they should ask the question, "Will the resulting action benefit the team as a whole and further the accomplishment of corporate goals?"

Physio maintains a profit-sharing plan that provides a cash bonus based on Physio's performance. In addition, team members may invest in a savings plan that provides a match of 50 cents for each team member dollar invested, plus an additional amount based on the overall performance of Eli Lilly. Team members are also offered a retirement plan, psychiatric and orthodontia coverage, and both short- and long-term disability insurance. As a matter of policy, Physio allocates 3 percent of pretax profits to philanthropy—a rate three times the average in U.S. industry. And Physio is one of the rare companies with an adoption aid program: If a team member wishes to adopt a child, the company will reimburse up to a maximum of $1,500.

In 1983, Physio launched an innovative program to help people with developmental disabilities learn skills that would enable them to join the company as regular workers. Working with an outside firm, Trillium Employment Services, Physio added six disabled workers to its production line—in the final assembly area—and paid them through Trillium. The idea is that when they reach specified skill levels, they become full-fledged team members. The first to do so was Janice Adkins, who entered the program in September 1983 and became a Physio team member in May 1984. The Physio program has attracted national attention from people and organizations interested in finding ways to bring the disabled into the workplace.

To see the Physio spirit in action, you need to catch one of the quarterly pep meetings. Every three months the company holds a mass meeting open to all team members, on company time. At that session, team members are briefed on what's going on in the company—what sales were in the previous three months, new products in the pipeline, goals for the future. And it's a meeting carried on with a fair amount of hoopla. For example, it's not unusual to have the University of Washington marching band present for the occasion. Each year at one of the four meetings, a pancake breakfast is served, at which senior managers make the pancakes for the rest of the team.

Thanks to its success, Physio-Control has steadily expanded the size of its team. It went from 57 members in 1970 to 733 in 1978 and 1,100 early in 1983. Applications pour into the place at a rate of 1,200 a month these days because the company's reputation has spread. Many of the people hired are those recommended by current team members. Hunter Simpson himself makes it a point to spend one hour with every new team member, no matter what level. He seemingly never tires of telling the Physio-Control story. And walking through the plant with him, one is amazed to see how many people he can greet by first name—and they, in turn, address him as "Hunter." He claims to know half the work force by their first names.

Physio-Control people do not like to leave the team. The four people who were with the company when Hunter Simpson came aboard in 1966 were, amazingly, still with the company in 1984: Harold Kawaguchi, who's in charge of corporate resources; engineers Jack Howard and Ed Warrick; and Marcheta Ackenhausen, who is Simpson's secretary. The company has 400 team members with more than five years of service; Simpson has lunch with them twice a year. And there are 71 so-called moldly oldies, people who have spent more than 10 years with Physio; Simpson has dinner with them once a year. Not since 1967, when the company was in its infancy, has there been a layoff.

Main employment center   Redmond, Washington. Hunter Simpson has a deep and abiding affection for his alma mater, the University of Washington, a prime source of new team members. He has a policy that so far he has been able to maintain: "I never want any Physio facility to be more than 22 minutes away from the University of Washington."

Headquarters   Physio-Control Corporation
11811 Willow Road N.E.
Redmond, WA 98052
206-881-4000

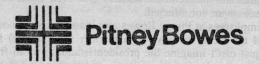

PITNEY BOWES INC.

Pitney Bowes makes nine out of every ten postage meters in the United States. U.S. employees: 21,600.

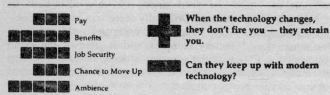

Pay

Benefits

Job Security

Chance to Move Up

Ambience

When the technology changes, they don't fire you — they retrain you.

Can they keep up with modern technology?

Some employees at Pitney Bowes like to contrast how their company has grappled with the new computer technology with what happened at NCR. Both companies dominate their industry with a major product line: Pitney Bowes is as synonymous with postage meters as is NCR with cash registers. A few years ago both companies recognized the need to update their machines from purely electromechanical to electronic. And both companies took steps to undertake that massive conversion.

That's where the analogy ends—happily for Pitney Bowes's Connecticut workers, not so happily for NCR's Ohio workers. NCR made a common business decision. Rather than try to do the expensive retooling in their Dayton plants and go to the trouble of retraining all their production workers, NCR built new factories in the Southwest and hired a fresh bunch of people. Thousands of assembly-line workers lost their jobs.

Pitney Bowes accomplished a similar conversion without laying off a single production worker, according to William Redgate, a vice-president of employee relations. The company set up a special training center in Stamford to teach people familiar with springs and gears how to solder chips on computer boards. At one point about 50 employees were assigned to work previously done by outside contractors—security guards and maintenance workers. But even those workers' paychecks were not affected.

Employees at Pitney Bowes aren't surprised the company bucked the trend to move to a warmer (or cheaper) locale. They just can't imagine the president standing up in front of them—as he does once a year—and making such an announcement.

Like other public companies, Pitney Bowes sends all stockholders an annual report and invites them to an annual meeting. Pitney Bowes also sends each employee an annual "Report to Jobholders" and since 1947 has also held an annual jobholder meeting. Originally there was just one meeting of the entire work force at the company's old red brick headquarters and factory complex within sight of the Long Island Sound. Because the company is so large now, it sets up several dozen jobholder meetings throughout the country, and about 250 to 300 employees attend each of the two- to three-hour meetings. The president himself usually attends about a third of these gatherings, and other high officials chair the others.

Jobholder meetings are not nearly so polite as the typical stockholder meeting. Employees usually prepare for them beforehand, and many prepare detailed questions. Those who submit the best oral and written questions receive a $25 savings bond. Questions run the gamut, from personal complaints to queries about the company's marketing strategies.

Rawlin A. Fairbaugh, vice-president of customer engineering who chairs some of the jobholder meetings in some of the outlying areas, told us that "you've got to learn how to stand up there and take it. Most managers at other companies wouldn't believe that we make ourselves that vulnerable." But Fairbaugh, like other managers and employees we talked with, strongly believes in the jobholder meetings. Communication is the name of the game at Pitney Bowes.

Despite its size, Pitney Bowes has managed to retain a family feeling. Indeed, at the firm's major manufacturing plants in Connecticut, many of the people are related to each other. As one plant worker told us, "It's almost like working for a small company, like a 10-million-dollar company instead of a billion-dollar corporation." Everyone is on a first-name basis, including the president. The current president and chairman, George B. Harvey, has been known to accompany a Santa Claus around the plants at Christmastime, shaking hands and talking informally with employees. Of the atmosphere at Pitney Bowes, Harvey likes to say: "A good place to work is a good place to get work done."

To help maintain the small company/family atmosphere, the company has a unique in-house mechanism for airing employee concerns called the Council of Personnel Relations, formed in 1942. The CPR parallels the organization of the company and consists of an equal number of managers and employees elected by their peers. Every other week all employees meet with their elected representative and a supervisor—the section-level council. Problems not settled by the section council are sent along to the department council, then to the division council, and then on to the main council, co-chaired by the company president and an employee elected by the representatives from the division council. The last three council levels meet once a month, one week after each other. Common issues of CPR meetings in 1984 were expanding benefits, creating an employee referral program for open jobs, and balancing production requirements with employee suggestions for quality improvements.

One ground rule is that the management has the final say. But the sessions are spirited. Al Salvino, an offset press operator who was CPR chairman in 1983, told us, "We bang heads, we are suggestive, but we do not threaten. It used to be who can scream the loudest." The process is more "professional" now, he said, partly because of a CPR training school for representatives that involves three-day and week-long programs.

Salvino and others involved in the CPR we talked with said the process is much less adversarial than a union grievance negotiation. "There are written procedures and policies, but we don't always go by what's on paper," Salvino explained. "If we had to do that there would be no need to have the CPRs. You'd just need a book."

The process is costly; Pitney Bowes estimates well over one million dollars a year. From the management's viewpoint the process has been worthwhile since it contends that CPR has helped the company maintain high morale, low turnover —and no unions.

From the employee viewpoint, it has been a success as well. Aside from resolving many personal issues and maintaining a means of exchanging opinions, the CPR claims to have been instrumental in introducing a dental plan, liberalizing early retirement and short-term disability benefits, introducing a health maintenance organization, and forming an alcohol abuse program.

Pitney Bowes has a long laundry list of generous and unusual benefits. There's a suggestion system, for instance, that allows employees to earn up to $50,000 for a cost-saving idea. An employee gets to keep *half* of the savings coming from an implemented suggestion (up to $25,000 a year for two years). And there's a preretirement education program, where any employee over the age of 50 is reimbursed up to $300 a year to take any course related to his or her retirement plans. Courses have ranged from real estate, golf, and tailoring to cake decorating, watercolor painting, and photography. (There is, incidentally, no mandatory retirement age at Pitney Bowes.) And there's an anniversary vacation policy that offers an extra month's vacation when someone completes 25 years with the company. That is, after 25 years someone would get five weeks' regular vacation plus another four weeks' anniversary vacation. The same month's anniversary vacation is offered every five years thereafter—on the thirtieth anniversary, thirty-fifth anniversary, and so on.

These benefits are in addition to an already generous benefits package. Hewitt Associates, a consulting firm, did a survey of Pitney Bowes's benefits compared with those offered by 16 other companies, including DEC, Eastman Kodak, GE, Honeywell, IBM, Sperry, 3M, United Technologies, and Xerox. It concluded that Pitney Bowes ranked between second and third among all of these companies for such items as pension, disability, and medical benefits.

One of the best benefits is the company's profit-sharing plan, paid every quarter since its introduction in 1946. The company takes 19 percent of the firm's operating profits during the quarter and divides it among the employees, according to their earnings during that period. The quarterly profit-sharing checks have meant a bonus of between 3 and 11 percent in recent years. For the second quarter of 1983, for instance, employees received checks equivalent to 6.47 percent of their quarterly income.

At Pitney Bowes at least, better communication has meant higher benefits—and job security.

Main employment centers   Six thousand work in and around Stamford. Other facilities include the Dictaphone manufacturing subsidiary in Melbourne, Florida, and plants in Johnson County, Kansas, and Dayton, Ohio.

Headquarters   Pitney Bowes Inc.
Walter H. Wheeler Jr. Drive
Stamford, CT 06926
203-356-5000

THE BEST EMPLOYEE HANDBOOK
Leo Burnett

Polaroid

POLAROID CORPORATION

Polaroid invented and developed the instant camera—and it holds 75 percent of this market. U.S. employees: 10,000.

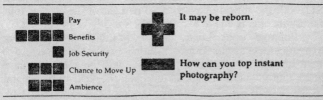

Pay ■■■□
Benefits ■■■□
Job Security ■
Chance to Move Up ■■■
Ambience ■■■

✚ It may be reborn.

■■ How can you top instant photography?

In 1979, Polaroid had nearly 21,000 employees worldwide. At the end of 1983, it had 14,500, including 10,000 in the United States. That's close to a one-third reduction in the work force. How can it be a good place to work? It still is, thanks to a heady atmosphere created and cultivated by the company's founder, Edwin H. Land.

The story goes that after Polaroid produced its first instant camera, Land called in one of his engineers and said, "I want you think about color." The scientist went away and thought about color for a year. Then he came back to Land and said, "I think I've got it." Polaroid has been a company where someone could work undisturbed for a year on a promising idea. There was never any question that this was the kind of creative effort that Edwin Land prized more than anything else. Polaroid headquarters in Cambridge is sandwiched between Harvard and the Massachusetts Institute of Technology—and that itself is a statement about what this company is about.

Along with developing the instant camera, Polaroid developed its own culture, considered a little quirky by straitlaced corporate types. It was an early leader in equal employment opportunity programs (8 percent of its salaried workers and 19 percent of its hourly force today are minori-

335

ties), and one result was the company's complete withdrawal from the South African market.

It established an employee committee to represent workers to management; members of the committee are elected by the employees (there's one representative for every 320 employees). Employees also get to choose by vote one paid holiday a year (would you believe Paul Revere Day?), in addition to the nine regular ones provided by the company. Polaroid began subsidized daytime child care for working mothers in 1971. The subsidy is graduated by income: if the employee comes from a family of six with a total income of $11,000, the subsidy comes to 80 percent of the cost; if total family income is above $25,000, the subsidy is 40 percent.

Polaroid, under Land, liked to do things differently. For example, it holds its annual meeting in unusual places, and with unusual programs. In recent years, the meetings have been held in such settings as the Polaroid plant in Needham, Massachusetts, Boston Symphony Hall, and Wellesley College. The financial community on Wall Street has never been fond of Polaroid because Land didn't like to talk to them; he also plowed money into research, which hurt short-term profits.

Another legacy from Land is an extraordinary emphasis on continuing education. The company picks up 100 percent of the tuition for job-related courses taken by employees. In 1983, 40 employees received undergraduate and graduate degrees under this program. Inside Polaroid itself more than 100 courses are offered to employees, ranging all over the lot: technical writing, oral communication, digital logic, basic English, coping with stress, making meetings work, management of change, college trigonometry, office skills, welding, blueprint reading, basic statistics. The courses are designed to help employees advance in their careers—or make career switches. Between 1983 and 1984, for example, 60 employees completed three-year retraining or apprentice programs to emerge as air-conditioning mechanics, electricians, instrument technicians, machinists, plumbers, and pipefitters, among others. More than 4,000 employees were enrolled in courses in 1983.

The problem with Polaroid is that the company was locked into one product, the instant camera, and into what was close to one-man rule under founder Edwin Land. That era has ended. Although Land is still the company's largest shareholder, he has retired from the company. And though instant photography is still the main revenue source, Polaroid has begun to explore other areas. In 1979, 9.4 million cameras were sold; by 1982, the number had dropped to 3.5 million. Meanwhile, Polaroid's industrial and technical business grew from 25 percent to 40 percent of total revenues.

Polaroid has been on a roller coaster before, but in the early 1980s it was forced into very drastic cutbacks in the employee rolls. Consistent with its longtime sensitivity to employee needs, however, it handled this crisis so well that there was little outcry from the work force. It tried, first of all, to get as many people as possible to accept early retirement packages. It set up outplacement offices to help laid-off employees get new jobs. It switched people to other jobs in the company. And it tried as much as possible to provide some continuity of income and benefits. For longtime employees, there was a severance payment that reached as high as one month's pay for every year of service, and their fringe benefits—health and life insurance—were continued for the same amount of months. Short-term employees who were let go also received generous treatment.

Polaroid has a strong profit-sharing plan, although the company has not been able to make contributions under the program during the 1980s because of poor corporate profits. But the future should be different. The company is committed now to moving into other areas besides instant photography. And it is trying to fashion a new management style in a post-Land era. One Polaroid veteran explained to us that in the past, life was exciting if "you were anointed by Land." On the other hand, if you didn't become part of his team, "you felt left out." Today, he said, "the mood is a little different. There are no more ups and downs. People have more control of their own destinies."

Polaroid is trying, in effect, to become a different kind of company, one that exploits its technology by making more mundane products instead of always looking for the flashy, new, breakthrough item. It's prepared to become a supplier of original equipment for other manufacturers instead of thinking only of mass consumer products. And, something Land would never have abided, Polaroid is even buying products from other companies—videotape, for example, from Sony—and putting its own name on it.

So it's a new ballgame in a company with a tradition of innovation. An employee survey taken in 1984 showed high satisfaction with workplace conditions but uncertainty about the future.

Main employment centers   Within a 100-mile radius of Boston—in Cambridge, Needham, New Bedford, Freetown, Norwood, and Waltham—9,500 people work for Polaroid.

Headquarters   Polaroid Corporation
549 Technology Square
Cambridge, MA 02139
617-577-2000

PRESTON TRUCKING COMPANY, INC.

A large trucking firm with a fleet that covers the northeast part of the United States. U.S. employees: 4,617.

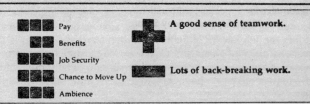

▪▪▪ Pay	✚ **A good sense of teamwork.**
▪▪ Benefits	
▪▪▪ Job Security	
▪▪▪ Chance to Move Up	▬▬ **Lots of back-breaking work.**
▪▪▪ Ambience	

"It's like the Giants or the Jets. If you don't play together, the line falls apart, and you lose. That's why we have to work in the same direction around here."

Sonny Muraco drives trucks for Preston from the Jersey City terminal. He was explaining why he likes Preston's version of quality circles, called "Performance Teams." Every few weeks Muraco and about 20 other Preston drivers sit down to brainstorm methods for improving their jobs. The terminal manager writes their ideas on a large sheet of paper, and the group votes for the best suggestions. The most popular ideas are implemented.

Preston may be the only company whose members of the Teamsters union and the International Longshoremen's Association regularly participate with their supervisors in such an exercise. Preston people seem to relish breaking down the traditional barriers between union and management. Everyone is called an "associate" instead of "employee."

Not that Preston's business is any different from other major truckers'. Its bright orange tractor trailers can be seen on highways throughout the Northeast or at the 85 Preston terminals from New York and Washington, D.C., to St. Louis and Chicago. In 1983 Preston ranked seventeenth among major motor carriers in terms of revenues (at $272 million that year). And the hectic pace around a Preston terminal resembles that of competitors such as Roadway Express and Consolidated Freightways. A few pounds short or a few minutes late spells the difference between profit and loss, so there's constant pressure about the smallest details. Charts adorn the walls, pointing to daily, weekly, and monthly totals.

Yet Preston has a distinctive style. How many other truckers (or American corporations, for that matter) quote the German philosopher Goethe in their annual report to stockholders? "Treat people as though they were what they ought to be and you help them become what they are capable of being." The report continues: "Preston People must be regarded as partners rather than as adversaries. The person doing the job knows more about it than anybody else. It is the responsibility of managers to ask for suggestions, to listen to possible solutions to specific problems, and to help implement productive change. Each employee has unlimited possibilities."

Besides using Performance Teams, Preston tries to tap these possibilities by "positive reinforcement." Instead of communicating to employees only when they make mistakes, supervisors are encouraged to reward good efforts with a pat on the back, or more formally, with letters of recognition or inscribed pens. "The ratio should be four-to-one, positive to negative," says Chuck Powell, who was Preston's northern New Jersey regional manager in 1983. "It's just the opposite of what's typical in an industry where people only get negative feedback."

"The idea is that we want our people to be self-starters," explains Tom English, terminal manager at Jersey City. "We ask a driver to set his own goal. Say he sets it at 1,800 pounds per hour. If he falls below it, we'll sit down and discuss why. We may decide to reduce it somewhat and try to reach the lower goal. If he goes higher than 1,800, we'll make sure to give him some kind of recognition, only if it is by telling him what a great job he's doing. We'll sit down and try to get him to raise his goal above 1,800. The idea is to try to get everybody to push up his output all the time."

In 1984 Preston started paying people bonuses for increasing productivity by becoming the first trucking company to adopt a Scanlon bonus plan. According to the plan, when efficiency improves over a preestablished level, 75 percent of the profit improvement goes to the associates and 25 percent to the company.

At the same time, Preston encourages all employees to take some responsibility for sales. In 1982 the company reported that 62.6 percent of Preston employees obtained additional shipments for the company. "The drivers are the best salesmen I've got," claims English.

A new Preston salesman, Charlie Wildman, who has been in sales for various trucking companies for 18 years, says, "There's not the great difference between Teamsters union people and the sales or management people that you see in other trucking companies." He attributes this to Preston's being "more of a team venture, more of a unification" than other truckers.

"Let's face it, if we don't pull together, we'll go down the tubes like those other truckers," says John Iannaci, a Preston driver in Jersey City for the last 15 years and member of Teamsters Local 560. "If we make money for the boss, he'll stay around to keep us on."

Main employment centers   Eighty-five terminals in Connecticut, Delaware, Illinois, Indiana, Maryland, Michigan, Missouri, New Jersey, Ohio, Pennsylvania, Virginia, and Washington, D.C.

Headquarters   Preston Trucking Company, Inc.
151 Easton Boulevard
Preston, MD 21655
301-673-7151

THE PROCTER & GAMBLE COMPANY

THE PROCTER & GAMBLE COMPANY

Procter & Gamble dominates the soap and detergent industry, makes other household and personal-care products, and ranks perennially as the nation's largest advertiser. U.S. employees: 39,900.

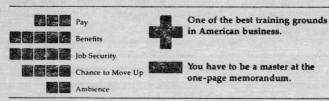

▓▓▓ Pay	✚	One of the best training grounds in American business.
▓▓▓▓▓ Benefits		
▓▓▓▓▓ Job Security		
▓▓▓▓ Chance to Move Up	▓	You have to be a master at the one-page memorandum.
▓▓ Ambience		

It's good to be with a winner, and if any company is a winner, it's Procter & Gamble. The pride and glory of Cincinnati, P&G is without question the most successful developer and seller of consumer products in the United States. Of the top ten best-selling household products in the American marketplace, six—Pampers, Tide, Charmin, Bounty, Cheer, and Downy—are P&G brands. What household does not have one of these brands on hand: Dash, Ivory, Comet, Cascade, Sure, Zest, Head & Shoulders, Prell, Folgers, Pampers, Duncan Hines, Scope, Crest?

In terms of sales volume P&G ranks as the thirty-second-largest company in the United States. Measured by profits, it's twenty-third. And, as anyone who watches television knows, it's always number one when it comes to advertising expenditures.

When you join P&G, you become part of a very disciplined organization that nurtures its people, moving them up from one rung to another. This is a company that lives and dies by performance. And just as the movement of brands is measured carefully, so is the movement of personnel.

If you write to P&G about job opportunities, you get

back a flier that announces: "We're looking for achievers . . . we seek exceptionally able college graduates who have already demonstrated a superior ability to achieve, and who possess the potential for rapid personal growth after they join us. . . . We hire at the beginning level and promote from within, strictly on the basis of performance." They're not kidding. No one ever comes into P&G at a middle- or top-management level who has garnered his or her experience at another company. It just doesn't happen.

This is an up-through-the-ranks company with a vengeance. When you look at the biographies of the top people at P&G and come to the entry "Business Affiliations Prior to Joining Procter & Gamble," it nearly always says, "None." The present chief executive officer, John G. Smale, did work three years at two other companies, but when he joined P&G in 1952, it was as an assistant brand manager, an entry-level job. His predecessor, Edward G. Harness, joined the P&G advertising department in 1940 after graduating from Marietta College.

There is a P&G way of doing things, and if you don't master it or at least feel comfortable with it, you're not going to be happy here, not to speak of being successful. The hallmark of this working style is thoroughness. P&G is legendary for researching a subject to death before it does anything — and that applies in all areas, whether it's launching a new brand or deciding where to put a new factory or buying some paper clips.

An almost unbelievable example of how the company does its homework was related in 1982 by the *Cincinnati Enquirer*, which told this story (attributed to Hercules Segalas, an ex-P&Ger who is now the foremost P&G watcher on Wall Street): "Procter's purchasers buy phosphates for its detergents from wholesale manufacturers. During the Arab oil embargo in the '70s, the wholesaler came to the company and said the shortage of petroleum had left him too little raw materials to meet the delivery schedule. To the wholesaler's disbelief, the Procter people had anticipated the problem *and* tracked down the materials he needed."

This is not a company for hip-shooters. Harness once said, "We don't go in for any of this 'let's-get-together-and-rap' nonsense." Gordon Wade, an ex-P&Ger who's now a consultant, told this story to the *Cincinnati Enquirer*: "When I first arrived there, fresh from Harvard, I kept wanting to say, 'In my judgment.' I can still hear the response, 'Your judgment's no better than the drunk in Lytle Park.' At Procter, they don't pay you for judgment. They pay you for removing judgment." *Fortune* once put it this way: "P&G resembles an Oriental juggernaut—careful, thorough, convinced of the utter righteousness of its cause, and willing to think in decades."

Some people who've left P&G describe the company as a "memo-driven organization" where all the decisions are made by committees. There is consensus management operating at P&G, but it's not clear whether the important decisions are being made by committees or it's simply that everyone thinks alike because everyone has grown up together in the same corporate family.

On the other hand, P&G stalwarts make the point that you get an opportunity to have responsibility early. P&G believes that "the best way to start to learn our business is to start to manage part of it." Craig Decker, a bearded personnel director who joined P&G in 1967, told us that he had been with the company for only two weeks when he was asked to make a recommendation on a $500,000 promotion program. Decker pointed out, with some humor, that this "enables you to get the mistakes out of the way when they don't cost much." The one-page memorandum is the butt of many P&G jokes—and it does exist. You are expected here to be able to distill your thoughts into a few choice paragraphs. One ex-P&Ger told us that she heard of one memo that was rewritten 47 times.

What kind of people work at P&G? Charles C. Carroll, a P&G executive, made a stab in 1978 at describing the members of the advertising department: "They are people with brains and ability to use them. . . . For example, more than eight out of ten of those who joined our various advertising departments just this year were in the top 10 percent of their high school class; over half were in the top 10 percent of their college class—from some very first-rate colleges—and more than one in ten were Phi Beta Kappa."

There's nothing fancy about the P&G headquarters building in downtown Cincinnati. The offices are efficient, comfortable—and spartan. The company cafeteria serves food that's undistinguished but inexpensive. And there are rules.

You are not permitted, for example, to have any alcoholic beverage at lunch when you eat outside, not even a glass of wine or beer. Charles Hedrick, manager of employee relations, points out that "there is nothing moral" in this regulation. P&G just feels that you can't make clear decisions when your head is clouded with alcohol—and so it doesn't want its people making such decisions under the influence. If you drink at lunch, you're expected not to return to the office.

Some companies take pride in hiring back people who left and found that the grass was not greener outside. Not Procter & Gamble. When you leave, you're out—for good. And many do leave, using their P&G training as a springboard for good jobs in other companies. Hedrick likens Procter & Gamble to the National Football League, providing the training for people who go on to the business equivalents of the old American Football League and the United States Football League.

In any case, there's an active group of P&G alumni. Former P&Gers fill the chairman's or president's post at more than 40 major companies. So numerous are the alumni, and so fond are they of their early days at P&G, that they gather together occasionally for alumni meetings. The biggest gathering was held in 1983 at the Field Museum of Natural History in Chicago. Some 400 showed up for a dinner party organized by John T. Thomas, an ex-P&Ger now with a Chicago headhunter, E. N. Wilkins & Co. The booklet distributed at this party listed the names of more than 800 ex-P&Gers scattered in the ranks of such big companies as General Foods, PepsiCo, and Kraft, and in many advertising agencies.

One alumnus, William E. Phillips, now runs Ogilvy & Mather, one of the nation's largest advertising agencies. He described the intensity of the working experience at Procter & Gamble: "You go to a strange town, work together all day, write memos all night, and see each other on weekends. You form a lot of friendships that way." And some blossom into marriages. When P&G alumni came together for a meeting in Los Angeles in the summer of 1982, among the attendees were Nancy Pullen, with United Vintners, and her husband, David Preuss, with Chlorox, and Melissa Sawyers, with the Foote, Cone & Belding ad agency, and her husband, Peter Sawyers, with Carnation.

Those who do leave Procter & Gamble give up one of the best benefits programs in U.S. industry. This is a company that grasped very early in its history the connection between its business welfare and its employees'. P&G has had for more than 100 years a regulation in its books that states: "It is declared to be the policy of the Company to recognize that its interests and those of its employees are inseparable." Many actions have flowed from this policy, to wit:

• In 1885, P&G began giving its employees Saturday afternoon off—with pay. Other companies thought P&G had lost its marbles.

• In 1887, the company instituted a profit-sharing plan. This is the oldest profit-sharing plan in continuous operation in American industry.

• P&G was one of the first companies in the nation to adopt comprehensive sickness, disability, and life insurance programs. That was in 1915.

• Since 1923, Procter & Gamble has "guaranteed" production people regular employment of "not less than 48 weeks." This does not mean that no one is ever fired at P&G. You cannot loaf your way through this organization. However, it does mean that established P&G workers can expect, assuming they do their jobs, regular employment.

• The company encourages stock purchases through a payroll-deduction plan. An estimated 20 percent of all P&G shares are owned by employees and retirees.

In a survey of 983 companies conducted in 1980 by the U.S. Chamber of Commerce, P&G ranked in the top 4 percent in terms of benefits paid to employees. Procter & Gamble is one of a handful of companies that offers an adoption aid benefit—you can get reimbursement up to $1,000 for the costs of adopting a child. It has a health plan that enables you to flash a card in your pharmacy and then pay a maximum of $2 for a prescription. It recently adopted a program that matches employee gift contributions to colleges on a two-for-one basis. And it now has a flexible benefits program that helps employees tailor their own package. Under this program, you get a credit, based on your salary, which you can then take in cash or apply to various programs as you see fit. You can also, if you wish, trade in vacation time for credits.

It's a program designed to keep Procter & Gamble ahead

of the competition. P&G likes to stay ahead, whether it's selling detergents or offering employees the best compensation-and-benefits package.

Main employment centers   Some 12,500 people work in the Cincinnati headquarters area, including the Ivorydale factory, the company's oldest production facility. Another 22,000 work outside the United States. The company is putting up a new, 17-story building in downtown Cincinnati that will be a twin to the one now serving as headquarters. To be completed in 1985, the new building will be connected to the old one by glass bridges and a tunnel. Other major United States plant cities are Mehoopany, Pennsylvania, 2,900, and Green Bay, Wisconsin, 2,000—both are paper plants. P&G operates 50 plants in 24 states.

Headquarters   The Procter & Gamble Company
301 East 6th Street
P.O. Box 599
Cincinnati, OH 45201
513-562-1100

WHERE GAS IS SOLD AT COST

Federal Express
Liebert
Linnton Plywood

Merle Norman
Cosmetics

Publix super markets, inc.

PUBLIX SUPER MARKETS INC.

Publix operates the largest supermarket chain in Florida. Employees: 35,000.

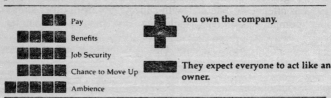

Pay	**+** You own the company.
Benefits	
Job Security	
Chance to Move Up	They expect everyone to act like an owner.
Ambience	

"Publix represents something. It's not like working for Kroger or Winn-Dixie or someplace like that. When you work for a company like Publix, you try to make sure to behave well even when you are off the job."

Like other employees we talked with, John Siske feels there's something special about working for Publix. He works in a Publix store in Miami Beach. His job title is "Third Person," meaning he's sort of a troubleshooter, a jack-of-all-trades. He started with the chain as a part-timer while in school (a common way people join the company) and has been a full-time employee since completing Dade Junior College five years ago.

"I plan to be here until I retire," Siske told us. "They will have to drag me out of here." Why? "It's fun to work here. Time passes so quickly every day. You enjoy the customers."

The remarkable esprit Publix employees exhibit is not the only unusual feature of this Florida chain of 276 supermarkets. It is also one of the largest employee-owned companies in America. And it is one of the most profitable supermarket chains in the land. Though its 1983 sales of $2.8 billion made Publix the eleventh-largest supermarket chain in the country, it ranked seventh in profits and first in profit per dollar of sales. Publix netted 2 cents per dollar of sales compared to 1.6 cents for runner-up Winn-Dixie. Publix's return was twice that of the national sales leader, Safeway.

Publix employees attribute this performance to employee ownership and the maintenance of a small-company style.

A. J. Montgomery, a personnel director, went to work for Publix in 1958 at the age of 38. He previously had managed his family-owned grocery store in Augusta, Georgia. But, like everyone else at Publix, he had to start at an entry-level job, stocking shelves and bagging groceries. He was hired for a new store, Publix's forty-first. The night before the store's grand opening, Montgomery and the other new employees attended a banquet with supervisors from other stores and company officials, including chairman and founder George Jenkins.

The opening-night banquet is still a tradition at Publix. It is also part of the company culture for Jenkins to show up the next day to help at the store along with other executives from the headquarters in the central Florida city of Lakeland. Jenkins bags groceries for customers who have no idea who is waiting on them.

Montgomery was surprised at the folksy attitude. "Since Publix was such a large chain, I thought I would just be a number, and it would be about ten years before I would be accepted. But that first night I met George Jenkins and the other top people. It was more like they were welcoming us into their family."

Publix employees often talk about their company as a family, albeit a very big one. For one thing, many Publix people are related. A recent company magazine showed pictures of the 26 sets of twins who work for Publix.

Once a year the company sponsors "Publix Night" at Disney World. Thousands of employees and their families from all over the state converge on Orlando. The entire park is made available to them.

Year-round, dozens of Publix employees participate in the company sport, golf. Company founder Jenkins is so devoted to the game that he built a par-three, nine-hole golf course next door to the company's Lakeland warehouse so employees could play a quick round whenever possible. Jenkins also had a golf course built nearby, Lone Palm Country Club.

Golf also plays a central role in the life of many Publix employees who work far from Lakeland. It is traditional, for instance, for Publix store managers to take Wednesday off to play golf. (They usually work on Saturdays instead.) The practice was so well known that a ring of thieves regularly stole loads of food from one Miami store on Wednesday afternoons until apprehended by a nongolfing supervisor.

You should not expect to find many of the Publix managers spending much time at the nineteenth hole after their golf rounds, however. Though all store managers aren't practicing Southern Baptists, some say that most were as recently as the early 1960s. Publix still exibits a straitlaced streak. The company handbook specifically states that the "use of profanity cannot be tolerated" in the sales area. Dress for sales personnel is described in detail: women are to wear "comfortable, neat, low-heel shoes. . . . Very moderate makeup and cosmetics. . . . Jewelry should be inconspicuous." Men are to make sure their "fingernails [are] clean and close-clipped. . . . Shoes shined and neat."

Publix also states that it expects "enthusiasm" from all its employees: "Entering wholeheartedly into the promotion of Publix, both as a successful business enterprise and as a group of dedicated people, will bring greater enjoyment in your immediate task and will mark you as worthy of assuming greater responsibilities."

Above all else, Publix demands that employees devote themselves to making "Shopping a Pleasure" for the customers. Walls of its stores and warehouses are full of such slogans: "Publix People Make the Difference"; "Carry-Out Service Is Our Publix Policy—No Tipping, Please"; "A Smile Costs Nothing, But Its Value Is Priceless;" "Publix Will Be a Little Better Place to Work—Or Not Quite as Good—Because of You."

Training takes place on the job. Trainees learn such policies as always giving the customer a refund. Absolutely everybody starts at the bottom. All 401 truck drivers worked their way up through the warehouse. Hiring people from outside Publix for almost any job is almost unthinkable.

This single-minded devotion to selling groceries is the secret to Publix's profitability. Since employees are Publix's only shareholders, the company has been extremely good for those who work there. To start with, each quarter a store sets aside 20 percent of its profits to be split among the employees. On top of that, employees earn a Christmas bonus usually equal to two weeks' pay. One disadvantage is that employees have to work there 15 years before they get three weeks' paid vacation.

Publix also has a profit-sharing fund into which it puts 10 percent of annual profits, dividing them among all employees with more than 1,000 hours of service. In recent years, this has meant an employee bonus of between 6 and 8 percent of annual salary. The employee has access to this money when he or she retires or leaves the company. The company claims that although the typical base pay is about the same as the average paid to workers at other Florida supermarket chains (between $6.50 and $7.00 an hour), the combination of the Christmas bonus and various forms of profit-sharing means that Publix employees make far more than their Florida competitors.

One of the biggest advantages to working at Publix is the right to buy stock. In fact, the company encourages employees to buy shares of stock on their own, and over 7,000 are shareholders. The stock is their personal property, even if they leave Publix, but it can only be sold back to the company at the prevailing price. There are limits—only 5 shares after the first year, 10 shares after two years, 20 shares after three, 40 after four, and 100 for five years or more. Those who have been able to save enough money to purchase Publix stock have had a genuine bonanza. A share of stock bought in 1960 for $10 was worth about $360 in 1983. Between 1981 and 1984 the stock doubled in value.

As a result, many longtime Publix employees have retired with a considerable sum of money. "It is not uncommon for people around here to retire with a half-million dollars," said Benny Brown, director of meat operations.

Or, as advertising manager John Bernard put it: "We have a piece of the pie. It's easy to see the fruits of your labor when you work for Publix."

Publix is a highly unusual company in at least two other respects. Although it's completely privately owned, it issues an audited annual report to its "employee stockholders" that discloses the same kind of financial information reported by companies which are publicly owned. And the stock of the company is widely held by employees. Founder George W.

Jenkins is believed to hold no more than 5 percent. The Jenkins family (there are four members who are active officers) may have no more than 20 percent. Employees hold the rest. If Publix ever does go public, a lot of instant millionaires would be created here.

Main employment centers   Stores throughout Florida. Warehouse distribution centers in Lakeland, Miami, Sarasota, and Jacksonville. The company serves a free, cafeteria-style lunch to all warehouse and office employees at those four locations. Sixty percent of all employees are part-time.

Headquarters   Publix Super Markets, Inc.
Box 407
Lakeland, FL 33802
813-688-1188

Quad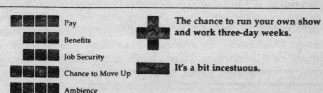

QUAD/GRAPHICS INC.

Quad prints national magazines and catalogs. Employees: 1,400.

▪▪▪▪ Pay	✚ The chance to run your own show and work three-day weeks.
▪▪▪ Benefits	
▪▪▪ Job Security	▪▪▪ It's a bit incestuous.
▪▪▪▪ Chance to Move Up	
▪▪▪ Ambience	

In mid-1969, Harry Quadracci found himself in an untenable position. He was the labor negotiator for a large Wisconsin printing company in the throes of a bitter 14-week strike. He had long opposed the tough-nosed, bottom-line, antilabor thinking of the company's board of directors. And during the strike, he also found himself in the middle of a conflict between the printer's high-level management and the board about how to respond to the crisis. So he quit and formed his own printing company—one with a different style of labor relations.

Quadracci founded Quad/Graphics in 1970 using capital from a second mortgage on his summer home. Believing that magazines would soon use only color photos (just as television had moved from black and white to color), Quadracci bought a state-of-the-art, full-color printing press. He housed it in a former warehouse in a rural area outside Milwaukee.

After some lean times, the business started to prosper. Fourteen years later Quad prints more than 100 different national magazines and catalogs, including the Midwest edition of *Newsweek*, advertising pages for *Time*, *U.S. News & World Report*, and *Playboy*, and regular monthly issues of *Black Enterprise*, *True Story*, *Beauty Digest*, *Mother Jones*, and *Four Wheeler*. The work force has grown from 11 to 1,400. The one web press was joined by nine others in a printing plant now five football fields in length. And the one plant was joined by two others, one in nearby Sussex, another in Saratoga, in upstate New York.

From the outset, Quadracci, an ex-lawyer, structured his company like a typical law firm. He talks of his employees as "partners," and like a law firm, which is owned by the partners, Quad is mostly employee-owned. Quadracci calls his philosophy "Theory Q" as opposed to the traditional American, top-down Theory X or the Japanese management, Theory Z. It's not so much a coherent philosophy as a hodge-podge of Quadracci's ideas about how to run a business. He expounds his thinking to other partners in "Think Small" seminars. Chief among his notions is an aversion to organizational charts, job descriptions, time clocks, and committing policies and procedures to paper. Communications with employees should be "personal, vocal, and spontaneous."

Quadracci considers all employees to be "students" hired by "sponsors" and directed by "mentors," rather than by bosses. Before employees become mentors themselves, "they must go through our boot camp and be brainwashed into our culture." Boot camp lasts about one year and is not so much a formalized training program as an on-the-job absorption of Quad's way of doing things. A high percentage of employees also participate in the wide variety of training courses conducted in-house by the more experienced employees. The accent is on quality and treating printing as a profession.

What seems to tie much of Quadracci's thinking together is his belief that a successful business is based on trust. Once a year Quad demonstrates this faith by what's called the "Spring Fling and Management Sneak." All managers leave the plant to have meetings and then go to the Milwaukee Art Museum. (Quadracci is an art enthusiast, as the numerous original paintings around the facility testify. There are even art posters in the men's locker room.) For 24 hours, normal printing operations continue without the presence of any managers. "We trust them," Quadracci explained. "But we also hope the mistakes will be small ones." *Inc.* called the technique "management by walking away."

Quad's loose managerial style contrasts sharply with traditional, unionized printers, according to Kent Underberg, a supervisor in the plate department. Underberg held a similar position at W. A. Krueger (the printing company Quadracci quit to form Quad/Graphics). "Here you get a chance to do things your own way. There they got on your case all the time. Here you act as your own boss. You don't just punch a time clock."

Tom Frankowski, who operates a Mizo plate machine, appreciates the lack of rigid work rules. "It's an open field here," he said. "I don't just do one thing, like in union shops. I'm allowed to do everything in this department, so I can learn more about printing and get ahead in my career."

Frankowski especially likes Quad's three-day work week. Shifts are 12 hours long, and since the plant never shuts down, everyone works alternate Sundays. Sunday work is paid double-time, so hourly employees get a weekly average of 48 hours of pay for 42 hours of work. (After four years, Frankowski's pay was $12.60 an hour in 1983.) On his day off, Frankowski frequently goes on fishing or hunting trips. The company sponsors several sporting activities, including bowling, trap shooting, softball, and running.

Once a year, Frankowski and a dozen or so people from his department go to Quad's lodge, located on a nearby lake, for a Quad tradition called a "Think Small Dinner." The employees enjoy a first-class catered meal with wine and beer. They can also go out on the lake in one of the two Quad sailboats. "It makes for a good work environment because it loosens everybody up," says Frankowski.

Another Quad tradition is promoting all new managers for the year at the company Christmas dinner party. In 1982, 21 new managers were promoted at a black-tie dinner for all employees held at the Pfister Hotel in downtown Milwaukee. Quadracci handed new supervisors a white sailor's cap with the bright Quad/Graphics logo to symbolize their becoming crew members of the company ship (considered to be the *H.M.S. Printafore* because of a spoof on the Gilbert and Sullivan play presented by various employees at an earlier Christmas party). The 1984 Christmas party, a catered sit-down dinner for 2,200 employees and their guests, was held at the new plant in Sussex. The theme of the party was a circus parade. All the managers dressed as clowns; Quadracci dressed as a ringmaster and rode into the gathering on an elephant.

Quad's managers have an unusual amount of latitude. Each division operates as its own business. For instance,

Quad's fleet of 10 Peterbilt trucks hauls most of the printed magazines. Several years ago, Quadracci suggested that the truckers find loads for their return trips. When the truckers asked what they should carry, Quadracci reportedly shrugged and told them to figure it out for themselves, saying they were now a separate division, DuPlainville Transport, Inc.

"Believe me, it was a big challenge for everybody," fleet manager Larry Lynch told *Inc*. "We got stung a few times [by loads and destinations that were not as promised], but we got rolling."

When the new entrepreneurs are operating, Quadracci is loath to intervene. There are stories of how he has been reprimanded with his own philosophy when he has tried. Quadracci once urged the rehiring of an employee who had been fired with four others who were smoking marijuana during lunchtime. Quadracci argued with the bindery managers that the employee in question should not have been dealt with so harshly since he had only been an innocent bystander. The managers disagreed, saying the young man had "violated their trust," the worst possible offense. Quadracci backed off.

One unusual perk available to all managers is a free trip to New York City. The company picks up the tab for airfare for two and provides use of the company's apartment on 57th Street. Such trips help acquaint the work force of mostly local Wisconsin youth with the home base of most of the company's magazine customers. About 20 managers a year take advantage of this opportunity.

In the plant, managers wear uniforms that appear identical to those of everyone else, except that the name tag states their last name instead of their first name. (Plant employees get a clean, dark blue uniform daily.) In addition to their salary (average of all managers is $35,000), they receive an annual bonus from the company's profits. It typically amounts to an additional 10 to 12 percent of their base salary, according to Jeanne Kuelthau, the corporate secretary.

The company also places some corporate profits into the employee stock-ownership program. The ESOP owns about 20 percent of the company's stock. (Quadracci and other founding employee shareholders hold another 60 percent, while outsiders possess the remaining 20 percent.) An employee typically has the equivalent of 8 to 9 percent of his or

TRUST IN TRUST AT QUAD/GRAPHICS

• The Trust of Teamwork. Employees trust that together they will do better than as individuals apart.
• The Trust of Responsibility. Employers trust that each will carry his/her fair share of the load.
• The Trust of Productivity. Customers trust that work will be produced to the most competitive levels of pricing, quality and innovation.
• The Trust of Management. Shareholders, customers and employees trust that the company will make decisive judgments for the long-term rather than the short-term goals or today's profit.
• The Trust of Think-Small. We all trust in each other: we regard each other as persons of equal rank; we respect the dignity of the individual by recognizing not only the individual accomplishments, but the feelings and needs of the individual and family as well; and we all share the same goals and purposes in life.

her base salary contributed into the ESOP. When they leave the company they receive cash for their stock.

Quad has no centralized personnel department; most hiring is done by individual managers. They typically hire people recommended by others already working at Quad. Often this has meant hiring relatives of other Quad employees. In fact, at the end of 1984, Quad's in-house newspaper claimed that the company's "*Ouchi* rating" was a whopping 39.5 percent. (*Ouchi* in Japanese translates roughly to "part of the family.") Of the 1,400 employees at the time, 554 were related, including 35 husbands, 35 wives, 134 brothers, 38 sisters, 55 cousins, 12 nephews, 3 nieces, 15 mothers, 23 fathers, 30 sons, 13 daughters, 1 grandparent, 139 in-laws, 13 uncles, and 2 aunts. Another notable figure: the median age was 27.

Quad does not forbid smoking but pays employees $30 to attend a seminar devoted to kicking the habit. Anyone who doesn't smoke for a year gets a bonus of $200.

Main employment centers   Pewaukee and Sussex, Wisconsin; Saratoga, New York. Quad also has small sales offices in New York, Los Angeles, and Boston.

Headquarters   Quad/Graphics Inc.
DuPlainville Road
Pewaukee, WI 53072
414-691-9200

BEST EMPLOYEE SUGGESTION SYSTEMS

Eastman Kodak   Maytag
IBM

RAINIER BANCORPORATION

RAINIER BANCORPORATION

Rainier operates a commercial bank that's the second-largest in the state of Washington and thirty-ninth-largest in the nation. U.S. employees: 5,200.

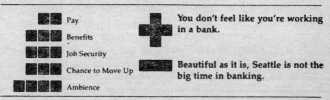

■■■ Pay	**You don't feel like you're working in a bank.**
■■■ Benefits	
■■■ Job Security	
■■■ Chance to Move Up	Beautiful as it is, Seattle is not the big time in banking.
■■■■ Ambience	

Part of the ambience of this company comes from its location, Seattle, a city regularly rated as one of the most salubrious cities in the country in which to live. And it is a wonderful city, framed by mountains and water. Seattle has a sea-air briskness, ferryboats that ply Puget Sound, a great college campus (the University of Washington), and, towering above everything to the south, Mount Rainier. When it's not raining, which is often, it's exhilarating. But why come here to work in a bank, which is basically what Rainier is? The best ones to answer that question are the people who work there.

Marty Morris, a black, made a career switch when he came to Rainier in 1980. Previously, he had worked as an assistant city planner in San Diego. "Coming to Seattle—and to Rainier—was the first time I'd ever really planned a major change in my life," he said. "Before that, things just seemed to happen." A native of Arkansas and a graduate of Southern Illinois University, Morris became a personal banker at Rainier by going through the bank's Individual Development Program. This is a special Rainier program that provides entry-level management training, especially for people making career changes. The training can run from three months to two years. Some 50 people go through it every year.

What does Morris like about Rainier? "I'm given a great deal of freedom and latitude. People will give you your head here if they think you can run with it." Those are not the words you usually hear when banks are being described, but they are echoed by other Rainier employees, who cite the openness of the bank, the accessibility of top managers (they're called by their first names), and the ability to advance through the ranks, no matter what level you come in at. Morris, for example, came in as a commercial loan trainee.

Roxane Engelhardt-Cerf supervises tellers at the main Rainier office in downtown Seattle. Previously, she worked at the Bon Marché department store in Seattle. She says the people at Rainier are "friendlier." She also says that the management "seems to care about what people are doing here."

Shelly Silverthorne works in personnel at Rainier, and you would expect her to be a booster. She reported that she moved up four levels in her first two years with the bank. "We post jobs here," she points out, "and people aren't trapped in these jobs for years and years."

Bruce Emry came to the public relations department of Rainier after stints with Georgia-Pacific, Puget Sound Power & Light, and the PR agency Hill & Knowlton. "This is the best," he declares, with no hesitation. Why? For one thing, according to Emry, at the other companies where he worked, the quality of management dropped off sharply beyond the chief executive officer level. "Here," he said, "they're solid all the way through." Emry added that at Rainier he can be more of a risk taker—entrepreneurial, if you will—because he knows he is not going to be jumped on for a mistake, as he was in previous jobs. "Not that it's easy," he said. "I never worked so hard in my life."

There's a family feeling at Rainier that you can sense as you walk through the halls. And soon you learn that this is more than a metaphor. So many relatives—husbands and wives, brothers and sisters, cousins—work for Rainier that employees call it "Nepotism City."

It's what you might expect in a company headed by someone who keeps on a chair in his office a large soft-sculptured gorilla. G. Robert Truex, Jr., came to Rainier in 1973 from San Francisco where he was executive vice-president of the Bank of America. (He used to upset the brass there by driving a Jaguar to work. How unbankerly!) In his last position at the Bank of America, Truex headed up the social responsibility functions, and so he brought to Rainier a commitment to the community that has manifested itself not only in philanthropic and voluntary programs but in day-to-day operations.

Three years after he came to Rainier, Truex expressed his philosophy as follows: "Our goal is not to be the biggest. That kind of thinking leads to foolishness. But while it may sound utopian, there is no reason why we cannot be the best performer in the country." It's a message that has reached the staff at Rainier.

When Truex took the reins, the bank holding company operated under various names: National Bank of Commerce, Coast Mortgage Company, Commerce Credit Company, International Bank of Commerce, Commerce Finance Company. He united them all under the Rainier name. He then startled the staid Seattle establishment by moving Rainier into a daring new headquarters building designed by the Japanese architect Minoru Yamasaki. Opened in 1977, the Rainier Bank Tower is a 40-story structure that sits on a pedestal. It was criticized at first for looking like a building that would topple over. Now it has taken its place in Seattle as a downtown landmark.

Yes, Bob Truex has brought a sense of excitement to Rainier—and Seattle. And that excitement is reflected in the way employees talk about the bank. Salaries of these employees have also been increased steadily since the early 1970s. They were increased 10 percent in 1976—wages and fringe benefits—to reach an average of $13,000 a year per employee. They are now $22,000 a year, which is above average in the banking business.

People who work for companies normally get a chance to buy the company's products at reduced prices. Rainier doesn't allow its employees to buy money at reduced prices, but it does offer these in-house benefits: two free personal checking accounts, free checks, money orders and cashier's checks without service charges, travelers' checks with no commission, VISA accounts at reduced rates, bank and government securities available for purchase at a reduced fee, discounts on loans, and reduced rates for trust department services.

The bank also has a strong benefits program that includes:

- 90 percent coverage of medical costs up to the first $1,500, 100 percent after that;
- Psychiatric care—up to $30 per visit, $1,000 annual limit;
- Chiropractic care—$9 per visit;
- A 401K pension thrift plan that allows employees to salt away pretax money, with the company (depending on its return of equity) matching these savings, dollar for dollar, up to 6 percent of the employee's salary. The match begins at 25 percent when Rainier earns 13.5 percent on equity and moves up to a 65 percent match when return on equity reaches 16.5 percent. In 1984, the bank's return was 14.9 percent, bringing a 35 percent match.

Main employment centers   Seattle has three-quarters of the employees but Rainier National Bank has 136 offices in the state of Washington. After Seattle, the biggest employment center is Hong Kong, where there are nine offices. In 1983, Rainier bought Peoples Bank and Trust Company of Alaska and promptly changed its name to Rainier.

Headquarters   Rainier Bancorporation
1301 Fifth Avenue
Seattle, WA 98101
206-621-4111

RANDOM HOUSE—

RANDOM HOUSE, INC.

One of the nation's largest book publishers. U.S. employees: 1,600.

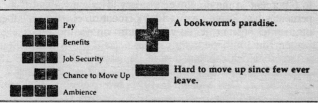

Pay	■■		A bookworm's paradise.
Benefits	■■■		
Job Security	■■		
Chance to Move Up	■■		Hard to move up since few ever leave.
Ambience	■■■■		

Random House attracts the kind of people who eagerly look forward to meeting Donald Klopfer, who founded Random House in 1925 with Bennett ("What's My Line?") Cerf. Klopfer can talk for hours about the famous authors Random House has published: Sinclair Lewis, Eugene O'Neill, James Michener, Robert Penn Warren, Truman Capote, Ayn Rand, and John Updike, to name a few. Every month, newly hired employees assemble in Klopfer's office and hear him talk about life over the years at Random House.

Klopfer's audience invariably loves the informal gathering. One who enjoyed it was Joshua Odell, a publicist for Alfred A. Knopf, one of a half-dozen imprints owned by Random House. Others include Pantheon, Ballantine, Del Rey, Fawcett, Vintage, Villard, Times Books, and Modern Library. A recent college graduate, Odell jumped at the chance of getting a job with Random House because of its reputation as America's premier publisher. "I was especially attracted by the tradition of Knopf. It had published all the people I read while I was growing up, like Thomas Mann, Albert Camus, Jean-Paul Sartre, and H. L. Mencken." He appreciates a perk available to all employees: they can select up to 10 free books a year and buy any other Random House book at a 50 percent discount.

363

A self-described "book person," Odell's reverence for the printed word typifies many of the people who work in the Random House building on East 50th Street in New York, not far from the buildings housing other publishers such as Doubleday, Harper & Row, and Macmillan. Because everyone, from receptionists and messengers to the most senior editors, shares an interest in books, job functions are not rigidly separated. It's common, for instance, for editors to solicit or hear opinions from a wide variety of people in what some refer to as "the Random House family."

It's also common for employees to call president Robert Bernstein and other top Random House executives by their first names. To break down barriers within the ranks even further, Random House's president hosts about a dozen "State of the House" luncheons during January and February. Bernstein, who joined the company in 1957 and became president shortly before Cerf's death in 1971, briefs groups of 30 to 40 employees at a time.

Knopf editor Ann Close appreciates the company's informality. A southerner, Close previously edited books for Harper & Row and Macmillan. "It's very human around here," she said. "There are no corporate rules or petty harassments like having to sign in and out or clean off your desk at the end of the day."

Quite the opposite. Random House is not the place for someone who likes a tidy workplace. Almost all editorial offices seem to be cluttered with manuscripts, books, correspondence, memos, and assorted other pieces of paper. Editors show up pretty much when they want to in the morning and leave when they want in the evening.

Close says that because of Random House's atmosphere, there is very little turnover. "No one leaves," she said, "so it's hard for younger people to move up."

Indeed, the top editors at Random House are sometimes referred to as "Members of the Club," and most have been in place since the mid-1960s. But some insist that things are opening up. They say the house offers increasing opportunities as a result of recent acquisitions (such as Times Books) and the firm's rapid growth—with sales estimated to have doubled since 1979 (from about $150 million that year to over $300 million in 1984). And they point to the successful Ballantine mass-market paperback division, whose woman president was 40 in 1984, vice-president of sales was 31, and vice-president of finance was 30. In 1984, the company hired 44-year-old Howard Kaminsky from Warner Books to head the Random House trade books division, the firm's flagship imprint. Kaminsky, who began his publishing career with Random House, was described by *Manhattan, Inc.* as "outspoken and irrepressible," having "a comic sensibility the Random House cofounder might have enjoyed."

Klopfer thinks that the secret to Random House's ability to attract and maintain top-flight editors is related to the element of trust that has always been part of the company. He said that people considered him and Cerf "nuts" to set up the company so that each owned 50 percent of the stock. And until Cerf died, both drew the same salaries. But he insists that the arrangement forced them to talk their problems out and to develop faith in the other's judgment. "We have a business that consists entirely of people. It's always been a very personal business," said Klopfer, who maintains an open-door policy for any employee with a problem.

Random House strained to keep its informal, relaxed style after Cerf and Klopfer sold the company to RCA in the late 1960S. "When RCA took us over, they promised not to interfere with the editorial side of the business. And they didn't. But they made our executives waste a lot of time reporting to them in quarterly business meetings and such. It was ludicrous." Klopfer much prefers being part of Newhouse, which bought Random House in 1980.

Most Tuesday afternoons, Bob Bernstein can be seen leaving his office on the twelfth floor of the Random House skyscraper and walking to the Four Seasons or another restaurant in midtown Manhattan. That's where Random House's president lunches with Si Newhouse. Newhouse heads the $1-billion-a-year publishing empire that also owns *Vogue*, *Mademoiselle*, and *House & Garden* magazines, 29 major metropolitan newspapers, and the *Parade* Sunday newspaper supplement. The low-key Tuesday lunches represent Newhouse's way of keeping abreast of Random House, according to Bernstein.

"Newhouse doesn't believe in structure," Bernstein explained to us. "Too much structure is the death knell of American corporations." He prefers a company patterned along the lines described in Robert Townsend's best-selling book (published by Knopf, of course), *Up the Organization: How to Stop the Corporation from Stifling People and Strangling Profits*. Among other recommendations, Townsend urges companies to promote from within and to get rid of policy manuals, job descriptions, and layers of bureaucracy.

For his part, Bernstein makes sure that people who perform staff functions such as public relations or administration wear other hats as well. For example, the company's vice-president for corporate affairs, William T. Loverd, also directs publicity for Knopf.

Like Townsend, Bernstein expresses his publishing and business philosophy in pithy sayings:

"The one thing you cannot be in publishing is consistent."

"Publishing keeps you humble because the authors are always the experts in their field. The only thing we may know more about is the details of publishing."

"All the ideas of the world pour into this place. The in-depth investigation of ideas in America is done through books. The distributors of ideas are the bookstores."

Bernstein acknowledges that publishing has paid much lower than other industries in the past, though he says it is competitive today. (Random House claims to pay its people as well as or better than any other publisher.) Bernstein reflects, "If editors could book hours like lawyers, they would be the highest-paid people in the United States."

Main employment centers About 600 work at the New York headquarters, while 400 are part of the sales force located throughout the country. Another 600 work in the book distribution center at Westminster, Maryland.

Headquarters   Random House, Inc
201 East 50th Street
New York, NY 10022
212-751-2600

Raychem

RAYCHEM CORPORATION

Raychem uses radiation chemistry—bombarding plastics and other materials with high-energy electrons—to produce thousands of products like corrosion-proof insulation materials (cables, wires, connectors). U.S. employees: 4,800.

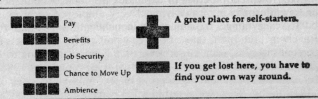

■■■■ Pay

■■■ Benefits

■■ Job Security

■■ Chance to Move Up

■■■ Ambience

A great place for self-starters.

If you get lost here, you have to find your own way around.

Some people are afraid of going to work for a company they never heard of. And they probably should be. But they can rest easy about Raychem, a company founded in 1957 in the proverbial garage near Stanford University. Raychem's home base is Menlo Park, a small town 30 miles south of San Francisco and bordering Palo Alto, home of Stanford University. There, in a campuslike industrial park sandwiched between the Route 101 Freeway and San Francisco Bay, Raychem has developed from radiation chemistry a $700-million-a-year business.

Because of its proximity to Silicon Valley, Raychem is sometimes taken for a high-tech company. It's not high-tech in the sense that it has nothing to do with computers or microelectronics or robotics or any of the other hot technologies people talk about these days. But Raychem did start out in life by exploiting a new technology—the bombarding of plastic with high-energy electrons—and it still plows a high percentage of its income back into research and development, trying to come up with commercially viable products. One out of every 10 employees works in research and development.

The products it has developed were not so much brandnew items as improved versions of older materials. There were coaxial cables, hookup wires, and connectors before

Raychem, but this company has been able to score by using its know-how in chemical radiation to produce more durable and effective versions—conductive polymers shape-memory alloys, fiber optics.

The pay at Raychem is good. Starting salaries average $20,000. The benefits are above average. Employees are encouraged to buy stock, and when they do, the company puts up $1 for every $3 invested by an employee. Two-thirds of Raychem's employees are stockholders.

One incentive that makes people inordinately interested in the overall performance of Raychem is a bonus scheme tied to how well the company does. Every employee receives a bonus every three months that's equivalent to one-half of Raychem's return on sales. In other words, if Raychem nets 8 percent on sales, each employee gets a bonus amounting to 4 percent of his or her salary. In the final three months of 1981, for example, Raychem had a profit of $9.5 million on sales of $131 million. That works out to a 7.3 percent return on sales. So, if you were a Raychem employee earning $20,000 a year or $5,000 a quarter, your paycheck was fattened by $180 (3.6 percent of $5,000). In 1983, the return on sales dropped to 5 percent. (It was 6 percent in 1984.)

Nineteen eighty-three was, in fact, a testing time for Raychem. The engine that had propelled the company to a spectacular advance over the previous 25 years stalled a bit, resulting in staff reductions at various levels. Randi Bolton, director of human resources, told us that the number of people let go amounted to less than the number usually lost through attrition. Raychem, she volunteered, was going through an "organizational refocusing. It's what happens when a high-growth company grows too fast." As for the people who had to leave, Bolton said Raychem offered all of them "very elegant terms." (In 1984, employment increased by 3 percent.)

It was in talking to Raychem people during this difficult period that we gleaned some special characteristics of the company. One staffer who had been there for two years made the strong point that Raychem is the wrong place for anyone who needs a lot of structure. The pay scale is high—she left a $24,000-a-year job to land a $38,000-a-year position with Raychem. But once she was hired, she found that it wasn't easy for her to learn the new skills she expected to acquire.

"Other companies have career paths," she said. "Not here. There is no specific ladder you can climb. And you're not going to find mentor relationships."

On the other hand, she was quick to add—and others at Raychem confirmed—that once you're hired, you virtually have a license to look inside and outside the company to fashion your next position. So people at Raychem are expected to build their own careers, using individual initiative. And you can cross departmental lines to do it.

Eric Keller, a graduate of the business school at the University of California at Berkeley, came to Raychem in 1980 and calls it "one of the best assemblages of bright people I have ever encountered." It's possible—indeed it may be necessary—to move around here. Keller cites the example of a woman who joined Raychem's treasurer's department after stints at Price Waterhouse and Wells Fargo. After a year she decided she really wanted to work in production—and that's where she is today, by choice.

It's apparently not an advantage at Raychem to be a specialist. You have to try to do other things, and you have to do the pushing. It's a company where the emphasis is on the individual rather than the group. Keller, who likes to travel, was controller of the international division in 1983. He calls himself finance manager of the American-Pacific division. "Titles don't mean a lot here," he told us. "And career paths are not easy to make out. Am I moving up or down?"

We were impressed, in interviews conducted in 1984, with the diversity of people at Raychem and their obvious satisfaction in being able to follow their particular bents, whatever they might be. Don Foley used to work at the telephone company before coming to Raychem in 1966. Now he says he couldn't imagine anyone preferring to work at another company. Foley is a burly, earring-clad machine builder—and he's heavily tattooed. He enjoys the freedom he has found in Raychem's central engineering department. Stephen Powell, a blond, bespectacled chemical engineer, joined Raychem fresh out of Stanford in 1982. Raychem helped him get his Ph.D. He works in research, and he's pleased at being able to devote up to 20 percent of his time pursuing his own notions in the laboratory. And he concedes, not so happily, that "parties break out here at the drop of a hat." Phyllis Hampton is a young, bubbly black woman who was trained in psychology and worked previously at Goodwill Industries. She has worked in several different departments at Raychem—"people are helpful, they will show you how to do it if you ask" —before finding a home in the research laboratory where Powell also works. Raychem is helping her get a degree in chemistry.

One constant at Raychem has been Paul M. Cook. An MIT chemical engineer, he started the company after working for the Atomic Energy Commission, where he sensed the commercial possibilities of plastic bombarded by high-energy electrons. Cook was wearing bow ties in 1957—and he still is today.

Robert M. Halperin, a mechanical engineer, joined Raychem two months after Cook started the company (he was the seventh employee), and the two have worked in tandem ever since, Halperin being responsible as executive vice-president for the business side. But it wasn't until 1983 that Cook moved up from president to chairman and gave the president's title to Halperin.

Raychem may not be widely known, but if you are in its orbit, you certainly feel its presence. The company has developed its own procedures and styles almost the way a family does. Things have to be done in a certain way. For example, even though it sells no products to consumers, Raychem is concerned about how it looks; it maintains a strong corporate identity program. If you see a memorandum or a truck or a product manual or a pamphlet or a poster, you'll know instantly if it's from Raychem.

A communications design center sets corporate graphic standards and supplies materials to ensure that the company always "dresses" in the same way. Raychem has adopted a single typeface, Helvetica, for all print communications. The Raychem logo is always printed in red unless it's being placed against a red background, and then it can be white. The logo must be used in prescribed ways: on the cab of a truck, for instance, it must be placed on the door "below any breaks in the surface contour such as chrome strips, raised areas and mouldings."

Not only are its graphic standards high, but Raychem is concerned about attracting top-flight professional people. That's the reason it decided to have its stock listed on the New

Raychem's Work Environment

We believe that people work best in an atmosphere which is vigorous and stimulating rather than unnecessarily limiting. To provide this atmosphere, we encourage each employee to become involved with the job, to find better ways of doing it, and to make his or her ideas heard.

We attempt to select managers who are involved and enthusiastic and who can spark enthusiasm in those with whom they work.

We encourage our managers to define and communicate important directions, and to give each person the freedom to work within his or her own style towards the common goal.

We rely on the competence and integrity of each manager to ensure that good ideas are heard and used.

We maintain an open-door policy which protects the right of each individual to discuss his or her ideas or problems with anyone in the company.

We encourage outstanding performance and strive to recognize and reward it.

We attempt to provide a safe and pleasant working environment.

We insist that fairness and integrity permeate all decisions we make concerning our people, our products, and our customers.

York Stock Exchange in 1982. It wanted greater visibility. Raychem is careful about whom it hires. It's not unusual for an engineer to see 10 to 12 managers, each interview consuming an hour, before a hiring decision is made. Keller remembers one person who went through 36 interviews.

When the company was 25 years old in 1982, it held a gigantic community party to which it invited all its employees and their families as well as special guests; it was a day-long celebration at its 140-acre plant site. Everyone was given a steak dinner. There was continuous entertainment for seven hours, featuring headline acts such as Maria Muldaur, Jules Broussard, and Back in the Saddle. There were 15 carnival rides, including a Ferris wheel and a merry-go-round. It was a birthday party that cost at least $25,000, designed to impart a family feeling to a company where the emphasis is on the individual.

Main employment centers   4,300 in Menlo Park. Another 250 work in Research Triangle, North Carolina, and 250 work in Pennsylvania. Some 4,200 work overseas, mostly in Western Europe.

Headquarters   Raychem Corporation
300 Constitution Drive
Menlo Park, CA 94025
415-361-3333

Reader's Digest

READER'S DIGEST ASSOCIATION

Publisher of the most popular magazine in the world. U.S. employees: 3,950.

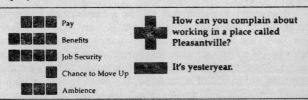

▮▮▮ Pay	How can you complain about
▮▮▮▮ Benefits	working in a place called
▮▮▮ Job Security	Pleasantville?
▮ Chance to Move Up	▮▮ It's yesteryear.
▮▮▮ Ambience	

The last day of 1981 was the scene of a remarkable gathering at the spacious, landscaped Pleasantville, New York, estate where *Reader's Digest* makes its headquarters. It was a farewell party for a retiring employee, Rose Mattagrano. One hundred and twenty-five Digesters, as they like to call themselves, showed up to say goodbye. Mattagrano was leaving the company after 38½ years of service, all in the same department—customer mailing. That's remarkable enough. Even more remarkable is the fact that Rose Mattagrano had never, in all those years, missed a single day of work because of illness. "I've been blessed with good health," she said, "and I never played hooky."

Playing hooky is not something you would expect to find at the Reader's Digest Association, a genteel, upright place that smacks of the "goodness" that seeps through the pages of the world's best-selling magazine (worldwide readership: 100 million). Indeed, employees who ride to work in the buses provided by the company are warned that the *Digest* "cannot be responsible if you miss the bus or are not picked up. If this happens, call the Transportation Department and explain the situation. If you do not work, it will result in the loss of a day's pay."

That may seem a little harsh or bureaucratic, but consider

this: do you know of another company that mounts its own bus service to bring employees to work and return them home at the end of the day? The 16 *Digest* buses pick up employees in 50 different towns within a 25-mile radius of Pleasantville. And the cost to each employee? Three dollars a week. The *Digest* has also made it possible for groups of employees to acquire their own vans to get to work. Parked in the *Digest* lot these days are 104-passenger vans. The Digesters who use a van to commute pay for it via payroll deductions. After three years they collectively own the van. (Socialism at the *Reader's Digest*?)

If you get the idea that this is a benevolent company, you're right. Although Pleasantville is only 40 miles from New York (the company has its own exit on the Sawmill River Parkway—Reader's Digest Way), you could be in another country. It's almost like entering a time warp. There's none of the hustle and bustle of Manhattan. It's quiet and restrained— even in the cavernous rooms where middle-aged women are seated before slots opening envelopes containing checks sent in by subscribers. With a U.S. circulation of 18 million, the *Digest* gets so much mail that it has its own zip code—and working there resembles working at the post office. Of the 2,500 people at Pleasantville, two-thirds are hourly wage workers.

The employees do toil in an uplifting environment, however. Headquarters is a Georgian-style structure that looks like a museum or a courthouse or a building on a college campus. And once inside, you could easily believe you were in a museum. Paintings by Chagall, Utrillo, Matisse, and Degas line corridors and office walls of editors and executives. A top editor at the *Digest* works in an office that has period furniture—wing chairs, a wooden desk, curtains, a soft pile rug. It's all rather subdued and elegant—precious, some people might think. It hardly resembles a place geared to anything nasty like deadlines. The loudest noises you're likely to hear at the *Digest* come from the company cafeteria at lunchtime. The cafeteria, recently redesigned, is a sunny, cheerful facility where you can get a substantial hot meal for as little as $1.75. During the warm months, employees take their lunches outdoors on the well-manicured lawns that surround the headquarters building. Toward one end of the *Digest* estate is a guest house that dates back to the American Revolution. It's used primarily to entertain visitors (and they make excellent martinis there).

The *Digest* cossets its employees with benefits, some unique to this company. You work a 35-hour week, starting at 8:30 in the morning, leaving at 4:00 in the afternoon. You get 16 paid holidays a year. During the month of May, the entire company shuts down every Friday, including those years when there are five Fridays in May. Why? The *Digest* people say: "May is such a pretty month." During your first year, you're entitled to two weeks of paid vacation. You get four weeks in your second year, plus an additional two weeks after 20 years of service, after 25 years, 30 years, and so forth (in other words, someone with 25 years' service gets eight weeks). There are plenty of "Rose Mattagranos" at the *Digest*. Every year the company holds a banquet for people who have been there for at least 20 years. In 1982, 125 people attended this affair—8 with 40 years of service, 5 with 35 years, 12 with 30 years, and 27 with 25 years. Of the group of 125, only 14 were men.

The Reader's Digest Association is privately held—and employees, except possibly for a few at the top, do not own any stock in it. But there is a profit-sharing plan that regularly augments an employee's salary by 14 percent a year; these funds are kept in a trust account for each employee. After six years it's fully vested—and you can leave with all of it.

The *Digest* may not be for everyone, but you'd like it if you're looking for a warm, homelike, family feeling. There are bowling teams and softball teams and volleyball and basketball teams (for both men and women). There's a Reader's Digest Chorus that rehearses every Tuesday between 4:15 and 5:30 P.M. and gives concerts throughout the year at hospitals, nursing homes, senior citizen centers, and on special occasions. The *Digest* wants its employees to be active, and so it will pick up 50 percent of the tab for any athletic club membership. It also wants employees to improve their minds, so it will reimburse them for 100 percent of tuition for any job-related courses, 75 percent for any "personal interest" course at an accredited school, and 50 percent for all other educational classes, from Weight Watchers to TM (transcendental meditation). The *Digest* is the kind of place where a security guard patrols the parking lot and lets you know if any of your tires are getting soft.

Also, at the north end of the *Digest* estate, there's a community garden with individual plots for which employees can sign up. If you come by on Saturday, you will see the Digesters taking care of their vegetable gardens. Since the establishment of the community garden in 1976, more than 500 employees have taken advantage of the facility to become part-time farmers. The *Digest*, in addition to providing the land, plows and fertilizes and puts on a winter cover. In 1983, it began charging $10 a plot to cover a small portion of its costs.

Will this place always remain the same? It may not. The *Reader's Digest* was founded in 1922 by DeWitt and Lila Wallace, both children of ministers. They worked together to build the Reader's Digest Association, proving a lot of experts wrong. They didn't accept advertising in the U.S. edition (they always did in the international editions) until 1955. It wasn't until recent years that they accepted advertising for wine and spirits. They have never accepted advertising for cigarettes—in fact, for many years they have carried articles on the dangers of cigarette smoking (but you can find vending machines dispensing cigarettes at the *Digest*). DeWitt Wallace died in 1981 at the age of 91. His widow died in May 1984 at the age of 94. A trust now holds her stock. The Wallaces had no children.

The Reader's Digest Association publishes books, sells records and cassettes, and has a division that's in the fundraising business.

Main employment centers Pleasantville, 2,500; New York City, 450. (The people employed outside Pleasantville are mainly involved in selling advertising space.) Some 7,000 employees, nearly all foreign nationals, are employed overseas. The *Digest* has 40 international divisions.

Headquarters Reader's Digest Association
Pleasantville, NY 10570
914-769-7000

RECREATIONAL EQUIPMENT, INC.

REI sells outdoor gear and clothing through its own stores.
Employees: 1,000.

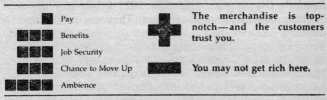

■ Pay	**+**	The merchandise is top-notch—and the customers trust you.
■■■ Benefits		
■■■ Job Security		
■■■ Chance to Move Up	■■■	You may not get rich here.
■■■■ Ambience		

Social experiments have always been part of the American scene, especially in the Pacific Northwest, a fertile breeding ground in the last century for communal societies and a nourishing environment in this century for a string of cooperative ventures. By far the most successful of these ventures is Seattle-based Recreational Equipment, Inc., known to everyone—employees, customers, competitors—as simply REI. We first learned about REI from customers who sang its praises as a place where the employees really know the merchandise. Then we had a clipping from the October 23, 1983, issue of *Forbes*, which, as a magazine for investors, rarely examines a company whose stock cannot be bought by the public. *Forbes* writer William Baldwin depicted REI as "the money-minded mountaineers," asking the question, "Who would expect a bunch of collectivist backpackers to know how to turn a profit?" and immediately answering that REI "has financials that would warm any money man's heart." Next, interviews with employees persuaded us that REI is not only good for its customer-owners but for the people who work there.

REI is the largest consumer cooperative in the nation. It logged sales of $94 million in 1984 through 10 stores in the western part of the nation and a mail-order catalog, five million copies of which go out every year. An REI store is the kind of place where you will find parkas, tents, sleeping bags, hiking boots, canteens—you get the picture. You will see some dress shirts featured in an REI catalog, and you can find books, cards, calendars, and chocolates in REI stores, but the heart and soul of REI consists of clothes and equipment for serious hikers and for the not-so-serious ones who aspire to hike or who just want to be dressed warmly in well-made clothing. REI was founded in 1938 by a bunch of mountain climbers who used it originally to import Swiss ice axes.

To be a consumer cooperative is to be owned by your customers. A customer joins REI with the payment of a one-time membership fee of $5. Aside from getting on the mailing list for a lot of literature, that membership qualifies the customer for rebates on everything he or she buys at REI—providing, of course, that the co-op makes enough of a profit to pay this dividend. The bylaws mandate that 85 percent of the profits be returned to customer-members in the form of a patronage dividend. It's a mark of how well REI is run that it has never missed a dividend payment. In 1984, on its sales of $94 million, REI cleared $9.3 million before taxes, which is an extraordinary return for a retailer. It paid a dividend of 12.7 percent, or $7.4 million, to its members. (In other words, they got back 12.7 percent of everything they had spent at REI during the year.) REI's membership-ownership base has tripled since 1976 and stood at 1.5 million at the start of 1985.

REI is a cooperative that works because it pays attention to running a good business and doesn't let politics (internal or external) interfere with its mission of delivering quality merchandise to its customers—at a profit. Many co-ops have foundered on the issue of whether they are in business to serve some social goals or make money.

When you walk into an REI store, you know right away it's not a reincarnation of Abercrombie & Fitch (even though the merchandise mix is similar). REI is the opposite of slick. It's a down-to-earth place where you are likely to be waited on by a jeans-clad youth wearing a plaid shirt. A serious dialogue goes on here between the customer and the salesperson. You may not want to scale Mount Everest, as did Jim Whittaker, REI's president from 1970 to 1979 (he was the first American to scale the Himalayan peak), but you might take some comfort in knowing that REI is the place to shop for those who do entertain such fantasies.

We were impressed in our interviews with REI employees in the Berkeley, California, store (the second-largest in the co-op's chain) by how closely and strongly they identified with the needs of customers. Assistant store manager Kevin Washington, a black and an ex-IBMer who has been with the Berkeley store virtually from its inception in 1975, said the customers "write to us" and "they feel like this is home to them." Kim Mayer, a part-time promotion coordinator, pointed out to us that REI people are very conscious of the importance of equipment working—you don't want a customer coming back to say, "You've ruined our trip." And Washington chimed in to add that selling the wrong kind of gear could result in serious injury, even death, to a customer. So REI people are not just interested in making the quick sale. Besides, they don't work on a commission basis.

REI people are certainly not working for top dollar. Stores are notoriously poor payers—and REI is no exception. Peggy Wheaton, a 32-year-old mother who joined REI-Berkeley on the sales floor in 1983, told us, "This is not the way to get wealthy, so there has to be something else that keeps us here." Part-timers—and they make up 60 percent of REI's work force—were being hired in 1984 at $4.28 an hour. Skilled mechanics, working on bikes and skis, were being hired for between $6.43 and $8.04 an hour, depending on previous experience. Secretaries in the Seattle headquarters were making $7.34 an hour. Full-timers are reviewed annually and given raises based on performance. The maximum pay in 1984 for a supervisor was $10.29 an hour; for a mechanic, $9.65 an hour; for a cashier, $8.61. (Add at least 15 percent to these rates if you work in the Anchorage store.)

Nikki Nichols worked part-time at REI from 1979 to 1981 and returned in 1983 to put in another year, again as a part-timer. Signing up again was, as she put it, "a statement in itself." She calls REI "a fun place to work." She liked it because it gave her a chance to meet kindred souls—people to "play with or go skiing or bicycling." The crew at REI is young (the average age is under 30), and they obviously like each other and have pride in what they're selling. But it's a little frustrating when you look at your paycheck. Nichols said that when she left in 1981, she was making $4.64 an hour. In 1983, she started again at the same rate, took six months to get to $4.85, and another six to reach $5.06.

The compensation improves markedly outside the hourly ranks. In 1984, assistant store managers were making up to $30,000 a year. Also, REI has special incentive programs for its managers—and these are keyed to meeting or exceeding goals. The top 40 people in the co-op are eligible for bonuses based on their individual performances. In 1982, for example, 33 managers shared a bonus pot of $661,000. Jerry Horn, who was president of REI from 1979 to 1983, worked himself up to $220,000 a year. Wally Smith, who succeeded him, told us that he does not make that much. Salaries of REI managers are not disclosed publicly.

Horn was recruited from Sears, Roebuck, but that was an exception to regular practice. The management ranks at REI are filled with people who have come up from below. Wally Smith, who was 37 years old in 1984, started working for REI in the Seattle store when he was 17 years old and a senior in high school. In 1975, when he was 27, he opened the Berkeley store for REI. Since 1982 the manager of the Berkeley REI has been Arleen Hiuga, who moved down from the Seattle store, where she had been assistant manager. She began working for the Seattle store as a part-timer in 1974. In 1984, she was all of 31 years old. She succeeded Roger Neale as the store manager in Berkeley—and Neale became manager of REI's largest store in downtown Seattle. Expansion has created new opportunities for the REI staff. REI's eleventh store was slated to open in Sacramento, California, in May 1985. Later in the year the twelfth store was to be opened in Cupertino, California. To manage the Sacramento store REI tapped Sandy Hilleary, who had been serving as retail coordinator of all the stores in Seattle headquarters. Replacing her was Kevin Washington, moving up from Berkeley.

When we talked to Arleen Hiuga in early 1985, she was on top of the world for having exceeded her sales projections by $1.1 million; the Berkeley store rang up $12.5 million of sales in 1984. She was also proud of REI's ''shrinkage,'' which is a retailing term denoting the difference between actual inventory and the inventory the books show that the store should have—the difference being partially the result of shoplifting by customers and stealing by employees. Shrinkage runs over 2 percent of sales in the U.S. retail industry; at REI it's four-tenths of 1 percent.

While the wages may be nothing to write home about, REI offers its full-timers (people who work over 1,000 hours a year) some generous benefits. In 1984, every employee received a turkey at Christmas. You get three weeks' vacation after your fourth year, four weeks after 10 years. You have your birthday off. You're entitled to a 30 percent discount on all REI products. If rental equipment (skis, bikes, tents, boots, etc.) is available, you can use it free of charge—an important benefit in a place where many people are outdoor enthusiasts. Premiums for medical and dental insurance, covering you and your dependents, are paid in full by REI.

The full-time employees—there were 380 of them at the end of 1984—also benefit directly from high earnings through a profit-sharing plan that augments their pay by up to 15 percent. In recent years the company contribution has been at the maximum level. In addition, there is a money purchase account, which obligates the company to lodge 5 percent of your pay in your retirement account every year, no matter what the profits were. These two retirement accounts vest fully after five years, meaning you can then take it all with you if you leave. There is also a cash option with the profit-sharing contribution that exceeds 5 percent—you can take half of it immediately in dollars.

REI is clearly an outfit on the move—its sales have nearly doubled since 1980—and that has brought some inevitable strain. Some purists feel they have strayed a little bit from their original mission. Nikki Nichols, for example, said she worked in the boot department when REI began stocking little canvas walking shoes that a housewife might wear in city parks. "What are we doing selling pink-and-green shoes?" was the reaction of some REIers, she said. Wally Smith's answer: "The demand for backpacking goods peaked in the 1970s. What responsible company doesn't change with the times? The trick is to grow while protecting your original product image—and I think we have done that."

Main employment centers   100 people work in a nondescript, two-story headquarters building two blocks from the Sea-Tac airport outside Seattle. 200 work in a mail order and distribution center at Tukwila, just a mile from headquarters (mail order accounts for 25 percent of REI's sales). Another 150 work in two small plants in Seattle that supply about

10 percent of REI's merchandise. The biggest store, in downtown Seattle, has 130 employees. Another 100 work in a windowless store in a Berkeley shopping center. The remaining 300 or so (employment peaks in December, drops to a nadir in February) staff the stores in Portland, Oregon; Carson, California; Minneapolis; Anchorage; Orange, California; Denver; Salt Lake City; and Bellevue, a suburb of Seattle. Stores are opening in 1985 in Sacramento and Cupertino, California.

Headquarters   Recreational Equipment, Inc.
3100 South 176th Street
Seattle, WA 98188
206-433-0771

REMINGTON
PRODUCTS, INC.

REMINGTON PRODUCTS, INC.

Remington is the sole U.S. manufacturer of electric shavers.
Employees: 1,100.

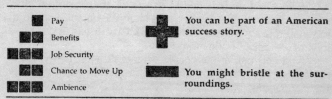

Pay	
Benefits	
Job Security	
Chance to Move Up	
Ambience	

You can be part of an American success story.

You might bristle at the surroundings.

Victor Kiam is the Lee Iacocca of the electric shaver business, and he has made this company a good place to work. In fact, he's probably responsible for the survival of Remington Products. If he hadn't bought the company in 1979 in a leveraged buyout (he put up less than $1 million of the $25 million purchase price), Remington probably wouldn't be around anymore. Under the previous owner, the giant Sperry Corp., maker of the Univac computers, Remington had piled up combined losses of $30 million for the previous five years. Under Victor Kiam, Remington has tripled its sales, more than doubled its market share, and is solidly in the black. And the Remington payroll has gone from 499 people to more than 1,100 at the start of 1985.

In the process Victor Kiam has become famous because of his strident television commercials declaring that "I liked the shaver so much, I bought the company." These commercials are not the products of a slick Madison Avenue advertising agency. They are done in-house, saving the company a lot of money. And in-house is a very precise description. Kiam does these commercials in his office (and the adjoining bathroom) in the seedy Bridgeport, Connecticut, headquarters of the company next to the dilapidated factory where the Remington shavers are produced.

It's a factory that dates back more than 50 years. No one

is quite sure how old it is. Although it's located right on Long Island Sound, it would certainly not win any "beautiful factory" awards. It's an airless, windowless structure where workers, most of them women, report each day at 7 A.M. to stations on a dreary assembly line where they put together the shavers Kiam promotes so enthusiastically on television. The plant is crowded—there's not even room for a cafeteria. Most workers brown-bag it for lunch. The line stops at noon for a half hour. Many employees eat right at their stations.

Bridgeport itself is not going to win any "beautiful city" awards. Situated midway between New Haven and Stamford, some 60 miles northeast of New York City, it has the helpless look of a bombed-out metropolis.

And yet, talk to the people who work here, as we did in the fall of 1984, and you quickly find that they like working for Remington, or rather for Victor Kiam, because he's the one who has made the difference—and they know it. Assistant treasurer Len Summa came aboard in 1982 after 12 years with a much bigger company, General Foods. He appreciates the lack of bureaucracy, the accessibility of Kiam, the ability to get a quick decision. He had been with Remington for three months and had done a 50-page report recommending, among other things, a change in the company's insurance broker. Kiam called him in and told him, "You're in charge, do it." Summa works next door to the shaver factory. He worked for a year and a half at General Foods before he visited a factory to see an actual product coming off a production line. Mike Dillella, a young computer programmer who used to work for Hartford Insurance, told us that at Remington he gets more of a chance "to do what I want to do."

Others we talked to—accountant Tom Parry, manufacturing coordinator Dick Zaino, and financial analyst Charles Kinney—echoed those sentiments. They had all worked for other companies, and they all praised Remington for being more open, more flexible, and friendlier. And they were unstinting in their praise for Victor Kiam. It's not every employee force that sings the praises of the boss. When CBS's Ed Bradley visited Bridgeport to do a "60 Minutes" segment, a production-line worker said this of Kiam: "He believes in us, just as we trust and believe in him."

The extraordinary part of the transformation wrought by Kiam is that it resulted from a change in the way people worked, not in the product itself, which was unchanged. Kiam chopped 70 managers from the payroll, thereby saving $2 million a year. He eliminated all company perks. No country club memberships. No company cars. He himself drives a 1976 Cadillac with more than 175,000 miles on it. ("It's dangerous too," says his wife, Ellen, who has her own business importing jewelry from China.) He works long hours, and he's a very visible boss, not just on television but on the factory floor, where he knows many workers by their first names. He closes down the line at least four times a year to address the troops. And he praises them to the sky, telling them, "You make the best product, and you can outproduce anyone in the world."

He also instituted profit-sharing and incentive programs that tie compensation to performance—individual performance and company performance. Just about everyone at Remington, from the chief financial officer to the plant manager and down to the assembly line employee, works on an incentive system that supplements their wages with bonuses pegged to how much they exceed norms. The bonus, for some people, can be as much as 100 percent of salary. In 1984, the base wage of factory workers was $5.54 an hour. But in the final quarter of the year, when the plant was going all-out to meet the demand provoked by the Kiam commercials, the average wage rose to $8 an hour. When we visited the plant in November, it was running an extra hour a day and an extra eight hours on Saturday—and the average factory hand was grossing $450 a week.

The workers are not represented by any union, which is unusual in this part of the country. The work force at Remington is 68 percent female, most of them married. It's 32 percent minority. And the average age is 42. Every Friday morning 10 or more factory workers meet for an hour with the plant manager, Nestor Squoros, and the personnel vice-president, Michael Duda, to make suggestions and air any complaints they may have.

It's the little things that count. After he bought the company in 1979, Kiam instituted the practice of handing out a turkey at Christmastime—and each year he added another item: cranberry sauce, a bag of stuffing, and chits cashable at a nearby liquor store for a bottle of white wine and a bottle of red wine. It takes a full day to bag the food—and all the bagging is done by Remington executives. Kiam also maintains a $25,000 discretionary fund to give instant cash recognition to workers who have been spotted by their supervisors doing an exceptional job. He calls these people to his office and hands out checks ranging from $200 to $500.

Do employees appreciate these touches? In 1982, when Remington's arch competitor, Norelco (decried in Kiam commercials as a company importing shavers that sell for higher prices than the Remingtons), bought the electric shaver business of Schick, Kiam brought an antitrust action. To support Kiam, 443 Remington employees dug into their pockets to pay for a full-page advertisement in the *Bridgeport Telegram* that told the public "we are behind Remington 100 percent." The ad was signed by each employee with his or her years of service listed. The roster ran alphabetically from Andrea Acevedo, who then had 12 years of service, to Stanley Zitowsky, a 21-year veteran. Other signers (and their service years) included Marion Battaglia (34), Mary Avery (41), Stephen Anderson (44), Mary Knapp (41), Wilma Palsco (45), and Charles Blydenburg (40).

It's appropriate to note that even before Kiam arrived in Bridgeport, there was a strong family feeling among the Remington employees. The company may not have been doing well, but people apparently did like to work there—at least they stayed around for a very long time. Walter DiGiovanni, who's president of the Remington manufacturing division, has been there 31 years. The company's chief research engineer, Dave Locke, has been there 34 years—and his brother worked in the plant for 40 years. (Their father helped develop the first electric razor.) The average Remington worker at the Bridgeport plant has been with the company 14 years, incredible when you keep in mind that employment there has doubled since 1979. In 1984, when the company held its twenty-third annual banquet for the Quarter-Century Club (members have worked at least 25 years for Remington), the printed invitation for the dinner showed 295 members, including 160 retirees. The banquet, held at Bridgeport's Algonquin Club, featured a menu of New England clam chowder, prime ribs, and New York cheesecake.

When Victor Kiam took over, Remington's market share was 19 percent. Now it's above 40 percent. The Bridgeport plant turned out nearly 5 million shavers in 1984, compared to 1.6 million in 1979. And one-third of the production is exported to 30 countries, including Japan, where the shaver is believed to be the only appliance sold with a "made in America" label. The Remington is the only electric shaver still made in the United States.

Bigger companies are now coming to Remington to find out how they do it. General Motors sent a team from its new Saturn unit to Bridgeport. And in late 1984 Mike Duda, who came to Remington in 1979 from Frito-Lay, took a call from General Motors of Canada, which was planning a new facility and wanted to send some people to Bridgeport to get some pointers. Here's an $80 billion company hoping to learn from a $150 million enterprise.

They might learn from Elena Wallace, who has worked in the Bridgeport factory since 1962. In 1984, she won a trip to Acapulco in a company contest tied to the theme, "What Makes Remington Good." Her winning entry was a poem dedicated to Victor Kiam. It said, in part:

He does all the things that a smart owner should . . .

There's a reason, of course, why we've gone to the top.
It's the big happy family we have in the shop.

So it's not just a whole that's the sum of its parts,
It's a good bunch of people who work from their hearts.

Main employment centers   Bridgeport, where 850 people work. Another 250 are scattered in 54 Remington retail stores across the country.

Headquarters   Remington Products, Inc.
60 Main Street
Bridgeport, Connecticut 06602
203-367-4400

ROLM Corporation

ROLM CORPORATION

The second-largest maker of computerized telephone exchanges (PBXs). U.S. employees: 10,000.

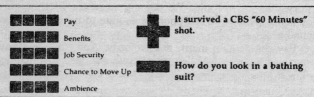

Pay	It survived a CBS "60 Minutes" shot.
Benefits	
Job Security	
Chance to Move Up	How do you look in a bathing suit?
Ambience	

When CBS's "60 Minutes" decided to do a special on the burgeoning Silicon Valley, the producers sent a camera crew to ROLM. The company's headquarters complex provides the perfect setting to record what many outsiders consider to be the California work style. In the middle of the campus-like facility is ROLM's million-dollar recreation center, complete with two heated swimming pools, sauna, Jacuzzi, steam room, tennis and racquetball courts, track, par course, and full-size indoor gymnasium for basketball and volleyball. In midafternoon it's common to see ROLM employees lounging by the pool, playing racquetball, or working out in a Jane Fonda-style exercise class.

ROLM is the only company in America with a "Great Place to Work" department. ROLM's "flex-flex time" program fosters the country club atmosphere. Some companies offer "flex-time," meaning employees have several options as to when to start and leave work. They can arrive at 8:00 A.M. or 9:00 A.M. or 10:00 A.M.—and leave after putting in eight hours. ROLM takes the concept a step further by stating that employees can work whenever they want to, subject to the approval of their immediate supervisor or work group. Though most choose to work conventional hours, some night owls can regularly be found in their offices long after midnight.

An icing on ROLM's "Great Place to Work" cake, the company gives all employees an unparalleled sabbatical program. After each six years at ROLM, any employee can take three months off *at full pay*. Or, if desired, the employee can take six weeks of at double pay. Needless to say, virtually everyone opts for this sabbatical as it's lost if not used.

Despite appearances, one ROLM executive insists, "This is no California hip, loosy-goosy place. ROLM has a very competitive atmosphere." Another official pointed out that although the company has never laid off anyone in its 13-year history, "we fire people. We do not guarantee lifetime employment. We believe it's poor for morale to have deadwood around here."

Pay is based on merit, not seniority. And, though many companies in Silicon Valley try to eradicate class distinctions by having open offices, ROLM builds as many closed offices as possible, claiming that executives and engineers prefer privacy.

At the same time, the company makes a serious effort to remain nonhierarchical. One of the principles of ROLM management is to "avoid bureaucracy." Another is to "use written communications only when it makes sense to do so." In 1983, the company had only 16 vice-presidents for 5,000 employees, making it the "most bottom-heavy company" in the high-tech industry, according to the *San Francisco Chronicle*.

These attitudes seem to make a difference to those in the ranks. We received an unsolicited letter from Andrea Nieman, an administrative assistant for ROLM in Santa Clara, who had heard about our project from a national newsletter for secretaries. She wrote: "ROLM recognizes that people are the greatest asset. There is no 'us' and 'them' attitude here; everyone is important. Upper management is visible and accessible. There is always time to talk, to find solutions, and to implement changes."

ROLM is highly decentralized. Hiring is done largely by the immediate supervisors rather than by the personnel department. So you have to relate well to your supervisor here. As a safety valve, all job openings are posted internally first, and movement to other departments is encouraged.

Run by engineers, the company's name is based on the initials of four Rice University electrical engineering graduates, who all attended Stanford in doctoral programs (Gene

---

ROLM's Goals

To Make a Profit
To Grow
To Offer Quality Products and Customer Support
To Create a Great Place to Work

"Great Place to Work" means:
1. Work should be a challenging, stimulating, and enjoyable experience.
2. The work place should be pleasant.
3. ROLM should have an environment where every employee can enhance one's self-image through achievement, creativity, and constructive feedback.

Therefore, every employee should have:
1. Equal opportunity to grow and be promoted
2. Treatment as an individual
3. Personal privacy respected
4. Encouragement and assistance to succeed
5. Opportunity to be creative
6. Evaluations based on job performance only

Employee's responsibilities include:
1. Being honest
2. Being helpful toward others to enhance teamwork
3. Performing to the best of his or her abilities
4. Helping to make ROLM a great place to work
5. Understanding and supporting ROLM's goals

Richeson, Ken Oshman, Walter Lowenstern, and Bob Maxfield). They started the company soon after completing their degrees. Now in their early forties, three of the men are still running the company; Oshman is president.

ROLM's founders discovered in 1969 that no one had produced an all-weather minicomputer. So, in a prune shed near Stanford's campus, they went to work to build a machine capable of withstanding temperatures as low as minus-100 degrees to plus-200 degrees Fahrenheit. In 1973, ROLM started making computerized telephone exchanges, the business that now accounts for 85 percent of its sales. Second only to AT&T, ROLM makes phone exchange equipment that serves from 24 to 4,000 extensions.

The company strives to win customers by quality rather

than price. "We are sort of an IBM-type company," one ROLM official explained to us in early 1983. "We are trying to be the best, not the cheapest. We want to make highly reliable equipment and provide top service. It's our objective to out-IBM IBM." Ironically, he told us that shortly before IBM bought a chunk of ROLM. By late 1983, IBM owned almost 20 percent of ROLM's stock, and the next year IBM picked up the rest, making ROLM a wholly owned IBM subsidiary.

From all early indications, IBM intends to leave ROLM's unusual culture intact. At a company-wide meeting held on the lawn of ROLM's headquarters, IBM's president, John Akers and vice-chairman, Paul J. Rizzo, told ROLM employees that they had no intention to "fill in the swimming pool [with cement]." And much to the amusement of those attending, ROLM's Oshman offered the IBMers a beer. Though IBM frowns on alcoholic beverages consumed during work hours, Rizzo and Akers toasted the acquisition.

Main employment centers   Manufacturing: Santa Clara, California; Austin, Texas; Colorado Springs, Colorado. Nearly half of ROLM's employees work in one of the company's 52 sales and service offices located throughout the country.

Headquarters   ROLM Corporation
4900 Old Ironsides Drive
Santa Clara, CA 95050
408-988-2900

RYDER SYSTEM, INC.

Ryder rents and leases trucks to individuals and businesses, leases airplanes, and owns a couple of small insurance companies. U.S. employees: 20,126.

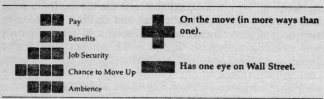

■■	Pay	✚	On the move (in more ways than one).
■■	Benefits		
■■■	Job Security		
■■■■	Chance to Move Up	■■	Has one eye on Wall Street.
■■■	Ambience		

When Ronald H. Dunbar arrived at Ryder in 1978 from Xerox, he was "appalled" at the weak compensation-and-benefits package. So he set about improving it. That's why he was hired. He's now executive vice-president in charge of human resources and administration at Ryder. The benefits have been expanded year after year. In 1984, for example, the company instituted an employee savings plan so that an employee can put aside up to 10 percent of his or her pretax earnings, and the company matches part of what is saved. Also that year, the firm started a "Take Care" health benefits program so that, among other things, employees receive more complete coverage of surgical costs when they obtain a second medical opinion. In 1983, the "sick pay" benefit was improved so that hourly employees receive full pay for five absences a year; previously, they were eligible for only 60 percent of their regular pay for a week's absence due to illness. In 1982, the dental coverage for orthodontic treatment was increased from $500 to $750. The 1981 changes included coverage of an additional 60 days of hospital care under major medical (the previous limit was 120 days in a 12-month period).

The Dunbar improvements reflect the Barnes-Burns transformation of this Miami-based transportation services company. Ryder was in the red to the tune of $20 million in 1974—and prospects looked bleak for everyone. Leslie O. Barnes arrived in 1975 from Allegheny Airlines and began a rebuilding program. M. Anthony Burns was already on board, having joined Ryder in 1974 as director of corporate planning; he was then only 30 years old. Together, they have refashioned Ryder so that it has a strong sense of direction—providing services for business—and it's making money. Burns succeeded Barnes as chief executive officer in 1983.

In the process Ryder has become a good place to work. You can catch the upbeat feeling in talking to employees. It's exciting to be with a company that's on the move. To be sure, there has been plenty of wheeling and dealing. Companies have been bought, companies have been sold—but it hasn't been a mindless exercise. In late 1983, for example, Ryder reached an agreement to sell its Truckstops of America division to Standard Oil of Ohio. It operates 34 full-facility truck stops in 17 states: gasoline and service around the clock, recreation lounges, restaurants—half of them have motels.

But it wasn't just a "cut-and-run" sale. Before the pending sale was announced, Ryder assembled in Nashville all the Truckstop managers and briefed them fully on what was going to happen and why it was happening. The session was videotaped so that the managers could take a tape with them to show to their people. Ryder then set up a toll-free telephone number that Truckstop employees could call to get answers to any questions they had. And Ryder also expressed to Sohio its concern that the Truckstop work force be treated well. It's not your everyday corporate divestiture.

The company being refashioned here is one that performs for other companies services they could do themselves but which Ryder thinks it can do more efficiently, like running a fleet of trucks or operating a fleet of airplanes. Most people assume that Ryder is a trucking company, since its distinctive yellow trucks can be seen on roads throughout the country. However, its main business is leasing trucks to companies. It also rents (there's a difference between renting and leasing) them to consumers who are moving household goods; but its main revenue source consists of companies which take long-term leases on vehicles owned and serviced by Ryder. So in this part of its business, truck leasing and renting, Ryder doesn't have many drivers. Where it does employ some 3,000 truck drivers is in its automotive carrier division, which picks up new cars from manufacturers and delivers them to dealers. You may have thought that the auto companies owned those long vehicle carriers but more often than not what you're seeing is a Ryder piece of equipment. Ryder carriers, for example, deliver about 40 percent of all the cars and light trucks produced by General Motors. The Teamster drivers are the only unionized group in the company.

We talked to people at Ryder's home base in Miami. The company has a tradition of promoting people through its own ranks. Donald Estes, who became president of the truck leasing division in 1983, started his career as a sales trainee at a truck rental office in Topeka, Kansas.

A number of employees we met cited the chances for advancement as the number one reason they like working for Ryder. Training programs exist on every level of the company. All job openings are posted, and they must be offered to qualified Ryder people before being advertised outside the company.

The company's roots go back to the depression when Jim Ryder started hauling freight in a black 1931 Model A Ford truck. He soon discovered that he could make more money by renting trucks to others. His first customer agreed to rent a truck at $37.75 per week and 9½ cents per mile. The fleet has expanded steadily ever since. Today, Ryder has nearly 97,000 trucks for hire at nearly 700 different locations across the United States. Ironically, founder Jim Ryder left the company in 1978 and later set up a competitor, Jartran, a name coined from his own.

In the Miami area, Ryder's 1,500 employees share an unusual level of camaraderie. Everyone communicates on a first-name basis. The company sport seems to be volleyball, and executives and nonmanagers often play on teams together. Also, many Ryder people are related to one another. Woody Donaldson works in the graphics shop; his father has worked for the company for 46 years, and he has five cousins who also work for Ryder.

There is no executive dining room at the company headquarters, located a few blocks west of Miami International Airport. Most of the nearly 1,200 employees who work there regularly eat in the company cafeteria, which faces a tropical garden. The five-story building surrounds the garden. When Ryder had its fiftieth anniversary celebration in 1983, employees shared a cake that was put in the middle of the garden. The cake was shaped like a truck and covered with yellow icing.

In terms of pay, Ryder does not rate highly. Dunbar told us that Ryder pays the going market rate for most of its jobs, neither higher nor lower than the average. But it has instituted pay-for-performance programs, enabling top performers to receive up to 20 percent more than others in their job category. Mechanics can receive 25 cents an hour more for each of the six levels of skill certification open to them.

The company has a stock purchase plan whereby any employee can buy up to 200 shares of Ryder stock over a two-year period at 85 percent of the price on either the opening date or the closing date, whichever is the lower price. Nearly 7,000 employees, over a third of the staff, have bought Ryder stock through the plan. The company also has an employee stock ownership plan. Since Ryder has performed well on the stock market during the past decade, some employees have been able to purchase their homes from profits made in stock sales. The company, under Barnes and Burns, is strongly oriented to the investment community.

There is a lot of pride in the company. Some employees assert that not only is Ryder the largest truck rental company but the best. They contend that it's not uncommon for people to join Ryder after having worked for U-Haul or Hertz, but that it's almost unheard of for the opposite to happen.

There was one ironic twist in recent Ryder history. Looking to expand, the company made a stab in 1983 at acquiring a big insurance broker (the company has some insurance operations), Frank B. Hall & Co. But Hall foiled the move by acquiring Jartran, the truck leasing company started by Jim Ryder, who sold it to Hall for $100—and has since started up a boat leasing company called Jarmada.

While the general pay levels at Ryder are not particularly high, they rise to the stratosphere in the executive suite. In 1984, Chairman Leslie Barnes and President Tony Burns received cash, bonuses, and other benefits that added up to $700,000 and $691,250 respectively, while the three top executive vice-presidents earned $442,916, $290,280, and

$279,485. Over the past five years, the five men at the top of Ryder have also made a total of nearly $6 million from their stock options. So if you get high enough in this company, you can really make a bundle.

Main employment centers   one thousand five hundred work in Miami. About half the employees work in the truck leasing and rental division, mostly in small offices scattered throughout the United States.

Headquarters   Ryder System, Inc.
3600 NW 82 Avenue
Miami, FL 33166
305-593-3726

BEST VACATION PLAN
Reader's Digest

SAGA CORPORATION

Saga feeds people—in colleges, hospitals, corporate dining rooms, and public restaurants—at more than 1,300 locations across the country. Employees: 58,000.

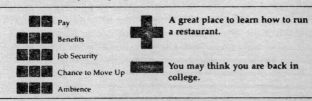

■■ Pay	✚ A great place to learn how to run a restaurant.
■■■ Benefits	
■■■ Job Security	
■■■ Chance to Move Up	You may think you are back in college.
■■■ Ambience	

Lunch is free at the Menlo Park, California, headquarters of Saga—and why not? The company is feeding thousands of people every day in cafeterias and restaurants all over the nation. A free lunch for employees is a logical fringe benefit. You would be paying for a Saga-prepared lunch if you ate at Goucher College in Towson, Maryland; the Rocky Mountain Hospital in Denver; Reed College in Portland, Oregon; the IBM facility in White Plains, New York; the Dart & Kraft headquarters in Northbrook, Illinois; or the Briercrest Bible Institution in Carenport, Saskatchewan. Saga has kitchens everywhere.

If you had visited Saga's headquarters a few years ago, you would have thought you were on a college campus. Saga's main business was feeding students at dozens of colleges and universities throughout the country, and company officials were *expected* to dress like students. Company executives wore bright pants, open sport shirts, and white bucks.

Saga still feeds students at 350 colleges and universities, but today school programs generate less than a third of the company's $1.2 billion in sales. The rest comes from Saga's restaurant chains (Black Angus, Velvet Turtle, Straw Hat Pizza) and contracts to provide food in hospitals and corporate dining rooms. The company added two new restaurant units in

1983: Grandy's, an upscale chicken chain with over 100 restaurants in the Midwest and South, and Spoons, a ten-unit hamburger chain out of Houston.

While Saga officials are more likely to be wearing three-piece suits these days, Saga retains some of the atmosphere of a collegiate fraternity. One reason: many of Saga's 4,000 managers joined the company as student-managers at one of its college dining halls. Another is that Saga has turned to the academic world for help in creating its internal training programs. Being close to Stanford University, the company developed strong links with the business school there. Illustrious behavioral psychologists from the National Training Labs, Esalen, and various universities have served as Saga consultants over the years. One was the famed Abraham Maslow.

The academic psychologists initially brought to Saga techniques such as encounter groups and T-groups to help employees discuss their feelings about working with each other. These practices became institutionalized at Saga over the years as the Organizational Development, or OD, program.

Saga is thus considered a preeminent training ground for persons involved in food service. Its management training is considered so strong that the company has thought of selling the service to other firms.

The restaurant business being what it is, the turnover is very high. More than half the people who work for Saga are part-timers. But the people who get to the top can be very young. In 1984, for example, there were more than half a dozen top executives—group heads or division heads—who were in their late thirties or early forties. Many managers do indeed begin their careers with the Saga restaurant at their college. Two of them—James W. Morrell, a member of the office of the president, and Robert C. Van Horn, president of the contract food services group—both came out of Kalamazoo College in Michigan. Another manager, Ralph A. Pica, president of the Black Angus chain, graduated from Hobart College in Geneva, New York, where Saga was founded.

You don't get a lot of benefits if you're just serving food in a college cafeteria operated by Saga, but the company does offer a strong program to people who become permanent corporate managers. There's life insurance, disability insurance, 100 percent reimbursement for job-related courses, a stock purchase plan (at 85 percent of the market price), and a profit-sharing plan that supplemented salaries by 8.7 percent in 1983. Saga was also quick to adopt a thrift plan made possible by new tax laws, enabling employees to sock away 10 percent of their income into a trust—before taxes.

Saga's campuslike complex at Menlo Park, where 500 people work, has one of the most extensive collections of modern art in California. Harry W. "Hunk" Anderson, one of the company's founders, has collected some 1,400 works of art. Major pieces are not confined to the lobbies and the offices of the senior executives, either. Oil paintings by major West Coast artists adorn walls above the desks of secretaries.

Anderson started the company in 1948 with William P. Laughlin and William F. Scandling, classmates at Hobart College. They pooled $1,500 and persuaded the school's administration that they could run the college's dining hall at a profit while offering students free, "unlimited seconds." Saga was serving nearly 100 colleges by 1962, the year they moved their headquarters to the West Coast. The three founders stepped aside for more professional managers in 1978, though they are still serving on the company's board of directors.

Professional corporate managers are at the top of Saga today (Chairman Charles A. Lynch is a former Navy quartermaster and executive for Du Pont and W. R. Grace). But the new managers have tried hard to keep the open, collegiate atmosphere within the organization while paying strict attention to the bottom line.

Main employment centers   Menlo Park, California; facilities in 48 states.

Headquarters   Saga Corporation
One Saga Lane
Menlo Park, CA 94025
415-854-5150

SECURITY PACIFIC CORPORATION

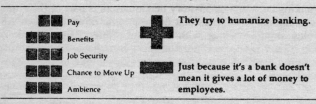

SECURITY PACIFIC CORPORATION

California's second-largest bank. Employees: 28,000.

▪▪	Pay	**They try to humanize banking.**
▪▪▪	Benefits	
▪▪▪	Job Security	
▪▪▪	Chance to Move Up	**Just because it's a bank doesn't**
▪▪▪	Ambience	**mean it gives a lot of money to employees.**

Japanese-style quality control circles in a bank? "Security Circles" are just one way Security Pacific is trying to "blend good employee relations concepts with West Coast culture," according to Irv Margol, executive vice-president and personnel director.

Started as a pilot project in 1982, Security Circles are volunteer groups of bank employees who meet regularly to talk about problems they've discovered on the job. One group, composed of employees who prepare monthly bank statements, figured out how to save $68,000. The program has since been expanded throughout the company.

Another unusual program is BOSS, or Black Officers' Support System. It started as an outgrowth of the movement of blacks into higher positions within the bank, a situation partly created by an affirmative action push several years ago. Sixty of Security Pacific's 1,734 vice-presidents are black. With the cooperation of the bank, many of these officers formed BOSS to help them learn the ropes in what has been a white-dominated world. BOSS sponsored a five-day workshop led by Price Cobbs, author of *Black Rage*. The group meets monthly. Similar groups have been formed by Asian and Hispanic bank officers. Security Pacific has 88 Hispanic and 59 Asian veeps.

400

Security Pacific has for the past several years led the banking industry in trend-setting personnel programs. It's no small accomplishment, considering Security Pacific's size: it is the country's eighth-largest commercial bank, second in the United States only to Bank of America in the number of banking offices, with more than 600 branches in California. It has nearly four million checking and savings account customers and 28,000 employees, does business in 24 countries on four continents, and serves 90 of the 100 largest industrial companies.

In most outward respects, Security Pacific resembles its banking cousins. Its 55-story headquarters is part of the clump of banking skyscrapers that dominate the downtown Los Angeles skyline, along with those of Wells Fargo, Bank of America, First Interstate, Crocker. But there seems to be a genuine effort here to make working different from the impersonal atmosphere associated with most banks.

Banks pay notoriously poorly. Security Pacific's pay scale is no exception, as beginning tellers received as little as $790 a month in late 1983. But Security Pacific tries to demystify the entire issue of pay by giving each new employee a card that indicates the salary ranges for all employees, in each of the 30 pay grades (ranging from $9,480 to $81,900). Bank employees know the details of everybody else's finances, so why not of each other's? The card also lays out the performance rating ranges within each grade. Thus, an employee working at grade nine can be paid anywhere from a minimum of $1,255 to $1,929 a month, depending on the performance rating from his or her supervisor.

The bank couples this openness with job posting. Every opening in the bank is listed in a weekly newsletter, with a complete job description, requirements, and—what makes it one of the best-read sections of the newspaper—the amount of the job-referral bonus. For suggesting a successful applicant for a job, a Security Pacific employee can earn anywhere from $50 to $500. The bonus has worked so well that the company virtually never relies on outside executive recruiters.

The bank's promote-from-within policy also means Security Pacific hires at least 50 percent of its management trainees from within the bank. To assist employees interested in management or in changing areas within the bank, Security

Pacific offers Career Strategies workshops, held on two consecutive weekends. Attendees range from regional vice-presidents to security guards.

Security Pacific's management seems concerned about the drudgery associated with many bank positions. Like many other banks, they're making an effort to automate and computerize the repetitive work. At the same time, Security Pacific has started a "job rotation" effort so that, for instance, those involved in opening cash one day may count it the next and pack it the following day. Similarly, the bank is experimenting with "job enrichment," trying to get people to do more than one function.

Security Pacific has other innovative policies: two social workers hired by the bank sit by a phone with a toll-free number to talk with employees who are having personal problems. Alcoholics, rape victims, or employees with drug or marital problems can call in total confidence and get referrals to counseling services. The company picks up the tab for up to a year's worth of counseling.

Security Pacific was one of the first major banks to offer a written grievance procedure to settle disputes between employees and their supervisors. It has a "Question Line" with a toll-free number to answer any job-related problem an employee is having. And, for those who wish to adopt a child, the bank offers adoption aid equal to maternity support.

Security Pacific seems to be making the effort to break down the rigidly hierarchical nature of a bank. The trend may accelerate as banks find themselves competing with other institutions in providing financial services to customers.

Main employment centers About two-thirds work in Southern California, and another third in the northern part of the state. Only 130 work outside California.

Headquarters Security Pacific Corporation
333 South Hope Street
Los Angeles, CA 90071
213-613-6211

Shell

SHELL OIL COMPANY

Shell is the eighth-largest oil company in the United States. Employees: 35,000.

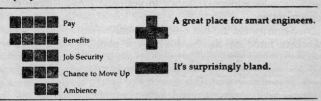

■■■■ Pay	✚ A great place for smart engineers.
■■■ Benefits	
■■ Job Security	
■■ Chance to Move Up	■ It's surprisingly bland.
■ Ambience	

Shell people like to think of themselves as the Ivy League of the oil industry. Not that most Shell employees come from Harvard or Yale; engineering graduates from Purdue and Georgia Tech are more typical. It's just that Shell thinks of itself as the elite, where the smartest people in the oil business work.

Shell may be headquartered in Houston, but its ranks are filled every year with people from all parts of the country. "We don't want to be provincial," explains Rod Maibe, a longtime professional recruiter for Shell. The policy isn't surprising. Shell itself has moved its home office twice—from San Francisco to New York in 1948, and from New York to Houston in 1970.

The life of many Shell employees is even more peripatetic. It's common for technical and managerial employees to transfer to a variety of locations during their careers. As the American arm of Royal Dutch Shell, the largest oil company in the world after Exxon, Shell Oil is concentrated almost exclusively in the United States. Three-quarters of all its employees work in Texas, Louisiana, or California. Most of the others belong to the marketing arm of the company, with offices scattered throughout the country. Service station operators are not Shell employees; they are self-employed and hire their own attendants and mechanics. In early 1985, Shell had 220 Americans working in overseas locations—150 of them in Saudi Arabia.

That Shell people are a little different from the types employed in other oil companies was remarked upon by Anthony Sampson in his book, *The Seven Sisters*. "Shell certainly appears more open-minded than the others, more prepared to discuss political problems, less confident of ultimate rightness. Its need to buy oil from others, ever since its beginnings, has forced it to live more continually on its wits...." Sampson was talking primarily about Shell people in Britain, but some of that character has rubbed off in America. As a self-contained American entity, Shell Oil has had to scrap hard for oil in the United States, and it has had to find end uses for the petroleum in this country, either in chemicals or in fuel pumps at gasoline stations. Even competitors would acknowledge that Shell has, over the years, mounted the most imaginative marketing and advertising programs in the industry. Shell engineers therefore have a closer feel for the consumer than competitors, although when you meet them face-to-face some still have a "Texas Aggie" literal-mindedness that drives some people up the wall.

The research division provides one of the few direct links to the Anglo-Dutch mother company which now owns more than 94 percent of Shell Oil's stock. Every year, six to eight United States Shell employees swap positions with their counterparts in the United Kingdom through an Exchange Scientist program. Shell's research complexes rank among the most desirable in the petroleum industry. Some 2,100 scientists and support people work in three centers—two in Houston devoted largely to oil, gas, and petrochemicals, and one in Modesto, California, for agricultural chemicals. The research facilities have universitylike environments. Staff members frequently present papers and attend seminars. Shell's research-and-development arm even publishes its own bimonthly magazine, *Quest*. One 1982 issue contained articles ranging from genetic engineering to a leak detection system for gas pipelines. Shell has a joint research effort with Cetus, one of the leading genetic engineering companies.

Much of the research involves Shell's chemical division. The largest chemical manufacturer among U.S. oil companies, Shell sells its industrial and farm customers a wide variety of products, including detergent alcohols, elastomers, epoxy resins, plastics, and agricultural chemicals such as herbicides and insecticides. Shell's chemical plants are located in Illinois, Louisiana, New Jersey, Alabama, and Ohio.

Shell places a premium on technical proficiency. Virtually all people in management come directly from the ranks. Promotion from within occurs throughout the organization. Since most new employees are hired because of their technical training, it means the top people at Shell are usually engineers or in related professions, rather than professional managers.

Paul Connolly, a relative newcomer to Shell with only six years at the company, explained that what he likes best is that the management is so technically oriented. An engineering graduate of Northern Michigan Tech, Connolly says that he has also been impressed by the informal avenues of communication. Though Shell has its share of paperwork, Connolly doesn't feel inundated by it.

The relative informality at Shell is also reflected in clothing. Like many others in Houston's headquarters office, Connolly doesn't wear a business suit and light shirt. When interviewed in the winter of 1983, he was wearing a black shirt with a white tie and no jacket. Shell's handbook for its headquarters staff even states explicitly that "there is no formal dress code." Recruiter Ron Maibe tells the story of one 10-year Shell veteran who was distressed to learn that he would have to wear a jacket and tie to conduct interviews for the company on college campuses. The man did not even own a necktie at the time.

All oil companies pay well and wrap their employees in such a comfortable blanket of benefits that few ever want to leave. Shell's savings and investment plan is the most generous in the petroleum industry. Here's how it works: after three years' service you may elect to have 2½ percent of your gross pay socked away in the company's Provident fund—and Shell will match your contribution dollar for dollar; after six years, the savings can be 5 percent of your compensation; and after nine years, it moves up to 10 percent, with the company matching dollar for dollar.

So, let's assume you have been with Shell for nine years and you're making $35,000 a year. You can have $3,500 of your pay banked—and the company will kick in another $3,500. Year after year, it can add up to big bucks. One of the newest features is that even if you decide not to save a dime, Shell will still come through with its contribution for you. In other words, for the nine-year employee earning $35,000, Shell will kick in $3,500 annually even if the employee saves nothing.

On top of this plan, there's a pension program whose entire costs are footed by Shell. In short, you could walk out of this company with a pile of cash. A 30-year-old earning $40,000 a year could retire at 65 with a $1.6 million lump sum—plus an excellent pension.

Main employment centers   Houston (13,000); Louisiana (6,950); California (4,340); Illinois (2,185).

Headquarters   Shell Oil Company
One Shell Plaza
Houston, TX 77002
713-241-6161

Southern
California
Edison
Company

SOUTHERN CALIFORNIA EDISON COMPANY

Edison provides electricity to nine million customers in central and southern California. Employees: 17,000.

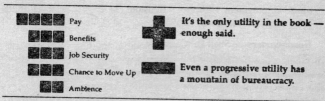

■■■■ Pay	✚ It's the only utility in the book — enough said.
■■■ Benefits	
■■■ Job Security	
■■ Chance to Move Up	■ Even a progressive utility has a mountain of bureaucracy.
■■ Ambience	

A utility that advocates solar and wind power? Southern California Edison shook up the electric industry in 1980 when it became the first and, to date, only major power company to go on record as saying that it would provide all its additional power needs through renewable and alternative energy sources: wind, geothermal, solar, fuel cells, and hydroelectric.

The company's innovative position extends to how it treats employees. Most utilities have the reputation of being highly bureaucratized. People are hired into one department and never leave it till retirement day. Not so at Edison. "Nobody ever stays in the same department where they're hired," claimed Claire Spence, who works in corporate planning and budgeting. Spence cited her own career. Hired as a steno in the safety division, she later became a statistical clerk and then a safety specialist. For a year and a half she worked full-time on the company's United Way campaign. Before moving to her current position, she was a conservation load planner.

Others at Edison agree that Spence's experience is the rule rather than the exception. The first female ''groundman'' (those who pass wires to the people who climb the poles) became a claims adjuster and then a customer service repre-

407

sentative, worked in the energy service division, and now works on the conservation staff.

Management encourages this lateral movement. Indeed, anybody who wants to get ahead at Edison must be used to moving from department to department. The 20 officers (vice-president and up) who constitute the executive management team have all worked in several different fields. The vice-presidents typically oversee an entirely different department from the one in which they were previously working.

Edison does not rely on the traditional grapevine to inform people of job openings. It regularly publishes a detailed listing of all the available positions, including any special job requirements.

With all the flow between departments, Edison employees often talk about the importance of gaining "visibility" within the company. There's a friendly, relaxed atmosphere at the company headquarters. Everybody seems to know everybody else. The headquarters occupies two recently built four-story buildings, each of which takes up an entire city block, and a separate data processing facility. But the buildings don't have an urban feel; they're located 15 miles east of Los Angeles, surrounded by employee parking lots and several acres of vacant company property. Unlike at many utilities, visitors need not wear badges, nor do the employees.

The utility's highly developed corporate communications program offers yet another vehicle for getting known around Edison. Not only are there weekly newsletters, but Edison has also launched its own video network. The company's communications department produces a regular half-hour company news program called "Horizons." The show is sent to 100 different Edison offices throughout the electric utility's service area.

Despite the homey atmosphere, Edison is big: the fourth-largest investor-owned electric utility in the United States. It serves more than nine million people in 800 cities and communities in central and southern California, though not in the city of Los Angeles. Edison, like many utilities, pays well. Entry-level journeyman linemen start at $30,000; entry-level groundmen, $15,000. Turnover is a low 5.6 percent a year. The average employee here has 12 years' service, the average retiree, 32 years'.

However, because it's government-regulated, like all

public utilities, Southern California Edison can't be as free-wheeling as it might like to be. It has to contend with mountains of paperwork—and it needs always to justify to the state Public Utilities Commission why it needs to make as much money as it does. That's the tradeoff for enjoying a monopoly service.

Edison was one of the first utilities to establish an employee medical plan. Eighty-two years ago the company decided to hire its own doctors to take care of its people. Today Edison has 12 staff physicians and part-time specialists. The utility pays 100 percent of all medical and hospital bills (after the employee pays a $120 annual deductible) as long as an employee goes to one of Edison's own doctors or those approved by the company.

One other perk associated with working for Edison: you get 25 percent off your electric bill.

Main employment centers   Rosemead, 3,425; San Onofre nuclear plant, 1,609; Alhambra office, 1,116. In the work force are 2,100 linemen, ground crew, or foremen; 4,000 clerical; 1,200 engineers; and 500 who work in energy conservation.

Headquarters   Southern California Edison Company
2244 Walnut Grove Avenue
Rosemead, CA 91770
818-302-1212

SPRINGS INDUSTRIES, INC.

The fourth-largest textile manufacturer in the United States, Springs sells more sheets and pillowcases than anyone else. Employees: 18,500.

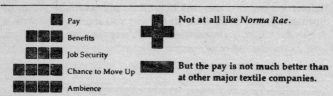

Pay
Benefits
Job Security
Chance to Move Up
Ambience

Not at all like *Norma Rae*.

But the pay is not much better than at other major textile companies.

Textile companies have long had lousy reputations as places to work—low wages, unhealthy working conditions, and unfeeling, if not tyrannical, management. One clear exception is Springs. Much of the difference can be traced to the founding family, which still owns nearly two-thirds of the company's stock. Elliott Springs, president from 1933 to 1959, left a unique legacy based on a genuine concern about "his people." Yes, there's a strong flavor of paternalism about Springs.

Elliott Springs—referred to as "the Colonel"—was possibly the most colorful character American industry produced in this century. To make the Springmaid label visible, he launched an advertising campaign the likes of which Madison Avenue had never seen before—or since. Hiring some of the best artists of the era, Springs created a series of risqué ads featuring lifelike drawings of beautiful, often scantily clad women. He used terms such as "hamper" and "lung lifter" to describe women's undergarments. And he loaded the ads with sexual double entendres: an Indian maiden alighting from a hammock which holds an exhausted Indian man, the headline reading, "A buck well spent." *Life* and the *Saturday Evening Post* rejected his ads as too shocking. But the ad campaign

410

paid off handsomely. Springmaid sheets went from thirteenth place to first, a position they still hold today.

In keeping with his style, the Colonel named Gypsy Rose Lee, the famous stripper, "vice-president of unveiling" for his short-line railroad. At the opening ceremony for a company facility, she removed her gloves to break a bottle of champagne over the new structure, saying, "This is all I will take off today."

Eccentricities aside, Elliott Springs also made a point of offering benefits not commonly provided to employees of other textile manufacturers. He believed that workers should have well-balanced meals while on the job, so he instituted a cafeteria system. Low-cost hot meals are available at most Springs plants for all three shifts. He also led the way with a profit-sharing plan, a vacation bonus, medical and life insurance, medical care, and clinics. The benefit plans have been changed and updated over the years. The Springs health-care plan today is considered a model for the textile industry. In recent years, the company has introduced a deferred compensation plan and a savings plan where the company matches employee contributions.

Begun in 1953, the Springs profit-sharing plan was for years the only such plan in the textile industry. In 1983, the company set aside $12.7 million for the plan. Salaried employees had an amount equal to 6.3 percent of their income put into their accounts, and hourly workers had 5 percent put into theirs. Springs has also improved hourly wages ahead of other textile manufacturers. In 1982, when the rest of the industry waited an extra six months before granting general wage increases, Springs didn't. The same happened again in 1983 and 1984 when others again lagged because of the slowing textile business.

Springs employees in South Carolina—in fact, anyone who lives in one of Springs's South Carolina plant communities—also have access to a remarkable number of recreational facilities. Springs Park covers 102 acres near the Springs mill town of Lancaster (population 9,000). The park boasts an Olympic-size swimming pool, miniature golf course, skating rink, and equestrian camp. The Colonel used to lead community singalongs in the park. The Leroy Springs Recreation Complex in Fort Mill has an indoor pool, gymnasium, racquetball and tennis courts, softball and soccer fields, meeting rooms for crafts classes and other activities, and a playground for children. There are golf courses in Fort Mill, Chester, and Lancaster.

For vacations, many Springs employees like going to Springmaid Beach on the Atlantic coast at Myrtle Beach, South Carolina. The facility offers motel rooms at reduced costs, a campground, a cafeteria, and a fishing pier.

These facilities are used by production-line workers and executives alike. The company frowns on frills such as executive dining rooms. Managers and hourly employees eat together in the same cafeterias.

Some people who have worked at Springs for many years claim that the family atmosphere has not changed, despite all the technological advances in the textile industry. Frances Reeves started working for Springs 35 years ago as a spooler in Springs's mill in Kershaw, South Carolina (population 2,000). "People used to look down on people who worked in cotton mills. They called us lintheads." That is no longer the case, says Reeves. Now a spooler tender in the Elliott plant in nearby Lancaster, Reeves makes about $8 an hour, including productivity incentives.

She thinks of working at Springs as "a family affair." For one thing, many relatives work there. Reeves's husband, for instance, also works for Springs, and she had to move to a different mill when he was promoted to supervisor because company policy prohibits one spouse from overseeing the work of the other.

Like many other Springs employees, Reeves watched the Academy Award-winning movie *Norma Rae*, a 1979 Hollywood film that sympathetically depicts efforts to unionize a big southern textile mill. She said that there was "some similarity between *Norma Rae* and the way our plants used to be," but that the type of machinery seen in the film had not been used in Springs mills for decades. "When I started, they did not stress earplugs or dust protectors, but we have air conditioning and everything is filtered now."

Reeves also considers Springs's managers to be benevolent rather than like the bullies shown in the movie. She appreciates the personal attention people in her mill get. For instance, when her father died, someone from the company came to the funeral, even though her father didn't work for

Springs. She said that sort of concern is typical. Though unions have tried to organize at Springs, none has ever succeeded in getting enough support to force a vote.

Tommy Davis started with Springs as a sweeper in the Chester mill in 1967, shortly after graduating from Chester's segregated black high school. Because he "wanted to make a decent living," he began asking the maintenance technicians about how various machines worked. A plant supervisor noticed his interest and offered to help him train for a maintenance job. Today, Davis works as a personnel manager in Chester at a plant with 1,100 people. When he began with the company, he was the only black on his shift; now he estimates the ratio at close to 50-50. He contends his advancement has to do with his own efforts: "I do not feel I am a token." He thinks Springs offers people opportunity to advance and to grow, a sentiment echoed by several people we interviewed.

When we interviewed Davis in 1983, Springs had two plants in Chester. But the company closed the older one the following year partly because of the competitive pressures from Asian textile imports and the need to modernize. As it had done in two similar instances, Springs waited to phase out the plant until the newer plant could accommodate a new weekend shift. As a result, of the 500 people affected, all either retired or were placed in other Springs jobs.

Textiles have been part of Jerry Nealy's family since his greatgrandfather worked in a mill. His grandfather worked as an overhauler; his grandmother as a fly-frame tender; and his mother as a spooler—all for Springs in Chester. He was willing to put sentiment aside when he graduated from the University of South Carolina, and he applied to all the major textile companies. But Springs stood out. He said it has the reputation in the industry as the technological leader. (It is currently in the midst of investing $175 million in new textile technology.)

Springs also is supposed to be the best place in the industry to learn textile management, according to Nealy. About 70 percent of plant supervisors come up through the ranks; another 10 percent are hired from other companies; the remaining 20 percent or so are hired straight out of college. Those management trainees must start right on the production floor, working for several months on the machines with the regular hourly workers. Nealy passed through his training and is now a shift supervisor of a small department in the Lancaster plant.

Not all Springs people were brought up in one of the company's mill towns, though a high percentage are local people. Jennifer Scott joined Springs's data-processing department after 12 years' experience with different firms in Florida. She commutes to the Fort Mill office from Charlotte. She was immediately charmed by the traditions at Springs. "I could sit here for hours and listen to stories about the Colonel. It makes you feel like part of the family."

She especially likes the story about how the Colonel was once racing through a small South Carolina town on his way to one of the mills. The local sheriff flagged his car down (Springs liked driving European sports cars). The officer fined him $25 for speeding. The Colonel pulled out his wallet and said, "Here, you'd better take fifty. I plan to come back this way after lunch."

"Even though Springs is a large company," Scott says, "I like it because it's a company with character."

The Colonel's spirit still lives at Springs's corporate offices in Fort Mill, South Carolina, a town of 4,000 about 15 miles south of Charlotte, North Carolina. It is clearly part of the Deep South; the municipal park has several Civil War statues—one to the community's two dozen Confederate war dead, another to soldiers' wives, and yet another to the slaves who kept the home front intact during the fighting. A few blocks from the park, Elliott Springs built the company's red brick corporate headquarters. He had the windows set at a 45-degree angle like those of the Zeppelin dirigible he took home from Europe after the First World War. On the walls hang posters of the original artwork for the Colonel's Springmaid ads. Along one hallway hang paintings by Grace Drayton, most famous for her baby-faced Campbell's Soup kids. The Colonel's collection includes a "Mona Lisa" and a "Napoleon," both done in the same pose as the classics but with Drayton's distinctive cherubic expressions.

Many employees enjoy peeking in the Colonel's office, still kept as he left it and used as a conference room. The room's main attraction is the Colonel's wooden desk. Sitting behind it he could, at the push of a button, raise a conference table out of the floor. Longtime Springs executives say they learned to jump out of their chairs when a meeting was completed. The Colonel would abruptly adjourn a meeting, push a button, and the conference table would drop back into the floor.

Main employment centers   All textile manufacturing is done within 100 miles of the Fort Mill headquarters in small towns in South and North Carolina. Some 315 marketing employees work out of Springs's 21-story New York City office at 104 West 40th Street. Subsidiary divisions have plants in Alabama, California, Georgia, and Wisconsin.

Headquarters   Springs Industries, Inc.
205 North White Street
P.O. Box 70
Fort Mill, SC 29715
803-547-2901

Steelcase

STEELCASE INC.

Steelcase is the world's largest manufacturer of office furniture. Employees: 10,000.

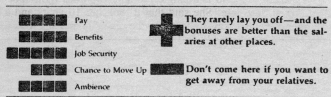

■■■■ Pay	✚ **They rarely lay you off—and the bonuses are better than the salaries at other places.**
■■■ Benefits	
■■■■ Job Security	
■■■ Chance to Move Up	**Don't come here if you want to get away from your relatives.**
■■■■ Ambience	

Kate McKenna started working for Steelcase in its file plant (where they make file cabinets) during the summer of 1979, when she was 29 years old. Her father, Paul Sherman, already worked there—as a foreman. He worked in the front of the plant, she worked in the back. And her husband, Charles McKenna, also worked there as a forklift operator. He had been there 12 years when his wife signed on as a welder. Kate watched the bulletin board for new openings, and she posted successfully for an office job in January 1981. Now she helps keep track of the torrent of job applications that pour in every day to this Grand Rapids, Michigan, firm, which has to be one of the least known corporate giants in the land.

While Steelcase may not be a household name in America, such is its local reputation as an excellent place to work that it receives 30,000 applications a year, just for salaried and skilled positions. According to McKenna, more than 200,000 applications have flowed into the company over the past four years. Incidentally, McKenna has more than just a father and a husband working at Steelcase. All told, she counts 18 relatives on the company payroll—and two others have their applications in. It's not easy to get a job at Steelcase, but it helps to be a relative. Three hundred husband-and-wife teams work here.

Les Clark, a systems plant manager who has put in 35 years at Steelcase, started as a stockroom clerk and worked his way up. Now a thousand people work for him. Three of his five children work at Steelcase, and he would be happy "to have five out of five" there. He recalls a time two years ago when Steelcase, looking to hire a hundred people, put up an internal notice that applications would be taken two days later between 5:30 and 7:00 P.M. On the appointed day and hour more than a thousand people were lined up around the block, causing a huge traffic jam.

Darlene Garland is a single mother who does light spot-welding at Steelcase. She said that it took her 10 years and a number of applications to "get into the place"—and she took a pay cut to come to Steelcase. However, considering the benefits, within a year she was making well over what she made on the previous job.

Jurgen Nitzsche, an immigrant from Germany, had been with Steelcase for 19 years at the end of 1984, and he told us that "this is best I ever worked for," including the several companies he worked for in Germany. Nitzsche started as a tool-and-die maker and now works in the engineering department. He also serves as a liaison with the German company in which Steelcase has a 50 percent interest. Nitzsche talks enthusiastically about Steelcase as being "a big family." His daughter, Patrice, graduated from high school in June 1984 and worked that summer in a Steelcase factory to earn money to go to college. She made $2,500. In 1981, his mother, who had remained in Germany, was in bad shape from a bout with cancer, and Nitzsche wanted to be with her. Steelcase allowed him to go to Germany for four weeks, keeping him on the payroll the whole time. He repaid the time, a week a year, from his future vacation allowance.

Why are these people—and others we talked to—so happy with Steelcase? The short answer is that this company has an extraordinary dedication to turning out quality products—and a by-product of that dedication is an iron determination to do right by its people, on the theory that such treatment will build a work force that's also dedicated. It's a determination that was built into the company at its inception in 1912 as a maker of fireproof safes. The founders of the company—and their descendants—never sold stock outside their families (to the public or to employees), but they made a point of paying top wages, and it's still Steelcase policy that its workers be "among the higher paid in the community."

In Grand Rapids, where it's now the second-largest employer, that means being on a par with, or topping, the city's largest employer, General Motors, which is unionized, whereas Steelcase is not. On top of their base wages, Steelcase employees get incentive pay keyed to their specific performance; and on top of that, they get cash bonuses, paid quarterly and yearly, based on the profit made by the company; and on top of that, they participate in the deferred profit-sharing plan, which salts away money for their retirement. In 1984, the average W-2 slip issued to hourly Steelcase employees showed income in the neighborhood of $31,000. That includes the incentive pay and the discretionary bonuses. In the 1974-84 period bonuses averaged out at more than 60 percent of base pay. The $31,000 does not, of course, include the profit-sharing contribution. The Internal Revenue Service puts a cap on contributions to a deferred profit-sharing trust—they can never be more than 15 percent of an employee's total compensation. It's a measure of Steelcase's profitability that since the plan was started in 1941, the maximum contribution has been made every year except one, when the payout came to 14.8 percent.

Money isn't everything. Beyond the high pay, Steelcase offers this rich panoply of benefits:

• Comprehensive medical, dental, and life insurance for employees and their dependents, with the company now offering a flexible benefits program enabling people to tailor their benefits to their specific needs;

• Camp Swampy: a 1,700-acre recreation area 60 miles north of Grand Rapids where there are 42 campsites available free of charge to employees, their families, and their guests;

• A day-care program that has achieved national recognition. Steelcase employs two coordinators full-time to screen all the child-care providers in the Grand Rapids area and direct interested employees to the most convenient and appropriate provider. The company also assists the qualified providers by lending them equipment and offering them technical aid. More than 200 Steelcase families use the program;

• Tuition reimbursement for job-related courses;

• An open-door policy. You can go above your supervisor's head to management if you're not satisfied with any answer to complaints;

• A minihospital staffed by 19 nurses and two physicians. In addition, Steelcase employs a psychologist and two social workers to counsel people on their personal problems —and this free service is available confidentially on company time or after hours; and

• An innovative food-service program that builds nutrition and variety into daily menus. This program was headed up in 1984 by 31-year-old Craig Smith, a graduate of the hotel management school at Michigan State University—and Smith had on his staff a dietician and five chefs, all graduates of degree programs. Smith seemed to be knocking himself out trying to make Steelcase employees, who are mostly meat-and-potatoes people, aware of nutritional values. He put celery and carrot sticks on coffee wagons, he prepared everything fresh, and he listed on his menus the caloric content of each item. Here, for example, is how one slice of the menu looked on January 28, 1985: Seafood platter (485 calories), Chicken Tahitian (310 calories), beef stew (515 calories), cream of vegetable soup (125 calories), chicken soup (65 calories), turkey sandwich (255 calories), club sandwich (345 calories). Representatives from Ford, Upjohn, and other companies have trekked to Grand Rapids to see what they could learn—or copy—from Craig Smith.

Steelcase's relations with its employees have been so good that the company has never experienced a work stoppage of any kind.

In 1983, Matt Gryczan and Jim Mencarelli, two reporters for the *Grand Rapids Press*, visited Steelcase and spotted this notice posted in several plants: "The schedule must be met! It is our boss! We must fight to the absolute limit to ship quality products, on time. Any action is warranted to accomplish this end." Jack Stegmier, Steelcase's senior vice-president for operations, explained that meeting the schedule was "one rule. The other is, each plant manager must know every employee by his name. If you meet the schedule, you're treating the customer right. If you know your employees by name, you become aware of how important they are to your success."

Jurgen Nitzsche told us much the same thing. "One

time," he recalled, "Bob Pew [Steelcase's chairman] came into the factory and a new employee addressed him as 'Mr. Pew.' He said, 'My name is Bob.'"

If business success is a measure, these policies work. Steelcase is a spectacular success story. It began making the nation's first metal desks in 1915. It started to make file cabinets in 1919. In the late 1930s it teamed with architect Frank Lloyd Wright to build the task-oriented, rounded furnishings that went into the ultramodern Johnson Wax headquarters in Racine, Wisconsin. During World War II it did nothing but make furniture for the U.S. Navy. It pioneered by building a strong exclusive-dealer network, gaining a reputation for supporting its dealers as well as it treats its workers. Among other products, every year Steelcase turns out 1.2 million chairs, 105,000 tables, 500,000 filing cabinets, and 590,000 unit assemblies. Steelcase furniture is not avant-garde or fancy. It's functional and well made. And the company has forged to the head of its industry by listening carefully to what its customers say. It owns two corporate jets primarily to fly customers and dealers into Grand Rapids. Today, Steelcase, as trendy as the next one, styles itself not so much a furniture maker as a designer and builder of complete office systems. Another reason for its success: it was in the right place at the right time—making office furniture in the midst of an explosion in the white-collar population. But so were other companies—Globe-Wernicke, General Fireproofing, Sperry Rand—and they failed to grasp the opportunity.

The emphasis on quality and pride in workmanship extends to Steelcase's truck fleet, which comprises 97 tractors and 213 trailers. It's one of the largest truck fleets in the country—and it boasts the best safety record of any private fleet. Steelcase has such a rigorous maintenance program that some of its trucks last one million miles. Its vehicles are kept in spotless condition. New drivers are required to spend their first six months on the job doing nothing but washing trucks. Drivers have their names on door panels. In 1984, a new driver, 30-year-old Paul Rosendahl, was so impressed with the pride and spit and polish that he recorded a song, "Blue and Chrome," to salute the Steelcase trucks.

Most people have never heard of Steelcase, but it's big. In 1984, its sales went over the $1 billion mark, which would easily qualify the company for the Fortune 500. It's one of the

nation's largest privately owned enterprises. And because of
its growth, it has become an ever-increasing source of employment. In 1959, it employed 1,000 persons. By 1973, it
was employing 5,000. Today, it has 10,000 on the payroll.
And they never seem to want to leave. In 1984, the company
inducted 70 members into its 25-Year Club. That brought to
526 the number of active or retired employees with more than
25 years' service. More than one-third of the Grand Rapids
work force has been with the company for more than 10
years. As of the end of 1984, the average service of all employees was nine years, but that understates the longevity because Steelcase doubled its employment in the previous
decade. So here's a better way to look at it:

• Of the people working for Steelcase at the start of
1975, 88 percent were still with the company at the start of
1985; and

• Of the people working for Steelcase in 1970, 72 percent were still with the company in 1985.

One reason people stay around is that Steelcase hardly
ever lays off anyone. It went for 58 consecutive years—until
1970—without a production layoff. It then let 600 people go;
all were recalled after three months. Another 1,200 were laid
off in 1975—and all were recalled after six months. Nine
hundred were laid off in 1983—and they were all recalled
after five months.

Apparently, Steelcase has always been a company with
strong discipline. Walter Idema, one of the founders, was said
to have weighed himself every day—and if he was a pound
overweight, he took it off immediately. Today, the company
retains a rigidity based on rules of conduct. Hourly employees
receive a 114-page handbook that spells out meticulously the
rules and regulations they're expected to abide by. You're advised, for example, not to have friends or relatives call you
during work hours "except in case of emergency." You're advised that "you are entitled to two 10-minute break periods for
each full shift," that "you may not leave your plant's parking
area during break periods," and that "you are required to
punch out on your daily and weekly time cards for lunch
breaks when you leave the immediate plant area." Truck
drivers are not permitted to have beards or mustaches. To en-
force behavioral standards, there is a system of penalties for
conduct violations. You're assessed 10 points for an unex-

cused absence and 5 points for failing to report an absence by calling in two hours before your shift starts. Class I offenses, calling for point penalties ranging from 1 to 60, include such actions as failing to punch in, gambling, horseplay, or unauthorized use of a company telephone; Class II offenses, calling for penalties of 60 to 120 points, include such actions as careless workmanship, destruction of property, theft up to $10, or reckless driving; and Class III offenses, bringing penalties of 80 to 110 points, include such actions as being under the influence of alcohol or drugs, assaulting a supervisor, or drinking on company time. If you accumulate 60 points, that brings a verbal warning; 85 points, an infraction letter that advises you are excluded from the internal job-switch request program; 120 points, a three-day disciplinary layoff and a 5 percent reduction in pay; 140 points, a five-day layoff; 160 points: discharge.

So Steelcase is a good place to work, but it may not be for the free spirit.

Main employment centers   Grand Rapids, where 7,000 are employed. Another 1,000 are employed in a plant at Tustin, California, and 1,500 more are employed in plants located in Fletcher, North Carolina; Athens, Alabama; Grand Prairie, Texas; and Lowell, Michigan. Steelcase has two plants in Canada, where 500 are employed, and it has 50–50 ventures with companies in France, Germany, and Japan.

Headquarters   Steelcase Inc.
Post Office Box 1967
Grand Rapids, MI 49501
616-247-2710

TANDEM

TANDEM COMPUTERS INCORPORATED

TANDEM COMPUTERS INC.

Tandem Computers makes fail-safe computer systems. U.S. employees: 4,000.

▟▟▟▟ Pay	➕	**Lots of freedom, few rules.**
▟▟▟▟ Benefits		
▟▟▟▟ Job Security		
▟▟▟▟ Chance to Move Up	▟▟▟	**Hard to predict the future of this company.**
▟▟▟▟▟ Ambience		

A hallowed institution at Tandem Computers' Silicon Valley headquarters is the Friday afternoon "beer bust." All employees—from the president to assemblers—go to the patio area outside the company cafeteria near the swimming pool and tennis courts to tip a few free cans of beer and talk informally.

It's part of Tandem Computers' conscious policy of promoting communication and egalitarianism within the ranks. Tandem Computers has no reserved parking slots at company facilities, no executive dining rooms, no time clocks or badges, and no organization charts. As Becky Deanda, an accounts payable supervisor, told us: "You have to be flexible to work here. There are no policies. The benefit of the doubt is always for the employee. They trust the employee."

Credit for Tandem Computers' enlightened personnel policies goes to its founder-president, James G. Treybig, called "Jimmy" by everyone at Tandem Computers. He specifically models his company on the Japanese concept of *heiwa*, meaning a state of unity and tranquillity. "We are trying to create a condition of equality among the people here. I know, and we all know, that everything isn't equal, but there are times when we should do things which are."

The quotable Treybig, an engineer who once worked at nearby Hewlett-Packard, once said the reason the company

423

goes to such lengths is to foster a creative atmosphere: "Creativity comes from sharing ideas. An idea may be sparked by an individual, but then it must be built on and modified and improved by the group until it becomes something really significant. That's why I say the environment nurtures creativity." Treybig makes a special effort to hear new ideas (and complaints). Like other Tandem Computers executives, Treybig regularly eats in the company cafeteria with the rest of the troops and attends the Friday afternoon beer bust. And if any employee wants to meet the president, he or she can simply sign up in Treybig's appointment book. No secretary or assistant screens these requests.

Bob Marshall, Tandem Computers' senior vice-president, told us that Treybig's philosophy means a great deal to the company's engineers and programmers: "We do not penalize people for not wanting to manage. We do not restrict an engineer's salary since his contribution may be more than his manager's." Marshall contrasted Tandem Computers with his experiences several years earlier at Xerox. "An engineer there could not make more than $45,000 without getting a special dispensation."

We talked with Roland Findlay, a software programmer who previously worked with Data General and Four-Phase, among other computer firms. He appreciates Tandem Computers' unstructured environment and lack of bureaucracy: "There are only three levels between me and the president of Tandem Computers. At Four-Phase there were seven levels."

More important for Findlay is that "people stay off my back here. I don't like meetings and I don't like memos. At Tandem Computers I don't get any memos and I only go to one meeting a week, and it lasts just one hour."

Tandem Computers makes a point of saying it hires only the best. They say they like to hire people "who come into the job running." So the company usually requires job candidates —even for minor clerical positions—to be interviewed and reinterviewed three or four times over a span of weeks. Any employee who refers a successful job candidate receives a bonus of $500.

Tandem Computers makes it a point to promote from within (a rarity among Silicon Valley high-tech firms). The vast majority of middle managers moved up from nonsupervisory positions. Of the top 19 executives, 12 were promoted from within.

Founded in 1974, Tandem Computers makes fail-safe computer systems. Tandem Computers' computers link more than one central processor so that if one breaks down, another takes its place. As a consequence, the banks, manufacturing companies, and airlines that buy Tandem Computers' products don't have to worry about computer breakdowns or about losing data. An astonishing financial success, Tandem Computers has doubled its sales almost every year, with 1984 sales of more than $500 million. The work force has multiplied accordingly, with four times as many employees by the end of 1984 as in 1980.

In late 1982, however, the recession hit Tandem Computers. Faced with declining orders, the top managers decided that rather than lay off anyone, they would require everyone to take two-and-a-half days of forced, unpaid vacation in November. How the cutback was announced illustrates the company's unusual commitment to high-tech communications with the employees.

For one thing, most employees have computer terminals sitting on their desks (linked to Tandem Computers mainframe computers). For another, Tandem Computers' major facilities are linked by an elaborate teleconferencing network. At the headquarters is a full-size TV studio and a large microwave dish. So, the forced vacation and its rationale were announced the same morning in two ways. A long memo was waiting on everybody's computer terminal. Since everyone is linked together on the same computer system, people were also able to express their reactions to the cutback by writing their own memos, which could also be read by any other Tandem Computers employee. Treybig also made himself available for dialogue through the teleconferencing network. Employees have regular company-wide teleconferences once a month.

One of the golden benefits at Tandem Computers is a company-paid sabbatical of six weeks for each four years of service (in addition to regular vacations). All employees are eligible for it. All employees also qualify for stock options, making Tandem Computers one of only a handful of American corporations to offer options to everyone in the firm—managers and rank-and-file employees alike. When Tandem

Computers first sold shares to the public in 1977, all employees were given the right to buy at a future date up to 300 shares of Tandem Computers stock at the initial offering price. Every year since then, all employees have annually been given 100 share options. Employees also can devote up to 10 percent of their income to purchase company stock at 85 percent of the market price. The company picks up the other 15 percent of the price. Tandem Computers employees have taken advantage of the stock options and stock purchase plans, as they hold between 20 and 25 percent of the company's shares.

Another unusual benefit is "TOPS," or Tandem Computers Outstanding Performers. Every year the company awards free vacation trips to about 5 percent of the employees, nominated by their co-workers. Each trip is limited to 50 employees, selected to be a cross section of the work force. In 1983, for instance, TOPS trips were planned for the Mardi Gras in New Orleans, a rodeo in Calgary, and Hawaii.

Main employment centers   Cupertino; Reston, Virginia; and Austin, Texas.nother 1,200 work overseas.

Headquarters   Tandem Computers Inc.
19333 Valco Parkway
Cupertino, CA 94014
408-725-6000

TANDY CORPORATION

TANDY CORPORATION

America's largest retailer of consumer electronics. U.S. employees: 27,000.

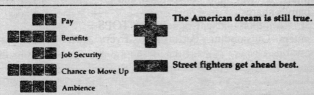

▓▓ Pay	✚ **The American dream is still true.**
▓▓▓▓ Benefits	
▓▓ Job Security	
▓▓▓ Chance to Move Up	▓▓ **Street fighters get ahead best.**
▓▓ Ambience	

Charles Tandy was a proud man. Of course, he had a lot to be proud of. He took a bankrupt chain of electronics stores in New England called Radio Shack and in less than 20 years built it into one of the biggest retailers in the world. At the time of Tandy's death in 1978, more Radio Shack stores (over 8,000) dotted the highways of the world than either McDonald's restaurants or 7-Eleven shops. The chain was selling over $1 billion a year in stereos, CB radios, and personal computers (over $2.5 billion by 1984). Indeed, there was much for any man to be proud of, but people who knew Charles Tandy say he was proudest of having made millionaires of about 60 of his employees.

David Beckerman, vice-president of advertising for Radio Shack, became a millionaire from his Tandy stock in 1971. He still remembers the day: "I went over to Charles's apartment with a bottle of Dom Perignon champagne. I told him of my good fortune. Then I said, 'For eight years I've wanted to be in a position to tell you to go———yourself. But now that I can, I have lost the desire.' We both had a big laugh and I popped open the bottle and we enjoyed the French champagne."

Not all the Tandy millionaires are high-level executives, either. They all simply believed the blustery Texan when he told them, "Stick with me and I'll make you rich." In the

427

beginning, he almost had to twist arms to get employees to invest their money in Tandy stock. Those who did have had an amazing payoff. For every $6 invested in Tandy stock in 1963, you would have had $4,200 in mid-1983.

One who believed Charles Tandy was a receiving clerk in a Radio Shack warehouse in Boston. His base pay on retirement was $5.05 an hour—about $10,500 a year. Starting in 1965, he had systematically put a small percentage of his income into the company's stock purchase program. When he retired 18 years later, he was worth $480,000. Invested prudently, the retired clerk's nest egg can draw nearly $50,000 a year for the rest of his life.

Today, an eight-foot-tall bronze statue of Charles Tandy (with a foot-long cigar between the fingers of his right hand) stands on the grounds of the Tarrant County Courthouse in downtown Fort Worth, Texas. And his spirit still dominates much of what goes on at the Tandy Center, a few blocks from the courthouse.

Tandy, for instance, insisted on answering his own phone. "There's no room for big shots around here," he used to tell his people. You can still telephone any Tandy executive, including the president. All you need to do is call the main switchboard number. If the executive is in his or her office, the call will be put straight through, without being screened first by a secretary. An occasional irate customer has been surprised to find his call connected directly to John Roach, the current Tandy president. "That's what you get for answering your own phone," Roach once explained to a reporter. "Sometimes you get someone who's not too happy. But that's what keeps you in tune with the world."

Keeping in tune means maintaining contact with "Mr. and Mrs. America," explained Beckerman. "We are not elitists. We know where our bread-and-butter is." Despite the high-tech products, the company projects a down-home image. The company headquarters is, after all, in a city that calls itself "Cow Town" and is famous for its rodeos.

The open door is another Tandy doctrine. The employee handbook puts it explicitly: "Any employee is welcome to walk through the door of any member of management to discuss business-related problems. There are no closed doors in our corporation." The policy even extends to the architecture of the Tandy Center in Fort Worth. Top executives work in offices with glass walls and doors, accentuating everyone's accessibility.

Promotion from within is another part of the Tandy tradition. One of the few exceptions to the rule was a man brought in as vice-president for administration in the mid-1970s, but he didn't fit in and lasted only a few years before being given the ax. His firing was a rarity around Tandy, though. Charles Tandy preferred to move people to jobs with less responsibility rather than get rid of them entirely.

The promote-from-within gospel is especially apparent in the company-owned Radio Shack stores. (Of the 6,563 Radio Shacks in the United States in 1983, 4,565 were company-owned, 100 were franchises, and 1,898 were dealer-owned.) Nobody becomes a Radio Shack store manager without first having spent time on the floor selling equipment. And those promoted to district manager and regional manager all come from the store manager ranks.

The company spends a lot of time teaching its salespeople about the equipment they sell, but they learn by selling on the sales floor, as Tandy believes the best way is to "learn while you earn." Because all new Radio Shack sales employees are considered potential store managers, they learn everything about running a small retail establishment, from opening the store in the morning, to ringing up sales, to putting up in-store displays, to balancing the books, to closing up at night. Everybody does every job in a Radio Shack store. There are no cashiers. It's difficult to know who is the manager.

The company considers each Radio Shack a separate "profit center." Salespeople are paid the higher of either $5 to $6 an hour or a sales commission of 6 percent. A retailing analyst told *Business Week* that as a result Tandy salespeople "tend to be more street fighters than you would find at other companies."

In company-owned stores, managers are paid a modest base salary and receive a bonus based on the profitability of the store. So, if a store's profitability increases 10 percent over the previous year, the manager gets an extra 10 percent on top of last year; if 15 percent, then he gets an extra 15 percent; and so on. The typical Radio Shack store manager makes over $50,000. In 1983, the highest-paid store manager received a $160,000 *bonus*. With other income, he made well in excess of a quarter-million dollars. On the down side, store managers themselves have to pay for store losses resulting from shoplifting and bad checks.

Bonuses are a way of life at Tandy. With each unit considered a profit center, there are more than 10,000 entities within the company preparing monthly profit-and-loss statements. Except for some hourly manufacturing, distribution, and clerical people, no two people can expect to have the same paycheck at Tandy.

In the company's early years, Charles Tandy used to deliver lectures on the virtue of owning a piece of the company whenever he delivered annual bonuses. He then would present a bonus check with one hand while holding shares of Tandy stock in the other.

The program is more sophisticated today, but the intent is the same. Under the Tandy Corporation Stock Purchase Program, all employees can put between 1 and 10 percent of their monthly income into Tandy stock. The company matches between 40 and 80 percent of the employee contribution. (For those with less than three years with the company, Tandy puts in 40 percent; between three and five years, 60 percent; over five years, 80 percent.) For example, a six-year Tandy veteran who had $100 a month deducted from his or her paycheck would have an extra $80 put in by the company. In mid-1983, with Tandy stock selling for $60 a share, that would mean the employee would have bought three shares of Tandy stock. Once a year, the company physically distributes the Tandy stock certificates purchased during the year.

A whopping 75 percent of all Tandy employees participate in this stock-purchase program. They own about 25 percent of all Tandy stock. It seems everyone at Tandy can tell you how Tandy stock is doing on Wall Street. There is a big sign, for instance, inside the door of the Radio Shack Security Department on the third floor of the Tandy Center. The sign reads, "We Own a Part of Our Company," followed by the names of about two dozen employees, the entire staff of the department. Below their names is displayed Tandy's closing price on the New York Stock Exchange the previous day.

Main employment centers   Most of the 4,000 manufacturing employees work in the Fort Worth area. Another 1,700 work at Tandy Center headquarters. There are eight distribution facilities throughout the country (900 employees), and over 6,500 Radio Shack stores, employing a total of 19,000 people. Some 1,000 work as service technicians, and 6,000 work overseas.

Headquarters   Tandy Corporation
500 One Tandy Center
Fort Worth, TX 76102
817-390-3011

COMPANY-PAID SABBATICALS

Intel
Moog

ROLM
Tandem Computer

COMMITTED TO EXCELLENCE

TEKTRONIX, INC.

Tek (nobody calls the company by its full name) makes more than 700 electronic instruments for display measurement and control, including the CRT oscilloscope, of which it is the largest producer. U.S. employees: 16,400.

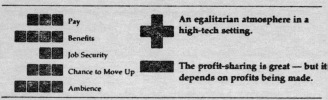

■■■ Pay	╋ An egalitarian atmosphere in a high-tech setting.
■■■■ Benefits	
■ Job Security	
■■■ Chance to Move Up	■■■ The profit-sharing is great — but it depends on profits being made.
■■■■ Ambience	

In the spring of 1983, dozens of Tek employees were shocked to read in the *Portland Oregonian* of a significant increase in the income of company president Earl Wantland. Since several hundred employees had been laid off over the previous six months, those reading the notice were outraged.

Within hours the company's area reps—local representatives of a formal communications structure within Tek—were besieged by demands for a full explanation. The task of finding an answer fell to Valerie Cullen, a junior electronics technician. She was serving a nine-month term as one of nine panel members representing the plant work force. She estimated that the panel received a dozen calls and several formal letters from area reps the day the newspaper article appeared. By the end of the first day, she had talked with Wantland himself and was able to relay his side of the story through the area representatives and the company newsletter. (His pay increase related to stock options granted five years earlier but not reported until 1983—a fact the newspaper article did not mention.)

Cullen thinks the forum provided by Tek's unique area rep program has importance beyond defusing situations that are potentially harmful to company morale. Once a month, area reps organize 40-minute educational sessions for the Tek employees they represent. These sessions familiarize employees with different aspects of the company and include tours of other Tek facilities, films and videotapes, and speeches on company research or policies by any of about 75 officials or researchers. To Cullen, the area rep activities are an extension of the company's philosophy that "everybody here is an employee. We just have different jobs."

Every year Tek's president gives a "State of the Company" address and then exposes himself to questions from the floor. And they can be zingers. Some of the ones tossed at him in 1983 were:

"Can 'pay for performance' still be considered Tek's policy for production workers with the economy the way it is now?"

"Will there be more money for merit raises?"

"How come when Wilsonville was number one and doing great, all of Tektronix profited, but now that our sales are down, only Wilsonville is told, 'Okay, no raises for you'?"

"If we can't have athletic facilities, couldn't we at least have showers and locker rooms so that those who want to can ride bikes to work or run during lunch break?"

Wantland answered all of them. We won't give all his replies, but here's what his answer was to the last question above:

"If we were to try to accommodate the interests of all the interested Tek people, we'd probably have the biggest sports complex in the state. Frankly, I've never been able to see that as a high enough priority to invest that large an amount of money on."

Despite its size (it's Oregon's largest private employer), Tek is aggressively egalitarian. There are no marked parking spaces in any of its facilities, for instance. In the corporate office, located in an ordinary-looking two-story suburban office building across the street from a big shopping center, the top officers don't even have their own offices. Spaces in the large room are marked off with four-foot-high room dividers.

Tek has worked hard over the years at keeping this informality. You won't find many companies that have issued to employees a handbook, as Tek has, that states:

"Teks started out calling one another by first names, and

never found any reason to change. So our chairman of the board is still just 'Howard' to everyone here, and no one will call you 'Ms.' or 'Mr.' or some other title either . . . and you can't always tell by looking who is the manager—most Teks, whether engineers or on the production line, dress comfortably and casually."

The company also tries to carry out this informality in its communications to shareholders. You won't find many companies issuing an annual report that opens the way the Tek 1983 report did:

"That dill-pickle look on your face says you have just read our highlights, as they are euphemistically called. They once again reflect a tough year. Our earnings took a pasting."

During the early years of Tek's life the company also stretched its egalitarian policies to include a "no cash register" cafeteria. Prices were posted, and employees were trusted to leave the correct amount. The policy was scrapped in the mid-1970s when the company brought in an outside caterer, but the spirit lives on.

Virtually anyone who has worked elsewhere notices the relaxed atmosphere at Tek. Joe Parret worked for Boeing in Seattle for 11 years before joining Tek. "At Boeing there was nothing you could do that could not get you fired. They had seven books full of rules and regulations, and if somebody wanted to can you, they only had to find the proper code. But here at Tek, the only equivalent is a small booklet. There are very few company-wide procedures here."

Parret heads manufacturing at Tek's plant in the Portland suburb of Wilsonville. There are no time clocks there. People in the manufacturing plants fill out detailed weekly time sheets, which are used more to keep tabs on production techniques than to monitor absenteeism. Like most of Tek's other facilities, it looks more like a college campus than a factory. Long, winding sidewalks connect several sprawling red brick buildings nestled among tall pine trees. Adding to the campus appearance the day we visited were several employees playing a game called Frisbee golf, in which the Frisbees are thrown at stakes arranged on the lawn in front of one of the plants.

Ray Kiger, a manufacturing technician, likes the informal atmosphere at Tek: "I worked for a company in Denver where you did not even know who owned it or anything. You just had to punch the time cards in and out every day." By contrast, he finds Tek "kind of like a high school where the teachers are out to teach you. When I came here, I didn't know that much about what I was supposed to do. But people here teach you everything."

Chuck Powell has found the same kind of learning environment at Tek: "I had fourteen different jobs since I got out of the Army. They don't treat you like a piece of equipment here. They will listen and they promote from within. They're more than willing to train you." He has taken advantage of Tek's program that reimburses employees 100 percent for job-related classes and 50 percent for other classes.

Tek encourages promotion from within by issuing a weekly newsletter that details all openings in the company, including pay scales. It goes to employees in all of Tek's plants in the Portland area. When the company's business was off between 1980 and 1983, Tek laid off nearly 800 people (out of more than 20,000) but was able to relocate another 800 also targeted for layoffs within the company itself, partly through the weekly classifieds. A number of others over age 50 took early retirement at a cost to the company of $10 million.

At the annual employee question-and-answer session in 1983, Tek broke down how many people it has in upper salary grades. In grade 24, which means salaries ranging from $40,500 to $60,890, there are 143 people; in range 26, $47,350 to $71,020, there are 25 persons; in range 28, $55,230 to $82,840, there are 10 people; in range 29, $59,650 to $89,470, five persons; and in range 30, $64,420 to $96,630, eight persons.

Tek benefits are super. The company has one of the most liberal profit-sharing plans in American industry, allocating 35 percent of its pretax earnings to be divided among employees according to a complicated formula that works out to 13.75 percent being distributed in cash (it's reflected in every other biweekly paycheck), 7.5 percent lodged in a retirement trust, and the remaining 13.75 percent distributed according to the wishes of the employee (it can be taken in cash or deferred as part of a retirement trust). The company also has a stock-purchase plan that enables Tek people to buy Tek stock at a 20 percent discount.

Profit-sharing can provide a considerable boost to salaries—as much as 20 percent—but it depends, of course, on the company's making money. Here's how the company's profit-sharing contribution has looked in recent years: 1979, $62.6 million; 1980, $63.4 million; 1981, $61.6 million; 1982, $55.2 million; 1983, $29.3 million; 1984, $45.4 million.

Main employment center   Fourteen thousand and five hundred of 16,400 U.S. employees work in the Portland area. Another 4,000 work overseas.

Headquarters   Tektronix, Inc.
P.O. Box 500
Beaverton, OR 97077
503-627-7111

TENNECO INC.

A conglomerate with interests in oil, natural gas, shipbuilding, tractors, auto parts, and agribusiness. U.S. employees: 73,000.

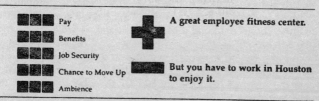

▮▮▮ Pay	✚ A great employee fitness center.
▮▮▮ Benefits	
▮▮▮ Job Security	
▮▮▮ Chance to Move Up	▮▮ But you have to work in Houston
▮▮▮ Ambience	to enjoy it.

As you walk into the Ten-Ten Garage, across the street from Tenneco's headquarters in downtown Houston, you can see a small sign reading, "Shoe Scraper. Courtesy of Tenneco Running Committee." The scraper itself gets plenty of use, as dozens of Tenneco employees regularly run a jogging course between downtown and the West Loop along the Buffalo Bayou. The company sponsors the annual Tenneco Houston Marathon.

The well-worn scraper is only a hint of the activity on the top two floors of the garage, home of the Tenneco Employee Center. An employee cafeteria, various meeting rooms, and a block-long indoor patio garden with live trees are located on the ninth floor. The floor below is devoted to the center's health and fitness facility, one of the best in corporate America. It includes four racquetball courts, exercise rooms with Nautilus equipment, an all-purpose athletic room, saunas, Jacuzzi pools, and a one-fifth-mile banked jogging track that circles the eighth floor.

About 600 Tenneco employees use the center each day, according to Mark Landgreen, Tenneco's "health and fitness manager," who oversees a staff of 11. He added that the center is visited regularly by about half of the 3,700 people

437

who work for the conglomerate in downtown Houston. Open to all employees, the center provides all the clothing needed for a good workout, including socks and athletic supporters.

Before participating in the fitness center, employees must take a complete medical test. The center has its own computer program to help employees keep track of their progress. They punch details of their daily workouts into one of five terminals and obtain a printout once a month.

When Tenneco chairman James L. Ketelsen formally opened the center in early 1982, he explained that the company spent over $11 million to build it, partly "because we're in a tight labor market in this city and we want to compete for the best people." Ketelsen added, "We have a commitment to making Tenneco a good place to work and, if we can, the best place to work."

Long before the center was constructed, Tenneco had its own country club, Tennwood, located northwest of Houston near the town of Hockley. Free to all Tenneco employees, the club features a 27-hole golf course, a swimming pool, tennis courts, an outdoor dance floor, and fishing lakes. The company opened Tennwood in the mid-1950s.

Tenneco has developed a progressive approach to Houston's nightmarish traffic. In addition to a large fleet of vans, the company covers most of the cost for monthly bus passes and subsidizes part of the parking expenses for car pools.

While some of Tenneco's oil company competitiors in Houston place a premium on paying top dollar to attract top employees, Tenneco has a different philosophy. "We pay well, but we do not believe that pay and benefits are the primary motivators," said David Knoll, corporate director of personnel. "It's more important that people have a feeling of purpose, self-accomplishment, and belonging."

Since becoming chairman in 1978, Ketelsen has devoted nearly a third of his .ime to getting Tenneco employees involved in community affairs. More than 1,500 now participate in a variety of volunteer programs ranging from work with disabled children, the retarded, and the elderly to fundraising telethons on the local educational TV channel. In 1982, Tenneco received a presidential citation for its volunteer efforts—the only private company so honored.

Knoll pointed to the numerous clubs and classes offered

to Tenneco employees that promote the sense of belonging. At the new center, for instance, the company offers classes on prenatal care and parenting because, Knoll says, "we have a holistic approach to employees." Tenneco's liberal pension plan is estimated to be 20 percent fatter than at most Fortune 500 companies, according to *Money*.

Tenneco is one of America's biggest companies, with 1984 sales of over $15 billion, but it is the youngest of the top 25 companies in the Fortune 500. Founded as a gas pipeline company in 1943, Tenneco grew by buying other companies —a gas company, a packaging company, one of the biggest landowners in California (Kern County Land Company), a couple of manufacturers (J.I. Case farm equipment, Monroe shock absorbers, Walker auto exhaust), a shipbuilder (Newport News Shipbuilding), and some life insurance companies (Philadelphia and Southwest). In all, Tenneco has more than 300 companies in its fold.

Because of its youth, the company is relatively unstructured, especially when compared with many other companies its size. David Knoll ascribed it to a kind of "Texas oil patch mentality" that pervades the company. To Knoll, "the impression at Tenneco is that the sky is the limit."

Movement among the various subsidiaries is becoming increasingly common. The chairman came from J.I. Case; the president, from Newport News Shipbuilding; and other top officers, from the pipeline and gas affiliates. The subsidiaries outside of Houston, however, do not have facilities comparable to Tennwood or the Tenneco Employee Center.

Main employment centers   Houston area (9,400); Virginia (shipbuilding, 26,700); Wisconsin (Case, Walker, and Monroe, 16,300); Illinois (packaging, 6,700); Louisiana (oil, 6,200); Bakersfield, California (agribusiness, 4,300); Dallas (life insurance, 1,600); Philadelphia (life insurance, 1,100). Of the 103,000 total employees, 30,000 work overseas.

Headquarters   Tenneco Inc.
Tenneco Building
Houston, TX 77002
713-757-2131

Time Inc.

TIME INC.

Time Inc. is the nation's largest magazine publisher, the largest company in the cable TV industry, and the second-largest book publisher. Employees: 20,000.

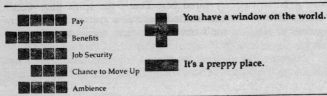

■■■■ Pay	**You have a window on the world.**
■■■■ Benefits	
■■■ Job Security	
■■ Chance to Move Up	■■ **It's a preppy place.**
■■■ Ambience	

Good pay. Super benefits. A sense that you're surrounded by a lot of bright people. A family atmosphere in a big corporate setting (if you leave, the chances are good you can come home again). These advantages—and more—are yours when you work at Time Inc.

Not that it's easy to land a job here. Applications flood into Time's Rockefeller Center headquarters at the rate of 250 to 300 a week. Satisfied employees are always recommending friends, relatives, and lovers.

Stuart Emmrich and Susan Spillman, two *Advertising Age* reporters, once characterized Time Inc. as a place "where your personal and business lives will be blended in a way that shapes friendships, romances, and living arrangements." They quoted a former Time Incer as saying: "Time Inc. is very much like college. And very much like dorm life." That's because parties are always breaking out at Time, for almost any occasion. In early 1983, there was a "block" party held when *Money* staffers moved from the twenty-ninth to the thirty-third floor of the Time & Life Building in Rockefeller Center.

Time people tend to stay with the company for life. And they get a chance to move around quite a bit. Marshall Loeb, managing editor of *Money*, used to be a business editor of *Time*. William S. Rukeyser, who's now managing editor of

Fortune, was *Money*'s first managing editor. Reginald K. Brack, Jr., former advertising sales director of *Time* and former publisher of *Discover*, is now group vice-president—books of Time Inc.

This sliding, upward and laterally, happens at many levels of the company. It's encouraged. You are supposed to look for new challenges. Janet Indelli was hired in 1982 as a secretary for Home Box Office. Formerly a teacher of handicapped children, she made it clear during her interview that she didn't want to come to Time Inc. to be a secretary for the rest of her life. They hired her. That's the spirit they want. Several HBO producers started there as secretaries. The average age at HBO, Time's newest business, seems to be around 30.

The crew is older in the magazine wing of the company. An early 1985 rundown of 14 top people in the publishing wing showed this picture of longevity:

	Age	Years at Time Inc.
J. Richard Munro, president and chief executive officer	54	28
Ralph P. Davidson, chairman	57	31
Kelso F. Sutton, executive vice-president, magazines	46	24
Henry Grunwald, corporate editor-in-chief	62	41
John A. Meyers, publisher, *Time*	56	30
James Hoefer, publisher, *Fortune*	56	29
Philip G. Howlett, senior vice-president, magazines	57	27
James Heyworth, senior vice-president, magazines	42	18
William Kelly, publisher, *Money*	55	31
S. Christopher Meigher III, publisher, *People*	38	17
Charles A. Whittingham, publisher, *Life*	55	26
James B. Hayes, publisher, *Discover*	46	26
Reginald K. Brack, Jr., group vice-president, books	47	23
Robert Miller, publisher, *Sports Illustrated*	35	11

No wonder they call it a close-knit family. Even the people who leave stay in touch, with each other anyway, through a Time-Life Alumni Society whose ranks number more than

1,200. And the company doesn't mind rehiring renegades. Thayer Bigelow, who was elected Time's treasurer in 1982, at age 41 (and who is now the company's chief financial officer), left in the early 1970s for a venture that didn't pan out. He remembers calling Time Inc. and having this conversation:

"Well, I guess I'm on the beach."

"Would you like to come back here?"

"Well, sure."

"Can you come in tomorrow morning?"

Time Inc. people are tired of defending themselves against accusations that they run a postgraduate institution for Ivy Leaguers. It is less preppy than it once was, especially outside the ranks of the magazine division, but it's difficult to mount a defense when you examine the pedigrees of the top 50 officers and editors of Time Inc. and find that 20 of them graduated from a certifiable Ivy League school while another 10 hold degrees from such private institutions as Haverford, Trinity, Union, Wesleyan, Davidson, Colgate, and Stanford. Of the top 50 people, only six went to a state-supported college. It's this insularity that prompted former *Time* writer John Tirman to depict the place as follows in a 1981 article in *The Progressive*:

"These corporate executives, largely white, male, Ivy League and suburban, have a view of the world that is informed by a relatively simple faith in corporate management, military power and a fuzzy cultural pluralism. *Time*'s peculiar system of group journalism helps fix and perpetuate those attitudes, for the editors and writers need never leave the Time & Life Bldg.; they draw their understanding of the world from *Time* files, *People* portraits, and *Fortune* commentary."

Time Inc. people bristle at this kind of characterization, charging that it amounts to a "Remembrance of Things Past" —and there's some justice in this reaction. With its acquisitions of such companies as American Television & Communications and Book-of-the-Month Club, Time Inc. is no longer a monolithic culture. Only one-quarter of Time's 20,000 employees work in the magazine group. More than half now work in the video end, where the style differs markedly from publishing. "Home Box Office," a Time spokesperson told us, "is a version of a macho culture, characterized by deal-making, high-risk and quick feedback."

Inside the old cocoon, however, it's certainly cozy. Few companies can match the benefits Time Inc. people receive. Not every single employee is blessed with exactly the same benefits because some of the acquired companies (ATC and BMOC, for examples) retained benefit programs they had in place. But in general Time Inc. tries to make benefits applicable across the entire company. Here's a sampling.

• If you work past 8:00 P.M. in New York, you not only get $10 toward dinner but also the right to take a cab all the way home (even if home is New Jersey).

• You get free copies of all Time Inc. magazines.

• You and all the members of your immediate family are covered by a comprehensive medical and dental plan—and the company picks up the *entire* premium.

• Free physical exams after five years of service.

• The profit-sharing plan consistently deposits into your account 10 percent of your annual compensation, including bonuses. Your account is fully vested from the start, meaning that if you leave at any time, you take everything with you. (Most companies have it vest over a period of years—10 is typical—to induce employees not to leave.)

• The pension plan is supported entirely by the company.

• You can kick in from 3 to 10 percent of your salary to buy Time Inc. stock. Up to the 6 percent level, Time Inc. will match your $1 with 50 cents of its own.

• Parental leave of up to one year—for fathers or mothers (your job is guaranteed).

• All you have to do is flash your Time Inc. identity card and you gain free admission to the major museums in New York City.

• If you want to continue your education, and it's job-related, Time Inc. will pick up 100 percent of the tuition. If it's not job-related, the company will cover 75 percent of the tuition, provided the school is an accredited institution (so you can take dance courses at New York University). And the company will pick up 50 percent of the tab for membership in an athletic club, provided the club has a cardiovascular fitness program.

• A sabbatical after 15 years—half salary for at least three months and up to six months.

• You can get psychiatric care under a plan that has you

pay a deductible equivalent to 1 percent of your salary, after which the company will cover 60 percent of the cost up to a maximum of $7,000 a year.

To maintain all these benefits costs Time Inc. more than $60 million a year.

Time Inc. has made a determined effort to expand opportunities for women and minorities. As evidence of this determination, the company's affirmative action department publishes a quarterly newsletter, *Equal Time*. Twenty-two percent of Time's employees are now minority-group members—and 12.5 percent hold what are described as "management positions." The company has established annual Andrew Heiskell Awards to recognize employees who "make exceptional contributions to the advancement of equal opportunity." Women make up 52 percent of the Time Inc. staff, and they too have been moving into positions heretofore regarded as all-male preserves.

Time Inc. properties have usually been so successful that employees have not had to worry about layoffs. But in 1983, the company experienced its first magazine flop when *TV-Cable Week* was folded less than six months after it was launched. Within several weeks, 153 of the 248 employees had been relocated to other jobs in the company. An outplacement center helped 30 others find jobs elsewhere.

Time Inc. people talk a lot about the "quality of life" inside the company. It's something they are proud of. There are no written codes that sum it all up. You learn it by osmosis. Dick Munro, who became head of the company in 1980, embodies it. He's an informal, shirtsleeves kind of guy. In an in-house interview in 1983, he expressed the corporate philosophy: "You can talk about balance sheets, margins, and return on equity, but what really drives this company is the caliber of its people. There's an environment, a culture here, that separates us from a lot of other buildings on Sixth Avenue or wherever. So while we are trying to accomplish all the things we have set out to do, the main thing we don't want to lose sight of is caring for the people who work here. If there's one thing above everything else I've wanted to ensure, it's that this is still a company where people really want to come to work every morning."

Of course not everyone looks kindly on this culture,

especially in view of the *TV-Cable Week* failure. Flops always bring the critics to the surface. A postmortem by the *Wall Street Journal* in late 1983 quoted an unnamed Time Inc. executive as saying that the company will now have to get rid of its "traditional country-club culture." In a letter to employees, Munro responded: "I'd like to nail that one for the foolishness it is. Obviously Time Inc. could not have flourished so dramatically if it had been a country club. That's only an easy epithet for people who don't really understand us or grasp what sets us apart." And in the same letter, Munro took a stab at defining the "special character" of the company, to wit: "Call it style, compassion, magic, civility, excitement, whatever. Call it something as simple as treating people with decency and respect."

Main employment centers   Time's employment breaks down like this: video, 8,830; magazines, 4,540; books, 2,365; corporate and other, 2,880; and international, 2,400. Some 3,500 Time Incers work in the Time & Life Building in New York's Rockefeller Center. Home Box Office is based nearby at 1100 Avenue of the Americas. American Television & Communications is based in Denver and has 460 cable TV franchises in 31 states.

Headquarters   Time Inc.
Time & Life Building
Rockefeller Center
New York, NY 10020
212-586-1212

Viking
FREIGHT SYSTEM

VIKING FREIGHT SYSTEM, INC.

Viking is the largest carrier of freight by truck between points
in California. It also serves five surrounding states. U.S. employees: 2,200.

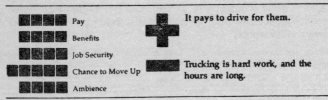

▮▮▮▮ Pay		
▮▮▮▮ Benefits	✚	It pays to drive for them.
▮▮▮ Job Security		
▮▮▮▮▮ Chance to Move Up	▬	Trucking is hard work, and the hours are long.
▮▮▮▮ Ambience		

"Most people spend approximately one-third of their
adult life working. Viking was founded on the idea that anything to which a person dedicates that much of his life should
be enjoyed."

That's the first thing new employees read in this trucking
company's handbook. They soon find out that Viking tries to
make the workplace pleasant, if not also enjoyable. Viking's
trucks are equipped with AM/FM radios and cassette decks—
something few other truckers provide. And, in contrast to the
typically spartan quarters of most trucking terminals, Viking's
off-duty rooms have pool tables, video games, and color TVs
with video cassette recorders.

Viking has grown rapidly since Dick Bangham left his
job at Memorex in 1966 and started making deliveries for the
telephone company in a four-year-old Chevy pickup. By the
late 1960s, Bangham's firm had generated enough business
customers to buy a tractor trailer for daily runs between the
San Francisco Bay Area and Los Angeles. During the 1970s
Viking's revenues increased at a head-spinning rate of 70 percent a year to over $100 million in 1984. In 1982 Viking
made its first expansion outside the state; by the end of 1984 it
was servicing Nevada, Arizona, Oregon, Washington, and
Idaho.

Bangham had been at Memorex in its early days. He knew that a small, new company that is fun to work for can change drastically with success. He told us, "They started bringing in new managers from the outside and stopped having monthly meetings of the staff. It lost a very close family atmosphere it had when it began."

To a remarkable degree Bangham appears to have retained the small company/family feeling at Viking. Once a month, he or one of the corporate officers goes to each of the system's 30 terminals to hold meetings with employees. After a management presentation, the floor is open to questions. "Almost anything is asked, from a driver complaining about a faulty heater on a truck to someone having a problem with collecting health insurance benefits," Bangham said.

Officers also pass out bonus checks at the monthly meetings. A form of profit-sharing, the bonus is calculated on the previous month's financial results. If the operating expenses are lower than the goal, employees divide three-quarters of the savings among themselves. The bonus checks can range anywhere from $15 to $200 a month, but they are not distributed when the goals are not met.

At one monthly meeting, an employee suggested a bonus for attendance and punctuality. The company took him up on it. Bonuses are now awarded every six months to anyone who was not absent or late more than three times and who was not involved in a preventable accident. This bonus can be significant: 30 cents an hour for dockworkers, 40 cents an hour for drivers, or between $400 and $500 per employee.

Such programs have helped keep Viking nonunion. Viking is, in fact, one of only three large trucking companies in the United States without a Teamster contract. (The other two are Central Freight Lines of Waco, Texas, and Overnite Transport of Richmond, Virginia.) Viking's base wage scale is slightly below the national Teamster master contract but roughly equivalent to local Teamster agreements in California. Company officials estimate that Viking drivers make between $35,000 and $45,000 a year, while the dockworkers earn from $19,000 to $29,000. Two Viking drivers have Ph.D. degrees, preferring to stay behind the wheel because it's so lucrative.

Bangham also pointed out that unlike most other trucking firms Viking has never laid off anyone. Employees have told managers they would rather cut back their hours during slack times than see anyone taken off the payroll.

This egalitarianism is reflected in the way people are promoted. With only two exceptions, Viking's principal officers started on the docks, loading freight, as did all terminal and operations managers. Even people with years of experience as over-the-road drivers must begin on the docks. After 30 days there, they can apply for work as drivers. The company has all trainees go through a two-week program at the Santa Clara headquarters. Managers are normally selected from the drivers; they, too, must go through a formal training course.

The company also sponsors a one-day orientation program for all employees after their first month on the job. Viking flies those working outside the San Francisco area to Santa Clara in one of the company's three small airplanes. Viking is headquartered about a mile from the San Jose airport, surrounded by dozens of newly built Silicon Valley plants. During the course of the orientation day, each new employee group spends about an hour with the president or one of the other top officers. Bangham thinks such sessions are important: "I don't like to cross the dock and have people turn their backs on me because they're afraid of me."

Turnover is high during the first year—between 19 and 25 percent, according to Terry Stambaugh, vice-president of industrial relations. The company hires mostly young people for whom Viking is their first or second job. They are often not prepared for the long hours and heavy physical labor involved in trucking. But after the first year, the turnover drops dramatically, to between 3 and 5 percent.

Viking encourages socializing among employees. Each spring the company tries to get Vikings to participate in truck roadeos. Instead of riding Brahma bulls, drivers vie in events like Off-Set Alley and the Serpentine (maneuvering a tractor trailer through a barrel course). Viking sets up a motor home at the regional and state roadeo competitions and offers huge barbecues to its drivers and their guests. In addition, the company gives special awards to drivers who win. Those who place first, second, or third in the regional roadeos get an all-expenses-paid weekend trip for two to Las Vegas or Lake Tahoe. Those who win at the state finals get a free trip for two to Hawaii; national roadeo winners get either $9,000 or a new Ford car of their choice.

The trophy case at the headquarters has more than 50 large roadeo trophies won by Viking drivers in the past few years. None has yet won a national roadeo event, but in 1982, Alan Lanier, from San Luis Obispo, came in third in the twin-trailer competition. The company gave him and his wife all-expenses-paid trips to Las Vegas and Hawaii—and $5,000 in cash.

Main employment centers   Santa Clara, Sacramento, and Los Angeles, California.

Headquarters   Viking Freight System, Inc.
3405 Victor Street
Santa Clara, CA 95050
408-988-6111

COMPANIES WITH EMPLOYEE VEGETABLE GARDENS

 **Control Data**
Reader's Digest

WAL-MART

WAL-MART STORES, INC.

Wal-Mart operates the nation's second-largest discount store chain. Employees: 85,000.

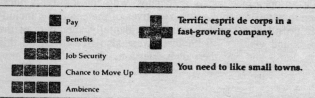

■ Pay		✚ Terrific esprit de corps in a fast-growing company.
■■■ Benefits		
■■ Job Security		
■■■■ Chance to Move Up		■■ You need to like small towns.
■■■ Ambience		

You might think you were at a revival meeting. It takes place in a gymnasium of Bentonville High School in Bentonville, Arkansas. Jammed into the place, sitting on folding chairs and bleachers, is an overflow crowd of 1,400 people who spend a good part of their time cheering and clapping. Facing the audience is a stage where some two dozen people are seated. Hosting the occasion is a balding, white-haired man, dressed in gray slacks and a blazer, who stops once in a while to shout greetings to friends of his in the audience. He introduces several people who make presentations to the group. One of them is Lou Holtz, head football coach at the University of Arkansas. On the wall, behind the people seated on the stage, hangs an enormous American flag. The front of the stage is draped with red-and-white bunting. Welcome to the annual shareholders meeting of Wal-Mart Stores.

There's probably not a corporate annual meeting to match it. The genial host—in effect, the head cheerleader—is Sam Walton, who founded this company in 1962 when he opened a Wal-Mart Discount City store in Rogers, Arkansas. It took 13 years for the company to build up the chain to 100 stores. Now it's opening 100 new stores a year.

Contributing to the overflow crowd at the 1983 annual meeting was a strong contingent of Wal-Mart people from the stores and divisions in 13 states. These people are called, in

J. C. Penney style, "associates" (Sam Walton began his retailing career as a management trainee at Penney's). In attendance were some 375 Wal-Mart associates. Some were there by virtue of being Regional All-Stars or top-performing department managers. Others were elected by their fellow associates to represent them.

The meeting began at 10:00 A.M. and ran for two hours. That was the business part. Associates and out-of-town guests were invited to a picnic lunch at the home of Sam Walton and his wife, Helen. It was a crowd of 800. In the afternoon there was an open meeting for associates, who could put any question they wished to the top executives of the company, including president Jack Shewmaker. Incidentally, members of the press and visiting stockholders were also free to attend this meeting—and ask their own questions. If Wal-Mart is anything, it's "open."

In the evening there was a company barbecue at scenic Blowing Springs Park in Bella Vista. Country-and-western recording stars Shelly West and David Frizzell performed, as did the Crystal Creek Band, composed of associates from the Wal-Mart warehouse at Searcy, Arkansas.

It didn't end there. The next morning, beginning at 7:30 A.M., there was what's called a "typical Saturday Morning management meeting" at the General Office building in Bentonville, where Wal-Mart is headquartered. Present for this meeting was the junior U.S. Senator from Arkansas, David Pryor (also a former governor of Arkansas). The out-of-town guests could then sign up for various recreational pursuits, including tennis, golf, fishing, or (what many chose) a canoe float down the Big Sugar Creek in Missouri.

The next day everyone went home.

This would be unusual behavior at other corporations. At Wal-Mart it goes on all the time. A rah-rah spirit has propelled the company into the fastest-growing store operation in the nation. And it's not small anymore. With sales of $4 billion in 1983, it ranked second only to K mart in the discount store field. It had 85,000 associates working in 745 stores at the end of 1984.

Wal-Mart pursued a unique marketing strategy as it fanned out from its first store in Rogers, Arkansas. It decided, first of all, that it would open only in towns with populations under 50,000. And it expanded methodically by moving into contiguous areas, town by town, state by state. When its discount operations came to dominate a market area, it moved to the adjoining territory. By the end of 1984, Wal-Mart had penetrated only 20 states—as far south as Florida and Texas, as far north as Illinois and Indiana, as far east as North and South Carolina, and as far west as New Mexico. The company uses its own trucks to distribute to stores.

The Wal-Mart concept is not unique. It sells nationally advertised, well-known brand-name merchandise at low prices. It honors all bank credit cards. It cheerfully gives refunds or credits or rain checks. What gives it special character is the way it has been able to involve associates in the company. They are more than just hired hands. The company doesn't pay extraordinary wages, nor are all its fringe benefits exemplary. For example, you get only one week's vacation after a year and you have to work 10 years before you're eligible for a three-week vacation. Your life insurance coverage starts at $5,000 and goes to $10,000 in the third year. At Christmas, part-time associates receive a $5 bonus; full-timers get $10, plus $5 for each additional year they've worked there, "providing the total bonus does not exceed one week's gross pay."

But Wal-Mart people are definitely roped into the affairs of the company by terrific profit-sharing and stock-purchase programs. The employee profit-sharing trust, one of the largest owners of Wal-Mart stock, has increased from $4.4 million in 1977 to $158.3 million in 1984. For 1984, the company's contribution to each associate's account represented 8.4 percent of his or her earnings for the year; if you were making $12,000 a year, the company credited your account with $1,008.

That may not seem to be such a terrific deal, unless you keep in mind the fact that the value of your account is tied closely to the performance of Wal-Mart stock, which has been a shooting star. Traded on the New York Stock Exchange, its price multiplied 20 times since 1977. Lucky indeed have been the Wal-Mart associates who have participated in the stock-purchase program. Nearly half the associates are buying stock through payroll deductions as low as $5 a paycheck. The company contributes to this stock-purchase program 15 percent of what you do. The luckiest Wal-Mart associate-stockholder is, of course, Sam Walton. *Forbes* ranked Walton as the second-richest man in America, worth $2.15 billion in late 1983.

Wal-Mart does everything it can to make its people feel part of a family. It hires locally, trains its people, encourages them to ask questions, and gives them stroke after stroke. Sam Walton seems to spend a good part of the year visiting stores. He's a very visible leader. He's the kind of person who likes to ride the highways in a Wal-Mart truck, talking to the driver. There are awards programs on top of awards programs. Here are some of them: Regional All-Star Teams, Special Divisions' All-Star Departmental Honor Roll, V.P.I. (Volume Producing Item) Contest, Department Sales Honor Roll, Shrinkage Incentive Program. Award winners have their names and pictures run in the company newspaper, *Wal-Mart World*, which reads a little like a high school sheet. One recent issue told how store 73 in Sapulpa, Oklahoma, was challenging all other Wal-Mart stores to beat the record its receiving crew set. They unloaded 842 pieces of freight in 17 minutes! The receiving crew worked in teams of four. Each team had one person on the truck, one person advancing the freight down the roller, and two unloading. The previous Wal-Mart record was set by store 359 in Fayetteville, Arkansas, which unloaded 1,356 pieces in 30 minutes, using 11 people. Yes, it is that kind of company. Enthusiasm is its middle name.

You get the flavor of the company from this recent message penned by founder Sam Walton to the troops:

"I'm continually amazed at your enthusiasm, the innovative ideas and promotions I see popping up throughout our Company. It's a disease, and usually it can be described as Wal-Mart Fever, and it does seem to be contagious. . . .

"On this trip, I've been to our Union, Missouri, store—what a great story our wonderful associates at Union have written—after the disastrous flood, completely resurrected after only 57 days! And then on to Washington, Eureka, and Pacific, Missouri. Then this morning I started at Pittsfield, Illinois, my first visit to that fine new store; and on to our 30,000 ft. stores in Louisiana, Missouri, as well as to Mexico, Missouri. I've just left our newly expanded and renovated store at Warrensburg, Missouri. All eight stores are really looking good. . . .

"I'm through the bird-hunting season. I've had a great

year. My two young setters, Buck and John, have done exceptionally well. Sue and Belle are really outstanding dogs also. . . .

"Thanks for 1982 and everything you're all doing to keep our Wal-Mart Company #1 and that Profit Sharing good for us all.

"Your friend, Sam Walton."

Main employment centers   Wal-Mart Stores are in 20 states in the South and Midwest, with the most in Texas (142), Missouri (82), Arkansas (70), Oklahoma (70), Tennessee (66), and Alabama (47).

Headquarters   Wal-Mart Stores, Inc.
P.O. Box 116
Bentonville, AR 72716
501-273-4000

VACATION SPOTS FOR EMPLOYEES

Hewlett-Packard
Johnson Wax
Springs Mills
Steelcase

WESTIN HOTELS

WESTIN HOTELS

Westin operates 52 upscale hotels in 10 countries, Employees: 28,000.

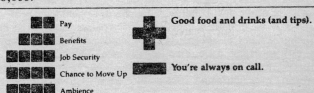

■■ Pay	✚ Good food and drinks (and tips).
■■■ Benefits	
■■■■ Job Security	
■■■■ Chance to Move Up	▬▬ You're always on call.
■■■■ Ambience	

There's a joke told at United Airlines. Two pilots are talking in the cockpit, and one says, "How do you get to be president of United Airlines?" The other answers, "Go to Cornell's hotel school." Since 1970, the route to the top of the nation's largest airline has been through its hotel subsidiary. Eddie Carlson, who began his career in the hotel business as a bellhop, was named head of United in 1970 shortly after he had negotiated the sale of Western International, as the hotel chain was then known, to United. And he brought with him to United another hotel man, Dick Ferris, then only 38 years old. Ferris became president of United in 1975. Ferris went to the hotel management school at Cornell, probably the most prestigious hotel training ground in the country.

Technically, Westin Hotels and United Airlines are both subsidiaries of a holding company, UAL Inc.—but they are, for the most part, quite separate. They are even headquartered separately—Westin in Seattle, United in Chicago. So, despite the dramatic moves by Carlson and Ferris, there's not much traffic between the two. However, there's a lot of movement within Westin, from one hotel to another, especially if you are on a management track. While Westin tries to maintain the individual character of its hotels—the Century Plaza in Los

455

Angeles, the St. Francis in San Francisco, and the Plaza in New York are all Westin entities—it grows its own professional managers who would be at home at any of them. Here, for example, were some of the 1983–84 moves:

• Christine Scala, controller at the Bellevue Stratford in Philadelphia, moved to corporate headquarters in Seattle as director of financial planning.

• Steve Caruana, sous-chef at the Westin Galleria in Houston, took the same post at the Westin in Chicago.

• When Westin opened a new 500-room hotel in Ottawa, 37-year-old Timothy Whitehead headed the staff as general manager. Whitehead joined Westin in 1972 as front office manager of the new Hotel Scandinavia in Copenhagen.

• Jeff Durham, who was senior assistant manager at the Shangri-La in Hong Kong, became senior assistant manager at the Westin Hotel in Detroit's Renaissance Center.

• Gloria Roberts, director of housekeeping at the Detroit Westin, took the same post at the Westin Crown Center in Kansas City.

• Gary Cope, reservations manager at the Westin Peachtree Plaza in Atlanta, transferred to Los Angeles as reservations manager for the Westin Bonaventure.

Westin is recognized as a hotel chain that runs a good show; namely, it has high standards—for all its establishments. It therefore often serves involuntarily as a training ground for other hoteliers. Pat Foley, president of Hyatt, Bill Hulett, president of Stouffer's, and Mike Lambert, executive vice-president of Four Seasons, all came out of Westin.

The hotel business is labor-intensive. Westin has roughly one employee for each room; 10 percent of the staff is management. The wage rates are not high, although Westin tries to pay 10 percent more than the competition. Even graduates of hotel schools—and Westin hires 60 to 100 of these every year—will earn only about $16,000 in their first assignment. Most of Westin's U.S. employees are represented by labor unions. At the St. Francis in San Francisco, for example, Westin negotiates with 9 different unions.

Westin has career-development programs to prepare people for both entry-level and upper-level positions. There are 12 entry-level programs in such areas as rooms, food and beverage, personnel, accounting, and marketing. These programs run 9 to 15 months and provide a general orientation as well as hands-on experience. A management-development program in place at the Westin in Seattle runs for a year and exposes the trainee to all areas of the hotel operation. Every employee is eligible to apply for these programs. A trainee is expected to have completed two to four years of college, with the proviso that "significant experience" can substitute for it. Among the other qualifications are willingness "to relocate and to work evenings, nights, and weekends." The hotel business is like that. The store never closes.

It may change in the future, but Westin traditionally has been a place where you did not need a college degree to climb to the top. Eddie Carlson never graduated from college, nor did Harry Mullikin, who became president in 1973 and chairman and chief executive officer in 1981; he started his career as an elevator operator at the Cascadian Hotel in Wenatchee, Washington.

To motivate its people, Westin has employee recognition awards of all kinds. There's the Carlson-Himmelman Award, presented annually for outstanding management achievements. Recipients get a trip around the world. There's the Thurston-Dupar Inspirational Award for employees who have not only excelled in their jobs but made important contributions in community service. Each hotel gives a Thurston-Dupar Award—and then a company-wide winner is selected. The corporate winner receives a two-week, expense-paid vacation for two at a Westin hotel, and $1,000 in cash plus airfare and expenses to attend the announcement ceremonies at the annual management conference. Trying to maintain fine restaurants in its hotels, Westin runs a three-year apprentice program for would-be chefs. Between 1974 and 1984, the program graduated 109 chefs. And then the Westin Hotel Academy of Master Chefs inducts into its ranks those Master Chefs who have worked at a Westin Hotel for at least five years.

To make up for the low wages, Westin employees do have access to perks that normally go with hotel service. There are, of course, tips for people who work in the food and beverage area. For most of the employees, there is also the opportunity to have free meals while at work. Free rooms are also available to you after one year's service. For example, if you have worked for Westin for 10 years, you and your immediate family can stay for 15 nights at Westin hotels during the year—free of charge. And you also get 20 percent off the cost of your meals. Any employee can always get 50 percent off any hotel room rate.

You cannot get discounts on travel with the sister company, United Airlines. And there's no profit-sharing program. However, for people ready to work hard, often at impossible hours, Westin offers career opportunities that can lead to your seeing a good part of the world. And many seem to like it. Of the 1,200 people employed at Westin's St. Francis Hotel in San Francisco, 700 have been with the hotel for more than 5 years, and overall, over 600 people have worked at Westin for more than 25 years. Every hotel holds an annual banquet honoring employees with more than 5 years' service.

Main employment centers   Westin has hotels in 21 U.S. cities. The four largest (by employee size) are: the Plaza in New York (1,300); the St. Francis in San Francisco (1,200); the Westin Bonaventure in Los Angeles (1,180); and the Westin in Detroit's Renaissance Center (1,080). Three hundred people work at Seattle headquarters.

Headquarters   Westin Hotels
The Westin Building
Seattle, WA 98121
206-447-5000

Weyerhaeuser

WEYERHAEUSER COMPANY

Weyerhaeuser owns 5.9 million acres of timberlands, and ranks as the nation's largest lumber producer and one of the biggest home builders. Employees: 40,000.

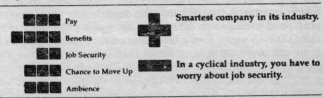

Pay	**+** Smartest company in its industry.
Benefits	
Job Security	
Chance to Move Up	In a cyclical industry, you have to worry about job security.
Ambience	

This is the class act in the timber industry. If you wanted to work in wood products, which can range anywhere from planting and taking care of trees to cutting them down and then processing them into salable products of all kinds (logs, lumber, plywood, shipping cartons, newsprint, disposable diapers), then Weyerhaeuser would have to be the company to look at first. It's one of the biggest, fattest cats in its industry but has a well-developed sense of responsibility to go with that size, so much so that an *Audubon* magazine article on the company was once titled "Best of the S.O.B.'s."

Weyerhaeuser stands out in an industry characterized by sluggish, slow-witted managers. With all those trees, they didn't have to be quick; they just cut them down. By contrast, Weyerhaeuser has usually taken a long-term approach to the resources under its control; and although it retains many of the vestiges of a family-owned enterprise, it deliberately seeks out—and usually finds—smart people to run the business.

Not just smart, but humane. You can sense the warmth, friendliness, and intelligence of the Weyerhaeuser managers by wandering around the company's beautiful headquarters facility, nestled in a glen midway between Tacoma and the Seattle-Tacoma airport. It's a breathtaking, five-story structure that overlooks a 10-acre lake and has a wonderful feeling of openness; there are virtually no doors in the place; there's a profusion of plants and wood (even the elevators have planked floors). Some 750 people work in this facility—lawyers, financial types, communications people, personnel experts, market analysts, long-range planners. They come from all over the country—Yale, Princeton, Iowa State, and the University of Nebraska are all represented at corporate headquarters.

One of the open-partitioned offices was occupied until recently by William Ruckelshaus, the first administrator of the Environmental Protection Agency. He became acting attorney general in the Nixon administration but lost his post after he refused to fire the special Watergate prosecutor, Archibald Cox. Weyerhaeuser hired Ruckelshaus in 1976 to head legal and corporate affairs. It's a mark of the respect Weyerhaeuser commands that when the Reagan administration rehired Ruckelshaus to head EPA in 1983, his nomination sailed through the Senate with nary a single naysayer. Ruckelshaus returned to Weyerhaeuser in 1985.

Of course, only a tiny percentage of Weyerhaeuser's employees get to work at corporate headquarters. Most work in mill towns near the extensive forestlands owned by the company. Some work in the forests themselves. (Outside of the U.S. Park Service, Weyerhaeuser is the biggest employer of foresters—it has more than 700.) Weyerhaeuser owns nearly six million acres of commercial forestland—about half of it in the Pacific Northwest (Washington and Oregon) where the company was born, the other half in the South. It's the only company in the industry that harvests enough wood to feed its own mills entirely; it doesn't have to buy any wood from outsiders.

Mill workers are a special breed, and Weyerhaeuser has tried to instill a special company pride in its operations, even though well over half of its employees are represented by unions. In many towns, Weyerhaeuser is the largest employer. Chuck Cooley, a supervisor at Weyerhaeuser's log mill in Cottage Grove, Oregon (population: 7,100), says, "We've got a damned fine crew here. We're just like family." Howard Beer, a bearded, wide-girthed, overalled man who looks like the prototype of a lumberjack, operates a bull edger machine at one of the Cottage Grove mills. As of early 1983, he had missed only one day in 27 years at the mill where his father, three brothers, four brothers-in-law, and three sons have all worked. At Marshfield, Wisconsin, where Weyerhaeuser makes doors, there are 47 husband-and-wife teams among the 960 workers, plus several third- and fourth-generation employees. When the pulp mill at Cosmopolis, Washington, celebrated its twenty-fifth birthday in 1982, on hand—as honored guests—were 71 employees who had been working when the plant opened in March 1957.

The tough aspect of working in the timber industry is that it's cyclical and relies on the housing industry (which is in turn highly dependent on low interest rates) and on the economy as a whole (when plants are not turning out products, they don't need shipping containers). The depression in the lumber and plywood industries forced two plant closings in 1984 (Livingston, Alabama, and Murfreesboro, Arkansas). Two other mills—Lewiston, North Carolina, and Beaumont, Mississippi—were sold. In the 1981–83 crunch, Weyerhaeuser had a rough time, although it fared better than most of its competitors. It did, over those two years, reduce its salaried force by 20 percent, which means 2,000 people left the company. They were mostly managers in the $25,000-to-$50,000-a-year range. The company felt it had become "overmanaged." Weyerhaeuser tried to help those who left. It kept them on the payroll for five months—and on top of that, it gave severance pay of a week's salary for each year of service. In addition, it set up 15 outplacement centers to help employees find new jobs. These were highly successful efforts (75 percent of the employees who went through the centers found new jobs). The cost of terminating those 2,000 was $63 million. But it saved Weyerhaeuser $150 million in annual overhead costs.

The benefits at Weyerhaeuser are good. The company pays the entire medical insurance premium for employees and all dependents. You can put between 1 and 10 percent of your annual pay into an investment growth plan—and for every dollar you contribute up to the 5 percent level, the company will add 70 cents, and it will then kick in 50 cents on every dollar up to the 10 percent level. Every year Weyerhaeuser buys stock for its employees. This costs the employee nothing. The allocation is based on a percentage of pay. In recent years, it has amounted to about 1.4 percent of pay. In other words, if you were making $25,000, the company would have bought you $350 worth of Weyerhaeuser stock, not such a great investment in recent years, but who knows what will happen in the future? You can cash in your shares after holding them for eight years.

Main employment centers   Of Weyerhaeuser's 40,000 employees, some 16,000 work in the states of Washington and Oregon, where the company's name is well known. In Washington, there are big plants at Everett and Longview. In Oregon, there are major facilities at North Bend, Springfield, and Klamath Falls. Weyerhaeuser plants are scattered through Arkansas (Dierks, Pine Bluff), Oklahoma (Craig, Valliant), Mississippi (Columbus), Alabama (Millport), and North Carolina (Plymouth, New Bern, Jacksonville). Weyerhaeuser operates in 44 states and 16 foreign countries.

Headquarters   Weyerhaeuser Company
Tacoma, WA 98477
206-924-2345

WORTHINGTON INDUSTRIES, INC.

Worthington processes steel for a variety of industrial uses and makes plastic products, undercarriages for subway cars, pipe fittings, and pressure cylinders (such as those used for barbecue grills). U.S. employees: 5,400.

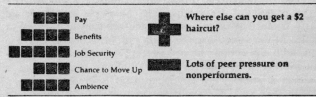

Worthington does not provide coffee breaks for its steel workers. Instead, free coffee is available at all times. The company assumes its employees are "team members" who can be trusted to decide for themselves when breaks are appropriate.

Worthington tries to make its people feel part of the team in a variety of ways. For one thing, workers have a hand in determining who will be on the team. Here's how it works. Most Worthington plants have an employee council composed of nonsupervisory workers. They are appointed to serve two-year terms. The plant manager chairs council meetings, and any topic can be discussed, including grievances against specific supervisors. One of the council's primary tasks is to vote on whether to accept a new employee into the profit-sharing and salary plan after he or she has worked at least three months. No one can achieve permanent status in the plant without a majority vote from his or her peers on the council. The company feels that an employee's peers are in the best position to say who should belong on the team.

Being part of the profit-sharing plan means more than just becoming a team member. Every three months, employees receive a check based on Worthington's profits for that quarter. The company sets aside 17 percent of its pretax profits to be divided among the employees. There are separate profit pools for production workers, administrators, truck drivers, and salespeople. Each person's share is determined by his or her base salary. (Production plant employees are on salary rather than hourly, and there are no time clocks.)

For production workers, the quarterly profit-sharing checks are a significant part of their annual income, accounting for as much as 45 percent of it. Managers typically depend even more on these incentives; nearly 60 percent of their annual compensation is derived from bonus payments.

The plan seems to work, as Worthington's productivity record is nothing if not admirable. Sales per employee are nearly triple that of the metal manufacturing industry as a whole. At the same time, the quality of Worthington's steel is high, with a rejection rate of 1 percent—far below the 4 percent average in the industry. The employee turnover rate is less than 2 percent, and absenteeism (at 2 percent) is among the lowest of all U.S. manufacturing concerns. Worthington's stockholders have benefited, too. Someone who had plunked down $7,500 to buy 1,000 shares of Worthington stock in 1968 would have shares worth $400,000 by late 1984.

Dean Saunders worked on the production line of an air-conditioning firm before being hired at Worthington's cylinder plant in Columbus, Ohio. "When I came here, I was hired at six dollars an hour, though I was making about ten dollars an hour at my previous job," Saunders told us. "But in the course of a year, I make more here at Worthington than I did there because of the profit-sharing."

More money was the least of the changes for Saunders: "When I first came to cylinder, I had to make a big adjustment. These guys work hard. They really hit it. Where I came from, we did not do 60 percent of what they do here. The air-conditioning work was a union job. When the company pushed us, the workers did less work. They would rebel and not work as hard. There was just a lot of deadwood around. You could not get fired."

Deadwood is not tolerated at Worthington, but Saunders and other Worthington employees consider their job security to be better than that at unionized plants. There is a saying at Worthington that the Eleventh Commandment is "Thou Shalt

Not Lay Off People." Like other companies in the steel industry, Worthington has faced sharp downturns in its business, but it has avoided layoffs by shifting people to other parts of the company. At times production workers can find themselves painting walls, sweeping floors, or repairing equipment.

Wendal Webb, who works in Worthington's processed steel plant in Columbus, was previously a shop steward at a unionized steel plant in California. He prefers Worthington: "At a union shop, you have one job. Here you do everything. You start on a line, and you learn to work on everything." Webb also likes Worthington's emphasis on quality. There are no quality control inspectors. "Nobody is standing over you. You are responsible for quality yourself."

New production workers tend to be young. It's frequently their first full-time job after high school—and some are recommended by people already working in the plant (often their relatives). Many brothers work together in the steel plants, but husband-and-wife teams are not permitted. The Worthington steel plants have virtually no women, whereas the company's four plastic manufacturing plants are predominantly female.

New sales personnel are expected to work four to six months in the plant before going into the field. The policy is unusual in the steel business, but it has created a sales force that is extremely familiar with the products they sell.

Company founder John H. McConnell says the key to Worthington's success was making it a "Golden Rule Company." The company has few written rules or regulations. There are no policy manuals, only some general guidelines that have been compressed to a one-page sheet. It states explicitly: "Our Golden Rule: We treat our customers, employees, investors, and suppliers as we would like to be treated."

Most managers have been promoted through the ranks. The president, Donal Malenick, started as a slitter machine operator in the steel plant. Both Malenick and McConnell make it a point to be visible. Workers in the Columbus facilities say they typically see Malenick several times a week. McConnell visits each plant and meets with small groups of employees on a regular basis.

In the unionized plants that Worthington has acquired in recent years, the unionized employees hear about the income

Worthington Industries' Philosophy

Our Golden Rule
    We treat our customers, employees, investors, and suppliers as we would like to be treated.

People
    We are dedicated to the belief that people are our most important asset.
    We believe people respond to recognition, opportunity to grow, and fair compensation.
    We believe that compensation should be directly related to job performance and therefore use incentives, profit sharing or otherwise, in every possible situation.
    From employees we expect an honest day's work for an honest day's pay.
    We believe in the philosophy of continued employment for all Worthington people.
    In filling job openings every effort is expended to find candidates within Worthington, its divisions, or subsidiaries.
    When employees are requested to relocate from one operation to another, it is accomplished without financial loss to the individual.

and benefits of their nonunion counterparts. (The unionized workers do not participate in the profit-sharing plans.) Unions have made no headway at organizing the company's original plants, and employees at five acquired facilities have voted to decertify their unions.

    Worthington officials make no effort to hide their antiunion bias. Before he started Worthington in the mid-1950s, McConnell worked in an Oldsmobile axle plant. He was offended that the union insisted that he and other workers spend eight hours doing what they could accomplish in five. So when he established his own company, McConnell was determined to avoid unions, believing they inhibit productivity.

    "I have no ill feelings toward unions," McConnell once said. "However, I've always believed that management organizes unions, unions do not organize unions. If you run your operation properly and if you are fair, honest, straightforward, and keep your people informed, your employees will not want to be represented by an outside party."

Worthington's corporate headquarters sits next to its processed steel and cylinder plants in an industrial park on the northern outskirts of Columbus. The somewhat austere three-story office building overlooks a pond stocked with fish. Some plant workers use it during their off-hours to fish for bluegill and bass.

One unusual perk available to the production workers: they can get haircuts on company time at barbershops located in the plants. The charge: $2.

Main employment centers   About 1,800, nearly half work in the Columbus area; 700 work in Upper Sandusky, Ohio; 600 in Malvern, Pennsylvania; 600 in Salem, Ohio; and 400 in Ashland, Ohio. Other locations have from 50 to 400 or fewer employees. Company facilities are also in Monroe, Mentor, and Mason, Ohio; Louisville, Kentucky; Chicago, Illinois; Rock Hill, South Carolina; Baltimore, Maryland; Claremore, Oklahoma; and Franklin, Tennessee.

Headquarters   Worthington Industries, Inc.
1205 Dearborn Drive
Columbus, OH 43085
614-438-3210

EPILOG: Why McDonald's Didn't Make It

How can a company that has a vice-president for individuality *not* be a good place to work? McDonald's, world's largest restaurant business, has such a position. It's filled by the company's former personnel director, James Kuhn, who's described as a "free spirit." His mission is to help employees escape the deadening hand of bureaucracy. He tries to loosen things up.

Kuhn works out of McDonald's headquarters at Oak Brook, Illinois, a suburb 42 miles west of Chicago's Loop on the way to Aurora. Having a vice-president for individuality is not the only unusual aspect of work life at McDonald's headquarters. It's a highly revved-up place where people seem to enjoy working long hours, a company for workaholic cheerleaders. And these people know they do not need an M.A. or M.B.A. or Ph.D. to get to the top. McDonald's does not recruit at graduate business schools. The route to the top can start on the firing line in a McDonald's store, serving Big Macs, bagging fries, making milk shakes. Fred L. Turner and Michael R. Quinlan, who were chairman and president, respectively, in 1983, did work their way up from the bottom: Turner from a grill station, Quinlan from the mailroom.

We visited McDonald's because people who had once worked in staff positions at Oak Brook strongly recommended the company to us. The people we met there praised it effusively. Ray Mines, one of the highest-ranking blacks in the company (in 1983 he was one of nine directors of national operations), told us how it is to work at McDonald's: "First you have to get McDonaldized. They take all the blood out of your veins and put ketchup in them. That's the truth. If you work hard, you can make it here. McDonald's is a very big corporation, but you're not a number. They know your name."

Helen Farrell joined McDonald's in 1973 after having taught at a community college in Nebraska. Hired as a paralegal staffer, she recalls that in her first month at McDonald's, she had a logistical problem in getting her two children transported from Texas, where they were with their father, to Chicago. She couldn't afford the air fare, and the bus and train schedules were complicated. She noticed from a posted schedule that the McDonald's plane was due to fly from Texas to Chicago—and so she called Ray Kroc's office (Kroc founded McDonald's) to ask whether her children could hitch a ride. Twenty minutes later Kroc himself called back to ask, "Now what's this about those children in Texas?" After she explained the situation, he said, "Have those kids at Love Field, and they'll be picked up." Farrell learned later that the plane's schedule had been changed to fly directly from Florida to Chicago without stopping in Texas. But Kroc rerouted it to pick up her children. "I'm going to do an awful lot for a company that does that for a nobody," Farrell told us.

McDonald's does a lot for the people who hang in there with the company. It has a strong array of benefit programs—profit-sharing (which typically augments your pay by more than 10 percent a year); an investment savings plan; a free physical exam every other year if you're under age 35, every year if you're over 35; a three-month sabbatical after 10 years' service. Some 50 employees are saluted annually for outstanding achievements. They receive President's Awards, which, aside from the prestige attached to them, come with a cash bonus equal to one-third of their pay.

All right, if it's so good, why isn't McDonald's one of the 100 best companies to work for in America? It certainly makes every list of the best-managed companies in the nation. It failed to qualify because we found, in checking at the local level where most employees work, that a McDonald's job is not an uplifting experience; it's certainly not a "people first" place.

McDonald's is the largest employer of teenagers in the country, and the profit squeezed out of the business by the parent corporation and the franchisees who own three-quarters of the outlets depends crucially on low wages (as low as possible) and an assembly-line operation that leaves the employee with little or no free time to think. Here are some comments given to us by teenagers working in McDonald's stores in California:

"McDonald's is a place where you work hard for little money. The one I worked at would only allow you a small french fries, a small drink, and large hamburger for six hours of work."

"The starting pay is $3.35 an hour. Every three months the employee gets reviewed to see if you get a five-cent, ten-cent, or fifteen-cent raise."

"They work you to death for cheap pay."

"Kids hate the job but they need the money."

"People leave all the time because the pay is low and lousy for the amount of work they put you through."

The McDonald's people at Oak Brook do not deny that the pay at the crew level is low. Nor do they deny that the kids have to work to a routine and are watched over carefully by their supervisors. What they say, in defense, is that this job is usually the first work experience for these teenagers, and the discipline will stand them in good stead. They claim that many teenagers work for McDonald's in high school and later return as full-timers. They insist that if you take all the hard stuff in the beginning and stay for the long haul, the rewards will be great. And then there is this ultimate justification: McDonald's creates jobs. Lee Dunham, operator of six McDonald's stores in New York City's Harlem area, says, "We give jobs to 400 people who otherwise wouldn't have them."

We debated among ourselves whether McDonald's belonged on our roster, deciding in the end that for most of the people who work for the company and its franchisees (well over 250,000), it's dehumanizing, similar to the experiences Charlie Chaplin encountered in *Modern Times*. We believe it's also true that for most of them, it leads nowhere. Peggy Stinnett, a member of the school board in Oakland, California, summed up what teenagers get from McDonald's in an interview with Seth Rosenfeld of Pacific News Service: "At the end of the semester, they're going to have a little experience at McDonald's and that's not going to buy them much."

In searching for good places to work, we wanted to select companies that are good for people in the lower ranks as well as in management. We clearly did not get to every last outpost of every company in this book, but all of the ones we finally selected did have in place a people orientation that was intended to flow through all the ranks, from top to bottom. McDonald's, on the other hand, seemed to embrace a system geared to exploiting people in the lower ranks.

THE 10
BEST COMPANIES
TO WORK FOR
IN AMERICA

Bell Labs
Trammell Crow
Delta Air Lines
Federal Express
Goldman Sachs
Hallmark Cards
Hewlett-Packard
IBM
Pitney Bowes
Time Inc.

...AND 5 RUNNERS-UP

Herman Miller	Northwestern	Publix Super
J. P. Morgan	Mutual Life	Markets
3M		

10 BEST-PAYING COMPANIES

Atlantic Richfield	Exxon	Linnton Plywood
Leo Burnett	Goldman Sachs	Shell Oil
Trammell Crow	Hewitt Associates	Steelcase
	Hewlett-Packard	

10 BEST FOR BENEFITS

Apple Computer	Trammell Crow	J. P. Morgan
Atlantic Richfield	Hewitt Associates	Procter & Gamble
Bell Labs	IBM	Time Inc.
	Johnson Wax	

10 BEST FOR JOB SECURITY

Delta Air Lines	Federal Express	Johnson Wax
Digital	Hallmark Cards	Proctor & Gamble
Equipment	Hewlett-Packard	Worthington
Exxon	IBM	Industries

10 BEST FOR CHANCES TO MOVE UP

Citicorp	Lowe's	Quad/Graphics
Federal Express	3M	Tandy
Gore	Nordstrom	Westin Hotels
	Procter & Gamble	

15 BEST FOR AMBIENCE

Advanced Micro	Hewlett-Packard	Northwestern
Devices	Kollmorgen	Mutual Life
Apple Computer	Los Angeles	Odetics
Delta Air Lines	Dodgers	Physio-Control
Doyle Dane	Merle Norman	Pitney Bowes
Bernbach	Cosmetics	Publix Super
Hallmark Cards	Herman Miller	Markets

THE 100 BEST BY INDUSTRY

Consumer Goods
Anheuser-Busch
Celestial Seasonings
Eastman Kodak
Fisher-Price Toys
General Electric
General Mills
H. J. Heinz
Johnson Wax
Johnson & Johnson
Mary Kay Cosmetics
Maytag
McCormick
Merle Norman Cosmetics
Polaroid
Procter & Gamble
Remington Products

Drugs & Health Care
Baxter Travenol
Johnson & Johnson
Marion Laboratories
Physio-Control

High Technology
Advanced Micro Devices
Analog Devices
Apple Computer
Bell Laboratories
Control Data
Digital Equipment
Electro Scientific
General Electric
Hewlett-Packard
Intel
IBM
Kollmorgen
3M
Moog
Odetics
ROLM
Tandem Computers

Tandy
Tektronix

Oil & Chemicals
Atlantic Richfield
Du Pont
Eastman Kodak
Exxon
H. B. Fuller
Gore
3M
Polaroid
Raychem
Shell Oil
Tenneco

Steel & Auto
Cummins Engine
Dana
Deere
Donnelly
Inland Steel
Nissan
Nucor
Tenneco
Worthington

Conglomerate
General Electric
General Mills
3M
Tenneco

Office Equipment
Apple Computer
Control Data
Digital Equipment
Eastman Kodak
Exxon
Hewlett-Packard
IBM
Liebert
Herman Miller

473

3M
Pitney Bowes
ROLM
Steelcase
Tandem Computers
Tandy

Clothing
General Mills
Gore
Levi Strauss
Olga
Springs Mills

Shelter
Armstrong
Trammell Crow
CRS Sirrine
Linnton Plywood
Weyerhaeuser

Utility
Southern California Edison

Media & Entertainment
Leo Burnett
Doyle Dane Bernbach
Hallmark Cards
Knight-Ridder
Los Angeles Dodgers
Quad/Graphics
Random House
Reader's Digest
Time Inc.

Retailing
Dayton Hudson
General Mills
Lowe's
Mary Kay Cosmetics
Merle Norman Cosmetics
Nordstrom

J. C. Penney
Publix Super Markets
Recreational Equipment
Tandy
Wal-Mart Stores

Banking & Finance
Citicorp
Control Data
A. G. Edwards
General Electric
Goldman Sachs
J. P. Morgan
Rainier National Bank
Security Pacific Bank

Insurance
Erie Insurance
Northwestern Mutual Life
J. C. Penney
Ryder
Tenneco

Transportation
Delta Air Lines
Federal Express
People Express
Preston Trucking
Ryder
Viking Freight

Restaurants & Hotels
General Mills
Saga
Westin Hotels

Aerospace
General Electric
Moog
Northrop
Odetics

THE 100 BEST BY LOCATION

Throughout the United States: Dayton Hudson; Delta Air Lines; Du Pont; Federal Express; General Electric; IBM; J. C. Penney; Pitney Bowes; Ryder; Saga; Tandy; Time Inc.; Westin.

Alabama: Lowe's; Nucor; Wal-Mart Stores; Weyerhaeuser.

Alaska: Atlantic Richfield; Nordstrom; Rainier National Bank; Recreational Equipment.

Arizona: Gore; Intel.

Arkansas: Baxter Travenol; Lowe's; Wal-Mart; Weyerhaeuser.

California: Advanced Micro Devices; Anheuser-Busch; Apple Computer; Atlantic Richfield; Citicorp; Exxon; General Mills; H. J. Heinz; Hewlett-Packard; IBM; Intel; Knight-Ridder; Levi Strauss; Los Angeles Dodgers; McCormick; Merle Norman Cosmetics; 3M; Nordstrom; Northrop; Odetics; Olga; Raychem; Recreational Equipment; ROLM; Saga; Security Pacific Bank; Shell Oil; Southern California Edison; Tandem Computers; Tenneco; Viking Freight; Westin Hotels; Weyerhaeuser.

Colorado: Atlantic Richfield; Celestial Seasonings; Citicorp; CRS Sirrine; Hewlett-Packard; Recreational Equipment; ROLM.

Connecticut: Hallmark Cards; Hewitt Associates; Pitney Bowes; Remington Products.

Delaware: Du Pont; Gore; Lowe's; Preston Trucking.

Florida: Anheuser-Busch; Citicorp; General Mills; IBM; Knight-Ridder; Los Angeles Dodgers; Lowe's; Pitney Bowes; Publix Super Markets; Ryder; Wal-Mart.

Georgia: Armstrong; Citicorp; Delta Air Lines; Lowe's; Herman Miller; Wal-Mart.

Idaho: Hewlett-Packard; H. J. Heinz.

Illinois: Baxter Travenol; Bell Laboratories; Leo Burnett; Deere; Exxon; Hewitt Associates; Inland Steel; 3M; Lowe's; Northrop; Shell Oil; Tandem Computers; Tenneco; Wal-Mart; Worthington Industries.

Indiana: Cummins Engine; Dana; Inland Steel; Lowe's; Maytag; Nucor; Wal-Mart.

Iowa: Deere; H. J. Heinz; Maytag; 3M; Wal-Mart.

Kansas: Hallmark Cards; Pitney Bowes; Wal-Mart.

Kentucky: General Electric; Fisher-Price Toys; Lowe's; Wal-Mart; Worthington Industries.

Louisiana: Exxon; Lowe's; Shell Oil; Wal-Mart.

Maine: Digital Equipment.

Maryland: Citicorp; Control Data; Erie Insurance; Gore; Lowe's; McCormick; Preston Trucking; Random House; Worthington Industries.

Massachusetts: Analog Devices; Delta Air Lines; Digital Equipment; General Electric; Hewlett-Packard; Kollmorgen; Northrop; Polaroid.

Michigan: Dana; Donnelly; Knight-Ridder; Herman Miller; Steelcase; Westin Hotels.

Minnesota: Control Data; Dayton Hudson; H.B.Fuller; General Mills; 3M.

Mississippi: Baxter Travenol; Lowe's; Wal-Mart; Weyerhaeuser.

Missouri: Anheuser-Busch; Citicorp; A.G.Edwards; Hallmark Cards; Marion Laboratories; 3M; Northrop; Wal-Mart.

Montana: Atlantic Richfield; Nordstrom.

Nebraska: Nucor; Wal-Mart.

New Hampshire: Anheuser-Busch; Digital Equipment.

New Jersey: Anheuser-Busch; Bell Laboratories; Exxon; Federal Express; Hewlett-Packard; Johnson & Johnson; People Express; Preston Trucking.

New Mexico: Intel; Levi Strauss; Wal-Mart.

New York: Anheuser-Busch; Citicorp; Cummins Engine; Doyle Dane Bernbach; Eastman Kodak; Fisher-Price Toys; General Electric; General Mills; Goldman Sachs; IBM; Kollmorgen; Moog; J. P. Morgan; J. C. Penney; Preston Trucking; Random House; Reader's Digest; Springs Mills; Time Inc.

North Carolina: Analog Devices; Armstrong; Baxter Travenol; Dana; IBM; Knight-Ridder; Lowe's; Raychem; Springs Mills; Wal-Mart; Weyerhaeuser.

Ohio: Anheuser-Busch; Cummins Engine; Dana; Delta Air Lines; General Electric; Johnson & Johnson; Knight-Ridder; Liebert; Lowe's; Pitney Bowes; Procter & Gamble; Worthington Industries.

Oklahoma: Dana; Wal-Mart Stores; Weyerhaeuser; Worthington Industries.

Oregon: Electro Scientific; Hewlett-Packard; Intel; Linnton Plywood; Nordstrom; Recreational Equipment; Tektronix; Weyerhaeuser.

Pennsylvania: Anheuser-Busch; Armstrong; Atlantic Richfield; Dana; Erie Insurance; H. J. Heinz; Hewlett-Packard; Johnson & Johnson; Knight-Ridder; Lowe's; Preston Trucking; Procter & Gamble; Tenneco.

South Carolina: CRS Sirrine; Cummins Engine; Eastman Kodak; Lowe's; Nucor; Springs Mills; Wal-Mart; Worthington Industries.

South Dakota: Citicorp; 3M.

Tennessee: Delta Air Lines; Eastman Kodak; Federal Express; Levi Strauss; Lowe's; Maytag; Merle Norman Cosmetics; Nissan; Wal-Mart Stores; Worthington Industries.

Texas: Advanced Micro Devices; Anheuser-Busch; Apple Computer; Atlantic Richfield; Trammell Crow; CRS Sirrine; Delta Air Lines; Eastman Kodak; Exxon; IBM; Intel; Johnson & Johnson; Levi Strauss; Lowe's; Mary Kay Cosmetics; 3M; Nucor; ROLM; Shell Oil; Tandem Computers; Tandy; Tenneco; Wal-Mart Stores.

Utah: Nordstrom; Nucor; Recreational Equipment.

Vermont: Digital Equipment.

Virginia: Anheuser-Busch; Kollmorgen; Lowe's; Preston Trucking; Tandem Computers; Tenneco; Time Inc.; Wal-Mart.

Washington: Hewlett-Packard; Nordstrom; Physio-Control; Rainier National Bank; Recreational Equipment; Tektronix; Westin Hotels; Weyerhaeuser.

West Virginia: Lowe's.

Wisconsin: Johnson Wax; 3M; Northwestern Mutual Life; Procter & Gamble; Quad/Graphics; Tenneco.

Wyoming: Atlantic Richfield; Exxon.